CW00545590

An Anthology of
CATHOLIC TEACHING ON EDUCATION

An Anthology of
CATHOLIC TEACHING
ON EDUCATION

Edited by
Leonard Franchi

Scepter
London – New York

This edition of *An Anthology of Catholic Teaching on Education* is published:
in England by Scepter (U.K.) Ltd., 21 Hinton Avenue, Hounslow
    TW4 6AP; e-mail: scepter@pobox.com;
in the United States by Scepter Publishers Inc., P. O. Box 211, New
    York, NY 10018; e-mail: info@scepterpub.org

ISBN-10: 0906138-69-8
ISBN-13: 978-0906138-69-4

© Translation of Church documents – Libreria Editrice Vaticana
© This edition – Scepter (U.K.) Ltd., 2007
Cover photograph: © Andrejs Pozarskis; Agency: www.dreamstime.com

All rights reserved. No part of this book may be reproduced, stored in a
retrieval system or transmitted, in any form or by any means, electronic,
mechanical, photocopying or otherwise, without the prior permission of
Scepter (U.K.) Ltd.

Nihil obstat: Fr Anton Cowan (Censor)
Imprimatur: Rt Rev Alan Hopes, V.G., Auxiliary Bishop in Westminster.
            Westminster, 25 April 2007, Feast of St Mark, Evangelist.

The Nihil obstat *and* Imprimatur *are a declaration that a book or pamphlet is
considered to be free from doctrinal or moral error. It is not implied that those
who have granted the* Nihil obstat *and* Imprimatur *agree with the contents,
opinions or statements expressed.*

Cover design, text revision and typeset by ISV Intermedia, and printed
in Thailand.

CONTENTS

PREFACE

This collection of official Catholic teaching on education is a rich body of work spanning almost a century. From *Acerbo Nimis* (1905) to *The Catholic School on the Threshold of the New Millenium* (1997) we see a responsive Church willing to engage with the challenges of particular eras. The totalitarian political ideologies which challenged the rights of the Church and of parents to educate their children were exposed for their flawed understanding of how education in truth must respect human dignity and freedom. Communism, Fascism and Nazism were all rejected. This was in part, because they failed to accept the central role of the family in the education of children and the irreplaceable contribution of religion to the comprehensive education of the person. We were reminded in *Divini Illius Magistri* (1929) that such education is also essential for the common good of the society in which the person lives. The acceptance of the key role of parents as the first educators was accompanied by a clarion call from the Church for teachers, priests and religious to assist parents in this regard. Later, in *Provido Sane Consilio* (1935) we were provided with a framework for the improved teaching of the faith along with a reminder to place catechesis at the heart of the Church's educational mission.

By the 1960's, various factors were at work in the Church. The most powerful agent of change in the Catholic Church during this century was the Second Vatican Council. Held in Rome between 1962-1965, it broke the Tridentine mould of Catholic life and was followed by radical developments, only some of which were intended. It is useful to recall that most young Catholics of today have little or no idea what Catholic life was like before the Council and Vatican II is for them as relevant as the Council of Chalcedon (A.D. 451).

Pope Benedict XVI, like his predecessor Pope John Paul II, is important as an accurate guide to the true meaning of Vatican II, which has to be seen in continuity with previous Church history;

certainly a development but not a radical break which invalidated the previous four hundred years of Catholic history.

A number of Conciliar teachings, including the *Decree on Christian Education* (1965), impinged directly on Catholic schooling. These teachings included a consideration of the rights of the family as paramount and the primordial role of the lay faithful in response to the changed makeup of Catholic teaching staffs. The essential role of the Church in Higher Education was also highlighted in *Gravissimum Educationis*. The two principal motifs of the Council were *"aggiornamento"*, bringing things up to date, and *"ressourcement"*, a return to the genuine sources i.e. New Testament and the Fathers. The tension between these two approaches remains at the heart of the differences today between gospel Christians in every denomination (sometimes called conservative or traditional) on the one hand and the liberals or radicals on the other. This tension continues to play out in Catholic schools and universities.

In the years following the Council, we experienced a situation where religious teachers were in a minority in many schools; a development which was covered adequately in an educational sense but crucially weakened the religious witness in schools. While many lay teachers were serious Catholics and an increasing number possessed theological qualifications, the balance changed. The teaching Church responded with *Catechesi Tradendae* (1979) and *Lay Catholics in Schools* (1982). These provided both an exposition of the ongoing dynamic between evangelisation and catechesis and a comprehensive treatise on the vocation of the lay Catholic teacher.

Later, the lay faithful had to increasingly step forward to replace the religious. Lay principals and the executive staff became responsible for the religious leadership of many schools, including the Catholic life of the schools. Many lay leaders are now perhaps more explicit about this than some of the religious principals of ten or twenty years ago.

While ours is a God of surprises we have only a limited capacity to transmit our tradition and preserve our identity. *The Religious Dimension of Education in a Catholic School* (1988) provided a valuable reminder of the holistic nature of education and that a Christian perspective encompassed education in both truth and virtue. Following within a decade was a fully integrated vision for Catholic education with the new *General Directory for Catechesis* (1997). This document provided an appropriate balance between the contextualization of catechesis in evangelisation as envisaged by *Evangelii Nuntiandi* (1975) and the appropriation of the content of the Catholic faith as presented in the *Catechism of the Catholic Church* (1992).

We are now in an age in which secularists strive to remove religion from the public domain and restrict it to private life, where individual religious choices reflect personal preferences unrelated to truth and general principles. Such forces see religion as simply another area for consumer choice. The document *The Catholic School on the Threshold of the Third Millennium* (1997) clearly rejected this notion and affirmed that any programme of education must place the integral education of the person at the centre and that this necessitated adequate religious and moral formation.

Today as always, our central concern as Catholics must be the presentation of the person of Jesus Christ, with his call to repent and believe. We espouse crucifixion Christianity which leads to the resurrection and believe that everyone stands under the four last things of death and judgement, heaven and hell. Catholicism calls to faith and reason as well as love and hope. This is now profoundly countercultural. This is the ongoing challenge for education in the Catholic tradition.

The decisions to believe in Christ are mysterious and individual. But parents and schools can impart religious knowledge, encourage patterns of clear thinking, constructive enquiry and a thirst for answers. We need to inculcate a respect for reason and tradition as well as call to faith, hope and love.

These are mighty tasks, but attempting them is a wonderful vocation. Especially in our challenging environment, catechesis, and evangelisation are not only a duty, but an adventure and challenge, truly one great work of the Holy Spirit. We need to support and urge one another to continue with all the wisdom and perseverance we can muster.

To conclude, I pose two series of questions to those immediately involved in the simmering milieu of Catholic education today.

Firstly, to educators:

• Do Catholic schools retain today a capacity to strengthen the faith and improve the morals of their students, as they did in the past?

• Are Catholic truths presented to your students sequentially and comprehensively over their years of schooling? Do students know what are the four or five fundamental truths of our faith? What is the place of student text-books in Religious Education?

• What strategies would overturn the assumption that all morality is relative? How can the truths about life, marriage, family and social justice be defended?

• What strategies might be adopted to strengthen the Christian faith and perhaps make converts among the non-Catholic students in our schools?

• What strategies would make Catholic schools more accessible to lower income families? Should our "elite" colleges offer more scholarships to the disadvantaged?

• Is it a concern that few Catholic schools are listed among the best academic schools?

• Is there sufficient diversity among Catholic schools?

• Should more be done for the religious education of Catholics in state-run schools?

• What must we do to prepare the next generation of leaders for truly Catholic schools?

• How can we attract committed Catholic school graduates into the teaching profession?

Secondly, to students:

• Do you pray when you are in trouble? How regularly do you thank God for the good things you have?

• Do you believe in the power of God's forgiveness? Do you ever go to the Sacrament of reconciliation?

• Do you believe some activities are right and some are plain wrong? Or is the grey of uncertainty the only moral colour?

• Have you a genuine concern for the underprivileged?

• Do you admire and value the Christian ideal of life-long marriage?

• Are the students who regularly practise their religion prepared to defend this and explain their faith, or are they cowed into silence in student discussion?

- Is there still discussion in each graduating year about which year-members might become priests or religious?
- When the time comes, what will you do to support the rich legacy of Catholic education that has been bequeathed to you?

Pope John Paul II should have the last word from his message at the start of the third Christian millennium "*Duc in altum! These words ring out for us today, and they invite us to remember the past with gratitude, live the present with enthusiasm and to look to the future with confidence: 'Jesus Christ is the same yesterday and today and forever'* (Heb 13:8)."

Amen to that.

+ Cardinal George Pell
Archbishop of Sydney
9 January 2007

FOREWORD

These documents from the Church's Magisterium, all issued in the 20th Century, are on the related themes of Catholic education (which includes the 'subject' of Religious Education) and catechesis. They have been collated and edited with a view to enabling Catholic educators to appreciate more fully the riches of the tradition in which they exercise their vocation. It should serve as a *vademecum* for all who have a locus in the mission of Catholic education: Bishops, priests, teachers, catechists and students.

Catechesis and Religious Education: some clarifications
Students of Catholic educational thought will appreciate the difference in emphasis between catechesis in general and the 'subject' of Religious Education as part of a school's academic syllabus. This dichotomy is clear in the Magisterial documents emanating from the latter half of the 20th Century.[1]

What is this difference? The Church argues that catechesis works in a context in which faith in Jesus Christ is accepted and needs developing. It is subsequent to the initial proclamation of faith – evangelisation – and allows the baptised to grow closer to God with the support of the faith community.

A familiar passage from the *Acts of the Apostles* – "and they devoted themselves to the apostles' teaching and fellowship, to the breaking of bread and the prayers"[2] – affords an insight into the world of early Christianity. We see a community learning from those in authority (*Apostles' teaching*), living charity (*fellowship*) and doing so in a culture of liturgy and devotion (*breaking of the bread and the prayers*). It is, indeed, a good model for all involved in catechesis.

Religious Education in schools, on the other hand, may not always have that dynamic and faith-filled approach which should underpin any *catechetical* enterprise. The reasons for this are many: e.g. students and staff may be at different stages of their faith journey. Yet, a good R.E. programme of studies in a Catholic school ought to allow for intellectual development in

---

[1] *Religious Dimension of Education in a Catholic School,* 1988, 68
[2] Acts 2:42

faith and critical reflection on the implications for living which flow from the key dogmatic principles of the Church.

This dichotomy between catechesis and Religious Education, must allow for fluidity. However, I would argue that a rigid compartmentalization of the two concepts is less than helpful. This, then, is the question to be answered: Is it possible for those involved in catechesis to learn from Catholic teachers and their approach to the teaching of Religious Education in schools? Similarly, would Catholic education in a Catholic school be enhanced if a more catechetical approach were adopted?[3] Is this possible, or indeed, desirable?

Selection of Documents

The documents selected for inclusion in this edition deal with Catholic education and catechesis. The following would be deemed broadly catechetical: *Acerbo Nimis,*[4] *Provido Sane Consilio,*[5] *Catechesi Tradendae*[6] and the *General Directory for Catechesis.*[7] The others – *Divini Illius Magistri,*[8] *Gravissimum Educationis,*[9] *The Catholic School,*[10] *Lay Catholics in Schools: Witnesses to Faith,*[11] *The Religious Dimension of Education in a Catholic School,*[12] and *The Catholic School on the Threshold of the Third Millennium*[13] – deal with the broader area of education in schools, the nature of Religious Education, the role of the Catholic teacher and the ethos and philosophy of Catholic education.

Structure of the Anthology

The documents chosen are arranged in chronological order. Each document is prefaced with a short introduction.

The Study Guide is based on some major themes in Catholic

---

[3] *General Directory for Catechesis,* Congregation for the Clergy, 11 August 1997, 60.
[4] *Acerbo Nimis*, Pius X, 15 April 1905.
[5] *Provido Sane Consilio*, Catechetical Office of the Holy See, 12 January 1935.
[6] *Catechesi Tradendae*, Pope John Paul II, Apostolic Exhortation, 16 October 1979.
[7] op. cit.
[8] Pius XI, Apostolic Encyclical, 31 December 1929.
[9] Second Vatican Council, *Declaration on Christian Education*, 28 October 1965.
[10] Sacred Congregation for Catholic Education, 19 March 1977.
[11] Sacred Congregation for Catholic Education, 15 October 1982.
[12] Congregation for Catholic Education, 7 April 1988.
[13] Congregation for Catholic Education, 28 December 1977.

education and catechesis. The documents provide a large canvas: these study notes should be seen principally as an initial point of contact with the texts.

The original paragraph numbers in each of the documents have been retained, and are referred to at the head of each document. Marginal numbers in bold have been added for this edition, for ease of reference.

Appendix 1 contains some detailed points from the Code of Canon Law which pertain to Catholic education and Catechesis. Appendix 3 is Paul VI's *Credo of the People of God.* It is a statement of the belief of Catholics, a profession of faith, "a creed which, without being strictly speaking a dogmatic definition, repeats in substance, with some developments called for by the spiritual condition of our time, the creed of Nicaea, the creed of the immortal tradition of the holy Church of God".

Appendices 2 and 4 are a collection of prayers and Scripture readings. These serve as a reminder that the study of Catholic Education is not simply a matter of learning information but should be a time of formation in faith: no formation is complete without prayer.

The Catechetical Office of the Holy See issued a "Questionnaire regarding the teaching of Christian doctrine" with its 1935 document *Provido Sane Consilio – On the Better Care for Catechetical Teaching.* This questionnaire appears in Appendix 5.

Acknowledgements

I would like to thank all at the Maryvale Institute, Birmingham and the Department of Religious Education, University of Glasgow, for the contributions they have made towards the publication of this work. Both institutions are leading lights in the fields of catechesis and Religious Education, and deserve to be valued highly by all Catholic educators.

A special thanks to Father John Keenan, Catholic Chaplain to the University of Glasgow, for his advice and helpful suggestions to me in the production of this Anthology.

His Eminence Cardinal George Pell, his busy schedule notwithstanding, quickly responded to my request to preface this work. And I wish to acknowledge this gratefully and to express my deep appreciation for his time and graciousness.

Leonard Franchi

CONTENTS OF THE DOCUMENTS[1]

---

[1] Marginal numbers are in **bold**

ABBREVIATIONS

I. Biblical abbreviations

Old Testament
Gen: Genesis
Ex: Exodus
Lev: Leviticus
Num: Numbers
Deut: Deuteronomy
Josh: Joshua
Judg: Judges
Ruth: Ruth
1 Sam: 1 Samuel
2 Sam: 2 Samuel
1 Kings: 1 Kings
2 Kings: 2 Kings
1 Chron: 1 Chronicles
2 Chron: 2 Chronicles
Ezra: Ezra
Neh: Nehemiah
Tob: Tobit
Jud: Judith
Esther: Esther
Job: Job
Ps: Psalms
Prov: Proverbs
Eccles: Ecclesiastes
Song: Song of Solomon
Wis: Wisdom
Sir: Sirach (Ecclesiasticus)
Is: Isaiah
Jer: Jeremiah
Lam: Lamentations
Bar: Baruch
Ezek: Ezekiel
Dan: Daniel
Hos: Hosea
Joel: Joel
Amos: Amos
Obad: Obadiah
Jon: Jonah
Mic: Micah

Nahum: Nahum
Hab: Habakkuk
Zeph: Zephaniah
Hag: Haggai
Zech: Zechariah
Mal: Malachi
1 Mac: 1 Maccabees
2 Mac: 2 Maccabees

New Testament
Mt: Matthew
Mk: Mark
Lk: Luke
Jn: John
Acts: Acts of the Apostles
Rom: Romans
1 Cor: 1 Corinthians
2 Cor: 2 Corinthians
Gal: Galatians
Eph: Ephesians
Phil: Philippians
Col: Colossians
1 Thess: 1 Thessalonians
2 Thess: 2 Thessalonians
1 Tim: 1 Timothy
2 Tim: 2 Timothy
Tit: Titus
Philem: Philemon
Heb: Hebrews
Jas: James
1 Pet: 1 Peter
2 Pet: 2 Peter
1 Jn: 1 John
2 Jn: 2 John
3 Jn: 3 John
Jude: Jude
Rev: Revelation (Apocalypse)

II. Documents of the Magisterium

AA: Second Vatican Council, Decree on the Apostolate of the Laity, *Apostolicam Actuositatem* (18 November 1965)

AG: Second Vatican Council, Decree on missionary activity in the Church *Ad Gentes* (7 December 1965)

CA: John Paul II, Encyclical Letter *Centesimus Annus* (1 May 1991): AAS 83 (1991) pp. 793-867

CD: Second Vatican Council, Decree on the pastoral office of Bishops in the Church *Christus Dominus* (28 October 1965)

CCC: Catechism of the Catholic Church (11 October 1992)

CCL: *Corpus Christianorum,* Latin series (Turnholt 1953 ff.)

CIC: *Codex Iuris Canonici* (25 January 1983)

ChL: John Paul II, Post-synodal Apostolic Exhortation, *Christifideles Laici* (30 December 1988): AAS 81 (1989) pp. 393-521

COINCATI: International Council for Catechesis, *Adult Catechesis in the Christian Community,* Libreria Editrice Vaticana, 1990

CSEL: Corpus Scriptorum Ecclesiasticorum Latinorum (Wn 1866 ff.)

CT: John Paul II, Apostolic Exhortation *Catechesi Tradendae* (16 October 1979): AAS 71 (1979), pp. 1277-1340.

DCG (1971): Sacred Congregation for the Clergy, General Catechetical Directory, *Ad normam decreti* (11 April 1971): AAS 64 (1972). pp. 97-176

DH: Second Vatican Council, Declaration on Religious Liberty, *Dignitatis Humanae* (7 December 1965)

DM: John Paul II, Encyclical Letter, *Dives in Misericordia* (30 November 1980): AAS 72 (1980) pp. 1177-1232

DV: Second Vatican Council, Dogmatic Constitution on Divine Revelation *Dei Verbum* (18 November 1965)

DS or Dz-Sch: H. Denzinger-A Schönmetzer, Enchiridion Symbolorum Definitionum et Declarationum de Rebus Fidei et Morum, Editio XXXV, Rome 1973

EA: John Paul II, Post-synodal Apostolic Exhortation *Ecclesia in Africa* (14 September 1995): AAS 88 (1996) pp. 5-82

EN: Paul VI, Apostolic Exhortation *Evangelii Nuntiandi* (8 December 1975): AAS 58 (1976) pp. 5-76

EV: John Paul II, Encyclical Letter, *Evangelium Vitae* (25 March 1995): AAS 87 (1995) pp. 401-522

FC: John Paul II, Post-synodal Apostolic Exhortation *Familaris Consortio* (22 November 1981): AAS 73 (1981) pp. 81-191

FD: John Paul II, Apostolic Constitution *Fidei Depositum* (11 October 1992) AAS 86 (1994) pp. 113-118

GCM: Congregation for the Evangelisation of Peoples, *Guide for Catechists* (3 December, 1993), Vatican City 1993

GE: Second Vatican Council, Declaration on Education, *Gravissimum Educationis* (28 October 1965)

GS: Second Vatican Council, Pastoral Constitution The Church in the Modern World. *Gaudium et Spes* (7 December 1965)

LC: Congregation for the Doctrine of the Faith, Instruction *Libertatis Conscientia* (22 March 1986): AAS 79 (1987) pp. 554-599

LE: John Paul II, Encyclical letter *Laborem Exercens* (14 September 1981), AAS 73 (1981), pp. 577-647

LG: Second Vatican Council, Dogmatic Constitution on the Church *Lumen Gentium* (21 November 1964)

MM: John XXIII, Encyclical Letter, *Mater et Magistra* (15 May 1961): AAS 53 (1961) pp. 401-464

MPD: Synod of Bishops, Message to the People of God, *Cum iam ad exitum* on catechesis in our times (28 October 1977) Typis Polyglottis Vaticanis 1977

NA: Second Vatican Council, Decree on the relationship of the Church with non-Christian Religions, *Nostra Aetate* (28 October 1965)

PB: John Paul II, Apostolic Costitution *Pastor Bonus* (28 June 1988) AAS 80 (1988), pp. 841-930

PG: Patrologiae Cursus completus, Series Graeca ed Jacques P. Migne, Paris.

PL: Patrologiae Cursus completus, Series Latina, ed. Jacques P. Migne, Paris.

PO: Second Vatican Council, Decree on Priestly Life and Ministry *Presbyterorum Ordinis* (7 December 1965)

PP: Paul VI, Encyclical Letter *Populorum Progressio* (26 March 1967) AAS 59 (1967), pp. 257-299.

RH: John Paul II, Encyclical Letter *Redemptor Hominis* (4 March 1979): AAS 71 (1979), pp. 257-324

RCIA: *Ordo Initiationis Christianae Adultorum*, Rite of Christian Initiation of Adults (R.C.I.A.) Editio Typica, Typis Polyglottis Vaticanis 1972

RM: John Paul II, Encyclical Letter *Redemptoris Missio* (7 December 1990): AAS 83 (1991), pp. 249-340

SC: Second Vatican Council, Constitution on the Sacred Liturgy *Sacrosanctum Concilium* (4 December 1963)

SYNOD 1985: Synod of Bishops (extraordinary meeting of 1985) Final Report *Ecclesia sub verbo Dei mysteria Christi celebrans pro salute mundi* (7 December 1985), Vatican City 1985

SCh: *Sources Chrétiennes,* Collectio, Paris 1946 ff.

SRS: John Paul II, Encyclical letter *Sollicitudo Rei Socialis* (30 December 1987) AAS 80 (1988), pp. 513-586

TMA: John Paul II, Apostolic Exhortation, *Tertio Millennio Adveniente* (10 November 1994): AAS 87 (1995) pp. 5-41

UR: Second Vatican Council, Decree on Ecumenism *Unitatis Redintegratio* (21 November 1964)

UUS: John Paul II, Encyclical Lettter *Ut Unum Sint* (25 May 1995): AAS 87 (1995) pp. 921-982.

VS: John Paul II, Encyclical Letter *Veritatis Splendor* (6 August 1993): AAS 85 (1993) pp. 1133-1228.

INTRODUCTORY NOTES TO THE DOCUMENTS

Acerbo Nimis, 1905, Encyclical Letter of Pope St. Pius X

Pope St. Pius X (1835–1914) became Pope in 1903 and took as his motto *instauare omnia in Christo* – to restore all things in Christ. As a priest and bishop he had shown much zeal for the religious formation of both priests and lay people. As Pope he is remembered in particular for his decree in 1910 that young children should receive their First Holy Communion soon after they had attained the 'age of reason' – thus affording the graces of the sacrament to children of 7-8 years.

The early years of the 20th Century were problematic for the Church in Europe as it contended with various political ideologies which did not fully accept the Church's rights with regard to education. This often led to Church-State tension. This short but powerful Encyclical of Pope St. Pius X has as its principal theme the importance of teaching Christian doctrine in the context of socio-political systems which were often not conducive to the aims of Christian education.

The Encyclical warns that 'ignorance in things divine' (para. 1) has grave consequences for the Church and society. Conversely, faithful instruction in matters of Christian religion can only have beneficial consequences for society. Particular mention is made of poorly catechised adults, yet in a nuanced way: those whose employers are reluctant to allow them time to take care of their basic family duties are far less culpable than those Christians of 'culture' who, despite their knowledge of the 'things of the world' (para. 2), live without religion.

As well as identifying the ideological sources of the problems faced by the Church, Pius X provides a framework for its resolution: priests and bishops, in accordance with the recommendation of the Council of Trent (1545–1563) are to take the lead in instructing the people 'the truths of religion' (para. 11) on a systematic basis. The Catechism of the Council of Trent (Roman Catechism) should be at the heart of this process.

The short Encyclical ends with a list of practical suggestions for catechetical instruction (paras. 19f).

Divini Illius Magistri, 1929, Encyclical Letter of Pope Pius XI

This long and comprehensive Encyclical from Pope Pius XI (1922–1929) is his response to the dangers posed to Christian education by the ideologies of Communism, Fascism and Nazism. He was no stranger to these political creeds. Although he was a scholar and head of the Vatican Library, he had been mandated by Pope Benedict XV (1914–1922) to take on a diplomatic role in Poland in 1918. This brought him into full contact with the diplomatic and political problems which assailed the continent of Europe at that time.

When he was elected Pope in 1922, Pius was keen to maintain some form of dialogue with the anti-religious ideologies of the time but this was not without difficulties. The philosophy of materialism was not a ready partner in dialogue. He established the feast of Christ the King in 1925 as a sign that the Church would not be subsumed by the all-consuming materialistic mentality which desired the neutering of Christian influence in social affairs.

Pius XI deals directly with the challenges facing Christian education in the Europe of the 1920s. As Communism, Fascism and Nazism sought to capture the minds and hearts of the young people of Europe, he argues that to remove Christianity from education is in effect to change the nature of education itself: 'there can be no ideally perfect education which is not Christian education' (para. 7). He upholds the primordial role of the family in education but reminds us that it is a role which is complemented by those of the Church and the State. He advises vigilance against ideologies which deny the importance of religion in the world of education. The three-part structure of Church, family and state provides an over-arching framework within which he develops his arguments.

Pius XI is also keen to stress the communitarian aspects of Christian education. He is aware that Christians should not form a clique and live apart from the world. As a passionate advocate of social reform, he reminds us that Christian education has, as one of its aims, the formation of good citizens who will, in turn, contribute to the common weal. He claims that good citizens cannot be formed without the contribution of Christian education (para. 54).

Contemporary educationalists may be interested to explore further his thoughts on co-education i.e. educating girls and boys together (para. 68) – which he deems 'harmful'.

Paragraphs 93-102 form a general conclusion to his thought and provide a neat synopsis on the true nature of Christian education.

Provido Sane Consilio – On the Better Care for Catechetical Teaching, Catechetical Office of the Holy See, 1935

This short document deals with catechetical provision for both young people and adults. It is worthy of inclusion in a compendium of teachings on Catholic education as it is a reminder of the need to put catechesis at the heart of the Church's educational mission.

It begins with an overview of the problems facing the Church, and in particular the Church's role *vis-à-vis* education, during the early years of the 20th Century. It draws heavily on the Encyclical *Acerbo Nimis* of Pope St. Pius X and it describes in blunt language (see para. 15) the difficulties faced by the Church in its educational work. The reader is left in no doubt as to the gravity of the situation in the inter-war years.

The document moves on through a number of short sections in which are contained more regulations and recommendations for catechesis. The section entitled *Specific Commands* sets out in some detail a strategy for remedying the situation: teachers, priests and bishops are asked to take the lead in this task. Paras. 32-35 provide an interesting and challenging set of measures which are recommended for use in dioceses.

The document ends with a questionnaire which should provide evidence of how each parish/community addresses the catechetical requirements of the community. This questionnaire is included in the Anthology as Appendix 5.

Gravissimum Educationis, Decree on Christian Education, 1965, Second Vatican Council.

The Second Vatican Council was convened by Pope John XXIII (1958-1963) in 1962 as a means of fostering a general spiritual renewal in the Church. It was also regarded as a means of dialogue with other Christian communities which were not in union with the See of Rome. This was the 21st Ecumenical Council in the history of the Church.

The Council Fathers produced sixteen documents on a wide range of issues, before closing in 1965 under Pope Paul VI (1963–1978). The key themes in these documents include the fostering of the lay vocation and dialogue with those who do not share the Catholic Christian faith.

The Decree on Christian Education, which was issued in 1965, is a concise document of only sixteen short sections. The social context has moved on considerably since the Papal Encyclicals of the first half of the 20th Century: technology and science have allowed more leisure time for much of the working population and the economic progress achieved (in Europe and North America) since the end of the Second World War in 1945 has increased the material prosperity of many citizens.

In summary, this document may be read as a re-statement of the basic principles of Christian education with the rights of the family as paramount. However, in contrast to earlier documents by Pope St. Pius X and Pope Pius XI, the tone is more nuanced with regard to the relationship between the Church and the State. In addition, emphasis is placed on the necessary role of the Church in Higher Education, in particular on the need for strong Catholic Universities.

The Catholic School, Congregation for Catholic Education, 1977

This is the first magisterial document on the nature of Catholic schools issued after the Second Vatican Council. It is a thoughtful unpacking of the ideals of Catholic education which had been adumbrated in *Gravissimum Educationis* in 1965.

The Catholic Church took some time to digest fully the pastoral importance of the Council's documents. In many ways, this is still going on today. We must also bear in mind that there were many changes in society at this time which had an impact on how Catholic schools undertook their mission. One of the challenges faced by the Council Fathers was how best to respond to cultural and social pluralism (para. 2).

The document addresses this problem directly by restating the importance of Catholic education in the wider mission of the Church. The objections of those who are not in favour of Catholic schools are answered. There is also an emphasis (para. 11) on how the Catholic vision of the human person is a solid reference point in a world marked by cultural pluralism.

There is no claim that this document is an exhaustive treatment of the nature and ideals of Catholic education. Rather, it should be read as a timely reminder that the promotion of these ideals in the culturally and socially pluralist milieu of the late 20th Century – as in the 21st Century – presents a challenge to all the baptised.

Catechesi Tradendae, Pope John Paul II, Apostolic Exhortation, 1979

For a multiplicity of reasons, catechesis had become an area of difficulty for the Church by the mid 1970s. The difference lay, broadly speaking, between competing strands of methodology: in the first place there were those who believed that the personal experience of the person/group to be catechised should be at the core of the process; on the other hand, many catechists and teachers still favoured the 'traditional' approach which focussed on the primacy of Revelation. Of course, such an analysis runs the risk of being deemed overly simplistic but it does convey the tension in the catechetical world at that time.

In 1971, the Congregation for the Clergy issued the *General Catechetical Directory*. This was an attempt both to contribute to the debate on catechetical methods and also to remind the Church that the caution which must be expressed *vis-à-vis* the development of new methodologies does not preclude their use entirely. This document is not included in this anthology as it was superseded by the *General Directory for Catechesis* in 1997.

John Paul II (1978–2005) wrote this Apostolic Exhortation not long after his election as Pope. The context of the document is the Fourth General Assembly of the Synod of Bishops in 1977 which had catechesis as its theme. This Exhortation is a synthesis of the recommendations made by the bishops at this Assembly.

It is a long document which will repay fruitfully serious study. John Paul II delineates some key points in the history of catechesis and explains clearly the nexus between catechetical endeavours and Christian mission. Catechesis is called 'a sacred duty' (para. 9) thereby leaving little room for doubt as to its place in the life of the Church.

It is essential to remind ourselves that catechesis involves the whole Church community and is not simply a process which happens in Catholic schools. Questions can be raised about the interface between catechesis and Religious Education in schools. However, Religious Education in a Catholic school, while not overly catechetical, must always be systematic, of good quality and seen to be something of value (para. 69).

Some references are made to *Evangelii Nuntiandi* (Evangelisation in the Modern World) a document written by Pope Paul VI in 1975. The role of catechesis in evangelisation is highlighted in para. 44:

"A means of evangelisation that must not be neglected is that of catechetical instruction. The intelligence, especially that of children and young people, needs to learn through systematic religious instruction the fundamental teachings, the living content of the truth which God has wished to convey to us and which the Church has sought to express in an ever richer fashion during the course of her long history. No one will deny that this instruction must be given to form patterns of Christian living and not to remain only notional. Truly the effort for evangelisation will profit greatly – at the level of catechetical instruction given at church, in the schools, where this is possible, and in every case in Christian homes – if those giving catechetical instruction have suitable texts, updated with wisdom and competence, under the authority of the bishops. The methods must be adapted to the age, culture and aptitude of the persons concerned, they must seek always to fix in the memory, intelligence and heart the essential truths that must impregnate all of life. It is necessary above all to prepare good instructors – parochial catechists, teachers, parents – who are desirous of perfecting themselves in this superior art, which is indispensable and requires religious instruction. Moreover, without neglecting in any way the training of children, one sees that present conditions render ever more urgent catechetical instruction, under the form of the catechumenate, for innumerable young people and adults who, touched by grace, discover little by little the face of Christ and feel the need of giving themselves to Him."

We can see how important it is, therefore, not to compartmentalize the notions of catechesis and evangelisation. Some see catechesis as subsequent to the initial proclamation on faith – which is called evangelisation – but here we can see some form of synthesis emerging.

Pope John Paul II was accustomed to ending his documents with an invocation to Mary. This Exhortation is no exception: she is called 'the first of the disciples', 'a living catechism' and 'the mother and model of catechists' (para. 73).

Lay Catholics in Schools: Witnesses to Faith, Sacred Congregation for Catholic Education, 1982

Following on from *The Catholic School* which was written in 1977, the Sacred Congregation for Catholic Education responded to a situation which had two distinct roots: a) the decline in the number of members of Religious Congregations who were involved in Catholic Education; b) societal developments which had brought about a worldwide increase in the number of schools. The number of lay people teaching in Catholic schools was, therefore, on the increase.

The document is a comprehensive treatise on the nature of the vocation of lay Catholic teachers. It takes the vision of the lay apostolate which had been central to the thought of the Second Vatican Council and develops it in the context of Catholic education. The Council Decree on the Apostolate of the Laity, *Apostolicam Actuositatem* (1965), explores the role of the lay person in the Church in theological terms. Much of what it says has a relevance to Catholic education, in particular with regard to the status and role of the Catholic educator. A short extract (from para 30) allows us to appreciate the depth of thinking it contains:

"Schools, colleges, and other Catholic educational institutions also have the duty to develop a Catholic sense and apostolic activity in young persons. If young people lack this formation because they do not attend these schools or for any other reason, all the more should parents, pastors of souls, and apostolic organizations attend to it. Teachers and educators on the other hand, who carry on a distinguished form of the apostolate of the laity by their vocation and office, should be equipped with that learning and pedagogical skill that are needed for imparting such education effectively."

Lay Catholics in Schools: Witnesses to Faith can be read as the application of the principles of the lay apostolate to the world of education. As such, any student who is preparing to teach in a Catholic school should see it as an *essential text* for study.

In summary, the key points are as follows: lay Catholic teachers have a specific vocation within the Church; the wider Church community has a duty to support and nourish this vocation.

The challenge for the Church now is to ensure that Catholic teachers have the opportunity to avail themselves of doctrinally-sound and stimulating formation which will enable them truly to enter into the necessary dialogue between faith and culture from firm doctrinal foundations.

The Religious Dimension of Education in a Catholic School,
Sacred Congregation for Catholic Education, 1988

This third document from the Sacred Congregation for Catholic Education in eleven years is a reflection on the nature of Catholic Education in the light of the previous two documents[1] on Catholic Education written in the years following the Second Vatican Council. This could be read as the final part of a trilogy! The thread running through this document is that the whole person – body and soul – has God as his final end. The title itself is revealing in that respect, suggesting that all education has a religious dimension. This accords with the Christian notion that all true education is, in effect, an education in virtue.

Parts I, II and III provide a profound meditation on the religious dimension of contemporary society, with particular reference to the world of young people. Part IV deals with the interface between religious instruction and catechesis (para. 68). There is a recognition of the tension that exists in this domain in schools which are viewed both as 'civic institutions' and a 'Christian community'. It would be helpful to ponder the key points of Part IV in the light of the words of *Catechesi Tradendae* (para. 69):

"Together with and in connection with the family, the school provides catechesis with possibilities that are not to be neglected. [...] This of course concerns first and foremost the Catholic school: it would no longer deserve this title if, no matter how much it shone for its high level of teaching in non-religious matters, there were justification for reproaching it for negligence or deviation in strictly Religious Education. [...] The special character of the Catholic school, the underlying reason for it, the reason why Catholic parents should prefer it, is precisely the quality of the religious instruction integrated into the education of the pupils. While Catholic establishments should respect freedom of conscience, that is to say, avoid burdening consciences from without by exerting physical or moral pressure, especially in the case of the religious activity of adolescents, they still have a grave duty to offer a religious training suited to the often widely varying religious situations of the pupils. They also have a duty to make them understand that,

---

[1] *The Catholic School,* 1977 and *Lay Catholics in Schools: Witnesses to Faith,* 1982

although God's call to serve Him in spirit and truth, in accordance with the Commandments of God and the precepts of the Church, does not apply constraint, it is nevertheless binding in conscience."

Part V provides a general summary, not just of the document, but of the general ideas of Christian education and formation which have been developed in the post-Conciliar documents.

This document is also an ideal core text for a group studying the nature and values of the Catholic school and the role and vocation of the Catholic teacher in that process.

General Directory for Catechesis, Sacred Congregation for the Clergy, 1997

In 1992, the Church issued the *Catechism of the Catholic Church*. This event was welcome in that it provided (and still provides) a sure reference-point for catechesis throughout the universal Church. Its traditional four-part structure of faith, sacraments, moral life and prayer (as well as a detailed Index) allows it to be regarded as a document worthy of study and application in all Catholic educational settings.

The *General Catechetical Directory* of 1971 had dealt with catechetical methodology *et al.* but a revision of this text was deemed necessary in order to adapt the teaching of the faith to new situations (para. 7). To this end, a group of experts in catechesis came together in the years following the publication of the *Catechism of the Catholic Church* to revise the 1971 *Directory*. The fruit of their substantial labours is the *General Directory for Catechesis*.

It is a work of some scholarship, lengthy yet clearly structured. The document is divided into five Parts, each of which has various Chapters on a variety of themes.[1] References are made to Scripture, the *Catechism of the Catholic Church* and to the major Magisterial documents on Catholic Education. Parts I and II are concerned with the major themes in catechesis and the remaining three parts have a more practical orientation. Part III offers clear guidance with regard to methodology and Christian pedagogy.

The document is addressed to those who have a locus in the mission of catechesis – especially bishops (para. 11). However, all Catholic teachers and catechists will profit from using it as part of their own personal and professional development and adapting its recommendations to the concrete situations in which they operate.

---

[1] see Contents Page

The Catholic School on the Threshold of the Third Millennium,
Congregation for Catholic Education, 1997

Twenty years after the publication of *The Catholic School*, the Congregation for Catholic Education published this reflection on the state of Catholic education at the end of the second millennium.

This short document does not shirk from identifying the problems faced by the world, the Church and Catholic education at this time. Multiculturalism, globalization, underdevelopment and a weakening of the faith of many Christians are some of the issues which have contributed to a crisis of values in society (para. 1). There is also mention made of the fact that, despite a number of documents of the Magisterium on the need for good catechesis and religious education, many young people are 'lacking in religious and moral formation' (para. 6). The question to be asked is: why is this so?

Another question asked is: If schools are increasingly viewed as places of training for employment and/or providers of certificates, how is it possible to have a vision of education which is truly Christian and which has the promotion of values at its core (para. 10)? This debate is still continuing.

Despite the existence of these challenges, Catholics are reminded that the way ahead must lie in a vision of education which places the integral education of the human person at the centre of any programme of studies. Christ Himself is the goal of this project (para. 4).

THEMATIC STUDY GUIDE

Introduction

This Study Guide has been designed to be of practical use for all who have an interest in Catholic education. There are two ways of familiarising oneself with the material in the documents contained in this volume. The first way is to read through the documents systematically in, for example, chronological order. The second way is to identify a specific theme and research how this theme is developed across the documents. The former is simple and straightforward. This Study Guide is designed as an aid for those who prefer the latter approach.

How To Use this Guide

Key themes in Catholic education have been identified. After a short introduction, some questions are posed. The intention of this is to focus the mind of the student on some possible implications of the theme.

The theme is then broken down into smaller sub-themes, each having a list of references which can be found in the text of the documents. *These references are not intended to be exhaustive but serve as initial points of contact with the documents.* It is recommended that students follow up references in the footnotes, both in Scripture and in related documents of the Church's Magisterium. The references given are to marginal numbers.

The documents in this volume are:

1905	*Acerbo Nimis*
1929	*Divini Illius Magistri*
1935	*Provido Sane Consilio*
1965	*Gravissimum Educationis*
1977	The Catholic School
1979	*Catechesi Tradendae*
1982	Lay Catholics in Schools
1988	The Religious Dimension of Education in a Catholic School
1997	General Directory for Catechesis
1997	The Catholic School on the Threshold of the Third Millennium

Theme 1: Pedagogy

'Pedagogy' refers to the way in which we teach our subjects. It is an area which arouses great debate in the wider educational world as well as in the world of catechesis and Religious Education.

Questions for Reflection
- Does our teaching in Religious Education require a specific method of teaching or can methods used in other disciplines be adapted fruitfully?
- Is there such a thing as 'Christian pedagogy'?
- Do we, as Catholic educators, reflect on our teaching and ask ourselves if we can improve our pedagogy?

References
The whole text of the *General Directory for Catechesis* is invaluable for this theme.

Christian pedagogy/Methods of teaching:	**33, 88, 90, 159, 228, 313, 320, 327, 333-337, 340, 507, 511, 590, 664, 670, 691-703, 711, 845, 848, 853**
Catechesis and communications media	**328, 712-714**
Catechesis and ecumenism	**314-316**
Catechesis and life experience	**304, 704**
Catechesis and sacraments	**305, 603**
Catechesis and theology	**343**
Catechesis as whole Church responsibility	**306, 772**
Catechumenate and Christian Initiation	**305, 603, 617-618, 640-642, 681**
Importance of personal contact	**376, 509**
Matching pedagogy to subjects	**228, 625, 700**
Memorization	**337, 706**
Systematic catechesis	**303, 603, 618**

Theme 2: The Teaching of Doctrine

All Christians are called to pass on the deposit of faith. This has been the case since the time of the first Christians.

Questions for Reflection

• Do we really understand the command given by Jesus in Matthew: 28:18-20?

• Why is it important to give a high profile to the teaching of doctrine?

• Have we fallen into the trap of believing that the teaching of doctrine is not an area of priority in Religious Education?

References

Acerbo Nimis and Catechesi Tradendae are both worth reading in their entirety.

Catechetical Renewal (post Second Vatican Council)	
Positive effects	**576, 579, 581**
Negative effects	**577-578, 580, 582**
Catechist, role of	**13-14, 26, 288, 701, 708, 782**
Catechesis of:	
Infants	**318, 729-732**
Children	**319, 733**
Adolescents	**320, 733**
Youth	**321, 734-737**
Content of Catechesis	**19-24, 303, 310, 312-343, 511-532, 592, 593, 632-637, 650, 660, 667**
Integrity of content	**312, 316, 334, 594-597, 663-664**
Importance of good catechetical material/ Catechisms	**14, 331-332, 334, 826**
Duties of bishops/priests	**7-12, 148-160, 174, 330, 345-346, 774, 776, 817-825**
Interface: Catechesis and RE	**240, 351, 504-507, 603, 625, 627, 731**
Teacher of Religion, role of	**412, 502, 533-534**
Teaching doctrine, consequences of not	**2, 6, 52, 137**
Teaching doctrine, importance of	**4, 16, 17, 131, 133, 179, 234, 236, 238, 240, 241, 351, 398, 411-414, 503-507, 610 b&c, 851**

Theme 3: The Catholic School – Philosophy and Special Features

Catholic schools exist for particular reasons. They have a particular philosophy which ought to underpin all that they do.

Questions for Reflection
- What should be the distinctive features of a Catholic school?
- How can Catholic schools be of benefit to the wider community?
- In what way should Catholic schools be a sign of contradiction to the wider world?

References
Please read carefully the whole of *The Religious Dimension of Education in a Catholic School* for an excellent overview of this theme.

Formation of the whole person	**224, 234, 371- 374, 470- 471, 492, 521, 526, 852, 857**
Distinctive nature of the Catholic School	**222-252**
Catechesis and the school	**351, 506, 625-627**
Atmosphere of liberty & charity	**183, 393, 462, 811**
Teaching to be under the direction of the Church	**108, 114, 625-626**
Animated by Gospel values	**183, 223-226, 238, 244, 459, 466, 812**
The promotion of virtue	**225-226, 367**
As an underpinning of the curriculum	
General	**494-495, 500-501**
History teaching	**495-496**
Literature and Art	**497-498**
Educational Science	**499**
Sex and Moral Education:	
Naturalism and premature sex education	**93-95**
Co-education	**96, 183**
Chastity, promotion of	**521**
The Catholic School and Social Justice	
Christian living provides good citizens	**82, 134, 532**
Christians as promoters of justice	**183, 202, 247, 251, 280, 311, 374, 407, 482-483, 625, 655**
Christian social ethic	**526**

Theme 4: Teachers

Good teachers are one of the keys to the success of Catholic schools. Indeed, to be a Catholic educator is more than just a profession: it is a God-given vocation.

Questions for Reflection
• What can teachers learn from Jesus, the master teacher?
• How can teachers be helped to understand more fully their vocation?
• In what way can teachers use 'promotion' and career advancement to serve the community?

References
Lay Catholics in Schools: Witnesses to Faith is a worthwhile text to read for this theme.

Catholic teachers, as a community of faith	**243, 389, 396, 411, 463, 468, 481, 854, 861**
Catholic teachers, religious and moral formation of	**116, 166, 183, 241, 267, 382, 415, 419-425, 534**
Formation for the service of catechesis	**585-589**
Importance of centres of formation	**419-421, 534**
Jesus as the model Teacher	**289-291, 689**
Schools for catechists and centres for higher learning for experts in catechesis	**800-804**
Teachers of religion	**155, 241, 383, 502, 512, 533-534, 625-626**
Teaching as a vocation	**180, 183, 370, 374, 392, 398, 415-416**
Witness of teachers	**183, 232, 277, 371, 380, 383-384, 387-388, 395, 463, 474, 509, 512, 515, 547, 861-862**

Theme 5: Cultural Pluralism and Dialogue

Early Christian writers faced up to the cultural implications of Christian living. How to deal with non-Christian belief systems was a key area for debate. How best to deal with other cultures is a question which is as old as Christianity itself.

Questions for Reflection
• What role should Catholic schools play in a plural state?
• How far can Christianity attempt to influence the wider culture?
• Can the Gospel be adapted to suit the prevailing culture?

References

Catholic schools as part of plural society	**182, 201-202, 255, 280, 369, 373, 402, 844, 848, 859**
Christian identity in a plural society	**200, 204, 251, 373**
Dialogue with culture	**204, 335, 375, 384, 385, 488, 490, 538b, 572-573, 857**
Inculturation of the Gospel	**661-663, 755**
Mutual respect with other non-Catholic educators	**405**
Non-Catholics students in a Catholic School	**184, 397, 443**
Split between culture and the Gospel	**452, 660**

Theme 6: Catholic Education and the State

Catholic schools should contribute to the common good of the community. Their relationship with the State ought to be harmonious.

Questions for Reflection
• Are there potential problems when Catholic schools have a close relationship with the State? What are they?
• Should Catholic teachers be employed by the State or by the Church?
• What should happen when Catholic schools are opposed to the agenda of the State?

References

Harmony between Church and State	**56, 71, 79-80, 369, 860**
Funding of Catholic Schools	**210, 270-271, 850**
State as Protector of the family's role in education	**71-72**
State as Protector of the child	**73**
State as Protector of education of youth	**74**

Theme 7: Family

The importance of the family in religious and moral education
cannot be over-emphasised. The family is the basic unit of society

Questions for Reflection
- Do we recognise that all educators of young people act *in loco
  parentis*?
- What can Catholic schools and parishes do to encourage
  catechesis and prayer within the family home?
- Are we active in support of the right of families to be
  recognised as the principal educators of their children?

References

Education as true work of the family	**58-68**
Family catechesis	**158, 240, 350, 628, 730, 807**
Good example of a well-ordered family life	**99, 101-102, 141, 178, 455**
Priority of the family over civil society	**40, 56, 181**
The family as principal educators	**178, 181, 262, 367-369, 469, 479-480, 778-779, 861, 863**

ENCYCLICAL, *ACERBO NIMIS*
Pope Pius X, on Teaching Christian Doctrine
15 April 1905

To the Patriarchs, Primates, Archbishops, Bishops and other Ordinaries in Peace and Communion with the Apostolic See.

Venerable Brethren, Health and the Apostolic Blessing.

1. At this very troublesome and difficult time, the hidden designs of God have conducted Our poor strength to the office of Supreme pastor, to rule the entire flock of Christ. The enemy has, indeed, long been prowling about the fold and attacking it with such subtle cunning that now, more than ever before, the prediction of the Apostle to the elders of the Church of Ephesus seems to be verified: "I know that . . . fierce wolves will get in among you, and will not spare the flock."[1] Those who still are zealous for the glory of God are seeking the causes and reasons for this decline in religion. Coming to a different explanation, each points out, according to his own view, a different plan for the protection and restoration of the kingdom of God on earth. But it seems to Us, Venerable Brethren, that while we should not overlook other considerations, We are forced to agree with those who hold that the chief cause of the present indifference and, as it were, infirmity of soul, and the serious evils that result from it, is to be found above all in ignorance of things divine. This is fully in accord with what God Himself declared through the Prophet Hosea: "And there is no knowledge of God in the land. Cursing and lying and killing and theft and adultery have overflowed: and

1

---

[1] Acts 20:29.

blood hath touched blood. Thereafter shall the land mourn, and everyone that dwells in it shall languish."[2]

2   2. It is a common complaint, unfortunately too well founded, that there are large numbers of Christians in our own time who are entirely ignorant of those truths necessary for salvation. And when we mention Christians, We refer not only to the masses or to those in the lower walks of life – for these find some excuse for their ignorance in the fact that the demands of their harsh employers hardly leave them time to take care of themselves or of their dear ones – but We refer to those especially who do not lack culture or talents and, indeed, are possessed of abundant knowledge regarding things of the world but live rashly and imprudently with regard to religion. It is hard to find words to describe how profound is the darkness in which they are engulfed and, what is most deplorable of all, how tranquilly they repose there. They rarely give thought to God, the Supreme Author and Ruler of all things, or to the teachings of the faith of Christ. They know nothing of the Incarnation of the Word of God, nothing of the perfect restoration of the human race which He accomplished. Grace, the greatest of the helps for attaining eternal things, the Holy Sacrifice and the Sacraments by which we obtain grace, are entirely unknown to them. They have no conception of the malice and baseness of sin; hence they show no anxiety to avoid sin or to renounce it. And so they arrive at life's end in such a condition that, lest all hope of salvation be lost, the priest is obliged to give in the last few moments of life a summary teaching of religion, a time which should be devoted to stimulating the soul to greater love for God. And even this as too often happens only when the dying man is not so sinfully ignorant as to look upon the ministration of the priest as useless, and then calmly faces the fearful passage to eternity without making his peace with God. And so Our Predecessor, Benedict XIV, had just cause to write: "We declare that a great number of those who are condemned to eternal punishment suffer that everlasting calamity because of ignorance of those mysteries of faith which must be known and believed in order to be numbered among the elect."[3]

---

[2] Hos 4:1-3.
[3] Instit., 27:18.

3. There is then, Venerable Brethren, no reason for wonder that the corruption of morals and depravity of life is already so great, and ever increasingly greater, not only among uncivilized peoples* but even in those very nations that are called Christian. The Apostle Paul, writing to the Ephesians, repeatedly admonished them in these words: "But immorality and every uncleanness or covetousness, let it not even be named among you, as become saints; or obscenity or foolish talk."[4] He also places the foundation of holiness and sound morals upon a knowledge of divine things – which holds in check evil desires: "See to it therefore, brethren, that you walk with care: not as unwise but as wise. . . Therefore, do not become foolish, but understand what the will of the Lord is."[5] And rightly so. For the will of man retains but little of that divinely implanted love of virtue and righteousness by which it was, as it were, attracted strongly toward the real and not merely apparent good. Disordered by the stain of the first sin, and almost forgetful of God, its Author, it improperly turns every affection to a love of vanity and deceit. This erring will, blinded by its own evil desires, has need therefore of a guide to lead it back to the paths of justice whence it has so unfortunately strayed. The intellect itself is this guide, which need not be sought elsewhere, but is provided by nature itself. It is a guide, though, that, if it lack its companion light, the knowledge of divine things, will be only an instance of the blind leading the blind so that both will fall into the pit. The holy king David, praising God for the light of truth with which He had illumined the intellect, exclaimed: "The light of Thy countenance, O Lord, is signed upon us."[6] Then he described the effect of this light by adding: "Thou hast given gladness in my heart," gladness, that is, which enlarges our heart so that it runs in the way of God's Commandments.

4. All this becomes evident on a little reflection. Christian teaching reveals God and His infinite perfection with far greater clarity than is possible by the human faculties alone. Nor is that all. This same Christian teaching also commands us to honour

---

* 'Uncivilised people' refers to non-Christian people; it is not a term that Christians would normally use now – Editor's note.

[4] Eph 5:34.

[5] Eph 5:15-16.

[6] Ps 4:7.

God by faith, which is of the mind, by hope, which is of the will, by love, which is of the heart; and thus the whole man is subjected to the supreme Maker and Ruler of all things. The truly remarkable dignity of man as the son of the heavenly Father, in Whose image he is formed, and with Whom he is destined to live in eternal happiness, is also revealed only by the doctrine of Jesus Christ. From this very dignity, and from man's knowledge of it, Christ showed that men should love one another as brothers, and should live here as become children of light, "not of revelry and drunkenness, not in debauchery and wantonness, not in strife and jealousy."[7] He also bids us to place all our anxiety and care in the hands of God, for He will provide for us; He tells us to help the poor, to do good to those who hate us, and to prefer the eternal welfare of the soul to the temporal goods of this life. Without wishing to touch on every detail, nevertheless is it not true that the proud man is urged and commanded by the teaching of Christ to strive for humility, the source of true glory? "Whoever, therefore, humbles himself . . . he is the greatest in the kingdom of heaven."[8] From that same teaching we learn prudence of the spirit, and thereby we avoid prudence of the flesh; we learn justice, by which we give to every man his due; fortitude, which prepares us to endure all things and with steadfast heart suffer all things for the sake of God and eternal happiness; and, last of all, temperance through which we cherish even poverty borne out of love for God, nay, we even glory in the cross itself, unmindful of its shame. *In fine*, Christian teaching not only bestows on the intellect the light by which it attains truth, but from it our will draws that ardour by which we are raised up to God and joined with Him in the practice of virtue.

5

5. We by no means wish to conclude that a perverse will and unbridled conduct may not be joined with a knowledge of religion. Would to God that facts did not too abundantly prove the contrary! But We do maintain that the will cannot be upright nor the conduct good when the mind is shrouded in the darkness of crass ignorance. A man who walks with open eyes may, indeed, turn aside from the right path, but a blind man is in much more

---

[7] Rom 13:13.
[8] Matt 18:4.

imminent danger of wandering away. Furthermore, there is always some hope for a reform of perverse conduct so long as the light of faith is not entirely extinguished; but if lack of faith is added to depraved morality because of ignorance, the evil hardly admits of remedy, and the road to ruin lies open.

6. How many and how grave are the consequences of ignorance in matters of religion! And on the other hand, how necessary and how beneficial is religious instruction! It is indeed vain to expect a fulfilment of the duties of a Christian by one who does not even know them.

6

7. We must now consider upon whom rests the obligation to dissipate this most pernicious ignorance and to impart in its stead the knowledge that is wholly indispensable. There can be no doubt, Venerable Brethren, that this most important duty rests upon all who are pastors of souls. On them, by command of Christ, rest the obligations of knowing and of feeding the flocks committed to their care; and to feed implies, first of all, to teach. "I will give you pastors according to my own heart," God promised through Jeremias, "and they shall feed you with knowledge and doctrine."[9] Hence the Apostle Paul said: "Christ did not send me to baptize, but to preach the gospel,"[10] thereby indicating that the first duty of all those who are entrusted in any way with the government of the Church is to instruct the faithful in the things of God.

7

8. We do not think it necessary to set forth here the praises of such instruction or to point out how meritorious it is in God's sight. If, assuredly, the alms with which we relieve the needs of the poor are highly praised by the Lord, how much more precious in His eyes, then, will be the zeal and labour expended in teaching and admonishing, by which we provide not for the passing needs of the body but for the eternal profit of the soul! Nothing, surely, is more desirable, nothing more acceptable to Jesus Christ, the Saviour of souls, Who testifies of Himself through Isaias: "To bring good news to the poor he has sent me."[11]

8

9. Here then it is well to emphasize and insist that for a priest

9

---

[9] Jer 3:15.
[10] 1 Cor 1:17.
[11] Luke 4:18.

there is no duty more grave or obligation more binding than this. Who, indeed, will deny that knowledge should be joined to holiness of life in the priest? "For the lips of the priest shall keep knowledge."[12] The Church demands this knowledge of those who are to be ordained to the priesthood. Why? Because the Christian people expect from them knowledge of the divine law, and it was for that end that they were sent by God. "And they shall seek the law at his mouth; because he is the angel of the Lord of hosts."[13] Thus the bishop speaking to the candidates for the priesthood in the ordination ceremony says: "Let your teaching be a spiritual remedy for God's people; may they be worthy fellow-workers of our order; and thus meditating day and night on His law, they may believe what they read, and teach what they shall believe."[14]

10   10. If what We have just said is applicable to all priests, does it not apply with much greater force to those who possess the title and the authority of parish priests, and who, by virtue of their rank and in a sense by virtue of a contract, hold the office of pastors of souls? These are, to a certain extent, the pastors and teachers appointed by Christ in order that the faithful might not be as "children, tossed to and fro and carried about by every wind of doctrine devised in the wickedness of men," but that practising "the truth in love," they may, "grow up in all things in him who is the head, Christ."[15]

11   11. For this reason the Council of Trent,[*] treating of the duties of pastors of souls, decreed that their first and most important work is the instruction of the faithful.[16] It therefore prescribes that they shall teach the truths of religion on Sundays and on the more solemn feast days; moreover during the holy seasons of Advent and Lent they are to give such instruction

---

[12] Mal 2:7.

[13] *Ibid.*

[14] Roman Pontifical.

[15] Eph 4:14, 18.

[*] 'Council of Trent' – this was the 19th Ecumenical Council in the history of the Church. It was in session from 1545-1563. The principal objectives of this Council were:

    a) to develop doctrine in response to the Reformation;

    b) to root out abuses which had crept into the life of the Church. – Editor's note.

[16] Sess. V, cap. 2, De Reform.; Sess. XXII, cap. 8; Sess. XXIV, cap. 4 & 7, De Reform.

every day or at least three times a week. This, however, was not considered enough. The Council provided for the instruction of youth by adding that the pastors, either personally or through others, must explain the truths of religion at least on Sundays and feast days to the children of the parish, and inculcate obedience to God and to their parents. When the Sacraments are to be administered, it enjoins upon pastors the duty to explain their efficacy in plain and simple language.

12. These prescriptions of the Council of Trent have been **12** summarized and still more clearly defined by Our Predecessor, Benedict XIV, in his Constitution *Esti minime.* "Two chief obligations," he wrote, "have been imposed by the Council of Trent on those who have the care of souls: first, that of preaching the things of God to the people on feast days; and second, that of teaching the rudiments of faith and of the divine law to the youth and others who need such instruction." Here the wise Pontiff rightly distinguishes between these two duties: one is what is commonly known as the explanation of the Gospel and the other is the teaching of Christian doctrine. Perhaps there are some who, wishing to lessen their labours, would believe that the homily on the Gospel can take the place of catechetical instruction. But for one who reflects a moment, such is obviously impossible. The sermon on the holy Gospel is addressed to those who should have already received knowledge of the elements of faith. It is, so to speak, bread broken for adults. Catechetical instruction, on the other hand, is that milk which the Apostle Peter wished the faithful to desire in all simplicity like newborn babes.

13. The task of the catechist is to take up one or other of the **13** truths of faith or of Christian morality and then explain it in all its parts; and since amendment of life is the chief aim of his instruction, the catechist must needs make a comparison between what God commands us to do and what is our actual conduct. After this, he will use examples appropriately taken from the Holy Scriptures, Church history, and the lives of the saints – thus moving his hearers and clearly pointing out to them how they are to regulate their own conduct. He should, in conclusion, earnestly exhort all present to dread and avoid vice and to practise virtue.

14. We are indeed aware that the work of teaching the **14**

Catechism[*] is unpopular with many because as a rule it is deemed of little account and for the reason that it does not lend itself easily to the winning of public praise. But this in Our opinion is a judgment based on vanity and devoid of truth. We do not disapprove of those pulpit orators who, out of genuine zeal for the glory of God, devote themselves to defence of the faith and to its spread, or who eulogize the saints of God. But their labour presupposes labour of another kind, that of the catechist. And so if this be lacking, then the foundation is wanting; and they labour in vain who build the house. Too often it happens that ornate sermons which receive the applause of crowded congregations serve but to tickle the ears and fail utterly to touch the hearts of the hearers. Catechetical instruction, on the other hand, plain and simple though it be, is the word of which God Himself speaks through the lips of the prophet Isaias: "And as the rain and the snow come down from heaven, and return no more thither, but soak the earth and water it, and make it to spring and give seed to the sower and bread to the eater: so shall my word be, which shall go forth from my mouth. It shall not return to me void, but it shall do whatsoever I please and shall prosper in the things for which I sent it."[17] We believe the same may be said of those priests who work hard to produce books which explain the truths of religion. They are surely to be commended for their zeal, but how many are there who read these works and take from them a fruit commensurate with the labour and intention of the writers? The teaching of the Catechism, on the other hand, when rightly done, never fails to profit those who listen to it.

15   15. In order to enkindle the zeal of the ministers of God, We again insist on the need to reach the ever-increasing numbers of those who know nothing at all of religion, or who possess at most only such knowledge of God and Christian truths as befits idolaters. How many there are, alas, not only among the young, but among adults and those advanced in years, who know nothing of the chief mysteries of faith; who on hearing the name of Christ can only ask? "Who is he. . . that I may believe in him?"[18] In

---

[*] Pope Pius is referring to the *Catechism of the Council of Trent*, also known as the *Roman Catechism.* – Editor's note.

[17] Is 88:10-11.

[18] John 9:36.

consequence of this ignorance, they do not consider it a crime to excite and nourish hatred against their neighbour, to enter into most unjust contracts, to do business in dishonest fashion, to hold the funds of others at an exorbitant interest rate, and to commit other iniquities no less reprehensible. They are, moreover, ignorant of the law of Christ which not only condemns immoral actions but also forbids deliberate immoral thoughts and desires. Even when for some reason or other they avoid sensual pleasures, they nevertheless entertain evil thoughts without the least scruple, thereby multiplying their sins above the number of the hairs of the head. These persons are found, we deem it necessary to repeat, not merely among the poorer classes of the people or in sparsely settled districts, but also among those in the higher walks of life, even, indeed, among those puffed up with learning, who, relying upon a vain erudition, feel free to ridicule religion and to "deride whatever they do not know."[19]

16. Now, if we cannot expect to reap a harvest when no seed **16** has been planted, how can we hope to have a people with sound morals if Christian doctrine has not been imparted to them in due time? It follows, too, that if faith languishes in our days, if among large numbers it has almost vanished, the reason is that the duty of catechetical teaching is either fulfilled very superficially or altogether neglected. It will not do to say, in excuse, that faith is a free gift of God bestowed upon each one at Baptism. True enough, when we are baptized in Christ, the habit of faith is given, but this most divine seed, if left entirely to itself, by its own power, so to speak, is not like the mustard seed which "grows up. . . and puts out great branches."[20] Man has the faculty of understanding at his birth, but he also has need of his mother's word to awaken it, as it were, and to make it active. So too, the Christian, born again of water and the Holy Spirit, has faith within him, but he requires the word of the teaching Church to nourish and develop it and to make it bear fruit. Thus wrote the Apostle: "Faith then depends on hearing, and hearing on the word of Christ";[21] and to show the necessity of instruction, he added,

---

[19] Jude 10.
[20] Mark 4:32.
[21] Rom 10:17.

"How are they to hear, if no one preaches?"[22]

17   17. What We have said so far demonstrates the supreme importance of religious instruction. We ought, therefore, to do all that lies in our power to maintain the teaching of Christian doctrine with full vigour, and where such is neglected, to restore it; for in the words of Our Predecessor, Benedict XIV, "There is nothing more effective than catechetical instruction to spread the glory of God and to secure the salvation of souls."[23]

18   18. We, therefore, Venerable Brethren, desirous of fulfilling this most important obligation of Our Teaching Office, and likewise wishing to introduce uniformity everywhere in so weighty a matter, do by Our Supreme Authority enact the following regulations and strictly command that they be observed and carried out in all dioceses of the world.

19   19. I. On every Sunday and holy day, with no exception, throughout the year, all parish priests and in general all those having the care of souls, shall instruct the boys and girls, for the space of an hour from the text of the Catechism on those things they must believe and do in order to attain salvation.

20   20. II. At certain times throughout the year, they shall prepare boys and girls to receive properly the Sacraments of Penance and Confirmation, by a continued instruction over a period of days.

21   21. III. With a very special zeal, on every day in Lent and, if necessary, on the days following Easter, they shall instruct with the use of apt illustrations and exhortations the youth of both sexes to receive their first Communion in a holy manner.

22   22. IV. In each and every parish the society known as the Confraternity of Christian Doctrine is to be canonically established. Through this Confraternity, the pastors, especially in places where there is a scarcity of priests, will have lay helpers in the teaching of the Catechism, who will take up the work of imparting knowledge both from a zeal for the glory of God and in order to gain the numerous Indulgences granted by the Sovereign Pontiffs.

23   23. V. In the larger cities, and especially where universities,

---

[22] *Ibid.*, 14.
[23] Constitution, *Etsi minime*, 13.

colleges and secondary schools are located, let classes in religion be organized to instruct in the truths of faith and in the practice of Christian life the youths who attend the public schools from which all religious teaching is banned.

24. VI. Since it is a fact that in these days adults need **24** instruction no less than the young, all pastors and those having the care of souls shall explain the Catechism to the people in a plain and simple style adapted to the intelligence of their hearers. This shall be carried out on all holy days of obligation, at such time as is most convenient for the people, but not during the same hour when the children are instructed, and this instruction must be in addition to the usual homily on the Gospel which is delivered at the parochial Mass on Sundays and holy days. The catechetical instruction shall be based on the Catechism of the Council of Trent; and the matter is to be divided in such a way that in the space of four or five years, treatment will be given to the Apostles' Creed, the Sacraments, the Ten Commandments, the Lord's Prayer and the Precepts of the Church.

25. Venerable Brethren, We decree and command this by **25** virtue of Our Apostolic Authority. It now rests with you to put it into prompt and complete execution in your respective dioceses, and by the power of your authority to see to it that these prescriptions of Ours be not neglected or, what amounts to the same thing, that they be not carried out carelessly or superficially. That this may be avoided, you must exhort and urge your pastors not to impart these instructions without having first prepared themselves in the work. Then they will not merely speak words of human wisdom, but "in simplicity and godly sincerity,"[24] imitating the example of Jesus Christ, Who, though He revealed "things hidden since the foundation of the world,"[25] yet spoke "all . . . things to the crowds in parables, and without parables . . . did not speak to them."[26] We know that the Apostles, who were taught by the Lord, did the same; for of them Pope Saint Gregory wrote: "They took supreme care to preach to the uninstructed simple truths easy to understand, not things deep and difficult."[27]

---

[24] 2 Cor 1:12.
[25] Matt 13:35.
[26] *Ibid.*, 34.
[27] Morals I, 17, chap 26

In matters of religion, the majority of men in our times must be considered uninstructed.

26 26. We do not, however, wish to give the impression that this studied simplicity in imparting instruction does not require labour and meditation – on the contrary, it demands both more than any other kind of preaching. It is much easier to find a preacher capable of delivering an eloquent and elaborate discourse than a catechist who can impart a catechetical instruction which is praiseworthy in every detail. No matter what natural facility a person may have in ideas and language, let him always remember that he will never be able to teach Christian doctrine to children or to adults without first giving himself to very careful study and preparation. They are mistaken who think that because of inexperience and lack of training of the people the work of catechizing can be performed in a slipshod fashion. On the contrary, the less educated the hearers, the more zeal and diligence must be used to adapt the sublime truths to their untrained minds; these truths, indeed, far surpass the natural understanding of the people, yet must be known by all – the uneducated and the cultured – in order that they may arrive at eternal happiness.

27 27. And now, Venerable Brethren, permit Us to close this letter by addressing to you these words of Moses: "If any man be on the Lord's side, let him join with me."[28] We pray and entreat you to reflect on the great loss of souls due solely to ignorance of divine things. You have doubtless accomplished many useful and most praiseworthy works in your respective dioceses for the good of the flock entrusted to your care, but before all else, and with all possible zeal and diligence and care, see to it and urge on others that the knowledge of Christian doctrine pervades and imbues fully and deeply the minds of all. Here, using the words of the Apostle Peter, We say, "According to the gift that each has received, administer it to one another as good stewards of the manifold grace of God."[29]

28 28. Through the intercession of the Most Blessed Immaculate Virgin, may your diligent efforts be made fruitful by the

---

[28] Ex 32:26.
[29] 1 Pet 4:10.

Apostolic Blessing which, in token of Our affection and as a pledge of heavenly favours, We wholeheartedly impart to you and to your clergy and people.

Given at Rome, at Saint Peter's, on the fifteenth day of April, 1905, in the second year of Our Pontificate.

Pope Pius X

ENCYCLICAL, *DIVINI ILLIUS MAGISTRI*
Pope Pius XI, On Christian Education
31 December 1929

To the Patriarchs, Primates, Archbishops, Bishops, and other Ordinaries in peace and communion with the Apostolic See and to all the faithful of the Catholic world.

Venerable Brethren and Beloved Children, Health and Apostolic Benediction.

1. Representative on earth of that divine Master who while embracing in the immensity of His love all mankind, even unworthy sinners, showed nevertheless a special tenderness and affection for children, and expressed Himself in those singularly touching words: "Suffer the little children to come unto Me,"[1] We also on every occasion have endeavoured to show the predilection wholly paternal which We bear towards them, particularly by our assiduous care and timely instructions with reference to the Christian education of youth. **29**

2. And so, in the spirit of the Divine Master, We have directed a helpful word, now of admonition, now of exhortation, now of direction, to youths and to their educators, to fathers and mothers, on various points of Christian education, with that **30**

---

[1] Mark 10:14.

solicitude which becomes the common Father of all the Faithful, with an insistence in season and out of season, demanded by our pastoral office and inculcated by the Apostle: "Be instant in season, out of season; reprove, entreat, rebuke in all patience and doctrine."[2] Such insistence is called for in these our times, when, alas, there is so great and deplorable an absence of clear and sound principles, even regarding problems the most fundamental.

31   3. Now this same general condition of the times, this ceaseless agitation in various ways of the problem of educational rights and systems in different countries, the desire expressed to Us with filial confidence by not a few of yourselves, Venerable Brethren, and by members of your flocks, as well as Our deep affection towards youth above referred to, move Us to turn more directly to this subject, if not to treat it in all its well-nigh inexhaustible range of theory and practice, at least to summarize its main principles, throw full light on its important conclusions, and point out its practical applications.

32   4. Let this be the record of Our Sacerdotal Jubilee which, with altogether special affection, We wish to dedicate to our beloved youth, and to commend to all those whose office and duty is the work of education.

33   5. Indeed never has there been so much discussion about education as nowadays; never have exponents of new pedagogical theories been so numerous, or so many methods and means devised, proposed and debated, not merely to facilitate education, but to create a new system infallibly efficacious, and capable of preparing the present generations for that earthly happiness which they so ardently desire.

34   6. The reason is that men, created by God to His image and likeness and destined for Him Who is infinite perfection realize today more than ever amid the most exuberant material progress, the insufficiency of earthly goods to produce true happiness either for the individual or for the nations. And hence they feel more keenly in themselves the impulse towards a perfection that is higher, which impulse is implanted in their rational nature by the Creator Himself. This perfection they seek to acquire by means of education. But many of them with, it would seem, too great

---

[2] 2 Tim 4:2:.

insistence on the etymological meaning of the word, pretend to draw education out of human nature itself and evolve it by its own unaided powers. Such easily fall into error, because, instead of fixing their gaze on God, first principle and last end of the whole universe, they fall back upon themselves, becoming attached exclusively to passing things of earth; and thus their restlessness will never cease till they direct their attention and their efforts to God, the goal of all perfection, according to the profound saying of Saint Augustine: "You created us, O Lord, for Yourself, and our heart is restless till it rest in You."[3]

7. It is therefore as important to make no mistake in **35** education, as it is to make no mistake in the pursuit of the last end, with which the whole work of education is intimately and necessarily connected. In fact, since education consists essentially in preparing man for what he must be and for what he must do here below, in order to attain the sublime end for which he was created, it is clear that there can be no true education which is not wholly directed to man's last end, and that in the present order of Providence, since God has revealed Himself to us in the Person of His Only Begotten Son, who alone is "the way, the truth and the life," there can be no ideally perfect education which is not Christian education.

8. From this we see the supreme importance of Christian **36** education, not merely for each individual, but for families and for the whole of human society, whose perfection comes from the perfection of the elements that compose it. From these same principles, the excellence, we may well call it the unsurpassed excellence, of the work of Christian education becomes manifest and clear; for after all it aims at securing the Supreme Good, that is, God, for the souls of those who are being educated, and the maximum of well-being possible here below for human society. And this it does as efficaciously as man is capable of doing it, namely by cooperating with God in the perfecting of individuals and of society, in as much as education makes upon the soul the first, the most powerful and lasting impression for life according to the well-known saying of the Wise Man, "A young man according to his way, even when he is old, he will not depart from

---

[3] *Confessions*, I, I.

it."[4] With good reason therefore did St. John Chrysostom say, "What greater work is there than training the mind and forming the habits of the young?"[5]

37   9. But nothing discloses to us the supernatural beauty and excellence of the work of Christian education better than the sublime expression of love of our Blessed Lord, identifying Himself with children, "Whosoever shall receive one such child as this in my name, receives me."[6]

38   10. Now in order that no mistake be made in this work of utmost importance, and in order to conduct it in the best manner possible with the help of God's grace, it is necessary to have a clear and definite idea of Christian education in its essential aspects, viz., who has the mission to educate, who are the subjects to be educated, what are the necessary accompanying circumstances, what is the end and object proper to Christian education according to God's established order in the economy of His Divine Providence.

39   11. Education is essentially a social and not a mere individual activity. Now there are three necessary societies, distinct from one another and yet harmoniously combined by God, into which man is born: two, namely the family and civil society, belong to the natural order; the third, the Church, to the supernatural order.

40   12. In the first place comes the family, instituted directly by God for its peculiar purpose, the generation and formation of offspring; for this reason it has priority of nature and therefore of rights over civil society. Nevertheless, the family is an imperfect society, since it has not in itself all the means for its own complete development; whereas civil society is a perfect society, having in itself all the means for its peculiar end, which is the temporal well-being of the community; and so, in this respect, that is, in view of the common good, it has pre-eminence over the family, which finds its own suitable temporal perfection precisely in civil society.

41   13. The third society, into which man is born when through Baptism he reaches the divine life of grace, is the Church; a

---

[4] Prov 22:6.
[5] *Hom. 60, in c. 18 Matth.: Quid maius quam animis moderari, quam adolescentulorum fingere mores?*
[6] Mark 9:37.

society of the supernatural order and of universal extent; a perfect society, because it has in itself all the means required for its own end, which is the eternal salvation of mankind; hence it is supreme in its own domain.

14. Consequently, education which is concerned with man as **42** a whole, individually and socially, in the order of nature and in the order of grace, necessarily belongs to all these three societies, in due proportion, corresponding, according to the disposition of Divine Providence, to the co-ordination of their respecting ends.

15. And first of all education belongs pre-eminently to the **43** Church, by reason of a double title in the supernatural order, conferred exclusively upon her by God Himself; absolutely superior therefore to any other title in the natural order.

16. The first title is founded upon the express mission and **44** supreme authority to teach, given her by her divine Founder: "All power is given to me in heaven and in earth. Going therefore teach ye all nations, baptizing them in the name of the Father, and of the Son, and of the Holy Spirit, teaching them to observe all things whatsoever I have commanded you, and behold I am with you all days, even to the consummation of the world."[7] Upon this magisterial office Christ conferred infallibility, together with the command to teach His doctrine. Hence the Church "was set by her divine Author as the pillar and ground of truth, in order to teach the divine Faith to men, and keep whole and inviolate the deposit confided to her; to direct and fashion men, in all their actions individually and socially, to purity of morals and integrity of life, in accordance with revealed doctrine."[8]

17. The second title is the supernatural motherhood, in virtue **45** of which the Church, spotless spouse of Christ, generates, nurtures and educates souls in the divine life of grace, with her Sacraments and her doctrine. With good reason then does St. Augustine maintain: "He has not God for father who refuses to have the Church as mother."[9]

18. Hence it is that in this proper object of her mission, that **46** is, "in faith and morals, God Himself has made the Church sharer

---

[7] Matt 28:18-20.
[8] Pius IX, Ep. *Quum non sine*, 14 July 1864.
[9] *De Symbolo ad catech., XIII.*

in the divine magisterium and, by a special privilege, granted her immunity from error; hence she is the mistress of men, supreme and absolutely sure, and she has inherent in herself an inviolable right to freedom in teaching.'[10] By necessary consequence the Church is independent of any sort of earthly power as well in the origin as in the exercise of her mission as educator, not merely in regard to her proper end and object, but also in regard to the means necessary and suitable to attain that end. Hence with regard to every other kind of human learning and instruction, which is the common patrimony of individuals and society, the Church has an independent right to make use of it, and above all to decide what may help or harm Christian education. And this must be so, because the Church as a perfect society has an independent right to the means conducive to its end, and because every form of instruction, no less than every human action, has a necessary connection with man's last end, and therefore cannot be withdrawn from the dictates of the divine law, of which the Church is guardian, interpreter and infallible mistress.

47   19. This truth is clearly set forth by Pius X of saintly memory: "Whatever a Christian does even in the order of things of earth, he may not overlook the supernatural; indeed he must, according to the teaching of Christian wisdom, direct all things towards the supreme good as to his last end; all his actions, besides, in so far as good or evil in the order of morality, that is, in keeping or not with natural and divine law, fall under the judgment and jurisdiction of the Church."[11]

48   20. It is worthy of note how a layman, an excellent writer and at the same time a profound and conscientious thinker, has been able to understand well and express exactly this fundamental Catholic doctrine: The Church does not say that morality belongs purely, in the sense of exclusively, to her; but that it belongs wholly to her. She has never maintained that outside her fold and apart from her teaching, man cannot arrive at any moral truth; she has on the contrary more than once condemned this opinion because it has appeared under more forms than one. She does however say, has said, and will ever say, that because of her

---

[10] *Ep. enc. Libertas*, 20 June 1888.
[11] *Ep. enc. Singulari quadam*, 24 Sept. 1912.

institution by Jesus Christ, because of the Holy Spirit sent her in His name by the Father, she alone possesses what she has had immediately from God and can never lose, the whole of moral truth, *omnem veritatem*, in which all individual moral truths are included, as well those which man may learn by the help of reason, as those which form part of revelation or which may be deduced from it.[12]

21. Therefore with full right the Church promotes letters, **49** science, art in so far as necessary or helpful to Christian education, in addition to her work for the salvation of souls: founding and maintaining schools and institutions adapted to every branch of learning and degree of culture.[13] Nor may even physical culture, as it is called, be considered outside the range of her maternal supervision, for the reason that it also is a means which may help or harm Christian education.

22. And this work of the Church in every branch of culture is **50** of immense benefit to families and nations which without Christ are lost, as St Hilary points out correctly: "What can be more fraught with danger for the world than the rejection of Christ?"[14] Nor does it interfere in the least with the regulations of the State, because the Church in her motherly prudence is not unwilling that her schools and institutions for the education of the laity be in keeping with the legitimate dispositions of civil authority; she is in every way ready to cooperate with this authority and to make provision for a mutual understanding, should difficulties arise.

23. Again it is the inalienable right as well as the indis- **51** pensable duty of the Church, to watch over the entire education of her children, in all institutions, public or private, not merely in regard to the religious instruction there given, but in regard to every other branch of learning and every regulation in so far as religion and morality are concerned.[15]

24. Nor should the exercise of this right be considered undue **52** interference, but rather maternal care on the part of the Church in

---

[12] A. Manzoni, *Osservazioni sulla Morale Cattolica*, c. III.
[13] *Codex Iuris Canonici* [1917], c. 1375. [All references to Canon Law, in this document, are to the 1917 Code of Canon Law, which is no longer in use. – Editor's note].
[14] *Commentar. in Matth., cap. 18*.
[15] C. I. C. [1917], cc. 1381, 1382.

protecting her children from the grave danger of all kinds of doctrinal and moral evil. Moreover this watchfulness of the Church not merely can create no real inconvenience, but must on the contrary confer valuable assistance in the right ordering and well-being of families and of civil society; for it keeps far away from youth the moral poison which at that inexperienced and changeable age more easily penetrates the mind and more rapidly spreads its baneful effects. For it is true, as Leo XIII has wisely pointed out, that without proper religious and moral instruction "every form of intellectual culture will be injurious; for young people not accustomed to respect God, will be unable to bear the restraint of a virtuous life, and never having learned to deny themselves anything, they will easily be incited to disturb the public order."[16]

53   25. The extent of the Church's mission in the field of education is such as to embrace every nation, without exception, according to the command of Christ: "Teach ye all nations;"[17] and there is no power on earth that may lawfully oppose her or stand in her way. In the first place, it extends over all the Faithful, of whom she has anxious care as a tender mother. For these she has throughout the centuries created and conducted an immense number of schools and institutions in every branch of learning. As We said on a recent occasion: Right back in the far-off middle ages when there were so many (some have even said too many) monasteries, convents, churches, collegiate churches, cathedral chapters, etc., there was attached to each a home of study, of teaching, of Christian education. To these we must add all the universities, spread over every country and always by the initiative and under the protection of the Holy See and the Church. That grand spectacle, which today we see better, as it is nearer to us and more imposing because of the conditions of the age, was the spectacle of all times; and they who study and compare historical events remain astounded at what the Church has been able to do in this matter, and marvel at the manner in which she had succeeded in fulfilling her God-given mission to educate generations of men to a Christian life, producing

---

[16] *Ep. enc. Nobilissima Gallorum Gens*, 8 February 1884.
[17] Matt 28:19.

everywhere a magnificent harvest of fruitful results. But if we wonder that the Church in all times has been able to gather about her and educate hundreds, thousands, millions of students, no less wonderful is it to bear in mind what she has done not only in the field of education, but in that also of true and genuine erudition. For, if so many treasures of culture, civilization and literature have escaped destruction, this is due to the action by which the Church, even in times long past and uncivilized, has shed so bright a light in the domain of letters, of philosophy, of art and in a special manner of architecture.[18]

26. All this the Church has been able to do because her mission to educate extends equally to those outside the Fold, seeing that all men are called to enter the kingdom of God and reach eternal salvation. Just as today when her missions scatter schools by the thousand in districts and countries not yet Christian, from the banks of the Ganges to the Yellow River and the great islands and archipelagos of the Pacific ocean, from the Dark Continent to the Land of Fire and to frozen Alaska, so in every age the Church by her missionaries has educated to Christian life and to civilization the various peoples which now constitute the Christian nations of the civilized world.   **54**

27. Hence it is evident that both by right and in fact the mission to educate belongs pre-eminently to the Church, and that no one free from prejudice can have a reasonable motive for opposing or impeding the Church in this her work, of which the world today enjoys the precious advantages.   **55**

28. This is the more true because the rights of the family and of the State, even the rights of individuals regarding a just liberty in the pursuit of science, of methods of science and all sorts of profane culture, not only are not opposed to this pre-eminence of the Church, but are in complete harmony with it. The fundamental reason for this harmony is that the supernatural order, to which the Church owes her rights, not only does not in the least destroy the natural order, to which pertain the other rights mentioned, but elevates the natural and perfects it, each affording mutual aid to the other, and completing it in a manner proportioned to its respective nature and dignity. The reason is   **56**

---

[18] *Discourse to the students of Mondragone College*, 14 May 1929.

because both come from God, who cannot contradict Himself: "The works of God are perfect and all His ways are judgments."[19]

57   29. This becomes clearer when we consider more closely and in detail the mission of education proper to the family and to the State.

58   30. In the first place the Church's mission of education is in wonderful agreement with that of the family, for both proceed from God, and in a remarkably similar manner. God directly communicates to the family, in the natural order, fecundity, which is the principle of life, and hence also the principle of education to life, together with authority, the principle of order.

59   31. The Angelic Doctor[*] with his wonted clearness of thought and precision of style, says: "The father according to the flesh has in a particular way a share in that principle which in a manner universal is found in God.... The father is the principle of generation, of education and discipline and of everything that bears upon the perfecting of human life."[20]

60   32. The family therefore holds directly from the Creator the mission and hence the right to educate the offspring, a right inalienable because inseparably joined to the strict obligation, a right anterior to any right whatever of civil society and of the State, and therefore inviolable on the part of any power on earth.

61   33. That this right is inviolable St. Thomas proves as follows: "The child is naturally something of the father . . . so by natural right the child, before reaching the use of reason, is under the father's care. Hence it would be contrary to natural justice if the child, before the use of reason, were removed from the care of its parents, or if any disposition were made concerning him against the will of the parents."[21] And as this duty on the part of the parents continues up to the time when the child is in a position to provide for itself, this same inviolable parental right of education also endures. "Nature intends not merely the generation of the offspring, but also its development and advance to the perfection of man considered as man, that is, to the state of virtue"[22] says the

---

[19] Deut 32:4: *His work is perfect; for all his ways are justice.*

[*] St Thomas Aquinas – Editor's note.

[20] *S. Th., 2-2, Q. CII, a. I.*

[21] *S. Th., 2-2, Q. X, a. 12.1*

[22] *Suppl. S. Th. 3; p. Q. 41, a. 1.*

same St. Thomas.

34. The wisdom of the Church in this matter is expressed **62** with precision and clearness in the Codex of Canon Law, can. 1113: "Parents are under a grave obligation to see to the religious and moral education of their children, as well as to their physical and civic training, as far as they can, and moreover to provide for their temporal well-being."[23]

35. On this point the common sense of mankind is in such **63** complete accord, that they would be in open contradiction with it who dared maintain that the children belong to the State before they belong to the family, and that the State has an absolute right over their education. Untenable is the reason they adduce, namely that man is born a citizen and hence belongs primarily to the State, not bearing in mind that before being a citizen man must exist; and existence does not come from the State, but from the parents, as Leo XIII wisely declared: "The children are something of the father, and as it were an extension of the person of the father; and, to be perfectly accurate, they enter into and become part of civil society, not directly by themselves, but through the family in which they were born."[24] "And therefore," says the same Leo XIII, "the father's power is of such a nature that it cannot be destroyed or absorbed by the State; for it has the same origin as human life itself."[25] It does not however follow from this that the parents' right to educate their children is absolute and despotic; for it is necessarily subordinated to the last end and to natural and divine law, as Leo XIII declares in another memorable encyclical, where He thus sums up the rights and duties of parents: "By nature parents have a right to the training of their children, but with this added duty that the education and instruction of the child be in accord with the end for which by God's blessing it was begotten. Therefore it is the duty of parents to make every effort to prevent any invasion of their rights in this matter, and to make absolutely sure that the education of their children remain under their own control in keeping with their Christian duty, and above all to refuse to send them to those

---

[23] C. I. C. [1917], c. 1113.

[24] *Ep. enc. Rerum novarum*, 15 May 1891.

[25] *Ep. enc. Rerum novarum*, 15 May 1891

schools in which there is danger of imbibing the deadly poison of impiety."[26]

64   36. It must be borne in mind also that the obligation of the family to bring up children, includes not only religious and moral education, but physical and civic education as well,[27] principally in so far as it touches upon religion and morality.

65   37. This incontestable right of the family has at various times been recognized by nations anxious to respect the natural law in their civil enactments. Thus, to give one recent example, the Supreme Court of the United States of America, in a decision on an important controversy, declared that it is not in the competence of the State to fix any uniform standard of education by forcing children to receive instruction exclusively in public schools, and it bases its decision on the natural law: the child is not the mere creature of the State; those who nurture him and direct his destiny have the right coupled with the high duty, to educate him and prepare him for the fulfilment of his obligations.[28]

66   38. History bears witness how, particularly in modern times, the State has violated and does violate rights conferred by God on the family. At the same time it shows magnificently how the Church has ever protected and defended these rights, a fact proved by the special confidence which parents have in Catholic schools. As We pointed out recently in Our letter to the Cardinal Secretary of State: "The family has instinctively understood this to be so, and from the earliest days of Christianity down to our own times, fathers and mothers, even those of little or no faith, have been sending or bringing their children in millions to places of education under the direction of the Church."[29]

67   39. It is paternal instinct, given by God, that thus turns with confidence to the Church, certain of finding in her the protection of family rights, thereby illustrating that harmony with which

---

[26] *Ep. enc. Sapientiae christianae*, 10 January 1890.

[27] C. I. C. [1917], c.1113.

[28] U.S. Supreme Court Decision in the Oregon School Case, 1 June 1925: "The fundamental theory of liberty upon which all governments in this Union repose excludes any general power of the State to standardize its children by forcing them to accept instruction from public teachers only. The child is not the mere creature of the State; those who nurture him and direct his destiny have the right coupled with the high duty, to recognize, and prepare him for additional duties."

[29] *Letter to the Cardinal Secretary of State*, 30 May 1929.

God has ordered all things. The Church is indeed conscious of her divine mission to all mankind, and of the obligation which all men have to practice the one true religion; and therefore she never tires of defending her right, and of reminding parents of their duty, to have all Catholic-born children baptized and brought up as Christians. On the other hand so jealous is she of the family's inviolable natural right to educate the children, that she never consents, save under peculiar circumstances and with special cautions, to baptize the children of infidels, or provide for their education against the will of the parents, till such time as the children can choose for themselves and freely embrace the Faith.[30]

40. We have therefore two facts of supreme importance. As We said in Our discourse cited above: The Church placing at the disposal of families her office of mistress and educator, and the families eager to profit by the offer, and entrusting their children to the Church in hundreds and thousands. These two facts recall and proclaim a striking truth of the greatest significance in the moral and social order. They declare that the mission of education regards before all, above all, primarily the Church and the family, and this by natural and divine law, and that therefore it cannot be slighted, cannot be evaded, cannot be supplanted.[31]

68

41. From such priority of rights on the part of the Church and of the family in the field of education, most important advantages, as we have seen, accrue to the whole of society. Moreover in accordance with the divinely established order of things, no damage can follow from it to the true and just rights of the State in regard to the education of its citizens.

69

42. These rights have been conferred upon civil society by the Author of nature Himself, not by title of fatherhood, as in the case of the Church and of the family, but in virtue of the authority which it possesses to promote the common temporal welfare, which is precisely the purpose of its existence. Consequently education cannot pertain to civil society in the same way in which it pertains to the Church and to the family, but in a different way corresponding to its own particular end and object.

70

---

[30] C. I. C. [1917], c. 750, & 2. S. Th., 2, 2. Q. X., a. 12.
[31] *Discourse to the students of Mondragone College*, 14 May 1929.

71   43. Now this end and object, the common welfare in the temporal order, consists in that peace and security in which families and individual citizens have the free exercise of their rights, and at the same time enjoy the greatest spiritual and temporal prosperity possible in this life, by the mutual union and co-ordination of the work of all. The function therefore of the civil authority residing in the State is twofold, to protect and to foster, but by no means to absorb the family and the individual, or to substitute itself for them.

72   44. Accordingly in the matter of education, it is the right, or to speak more correctly, it is the duty of the State to protect in its legislation, the prior rights, already described, of the family as regards the Christian education of its offspring, and consequently also to respect the supernatural rights of the Church in this same realm of Christian education.

73   45. It also belongs to the State to protect the rights of the child itself when the parents are found wanting either physically or morally in this respect, whether by default, incapacity or misconduct, since, as has been shown, their right to educate is not an absolute and despotic one, but dependent on the natural and divine law, and therefore subject alike to the authority and jurisdiction of the Church, and to the vigilance and administrative care of the State in view of the common good. Besides, the family is not a perfect society, that is, it has not in itself all the means necessary for its full development. In such cases, exceptional no doubt, the State does not put itself in the place of the family, but merely supplies deficiencies, and provides suitable means, always in conformity with the natural rights of the child and the supernatural rights of the Church.

74   46. In general then it is the right and duty of the State to protect, according to the rules of right reason and faith, the moral and religious education of youth, by removing public impediments that stand in the way. In the first place it pertains to the State, in view of the common good, to promote in various ways the education and instruction of youth. It should begin by encouraging and assisting, of its own accord, the initiative and activity of the Church and the family, whose successes in this field have been clearly demonstrated by history and experience. It should moreover supplement their work whenever this falls short of what is necessary, even by means of its own schools and institutions. For the State more than any other society is provided with the means put at its disposal for the needs of all, and it is only right that it use these means to the advantage of those who have contributed them.[32]

47. Over and above this, the State can exact and take measures to secure that all its citizens have the necessary knowledge of their civic and political duties, and a certain degree of physical, intellectual and moral culture, which, considering the conditions of our times, is really necessary for the common good.

48. However it is clear that in all these ways of promoting education and instruction, both public and private, the State should respect the inherent rights of the Church and of the family concerning Christian education, and moreover have regard for distributive justice. Accordingly, unjust and unlawful is any monopoly, educational or scholastic, which, physically or morally, forces families to make use of government schools, contrary to the dictates of their Christian conscience, or contrary even to their legitimate preferences.

49. This does not prevent the State from making due provision for the right administration of public affairs and for the protection of its peace, within or without the realm. These are things which directly concern the public good and call for special aptitudes and special preparation. The State may therefore reserve to itself the establishment and direction of schools intended to prepare for certain civic duties and especially for military service, provided it be careful not to injure the rights of the Church or of the family in what pertains to them. It is well to repeat this warning here; for in these days there is spreading a spirit of nationalism which is false and exaggerated, as well as dangerous to true peace and prosperity. Under its influence various excesses are committed in giving a military turn to the so-called physical training of boys (sometimes even of girls, contrary to the very instincts of human nature); or again in usurping unreasonably on Sunday, the time which should be devoted to religious duties and to family life at home. It is not our intention however to condemn what is good in the spirit of discipline and legitimate bravery

75

76

77

---

[32] *Discourse to the students of Mondragone College*, 14 May 1929.

promoted by these methods; We condemn only what is excessive, as for example violence, which must not be confounded with courage nor with the noble sentiment of military valour in defence of country and public order; or again exaltation of athleticism which even in classic pagan times marked the decline and downfall of genuine physical training.

78   50. In general also it belongs to civil society and the State to provide what may be called civic education, not only for its youth, but for all ages and classes. This consists in the practice of presenting publicly to groups of individuals information having an intellectual, imaginative and emotional appeal, calculated to draw their wills to what is upright and honest, and to urge its practice by a sort of moral compulsion, positively by disseminating such knowledge, and negatively by suppressing what is opposed to it.[33] This civic education, so wide and varied in itself as to include almost every activity of the State intended for the public good, ought also to be regulated by the norms of rectitude, and therefore cannot conflict with the doctrines of the Church, which is the divinely appointed teacher of these norms.

79   51. All that we have said so far regarding the activity of the State in educational matters, rests on the solid and immovable foundation of the Catholic doctrine of *The Christian Constitution of States* set forth in such masterly fashion by Our Predecessor Leo XIII, notably in the Encyclicals *Immortale Dei* and *Sapientiae Christianae*. He writes as follows: "God has divided the government of the human race between two authorities, ecclesiastical and civil, establishing one over things divine, the other over things human. Both are supreme, each in its own domain; each has its own fixed boundaries which limit its activities. These boundaries are determined by the peculiar nature and the proximate end of each, and describe as it were a sphere within which, with exclusive right, each may develop its influence. As however the same subjects are under the two authorities, it may happen that the same matter, though from a different point of view, may come under the competence and

---

[33] P. L. Taparelli, *Saggio teor. di Diritto Naturale*, 922; a work never sufficiently praised and recommended to university students (Cf. Our *Discourse* of 18 Dec. 1927).

jurisdiction of each of them. If follows that divine Providence, whence both authorities have their origin, must have traced with due order the proper line of action for each. The powers that are, are ordained of God."[34]

52. Now the education of youth is precisely one of those matters that belong both to the Church and to the State, "though in different ways," as explained above. Therefore, continues Leo XIII, "between the two powers there must reign a well-ordered harmony. Not without reason may this mutual agreement be compared to the union of body and soul in man. Its nature and extent can only be determined by considering, as we have said, the nature of each of the two powers, and in particular the excellence and nobility of the respective ends. To one is committed directly and specifically the charge of what is helpful in worldly matters; while the other is to concern itself with the things that pertain to heaven and eternity. Everything therefore in human affairs that is in any way sacred, or has reference to the salvation of souls and the worship of God, whether by its nature or by its end, is subject to the jurisdiction and discipline of the Church. Whatever else is comprised in the civil and political order, rightly comes under the authority of the State; for Christ commanded us to give to Caesar the things that are Caesar's, and to God the things that are God's".[35]

80

53. Whoever refuses to admit these principles, and hence to apply them to education, must necessarily deny that Christ has founded His Church for the eternal salvation of mankind, and maintain instead that civil society and the State are not subject to God and to His law, natural and divine. Such a doctrine is manifestly impious, contrary to right reason, and, especially in this matter of education, extremely harmful to the proper training of youth, and disastrous as well for civil society as for the well-being of all mankind. On the other hand from the application of these principles, there inevitably result immense advantages for the right formation of citizens. This is abundantly proved by the history of every age. Tertullian in his *Apologeticus* could throw down a challenge to the enemies of the Church in the early days

81

---

[34] *Ep. enc. Immortale Dei*, 1 November 1885
[35] *Ep. enc. Immortale Dei*, 1 November 1885

of Christianity, just as St. Augustine did in his; and we today can repeat with him: "Let those who declare the teaching of Christ to be opposed to the welfare of the State, furnish us with an army of soldiers such as Christ says soldiers ought to be; let them give us subjects, husbands, wives, parents, children, masters, servants, kings, judges, taxpayers and tax gatherers who live up to the teachings of Christ; and then let them dare assert that Christian doctrine is harmful to the State. Rather let them not hesitate one moment to acclaim that doctrine, rightly observed, the greatest safeguard of the State."[36]

82

54. While treating of education, it is not out of place to show here how an ecclesiastical writer, who flourished in more recent times, during the Renaissance, the holy and learned Cardinal Silvio Antoniano, to whom the cause of Christian education is greatly indebted, has set forth most clearly this well established point of Catholic doctrine. He had been a disciple of that wonderful educator of youth, St. Philip Neri; he was teacher and Latin secretary to St. Charles Borromeo, and it was at the latter's suggestion and under his inspiration that he wrote his splendid treatise on *The Christian Education of Youth*. In it he argues as follows: "The more closely the temporal power of a nation aligns itself with the spiritual, and the more it fosters and promotes the latter, by so much the more it contributes to the conservation of the commonwealth. For it is the aim of the ecclesiastical authority by the use of spiritual means, to form good Christians in accordance with its own particular end and object; and in doing this it helps at the same time to form good citizens, and prepares them to meet their obligations as members of a civil society. This follows of necessity because in the City of God, the Holy Roman Catholic Church, a good citizen and an upright man are absolutely one and the same thing. How grave therefore is the error of those who separate things so closely united, and who think that they can produce good citizens by ways and methods other than those which make for the formation of good Christians. For, let human prudence say what it likes and reason as it pleases, it is impossible to produce true temporal peace and tranquillity by things

---

[36] *Ep. 138.*

repugnant or opposed to the peace and happiness of eternity."[37]

55. What is true of the State, is true also of science, scientific **83** methods and scientific research; they have nothing to fear from the full and perfect mandate which the Church holds in the field of education. Our Catholic institutions, whatever their grade in the educational and scientific world, have no need of apology. The esteem they enjoy, the praise they receive, the learned works which they promote and produce in such abundance, and above all, the men, fully and splendidly equipped, whom they provide for the magistracy, for the professions, for the teaching career, in fact for every walk of life, more than sufficiently testify in their favour.[38]

56. These facts moreover present a most striking confirm- **84** ation of the Catholic doctrine defined by the Vatican Council:[*] "Not only is it impossible for faith and reason to be at variance with each other, they are on the contrary of mutual help. For while right reason establishes the foundations of Faith, and, by the help of its light, develops a knowledge of the things of God, Faith on the other hand frees and preserves reason from error and enriches it with varied knowledge. The Church therefore, far from hindering the pursuit of the arts and sciences, fosters and promotes them in many ways. For she is neither ignorant nor un-appreciative of the many advantages which flow from them to mankind. On the contrary she admits that just as they come from God, Lord of all knowledge, so too if rightly used, with the help of His grace they lead to God. Nor does she prevent the sciences, each in its own sphere, from making use of principles and methods of their own. Only while acknowledging the freedom due to them, she takes every precaution to prevent them from falling into error by opposition to divine doctrine, or from overstepping their proper limits, and thus invading and disturbing the domain of Faith."[39]

57. This norm of a just freedom in things scientific, serves **85** also as an inviolable norm of a just freedom in things didactic, or

---

[37] *Dell educaz. crist.*, lib. I, c. 43.

[38] Letter to the Cardinal Secretary of State, 30 May 1929.

[*] This is the First Vatican Council (the 20th in the history of the Church) which ran from 1869-1870. – Editor's note.

[39] First Vatican Council, Session 3, ch. 4.

for rightly understood liberty in teaching; it should be observed therefore in whatever instruction is imparted to others. Its obligation is all the more binding in justice when there is question of instructing youth. For in this work the teacher, whether public or private, has no absolute right of his own, but only such as has been communicated to him by others. Besides every Christian child or youth has a strict right to instruction in harmony with the teaching of the Church, the pillar and ground of truth. And whoever disturbs the pupil's Faith in any way, does him grave wrong, inasmuch as he abuses the trust which children place in their teachers, and takes unfair advantage of their inexperience and of their natural craving for unrestrained liberty, at once illusory and false.

86   58. In fact it must never be forgotten that the subject of Christian education is man whole and entire, soul united to body in unity of nature, with all his faculties natural and supernatural, such as right reason and revelation show him to be; man, therefore, fallen from his original estate, but redeemed by Christ and restored to the supernatural condition of adopted son of God, though without the preternatural privileges of bodily immortality or perfect control of appetite. There remain therefore, in human nature the effects of original sin, the chief of which are weakness of will and disorderly inclinations.

87   59. "Folly is bound up in the heart of a child and the rod of correction shall drive it away."[40] Disorderly inclinations then must be corrected, good tendencies encouraged and regulated from tender childhood, and above all the mind must be enlightened and the will strengthened by supernatural truth and by the means of grace, without which it is impossible to control evil impulses, impossible to attain to the full and complete perfection of education intended by the Church, which Christ has endowed so richly with divine doctrine and with the Sacraments, the efficacious means of grace.

88   60. Hence every form of pedagogic naturalism which in any way excludes or weakens supernatural Christian formation in the teaching of youth, is false. Every method of education founded, wholly or in part, on the denial or forgetfulness of original sin and

---

[40] Prov 22:15:

of grace, and relying on the sole powers of human nature, is unsound. Such, generally speaking, are those modern systems bearing various names which appeal to a pretended self-government and unrestrained freedom on the part of the child, and which diminish or even suppress the teacher's authority and action, attributing to the child an exclusive primacy of initiative, and an activity independent of any higher law, natural or divine, in the work of his education.

61. If any of these terms are used, less properly, to denote the necessity of a gradually more active cooperation on the part of the pupil in his own education; if the intention is to banish from education despotism and violence, which, by the way, just punishment is not, this would be correct, but in no way new. It would mean only what has been taught and reduced to practice by the Church in traditional Christian education, in imitation of the method employed by God Himself towards His creatures, of whom He demands active cooperation according to the nature of each; for His Wisdom "reaches from end to end mightily and orders all things sweetly."[41] **89**

62. But alas! it is clear from the obvious meaning of the words and from experience, that what is intended by not a few, is the withdrawal of education from every sort of dependence on the divine law. So today we see, strange sight indeed, educators and philosophers who spend their lives in searching for a universal moral code of education, as if there existed no decalogue, no gospel law, no law even of nature stamped by God on the heart of man, promulgated by right reason, and codified in positive revelation by God Himself in the ten commandments. These innovators are wont to refer contemptuously to Christian education as "heteronomous," "passive", "obsolete," because founded upon the authority of God and His holy law. **90**

63. Such men are miserably deluded in their claim to emancipate, as they say, the child, while in reality they are making him the slave of his own blind pride and of his disorderly affections, which, as a logical consequence of this false system, come to be justified as legitimate demands of a so-called autonomous nature. **91**

---

[41] Wis 8:1.

92   64. But what is worse is the claim, not only vain but false, irreverent and dangerous, to submit to research, experiment and conclusions of a purely natural and profane order, those matters of education which belong to the supernatural order; as for example questions of priestly or religious vocation, and in general the secret workings of grace which indeed elevate the natural powers, but are infinitely superior to them, and may nowise be subjected to physical laws, for "the Spirit breathes where He will."[42]

93   65. Another very grave danger is that naturalism which nowadays invades the field of education in that most delicate matter of purity of morals. Far too common is the error of those who with dangerous assurance and under an ugly term propagate a so-called sex-education, falsely imagining they can forearm youths against the dangers of sensuality by means purely natural, such as a foolhardy initiation and precautionary instruction for all indiscriminately, even in public; and, worse still, by exposing them at an early age to the occasions, in order to accustom them, so it is argued, and as it were to harden them against such dangers.

94   66. Such persons grievously err in refusing to recognize the inborn weakness of human nature, and the law of which the Apostle speaks, fighting against the law of the mind;[43] and also in ignoring the experience of facts, from which it is clear that, particularly in young people, evil practices are the effect not so much of ignorance of intellect as of weakness of a will exposed to dangerous occasions, and unsupported by the means of grace.

95   67. In this extremely delicate matter, if, all things considered, some private instruction is found necessary and opportune, from those who hold from God the commission to teach and who have the grace of state, every precaution must be taken. Such precautions are well known in traditional Christian education, and are adequately described by Antoniano cited above, when he says: "Such is our misery and inclination to sin, that often in the very things considered to be remedies against sin, we find occasions for and inducements to sin itself. Hence it is of the

---

[42] John 3:8.
[43] Rom 7:23.

highest importance that a good father, while discussing with his son a matter so delicate, should be well on his guard and not descend to details, nor refer to the various ways in which this infernal hydra destroys with its poison so large a portion of the world; otherwise it may happen that instead of extinguishing this fire, he unwittingly stirs or kindles it in the simple and tender heart of the child. Speaking generally, during the period of childhood it suffices to employ those remedies which produce the double effect of opening the door to the virtue of purity and closing the door upon vice."[44]

68. False also and harmful to Christian education is the so-called method of "co-education." This too, by many of its supporters, is founded upon naturalism and the denial of original sin; but by all, upon a deplorable confusion of ideas that mistakes a levelling promiscuity and equality, for the legitimate association of the sexes. The Creator has ordained and disposed perfect union of the sexes only in matrimony, and, with varying degrees of contact, in the family and in society. Besides, there is not in nature itself, which fashions the two quite different in organism, in temperament, in abilities, anything to suggest that there can be or ought to be promiscuity, and much less equality, in the training of the two sexes. These, in keeping with the wonderful designs of the Creator, are destined to complement each other in the family and in society, precisely because of their differences, which therefore ought to be maintained and encouraged during their years of formation, with the necessary distinction and corresponding separation, according to age and circumstances. These principles, with due regard to time and place, must, in accordance with Christian prudence, be applied to all schools, particularly in the most delicate and decisive period of formation, that, namely, of adolescence; and in gymnastic exercises and deportment, special care must be had of Christian modesty in young women and girls, which is so gravely impaired by any kind of exhibition in public.

96

69. Recalling the terrible words of the Divine Master: "Woe to the world because of scandals!"[45] We most earnestly appeal to

97

---

[44] Silvio Antonio, *Dell 'educazione cristiana dei figliuoli*, lib. II, e. 88.
[45] Matt 18:7.

your solicitude and your watchfulness, Venerable Brethren, against these pernicious errors, which, to the immense harm of youth, are spreading far and wide among Christian peoples.

98   70. In order to obtain perfect education, it is of the utmost importance to see that all those conditions which surround the child during the period of his formation, in other words that the combination of circumstances which we call environment, correspond exactly to the end proposed.

99   71. The first natural and necessary element in this environment, as regards education, is the family, and this precisely because so ordained by the Creator Himself. Accordingly that education, as a rule, will be more effective and lasting which is received in a well-ordered and well-disciplined Christian family; and more efficacious in proportion to the clear and constant good example set, first by the parents, and then by the other members of the household.

100   72. It is not our intention to treat formally the question of domestic education, nor even to touch upon its principal points. The subject is too vast. Besides there are not lacking special treatises on this topic by authors, both ancient and modern, well known for their solid Catholic doctrine. One which seems deserving of special mention is the golden treatise already referred to, of Antoniano, *On the Christian Education of Youth,* which St. Charles Borromeo ordered to be read in public to parents assembled in their churches.

101   73. Nevertheless, Venerable Brethren and beloved children, We wish to call your attention in a special manner to the present-day lamentable decline in family education. The offices and professions of a transitory and earthly life, which are certainly of far less importance, are prepared for by long and careful study; whereas for the fundamental duty and obligation of educating their children, many parents have little or no preparation, immersed as they are in temporal cares. The declining influence of domestic environment is further weakened by another tendency, prevalent almost everywhere today, which, under one pretext or another, for economic reasons, or for reasons of industry, trade or politics, causes children to be more and more frequently sent away from home even in their tenderest years. And there is a country where the children are actually being torn from the bosom of the family, to be formed (or, to speak more accurately, to be deformed and depraved) in godless schools and associations, to irreligion and hatred, according to the theories of advanced socialism; and thus is renewed in a real and more terrible manner the slaughter of the Innocents.

74. For the love of Our Saviour Jesus Christ, therefore, we implore pastors of souls, by every means in their power, by instructions and catechisms, by word of mouth and written articles widely distributed, to warn Christian parents of their grave obligations. And this should be done not in a merely theoretical and general way, but with practical and specific application to the various responsibilities of parents touching the religious, moral and civil training of their children, and with indication of the methods best adapted to make their training effective, supposing always the influence of their own exemplary lives. The Apostle of the Gentiles[*] did not hesitate to descend to such details of practical instruction in his epistles, especially in the Epistle to the Ephesians, where among other things he gives this advice: "And you, fathers, provoke not your children to anger."[46] This fault is the result not so much of excessive severity, as of impatience and of ignorance of means best calculated to effect a desired correction; it is also due to the all too common relaxation of parental discipline which fails to check the growth of evil passions in the hearts of the younger generation. Parents therefore, and all who take their place in the work of education, should be careful to make right use of the authority given them by God, whose vicars in a true sense they are. This authority is not given for their own advantage, but for the proper up-bringing of their children in a holy and filial "fear of God, the beginning of wisdom," on which foundation alone all respect for authority can rest securely; and without which, order, tranquillity and prosperity, whether in the family or in society, will be impossible.

75. To meet the weakness of man's fallen nature, God in His Goodness has provided the abundant helps of His grace and the countless means with which He has endowed the Church, the great family of Christ. The Church therefore is the educational

102

103

---

[*] 'The Apostle to the Gentiles' refers to St Paul. – Editor's note.
[46] Eph 6:4.

environment most intimately and harmoniously associated with
the Christian family.

104   76. This educational environment of the Church embraces the
Sacraments, divinely efficacious means of grace, the sacred ritual,
so wonderfully instructive, and the material fabric of her
churches, whose liturgy and art have an immense educational
value; but it also includes the great number and variety of
schools, associations and institutions of all kinds, established for
the training of youth in Christian piety, together with literature
and the sciences, not omitting recreation and physical culture.
And in this inexhaustible fecundity of educational works, how
marvellous, how incomparable is the Church's maternal
providence! So admirable too is the harmony which she maintains
with the Christian family, that the Church and the family may be
said to constitute together one and the same temple of Christian
education.

105   77. Since, however, the younger generations must be trained
in the arts and sciences for the advantage and prosperity of civil
society, and since the family of itself is unequal to this task, it was
necessary to create that social institution, the school. But let it be
borne in mind that this institution owes its existence to the
initiative of the family and of the Church, long before it was
undertaken by the State. Hence considered in its historical origin,
the school is by its very nature an institution, subsidiary and
complementary to the family and to the Church. It follows
logically and necessarily that it must not be in opposition to, but
in positive accord with those other two elements, and form with
them a perfect moral union, constituting one sanctuary of
education, as it were, with the family and the Church. Otherwise
it is doomed to fail of its purpose, and to become instead an agent
of destruction.

106   78. This principle we find recognized by a layman, famous
for his pedagogical writings, though these because of their
liberalism cannot be unreservedly praised. "The school," he
writes, "if not a temple, is a den." And again: "When literary,
social, domestic and religious education do not go hand in hand,
man is unhappy and helpless."[47]

---

[47] Nic. Tommaseo, *Pensieri sull 'educazione*, I, 3, 6.

79. From this it follows that the so-called "neutral" or "lay" school, from which religion is excluded, is contrary to the fundamental principles of education. Such a school moreover cannot exist in practice; it is bound to become irreligious. There is no need to repeat what Our Predecessors have declared on this point, especially Pius IX and Leo XIII, at times when laicism was beginning in a special manner to infest the public school. We renew and confirm their declarations,[48] as well as the Sacred Canons in which the frequenting of non-Catholic schools, whether neutral or mixed, those namely which are open to Catholics and non-Catholics alike, is forbidden for Catholic children, and can be at most tolerated, on the approval of the Ordinary alone, under determined circumstances of place and time, and with special precautions.[49] Neither can Catholics admit that other type of mixed school, (least of all the so-called "école unique," obligatory on all), in which the students are provided with separate religious instruction, but receive other lessons in common with non-Catholic pupils from non-Catholic teachers.

107

80. For the mere fact that a school gives some religious instruction (often extremely stinted), does not bring it into accord with the rights of the Church and of the Christian family, or make it a fit place for Catholic students. To be this, it is necessary that all the teaching and the whole organization of the school, and its teachers, syllabus and text-books in every branch, be regulated by the Christian spirit, under the direction and maternal supervision of the Church; so that Religion may be in very truth the foundation and crown of the youth's entire training; and this in every grade of school, not only the elementary, but the intermediate and the higher institutions of learning as well. To use the words of Leo XIII: "It is necessary not only that religious instruction be given to the young at certain fixed times, but also that every other subject taught, be permeated with Christian piety. If this is wanting, if this sacred atmosphere does not pervade and

108

---

[48] Pius IX, *Ep. Quum non sine*, 14 July 1864: *Syllabus*, Prop. 48; Leo XIII, Alloc. *Summi Pontificatus*, 20 August 1880, *Ep. enc. Nobilissima*, 8 February 1884, *Ep. enc. Quod multum*, 22 August 1886, *Ep. Officio sanctissimo*, 22 December 1887, *Ep. enc. Caritatis*, 19 March 1894, etc. (cf. C. I.C. cum. Fontium Annot., c. 1374).

[49] C.I.C. [1917], c. 1374.

warm the hearts of masters and scholars alike, little good can be expected from any kind of learning, and considerable harm will often be the consequence."[50]

109   81. And let no one say that in a nation where there are different religious beliefs, it is impossible to provide for public instruction otherwise than by neutral or mixed schools. In such a case it becomes the duty of the State, indeed it is the easier and more reasonable method of procedure, to leave free scope to the initiative of the Church and the family, while giving them such assistance as justice demands. That this can be done to the full satisfaction of families, and to the advantage of education and of public peace and tranquillity, is clear from the actual experience of some countries comprising different religious denominations. There the school legislation respects the rights of the family, and Catholics are free to follow their own system of teaching in schools that are entirely Catholic. Nor is distributive justice lost sight of, as is evidenced by the financial aid granted by the State to the several schools demanded by the families.

110   82. In other countries of mixed creeds, things are otherwise, and a heavy burden weighs upon Catholics, who under the guidance of their Bishops and with the indefatigable cooperation of the clergy, secular and regular, support Catholic schools for their children entirely at their own expense; to this they feel obliged in conscience, and with a generosity and constancy worthy of all praise, they are firmly determined to make adequate provision for what they openly profess as their motto: "Catholic education in Catholic schools for all Catholic youth." If such education is not aided from public funds, as distributive justice requires, certainly it may not be opposed by any civil authority ready to recognize the rights of the family, and the irreducible claims of legitimate liberty.

111   83. Where this fundamental liberty is thwarted or interfered with, Catholics will never feel, whatever may have been the sacrifices already made, that they have done enough, for the support and defence of their schools and for the securing of laws that will do them justice.

112   84. For whatever Catholics do in promoting and defending

---

[50] *Ep. enc. Militantis Ecclesiae*, 1 Aug. 1897.

the Catholic school for their children, is a genuinely religious work and therefore an important task of "Catholic Action." For this reason the associations which in various countries are so zealously engaged in this work of prime necessity, are especially dear to Our paternal heart and are deserving of every commendation.

85. Let it be loudly proclaimed and well understood and recognized by all, that Catholics, no matter what their nationality, in agitating for Catholic schools for their children, are not mixing in party politics, but are engaged in a religious enterprise demanded by conscience. They do not intend to separate their children either from the body of the nation or its spirit, but to educate them in a perfect manner, most conducive to the prosperity of the nation. Indeed a good Catholic, precisely because of his Catholic principles, makes the better citizen, attached to his country, and loyally submissive to constituted civil authority in every legitimate form of government.

113

86. In such a school, in harmony with the Church and the Christian family, the various branches of secular learning will not enter into conflict with religious instruction to the manifest detriment of education. And if, when occasion arises, it be deemed necessary to have the students read authors propounding false doctrine, for the purpose of refuting it, this will be done after due preparation and with such an antidote of sound doctrine, that it will not only do no harm, but will be an aid to the Christian formation of youth.

114

87. In such a school moreover, the study of the vernacular and of classical literature will do no damage to moral virtue. There the Christian teacher will imitate the bee, which takes the choicest part of the flower and leaves the rest, as St. Basil teaches in his discourse to youth on the study of the classics.[51] Nor will this necessary caution, suggested also by the pagan Quintilian,[52] in any way hinder the Christian teacher from gathering and turning to profit, whatever there is of real worth in the systems and methods of our modern times, mindful of the Apostle's advice: "Prove all things: hold fast that which is good."[53] Hence

115

---

[51] P.G., t. 31, 570.
[52] *Inst. Or.*, I, 8.
[53] 1 Thess 5:21.

in accepting the new, he will not hastily abandon the old, which the experience of centuries has found expedient and profitable. This is particularly true in the teaching of Latin, which in our days is falling more and more into disuse, because of the unreasonable rejection of methods so successfully used by that sane humanism, whose highest development was reached in the schools of the Church. These noble traditions of the past require that the youth committed to Catholic schools be fully instructed in the letters and sciences in accordance with the exigencies of the times. They also demand that the doctrine imparted be deep and solid, especially in sound philosophy, avoiding the muddled superficiality of those "who perhaps would have found the necessary, had they not gone in search of the superfluous."[54] In this connection Christian teachers should keep in mind what Leo XIII says in a pithy sentence: "Greater stress must be laid on the employment of apt and solid methods of teaching, and, what is still more important, on bringing into full conformity with the Catholic faith, what is taught in literature, in the sciences, and above all in philosophy, on which depends in great part the right orientation of the other branches of knowledge."[55]

116   88. Perfect schools are the result not so much of good methods as of good teachers, teachers who are thoroughly prepared and well-grounded in the matter they have to teach; who possess the intellectual and moral qualifications required by their important office; who cherish a pure and holy love for the youths confided to them, because they love Jesus Christ and His Church, of which these are the children of predilection; and who have therefore sincerely at heart the true good of family and country. Indeed it fills Our soul with consolation and gratitude towards the divine Goodness to see, side by side with religious men and women engaged in teaching, such a large number of excellent lay teachers, who, for their greater spiritual advancement, are often grouped in special sodalities and associations, which are worthy of praise and encouragement as most excellent and powerful auxiliaries of "Catholic Action." All these labour unselfishly with zeal and perseverance in what St. Gregory Nazianzen calls "the

---

[54] Seneca, Epist. 45: *invenissent forsitan necessaria nisi et superflua quaesiissent.*
[55] Leo XII, *Ep. enc., Insrutabli* 21 April 1878.

art of arts and the science of sciences,"[56] the direction and formation of youth. Of them also it may be said in the words of the divine Master: "The harvest indeed is great, but the labourers few."[57] Let us then pray the Lord of the harvest to send more such workers into the field of Christian education; and let their formation be one of the principal concerns of the pastors of souls and of the superiors of Religious Orders.

89. It is no less necessary to direct and watch the education of the adolescent, "soft as wax to be moulded into vice,"[58] in whatever other environment he may happen to be, removing occasions of evil and providing occasions for good in his recreations and social intercourse; for "evil communications corrupt good manners."[59]

117

90. More than ever nowadays an extended and careful vigilance is necessary, inasmuch as the dangers of moral and religious shipwreck are greater for inexperienced youth. Especially is this true of impious and immoral books, often diabolically circulated at low prices; of the cinema, which multiplies every kind of exhibition; and now also of the radio, which facilitates every kind of communications. These most powerful means of publicity, which can be of great utility for instruction and education when directed by sound principles, are only too often used as an incentive to evil passions and greed for gain. St. Augustine deplored the passion for the shows of the circus which possessed even some Christians of his time, and he dramatically narrates the infatuation for them, fortunately only temporary, of his disciple and friend Alipius.[60] How often today must parents and educators bewail the corruption of youth brought about by the modern theatre and the vile book!

118

91. Worthy of all praise and encouragement therefore are those educational associations which have for their object to point out to parents and educators, by means of suitable books and periodicals, the dangers to morals and religion that are often cunningly disguised in books and theatrical representations. In

119

---

[56] *Oratio II*, P.G., t. 35, 426.

[57] Matt 9:37.

[58] *Horat., Art. poet.*, v. 163: *cereus in vitium flecti.*

[59] 1 Cor 15:33..

[60] *Confessions* VI, 8.

their spirit of zeal for the souls of the young, they endeavour at the same time to circulate good literature and to promote plays that are really instructive, going so far as to put up at the cost of great sacrifices, theatres and cinemas, in which virtue will have nothing to suffer and much to gain.

120   92. This necessary vigilance does not demand that young people be removed from the society in which they must live and save their souls; but that today more than ever they should be forewarned and forearmed as Christians against the seductions and the errors of the world, which, as Holy Writ admonishes us, is all "concupiscence of the flesh, concupiscence of the eyes and pride of life."[61] Let them be what Tertullian wrote of the first Christians, and what Christians of all times ought to be, "sharers in the possession of the world, not of its error."[62]

121   93. This saying of Tertullian brings us to the topic which we propose to treat in the last place, and which is of the greatest importance, that is, the true nature of Christian education, as deduced from its proper end. Its consideration reveals with noon-day clearness the pre-eminent educational mission of the Church.

122   94. The proper and immediate end of Christian education is to cooperate with divine grace in forming the true and perfect Christian, that is, to form Christ Himself in those regenerated by Baptism, according to the emphatic expression of the Apostle: "My little children, of whom I am in labour again, until Christ be formed in you."[63] For the true Christian must live a supernatural life in Christ: "Christ who is your life,"[64] and display it in all his actions: "That the life also of Jesus may be made manifest in our mortal flesh."[65]

123   95. For precisely this reason, Christian education takes in the whole aggregate of human life, physical and spiritual, intellectual and moral, individual, domestic and social, not with a view of reducing it in any way, but in order to elevate, regulate and perfect it, in accordance with the example and teaching of Christ.

124   96. Hence the true Christian, product of Christian education,

---

[61] 1 John 2:16.
[62] *De Idololatria*, 14.
[63] Gal 4:19.
[64] Col 3:4.
[65] 2 Cor 4:11.

is the supernatural man who thinks, judges and acts constantly and consistently in accordance with right reason illumined by the supernatural light of the example and teaching of Christ; in other words, to use the current term, the true and finished man of character. For, it is not every kind of consistency and firmness of conduct based on subjective principles that makes true character, but only constancy in following the eternal principles of justice, as is admitted even by the pagan poet when he praises as one and the same "the man who is just and firm of purpose."[66] And on the other hand, there cannot be full justice except in giving to God what is due to God, as the true Christian does.

97. The scope and aim of Christian education as here described, appears to the worldly as an abstraction, or rather as something that cannot be attained without the suppression or dwarfing of the natural faculties, and without a renunciation of the activities of the present life, and hence inimical to social life and temporal prosperity, and contrary to all progress in letters, arts and sciences, and all the other elements of civilization. To a like objection raised by the ignorance and the prejudice of even cultured pagans of a former day, and repeated with greater frequency and insistence in modern times, Tertullian has replied as follows: "We are not strangers to life. We are fully aware of the gratitude we owe to God, our Lord and Creator. We reject none of the fruits of His handiwork; we only abstain from their immoderate or unlawful use. We are living in the world with you; we do not shun your forum, your markets, your baths, your shops, your factories, your stables, your places of business and traffic. We take shop with you and we serve in your armies; we are farmers and merchants with you; we interchange skilled labour and display our works in public for your service. How we can seem unprofitable to you with whom we live and of whom we are, I know not."[67]

98. The true Christian does not renounce the activities of this life, he does not stunt his natural faculties; but he develops and perfects them, by coordinating them with the supernatural. He thus ennobles what is merely natural in life and secures for it new

125

126

---

[66] Horat., *Od.*, 1, III, od. 3, v. 1: *lustum et tenacem propositi virum.*
[67] *Apol.*, 42.

strength in the material and temporal order, no less then in the
spiritual and eternal.

127   99. This fact is proved by the whole history of Christianity
and its institutions, which is nothing else but the history of true
civilization and progress up to the present day. It stands out
conspicuously in the lives of the numerous Saints, whom the
Church, and she alone, produces, in whom is perfectly realized
the purpose of Christian education, and who have in every way
ennobled and benefited human society. Indeed, the Saints have
ever been, are, and ever will be the greatest benefactors of
society, and perfect models for every class and profession, for
every state and condition of life, from the simple and uncultured
peasant to the master of sciences and letters, from the humble
artisan to the commander of armies, from the father of a family to
the ruler of peoples and nations, from simple maidens and
matrons of the domestic hearth to queens and empresses. What
shall we say of the immense work which has been accomplished
even for the temporal well-being of men by missionaries of the
Gospel, who have brought and still bring to barbarous tribes the
benefits of civilization together with the light of the Faith? What
of the founders of so many social and charitable institutions, of
the vast numbers of saintly educators, men and women, who have
perpetuated and multiplied their life work, by leaving after them
prolific institutions of Christian education, in aid of families and
for the inestimable advantage of nations?

128   100. Such are the fruits of Christian education. Their price
and value is derived from the supernatural virtue and life in Christ
which Christian education forms and develops in man. Of this life
and virtue Christ our Lord and Master is the source and dispenser.
By His example He is at the same time the universal model
accessible to all, especially to the young in the period of His
hidden life, a life of labour and obedience, adorned with all
virtues, personal, domestic and social, before God and men.

129   101. Now all this array of priceless educational treasures
which We have barely touched upon, is so truly a property of the
Church as to form her very substance, since she is the mystical
body of Christ, the immaculate spouse of Christ, and consequently a most admirable mother and an incomparable and perfect

teacher. This thought inspired St. Augustine,[*] the great genius of whose blessed death we are about to celebrate the fifteenth centenary, with accents of tenderest love for so glorious a mother: "O Catholic Church, true Mother of Christians! Not only do you preach to us, as is meet, how purely and chastely we are to worship God Himself, Whom to possess is life most blessed. You do moreover so cherish neighbourly love and charity, that all the infirmities to which sinful souls are subject, find their most potent remedy in thee. Childlike you are in moulding the child, strong with the young man, gentle with the aged, dealing with each according to his needs of mind of body. You do subject child to parent in a sort of free servitude, and set parent over child in a jurisdiction of love. You bind brethren to brethren by the bond of religion, stronger and closer than the bond of blood ... You unite citizen to citizen, nation to nation, yes, all men, in a union not of companionship only, but of brotherhood, reminding them of their common origin. You teach kings to care for their people, and bid people to be subject to their kings. You teach assiduously to whom honour is due, to whom love, to whom reverence, to whom fear, to whom comfort, to whom rebuke, to whom punishment; showing us that while not all things nor the same things are due to all, charity is due to all and offence to none."[68]

102. Let us then, Venerable Brethren, raise *our* hands and our **130** hearts in supplication to heaven, "to the Shepherd and Bishop of our Souls,"[69] to the divine King "who gives laws to rulers," that in His almighty power He may cause these splendid fruits of Christian education to be gathered in ever greater abundance "in the whole world," for the lasting benefit of individuals and of nations.

As a pledge of these heavenly favours, with paternal affection We impart to you, Venerable Brethren, to your clergy and your people, the Apostolic Benediction.

Given at Rome, at St. Peter's, the thirty-first day of December, in the year 1929, the eighth of Our Pontificate.

Pius XI

---

[*] St. Augustine died in AD 430. – Editor's note.

[68] *De moribus Ecclesiae catholicae, lib. 1, c. 30.*

[69] Cf 1 Pet 2:25.

PROVIDO SANE CONSILIO
On Better Care for Catechetical Teaching
12 January 1935

1. With truly far-seeing wisdom, the Catholic Church, the **131** guardian and teacher of divinely revealed truth, undertaking to fulfil her most holy office and duty, has always held that the imparting of the heavenly knowledge necessary for salvation through catechetical instruction must be placed among her most serious obligations. This work of bringing all men – particularly children and the poorly instructed adults – to know Christ our Lord and to learn His teachings, must be committed to the zeal and ministry of qualified teachers.

2. In this the Church surely acts with prudence. The **132** knowledge of a Christian is wholly contained in the words of the divine Redeemer: "This is everlasting life, that they may know you, the only true God, and him whom you have sent, Jesus Christ."[1] This knowledge is correctly and aptly contained in catechetical instruction wherein a summary of truths concerning God, Jesus Christ and His teachings and precepts are explained and presented to students according to their age, ability, and condition of life, Indeed, when this matter has been presented and clearly illustrated, no better way can be desired to provide a firm and certain norm of true belief and right living for the faithful.

"Let the little children come to Me"
3. Thus it is that in the Catholic Church catechetical **133** instruction has been and, indeed, should be held as that voice

---

[1] John 17:3.

through which divine Wisdom cries aloud in the streets: "Whosoever is a little one, let him come to me";[2] or like that lamp "shining in a dark place until the day dawns and the morning star rises in your hearts,"[3] or that "seed" and "leaven" of the Gospel whereby the whole Christian life springs into being and is nourished. Each of the faithful because of this instruction receives with profit the light of divine truth, the norm of divine law, and the help of divine grace; and he is able both to see what must be done and to gain the strength for its accomplishment. Religious instruction of this kind offers great advantages for all, but it is of special help in the years of childhood and adolescence, wherein lies the hope of adult life. Above all, then, catechetical instruction must be provided for children and youth, and they must be urged to take advantage of it. This is all the more necessary in an age in which the secular education of children and youth is eagerly planned and carried forward through a widespread pursuit of knowledge, manifold means of teaching, and improved methods of presenting matters to be learned. In the midst of such facilities for learning and such zeal for teaching, it must never be that the science of God and the all-important content of religion suffer neglect or omission.

134   4. It is evident, too, that the welfare of the nation itself is bound up with the Catholic instruction and training of children and youths. It is equally of vital interest to the state and to religion that citizens imbibe the Christian spirit as well as merely human knowledge and secular training.

135   5. It can thus be clearly understood why the Church, the teacher of Catholic truth and practice, out of love as well as prudence, speaks in the person of Christ and exclaims: "Let the little children come to me, and do not hinder them, for of such is the kingdom of God."[4]

Concern of the Holy See

136   6. The Roman Pontiffs as the supreme teachers and leaders of the Catholic Faith have always been fully cognizant of and attentive to all this, and they accordingly have never relaxed their

---

[2] Prov 9:4.
[3] 2 Pet 1:19.
[4] Mark 10:14.

vigilance and zeal in such an important matter.

7. There exists in our own time (if we may pass over more **137** ancient documents) a splendid proof of this diligence in the Encyclical Letter *Acerbo nimis* of Pope Pius X which appeared on 15 April 1905. In this encyclical the ever-vigilant Pontiff first set forth the advantages that flow properly and solely from catechetical instruction, and then he concluded that the Faith in our day grows weak and is almost dead chiefly because the work of teaching Christian doctrine is either performed carelessly or is entirely omitted. He thereupon enacted legislation to provide for the teaching of Christian doctrine not only to boys and girls but also to youths and to adults as well.

8. The Code of Canon Law (Book III, tit. XX, chap. I)[*] contains these same prescriptions practically in their entirety as set **138** forth in the canons (1329-1336). Here the provisions relating to catechetical instruction, made obligatory throughout the universal Church, are duly stated and proposed as law.

9. With the purpose of seeing how the catechetical provisions of the Code are being carried out and to stimulate their **139** enforcement when needful, Pope Pius XI, in a Motu proprio *Orbem catholicum* (29 June 1923), instituted within this Sacred Congregation of the Council a catechetical office, whose special work is to guide and to promote the catechetical movement everywhere throughout the Catholic Church.

10. The zealous activities of the bishops have been in **140** complete harmony with the commands and pleadings of the Supreme Pontiffs. In plenary and provincial councils, in diocesan synods, as well as in catechetical congresses both diocesan and national, they have earnestly endeavoured to improve the teaching of the catechism.

11. Despite the initial success of early beginnings, however, it is clear from the reports of the bishops themselves that there are **141** still many obstacles which prevent the full force and effectiveness of the teaching of Christian doctrine. We must surely deplore first of all the carelessness of parents, many of whom are ignorant of the things of God and who accordingly do little or nothing for the

---

[*] All references to Canon Law, in this document, are to the 1917 Code of Canon Law, which is no longer in use. – Editor's note.

religious education of their children. This is indeed a serious situation; for when the parents are either neglectful or deliberately opposed, there is practically no hope that the children will receive a religious training.

142   12. The condition is, even worse where, as is the case in some nations, the very right of the Church to direct the Christian education of children is called into question or even denied by reason of political policy. Then the parents, overcome by indifference or their own fickleness of mind or weakened by the pressure of circumstances, offer neither opposition to the unjust laws nor do they give attention or care to the catechetical instruction of their children.

143   13. In countries where Catholics and non-Catholics dwell together and mixed marriages among them are common, it often happens as a consequence of the intimate relationship of married life that both the parents and children grow to disdain religion or fall altogether from the Faith.

144   14. A further consideration is a general lack of interest on the part of the children and youth in religion. They are taken up with other things and are attracted by games and exercises of physical culture, or by worldly shows where not infrequently moral discipline is relaxed; and thus led away, even on feastdays, the result is failure to attend the parish catechetical instruction. Thereupon forgetfulness and neglect of the things of God, which we so much deplore, take root in early childhood and grow worse with the years.

145   15. This forgetfulness and neglect cause even greater harm to the Faith in view of the fact that ravening wolves have come into the world, not sparing the flock; likewise, pseudo-teachers given to atheism and the new paganism have made their appearance, giving expression to clever falsehoods and sheer nonsense by writings and by other means cunningly attempting to destroy the Catholic belief in God, in Jesus Christ, and in the divine work of the Church. With these are joined the individuals who possess a semblance of Christian learning and piety, yet burn with zeal to propagate unhappy Protestantism.* And with an ease that is

---

* 'Unhappy Protestantism': the choice of words indicates a certain tension between Catholic and non-Catholic Christians. – Editor's note.

almost unbelievable, they deceive those who are ignorant of or weak in Catholic doctrine – even also the simple and unwary faithful.

16. Although the bishops and those having the care of souls are striving diligently to overcome these difficulties, nevertheless this Sacred Congregation is bound to stimulate their zeal again and again; and their efforts do not exempt them from even greater attention and labour to a work upon which depends the eternal welfare of the sheep committed to their charge. **146**

Further Catechetical Regulations

17. It has, therefore, seemed opportune to this Sacred Congregation that all interested in religious education should be encouraged to new efforts, and that certain prescriptions should be enacted and promulgated which, if observed, will give grounds to hope that catechetical instruction will make greater progress in the future. **147**

18. In the first place let the bishops, mindful of the duty and office entrusted to them, exert even greater care and diligence than heretofore has been their custom, to encourage greater efforts and labour to spread catechetical instruction. "Let them see to it," therefore, in accord with Canon 336:2, "that the food of Christian doctrine be given to the faithful, especially to children and to the uninstructed, and that in the schools the education of children and youth be carried on according to the principles of the Catholic religion." Moreover, as provided in Canon 1336, "the Ordinary of the place has the right to legislate in his diocese in all matters that pertain to the instruction of the people in Christian doctrine," and, therefore, each Ordinary should consider in the Lord what preparations are to be made, what laws should be laid down for this most holy and necessary work, and by what means he can most easily and effectively carry out his plans in this matter. He shall bear in mind that, if the occasion warrants, he can punish those who are negligent or who refuse to obey with the penalties prescribed in Canons 1332:2 and 2182, and at the same time, as a reward to the zealous, he can intimate that special care and diligence exercised in the work of teaching catechism will be of greatest weight and importance in the conferring of parishes and other benefices. **148**

19. Pastors and others having the care of souls should ever **149**

bear in mind that catechetical instruction is the foundation of the whole Christian life, and to its proper performance all their plans, studies, and efforts should be directed. Let them, therefore, note well and put into effect all the prescriptions of Canons 1330, 1331, and 1332; thus in this work in particular they ought to become all things to all men that they may gain all men for Christ, and be able to show themselves as faithful ministers and dispensers of the mysteries of God. Let them carefully determine the souls who need to be nourished with milk, and those who have need of more solid food, but let all be offered that food of doctrine that gives growth to the soul and mind so that the Christian will not be ignorant of his religion, neither will he hold it merely as a gift from his forebears, but on the contrary he will possess it well understood and clearly analyzed in order that it enrich both himself and others.

150   20. In carrying out this most holy work, "let the pastor," in accord with Canon 1333:1, "employ the help of other clerics in the parish, and also if necessary, of devout lay persons, especially those who belong to the Confraternity of Christian Doctrine or a similar society established in the parish." All of these, whether asked or commanded, should freely, nay more, should most gladly give their assistance to this work – as joyful givers beloved of the Lord.

151   21. The help of members of religious communities, according to Canon 1334, should not be lacking in a work so helpful, so pleasing to God, and so necessary for souls, if the Ordinary of the place requires it. The religious themselves, on being called, should joyfully respond, and they should even desire to give assistance in order to gain the reward exceedingly great through the salvation of souls that is achieved also in this part of the Lord's field, where the harvest is great but the labourers are few.

152   22. Finally, effective help and loyal support in this matter is both expected and demanded from parents and guardians. The provision of Canon 1113 should be called to their attention that, "they are bound by a most strict obligation to provide to the best of their ability for the religious and moral as well as for the physical and civil education of their children," and this obligation is fulfilled, according to Canon 1335, when they see to it that their children receive catechetical instruction and also, by Canon

1372:2, in providing them with a Christian education.

23. All of the matters we have here treated in summary are **153** already well known and evident; nevertheless the old adage, "repetition is useful," must not be overlooked, especially when the subject is one that cannot be insisted upon too much.

Specific commands for the Catechetical Apostolate

24. In order, then, that all of this may more readily be carried **154** out in the entire world, this Sacred Congregation, with the approval of His Holiness, Pope Pius XI, commands that in all dioceses the following be observed:

25. 1. In every parish, besides the Confraternity of the **155** Blessed Sacrament, the Confraternity of Christian Doctrine, as the most important of all others, must be established in accordance with Canon 711:2, and it should embrace all who are capable of teaching and promoting catechetical instruction, especially teachers in the schools and all who are skilled in the science of teaching children.

26. 2. Using the Letter of this Sacred Congregation directed **156** to the Bishops of Italy as a norm, parochial classes in Christian doctrine should be established if they do not already exist. With the pastors themselves in charge of these classes, and with the employment of approved methods of teaching, children and youth will have opportunity to learn the fundamentals of the divine law and of the Faith. In order, moreover, to overcome the indifference of parents already referred to, who think their children are not obliged to attend the catechism classes of the parish because they are receiving religious instruction either at home or in the public schools, let the following be carefully observed:

27. a. Pastors shall not admit to reception of the sacraments of **157** Penance and Confirmation, as prescribed in Canon 1330, children who have not acquired sufficient knowledge of the catechism according to directives of the Decree of the Sacred Congregation of the Sacraments on 8 August 1910; and after they have received their First Communion, they must endeavour to learn the catechism more perfectly and with greater profit.

28. b. Pastors, preachers, confessors, and rectors of churches **158** shall take particular care to advise parents of the grave obligation which is theirs to see to it that, "all subject to them or under their

care are given catechetical instruction" (Canon 1335). On this subject, Pope Benedict XIV wrote as follows in his Encyclical *Etsi minime*, of 7 February 1742: "It is evident that the Bishop can and should in all earnestness recommend to preachers that in their sermons they impress upon the ears and minds of parents the importance of teaching their children the truths of our religion; and that if they are not fully capable of so doing, they should bring their children to the church where the precepts of the divine law will be explained."

159   29. c. Furthermore, let pastors and their assistants endeavour, so far as they can, to make the children eager to attend the parish catechism classes. To this end the most successful and tried means should be employed, for example, the celebration of a Mass for the children on all holy days, catechetical competitions, offering of attractive prizes, and the use of suitable projects and moderate forms of amusement.

160   30. d. Finally, let pastors carefully prepare the children so that they may be examined on their knowledge of religion by the bishop when he makes his pastoral visitation. The bishop will take this opportunity to call attention to the condition of religious instruction in the parish: what he feels needs correction, improvement, or special commendation.

161   31. 3. There is a danger that the religious training received in childhood will be forgotten with advancing age, for as Pope Benedict XIV has pointed out, "It is well known that not only the young and those reaching maturity are steeped in ignorance of the things of God, but also adults and old people are altogether destitute of the teachings of salvation; this is because they have never learned them, or having once learned them they have little by little forgotten them" (loc. cit.). Bishops, therefore, should carefully see to it that the provisions of Canon 1332 be scrupulously observed by the pastors. They are bound, according to this Canon, "to explain the catechism on Sundays and holy days to adults among the faithful in words suited to their capacity to understand." With this in mind, Pope Pius X, in his celebrated encyclical *Acerbo nimis*, ordered that "*the Catechism of the Council of Trent* should be used in such a way that over a period of four or five years the entire material would be covered which treats of the Apostles' Creed, the sacraments, the commandments, prayer, and the precepts of the Church," and the same holds true of the evangelical counsels, grace, the virtues, sin, and the last things.

Practical Means to be adopted

32. In addition to the above measures incumbent upon all, **162** this Sacred Congregation considers it opportune to point out to the Ordinaries some means which experience has proved to be well adapted to the end desired. The Ordinaries, therefore, will take care that all or at least some of the means which here follow are used according to the different needs and circumstances of each diocese.

33. 1. As is already provided for Italy in the Letter of this **163** Sacred Congregation on 12 December 1929, the Ordinaries will, if possible, set up a diocesan catechetical office, which under their supervision will direct all catechetical education in the diocese. The chief functions of this office will be to provide:

34. a. that in parishes, in schools, and in colleges, Christian **164** doctrine be taught by qualified teachers employing the traditional form of the Church;

35. b. that at stated times catechetical conventions and other **165** meetings in the interests of religious education shall be held for the purpose of discussion and study of the methods best suited for catechetical instruction, as has been noted in a decree of this Sacred Congregation on 12 April 1924;

36. c. that a special Course of Lectures on Religion be offered **166** each year to those who teach Christian doctrine in parochial and public schools, in order that they will increase in the quality and depth of their knowledge.

37. 2. The Ordinaries shall not fail to appoint competent **167** priest visitors each year to inspect all the schools of religion in the dioceses; they shall carefully report the results, the improvements, or the weaknesses in the religious instruction of the schools. Pope Benedict XIV wrote on this subject as follows: "It will be of greatest benefit for the education of the Christian people if visitors be chosen, some to visit in the city, others to go about in the diocese, making careful and exhaustive inquiry and informing the bishop who, thus made aware of the work being done by the pastors, may place praise or blame where it is deserved" (*loc. cit.*).

38. In order that the mind of the Christian people may be **168**

directed from time to time toward religious education, let a Catechetical Day be established in each parish, if this has not already been done. On this day, the Feast of Christian Doctrine is to be celebrated with as much solemnity as possible. On this occasion:

169   39. a. The faithful should be called together in the parish church, and having received the Holy Eucharist, they should pray to obtain greater fruit from divine teaching;

170   40. b. A special sermon should be preached to the people on the necessity of catechetical instruction. Parents are to be told about their duty to instruct their children in Christian doctrine and to send them to the parochial catechism classes, being mindful of the divine command: "And these words which I command you this day shall be in your heart. And you shall tell them to your children...."[5]

171   41. c. Books, pamphlets, leaflets, and other material suitable for the purpose should be distributed to the people;

172   42. d. A collection may be taken up for the promotion of catechetical works.

173   43. 4. In places where the scarcity of priests is such that the clergy themselves cannot satisfactorily perform the work of teaching Christian doctrine, the Ordinary should take active steps to supply capable catechists of both sexes to help the pastors to impart religious instruction in the parochial or in the public schools, even in the remote parts of the parish. A leading part in this work should be undertaken by all members of Catholic Action groups, These associations have already done much commendable work in this direction, and certain of them have very wisely provided in their constitutions that lectures in religion are to be conducted each year at which all their members must be present.

174   44. Members of other Catholic organizations and associations should not fail in this work, especially the societies of religious of both sexes that are specifically dedicated to the education of youth. To these His Holiness, Pope Pius XI, addressed his memorable Motu Proprio *Orbem catholicum*: "We earnestly desire that in all the principal centres of religious societies which are engaged in the teaching of youth, there be established, under the direction

---

[5] Deut 6:6-7

and guidance of the bishops, schools for select students of both
sexes, where they shall be trained in a suitable course of studies,
and upon examination be declared fit to undertake the teaching of
Christian doctrine and Bible and Church History." This surely
will be accomplished if, as reason itself persuades and demands,
the study of religion holds first place among the subjects pursued
by children and youth in our Catholic schools and colleges. Let
such instruction be given by priests skilled in teaching and
according to proved principles of pedagogy.

45. If these means and plans are used, and if all who are **175**
duty-bound give themselves vigorously and perseveringly to this
work – more holy and more necessary than any other – then it can
be hoped that the Christian people will be made secure through
holy and incorrupt doctrine against the attacks of error, becoming
an acceptable people, followers of good works. Then, too, they
will produce those wholesome results which the Roman Pontiffs
have repeatedly desired for the salvation of souls. Finally, with
the approval of His Holiness, Pope Pius XI, this Sacred Congregation, derogating in this respect from the above-mentioned Motu
Proprio *Orbem catholicum*, commands all bishops to submit an
accurate report every five years to this same Sacred Congregation
regarding catechetical instruction in their dioceses. They shall use
the questionnaire which follows and shall observe the order
prescribed in Canon 340:2 of the Code of Canon Law relating to
the report which must be submitted by each bishop on the state of
the diocese entrusted to him.

Given at Rome, on the Feast of the Holy Family of Nazareth,
12 January 1935.

I. CARD. SERAFINI, Prefect
I. BRUNO, Secretary
Catechetical Office of the Holy See

GRAVISSIMUM EDUCATIONIS, DECLARATION ON CHRISTIAN
EDUCATION
Second Vatican Council, Pope Paul VI
28 October 1965

Introduction

The Sacred Ecumenical Council has considered with care **176**
how extremely important education is in the life of man and how
its influence ever grows in the social progress of this age.[1]

Indeed, the circumstances of our time have made it easier and
at once more urgent to educate young people and, what is more,
to continue the education of adults. Men are more aware of their

---

[1] Among many documents illustrating the importance of education confer above
all apostolic letter of Benedict XV, *Communes Litteras*, 10 April 1919: A.A.S.
11 (1919) p. 172. Pius XI's apostolic Encyclical, *Divini Illius Magistri*, 31 Dec
1929: A.A.S. 22 (1930) pp. 49-86. Pius XII's allocution to the youths of Italian
Catholic Action, 20 April 1946: Discourses and Radio Messages, vol. 8, pp. 53-
57. Allocution to fathers of French families, 18 Sept 1951: Discourses and Radio
Messages, vol. 13, pp. 241-245. John XXIII's 30th anniversary message on the
publication of the Encyclical letter, *Divini Illius Magistri*, 30 Dec 1959: A.A.S.
52 (1960) pp. 57-S9. Paul VI's allocution to members of Federated Institutes
Dependent on Ecclesiastic Authority, 30 Dec 1963: Encyclicals and Discourses
of His Holiness Paul VI, Rome, 1964, pp. 601-603. Above all are to be consulted the Acts and Documents of the Second Vatican Council appearing in the first
series of the ante-preparatrory phase. vol. 3. pp. 363-364; 370-371; 373-374.

own dignity and position; more and more they want to take an active part in social and especially in economic and political life.[2] Enjoying more leisure, as they sometimes do, men find that the remarkable development of technology and scientific investigation and the new means of communication offer them an opportunity of attaining more easily their cultural and spiritual inheritance and of fulfilling one another in the closer ties between groups and even between peoples.

Consequently, attempts are being made everywhere to promote more education. The rights of men to an education, particularly the primary rights of children and parents, are being proclaimed and recognized in public documents.[3] As the number of pupils rapidly increases, schools are multiplied and expanded far and wide and other educational institutions are established. New experiments are conducted in methods of education and teaching. Mighty attempts are being made to obtain education for all, even though vast numbers of children and young people are still deprived of even rudimentary training and so many others lack a suitable education in which truth and love are developed together.

To fulfill the mandate she has received from her divine founder of proclaiming the mystery of salvation to all men and of restoring all things in Christ, Holy Mother the Church must be concerned with the whole of man's life, even the secular part of it insofar as it has a bearing on his heavenly calling.[4] Therefore she has a role in the progress and development of education. Hence this sacred synod declares certain fundamental principles of Christian education especially in schools. These principles will have to be

---

[2] Cf. John XXIII's Encyclical letter *Mater et Magistra*, 15 May 1961: A.A.S. 53 (1961) pp. 413-415; 417-424; Encyclical letter, *Pacem in Terris*, 11 April 1963: A.A.S. 55 (1963) p. 278 ff.

[3] Declaration on the Rights of Man of 10 Dec 1948, adopted by the General Assembly of the United Nations, and also cf. the *Declaration of the Rights of Children* of 20 Nov 1959; additional protocol to the Convention Safeguarding the Rights of Men and Fundamental Liberties, Paris, 20 March 1952; regarding that universal profession of the character of human laws cf. apostolic letter *Pacem in Terris*, of John XXIII of 11 April 1963: A.A.S. 55 (1963) p. 295 ff.

[4] Cf. John XXIII's Encyclical letter, *Mater et Magistra*, 15 May 1961: A.A.S. 53 (1961) p. 402. Cf. Second Vatican Council's Dogmatic Constitution on the Church, 17: A.A.S. 57 (1965) p. 21, and schema on the Pastoral Constitution on the Church in the Modern World, 1965.

developed at greater length by a special post-conciliar commission and applied by episcopal conferences to varying local situations.

1. The Meaning of the Universal Right to an Education   **177**

All men of every race, condition and age, since they enjoy the dignity of a human being, have an inalienable right to an education[5] that is in keeping with their ultimate goal,[6] their ability, their sex, and the culture and tradition of their country, and also in harmony with their fraternal association with other peoples in the fostering of true unity and peace on earth. For a true education aims at the formation of the human person in the pursuit of his ultimate end and of the good of the societies of which, as man, he is a member, and in whose obligations, as an adult, he will share.

Therefore children and young people must be helped, with the aid of the latest advances in psychology and the arts and science of teaching, to develop harmoniously their physical, moral and intellectual endowments so that they may gradually acquire a mature sense of responsibility in striving endlessly to form their own lives properly and in pursuing true freedom as they surmount the vicissitudes of life with courage and constancy. Let them be given also, as they advance in years, a positive and prudent sexual education. Moreover they should be so trained to take their part in social life that properly instructed in the necessary and opportune skills they can become actively involved in various community organizations, open to discourse with others and willing to do their best to promote the common good.

This sacred synod likewise declares that children and young people have a right to be motivated to appraise moral values with a right conscience, to embrace them with a personal adherence, together with a deeper knowledge and love of God. Consequently it earnestly entreats all those who hold a position of public authority or who are in charge of education to see to it that youth is never deprived of this sacred right. It further exhorts the sons of

---

[5] Pius XII's radio message of 24 Dec 1942: A.A.S. 35 (1943) pp. 12-19, and John XXIII's Encyclical letter, *Pacem in Terris* 11 April 1963: A.A.S. 55 (1963) p. 259 ff. Also cf. declaration cited on the rights of man in footnote 3.

[6] Cf. Pius XI's Encyclical letter, *Divini Illius Magistri*, 31 Dec 1929: A.A.S. 22 (1930) p. 50 ff.

the Church to give their attention with generosity to the entire field of education, having especially in mind the need of extending very soon the benefits of a suitable education and training to everyone in all parts of the world.[7]

178

2. *Christian Education*

Since all Christians have become by rebirth of water and the Holy Spirit a new creature[8] so that they should be called and should be children of God, they have a right to a Christian education. A Christian education does not merely strive for the maturing of a human person as just now described, but has as its principal purpose this goal: that the baptized, while they are gradually introduced to the knowledge of the mystery of salvation, become ever more aware of the gift of Faith they have received, and that they learn in addition how to worship God the Father in spirit and truth (cf. John 4:23) especially in liturgical action, and be conformed in their personal lives according to the new man created in justice and holiness of truth (Eph. 4:22-24); also that they develop into perfect manhood, to the mature measure of the fulness of Christ (cf. Eph. 4:13) and strive for the growth of the Mystical Body; moreover, that aware of their calling, they learn not only how to bear witness to the hope that is in them (cf. Pet 3:15) but also how to help in the Christian formation of the world that takes place when natural powers viewed in the full consideration of man redeemed by Christ contribute to the good of the whole society.[9] Wherefore this sacred synod recalls to pastors of souls their most serious obligation to see to it that all the faithful, but especially the youth who are the hope of the Church, enjoy this Christian education.[10]

179

3. *The Authors of Education*

Since parents have given children their life, they are bound

---

[7] Cf. John XXIII's Encyclical letter, *Mater et Magistra*, 15 May 1961: A.A.S. 53 (1961) p. 441 ff.

[8] Cf. Pius XI's Encyclical letter, *Divini Illius Magistri*, 1, p. 83.

[9] Cf. Second Vatican Council's Dogmatic Constitution on the Church, no. 36: A.A.S. 57 (1965) p. 41 ff.

[10] Cf. Second Vatican Council's schema on the Decree on the Lay Apostolate (1965), 12.

by the most serious obligation to educate their offspring and therefore must be recognized as the primary and principal educators.[11] This role in education is so important that only with difficulty can it be supplied where it is lacking. Parents are the ones who must create a family atmosphere animated by love and respect for God and man, in which the well-rounded personal and social education of children is fostered. Hence the family is the first school of the social virtues that every society needs. It is particularly in the Christian family, enriched by the grace and office of the sacrament of matrimony, that children should be taught from their early years to have a knowledge of God according to the faith received in Baptism, to worship Him, and to love their neighbour. Here, too, they find their first experience of a wholesome human society and of the Church. Finally, it is through the family that they are gradually led to a companionship with their fellowmen and with the people of God. Let parents, then, recognize the inestimable importance a truly Christian family has for the life and progress of God's own people.[12]

The family which has the primary duty of imparting education needs help of the whole community. In addition, therefore, to the rights of parents and others to whom the parents entrust a share in the work of education, certain rights and duties belong indeed to civil society, whose role is to direct what is required for the common temporal good. Its function is to promote the education of youth in many ways, namely: to protect the duties and rights of parents and others who share in education and to give them aid; according to the principle of subsidiarity, when the endeavours of parents and other societies are lacking, to carry out the work of education in accordance with the wishes of the parents; and, moreover, as the common good demands, to build schools and institutions.[13]

---

[11] Cf. Pius XI's Encyclical letter *Divini Illius Magistri*, 1, p. 59 ff., Encyclical letter *Mit Brennender Sorge*, 14 March 1937: A.A.S. 29; Pius XII's allocution to the first national congress of the Italian Catholic Teachers' Association, 8 Sept 1946: Discourses and Radio Messages, vol. 8, p. 218.

[12] Cf. Second Vatican Council's Dogmatic Constitution on the Church, 11 and 35: A.A.S. 57 (1965) pp. 16, 40 ff.

[13] Cf. Pius XI's Encyclical letter *Divini Illius Magistri*, 1, p. 63 ff. Pius XII's radio message of 1 June 1941: A.A.S. 33 (1941) p. 200; allocution to the first national congress of the Association of Italian Catholic Teachers, 8 Sept 1946:

Finally, in a special way, the duty of educating belongs to the Church, not merely because she must be recognized as a human society capable of educating, but especially because she has the responsibility of announcing the way of salvation to all men, of communicating the life of Christ to those who believe, and, in her unfailing solicitude, of assisting men to be able to come to the fulness of this life.[14] The Church is bound as a mother to give to these children of hers an education by which their whole life can be imbued with the spirit of Christ and at the same time do all she can to promote for all peoples the complete perfection of the human person, the good of earthly society and the building of a world that is more human.[15]

180   4. *Various Aids to Christian Education*

In fulfilling its educational role, the Church, eager to employ all suitable aids, is concerned especially about those which are her very own. Foremost among these is catechetical instruction,[16] which enlightens and strengthens the faith, nourishes life according to the spirit of Christ, leads to intelligent and active participation in the liturgical mystery[17] and gives motivation for apostolic activity. The Church esteems highly and seeks to penetrate and ennoble with her own spirit also other aids which belong to the general heritage of man and which are of great influence in forming souls and moulding men, such as the media

---

Discourses and Radio Messages, vol. 8, 1946: Discourses and Radio Messages, vol. 8 p. 218. Regarding the principle of subsidiarity, cf. John XXIII's Encyclical letter, *Pacem in Terris*, 11 April 1963: A.A.S. 55 (1963) p. 294.

[14] Cf. Pius XI's Encyclical letter, *Divini Illius Magistri*, 1 pp. 53 ff. and 56 ff.; Encyclical letter, *Non Abbiamo Bisogno* 29 June 1931: A.A.S. 23 (1931) p. 311 ff. Pius XII's letter from Secretariat of State to 28th Italian Social Week, 20 Sept 1955; *L'Osservatore Romano*, 29 Sept 1955.

[15] The Church praises those local, national and international civic authorities who, conscious of the urgent necessity in these times, expend all their energy so that all peoples may benefit from more education and human culture. Cf. Paul VI's allocution to the United Nations General Assembly, 4 Oct 1965: *L'Osservatore Romano*, 6 Oct 1965.

[16] Cf. Pius XI's motu proprio. *Orbem Catholicum*, 29 June 1923: A.A.S. 15 (1923) pp. 327-329; decree, *Provido Sane*, 12 Jan 1935: A.A.S. 27 (1935) pp. 145-152. Second Vatican Council's Decree on Bishops and Pastoral Duties, nos. 13 and 14.

[17] Cf. Second Vatican Council's Constitution on the Sacred Liturgy, no. 14: A.A.S. 56 (1964) p. 104.

of communication,[18] various groups for mental and physical development, youth associations, and, in particular, schools.

5. *The Importance of Schools*   **181**

Among all educational instruments the school has a special importance.[19] It is designed not only to develop with special care the intellectual faculties but also to form the ability to judge rightly, to hand on the cultural legacy of previous generations, to foster a sense of values, to prepare for professional life. Between pupils of different talents and backgrounds it promotes friendly relations and fosters a spirit of mutual understanding; and it establishes as it were a centre whose work and progress must be shared together by families, teachers, associations of various types that foster cultural, civic, and religious life, as well as by civil society and the entire human community.

Beautiful indeed and of great importance is the vocation of all those who aid parents in fulfilling their duties and who, as representatives of the human community, undertake the task of education in schools. This vocation demands special qualities of mind and heart, very careful preparation, and continuing readiness to renew and to adapt.

6. *The Duties and Rights of Parents*   **182**

Parents who have the primary and inalienable right and duty to educate their children must enjoy true liberty in their choice of schools. Consequently, the public power, which has the obligation to protect and defend the rights of citizens, must see to it, in its concern for distributive justice, that public subsidies are paid out in such a way that parents are truly free to choose according to their conscience the schools they want for their children.[20]

In addition it is the task of the state to see to it that all citizens are able to come to a suitable share in culture and are

---

[18] Cf. Second Vatican Council's Decree on Communications Media, nos. 13 and 14: A.A.S. 56 (1964) p. 149 ff.

[19] Cf. Pius XI's Encyclical letter, *Divini Illius Magistri*, 1, p. 76; Pius XII's allocution to Bavarian Association of Catholic Teachers, 31 Dec 1956: Discourses and Radio Messages, vol. 18, p. 746.

[20] Cf. Provincial Council of Cincinnati III, a. 1861: *Collatio Lacensis*, III, col. 1240, c/d; Pius XI's Encyclical letter, *Divini Illius Magistri*, 1, pp. 60, 63 ff.

properly prepared to exercise their civic duties and rights.
Therefore the state must protect the right of children to an
adequate school education, check on the ability of teachers and
the excellence of their training, look after the health of the pupils
and in general, promote the whole school project. But it must
always keep in mind the principle of subsidiarity so that there is
no kind of school monopoly, for this is opposed to the native
rights of the human person, to the development and spread of
culture, to the peaceful association of citizens and to the pluralism
that exists today in ever so many societies.[21]

Therefore this sacred synod exhorts the faithful to assist to
their utmost in finding suitable methods of education and
programmes of study and in forming teachers who can give youth
a true education. Through the associations of parents in particular
they should further with their assistance all the work of the school
but especially the moral education it must impart.[22]

183   *7. Moral and Religious Education in all Schools*

Feeling very keenly the weighty responsibility of diligently
caring for the moral and religious education of all her children,
the Church must be present with her own special affection and
help for the great number who are being trained in schools that
are not Catholic. This is possible by the witness of the lives of
those who teach and direct them,[23] by the apostolic action of their
fellow-students, but especially by the ministry of priests and
laymen who give them the doctrine of salvation in a way suited to
their age and circumstances and provide spiritual aid in every way
the times and conditions allow.

The Church reminds parents of the duty that is theirs to

---

[21] Cf. Pius XI's Encyclical letter, *Divini Illius Magistri*, 1, p. 63; Encyclical
letter, *Non Abbiamo Bisogno*, 29 June 1931: A.A.S. 23 (1931) p. 305, Pius XII's
letter from the Secretary of State to the 28th Italian Social Week, 20 Sept. 1955:
L'Osservatore Romano, 29 Sept. 1955. Paul VI's allocution to the Association
of Italian Christian Workers, 6 Oct. 1963: Encyclicals and Discourses of Paul
VI, vol. 1, Rome, 1964, p. 230.

[22] Cf. John XXIII's message on the 30th anniversary of the Encyclical letter,
Divini Illius Magistri, Dec. 30, 1959: A.A.S. 52 (1960) p. 57.

[23] The Church considers it as apostolic action of great worth also when Catholic
teachers and associates work in these schools. Cf. Second Vatican Council's
schema of the Decree on the Lay Apostolate (1965), nos. 12 and 16.

arrange and even demand that their children be able to enjoy these aids and advance in their Christian formation to a degree that is abreast of their development in secular subjects. Therefore the Church esteems highly those civil authorities and societies which, bearing in mind the pluralism of contemporary society and respecting religious freedom, assist families so that the education of their children can be imparted in all schools according to the individual moral and religious principles of the families.[24]

8. *Catholic Schools*

The influence of the Church in the field of education is shown in a special manner by the Catholic school. No less than other schools does the Catholic school pursue cultural goals and the human formation of youth. But its proper function is to create for the school community a special atmosphere animated by the Gospel spirit of freedom and charity, to help youth grow according to the new creatures they were made through baptism as they develop their own personalities, and finally to order the whole of human culture to the news of salvation so that the knowledge the students gradually acquire of the world, life and man is illumined by faith.[25] So indeed the Catholic school, while it is open, as it must be, to the situation of the contemporary world, leads its students to promote efficaciously the good of the earthly city and also prepares them for service in the spread of the Kingdom of God, so that by leading an exemplary apostolic life they become, as it were, a saving leaven in the human community.

Since, therefore, the Catholic school can be such an aid to the fulfilment of the mission of the People of God and to the fostering of the dialogue between the Church and mankind, to the benefit of both, it retains even in our present circumstances the utmost importance. Consequently this sacred synod proclaims anew what

184

---

[24] Cf. Second Vatican Council's schema on the Declaration on Religious Liberty (1965), no. 5.

[25] Cf. Provincial Council of Westminster I, a. 1852: *Collatio Lacensis* III, col. 1334, a/b; Pius XI's Encyclical letter, *Divini Illius Magistri*, 1, p. 77 ff.; Pius XII's allocution to the Bavarian Association of Catholic Teachers, 31 Dec. 1956: Discourses and Radio Messages, vol. 18, p. 746; Paul VI's allocution to the members of Federated Institutes Dependent on Ecclesiastic Authority, 30 Dec. 1963: Encyclicals and Discourses of Paul VI, 1, Rome, 1964, 602 ff.

has already been taught in several documents of the magis-terium,[26] namely: the right of the Church freely to establish and to conduct schools of every type and level. And the council calls to mind that the exercise of a right of this kind contributes in the highest degree to the protection of freedom of conscience, the rights of parents, as well as to the betterment of culture itself.

But let teachers recognize that the Catholic school depends upon them almost entirely for the accomplishment of its goals and programmes.[27] They should therefore be very carefully prepared so that both in secular and religious knowledge they are equipped with suitable qualifications and also with a pedagogical skill that is in keeping with the findings of the contemporary world. Intimately linked in charity to one another and to their students and endowed with an apostolic spirit, may teachers by their life as much as by their instruction bear witness to Christ, the unique Teacher. Let them work as partners with parents and together with them in every phase of education give due consideration to the difference of sex and the proper ends Divine Providence assigns to each sex in the family and in society. Let them do all they can to stimulate their students to act for themselves and even after graduation to continue to assist them with advice, friendship and by establishing special associations imbued with the true spirit of the Church. The work of these teachers, this sacred synod declares, is in the real sense of the word an apostolate most suited to and necessary for our times and at once a true service offered to society. The Council also reminds Catholic parents of the duty of entrusting their children to Catholic schools wherever and whenever it is possible and of supporting these schools to the best of their ability and of cooperating with them for the education of their children.[28]

---

[26] Cf. especially the document mentioned in the first note; moreover this law of the Church is proclaimed by many provincial councils and in the most recent declarations of very many of the episcopal conferences.

[27] Cf. Pius XI's Encyclical letter, *Divini Illius Magistri*, 1 p. 80 ff.; Pius XII's allocution to the Catholic Association of Italian Teachers in Secondary Schools, 5 Jan. 1954: Discourses and Radio Messages, 15, pp. 551-553; John XXIII's allocution to the 6th Congress of the Associations of Catholic Italian Teachers 5 Sept. 1959: Discourses, Messages, Conversations, 1, Rome, 1960, pp. 427-431.

[28] Cf. Pius XII's allocution to the Catholic Association of Italian Teachers in Secondary Schools, 5 Jan. 1954, 1, p. 555.

9. *Different Types of Catholic Schools*

185

To this concept of a Catholic school, all schools that are in any way dependent on the Church must conform as far as possible, though the Catholic school is to take on different forms in keeping with local circumstances.[29] Thus the Church considers very dear to her heart those Catholic schools, found especially in the areas of the new churches, which are attended also by students who are not Catholics.

Attention should be paid to the needs of today in establishing and directing Catholic schools. Therefore, though primary and secondary schools, the foundation of education, must still be fostered, great importance is to be attached to those which are required in a particular way by contemporary conditions, such as: professional[30] and technical schools, centres for educating adults and promoting social welfare, or for the retarded in need of special care, and also schools for preparing teachers for religious instruction and other types of education.

This Sacred Council of the Church earnestly entreats pastors and all the faithful to spare no sacrifice in helping Catholic schools fulfil their function in a continually more perfect way, and especially in caring for the needs of those who are poor in the goods of this world or who are deprived of the assistance and affection of a family or who are strangers to the gift of Faith.

10. *Catholic Colleges and Universities*

186

The Church is concerned also with schools of a higher level, especially colleges and universities. In those schools dependent on her she intends that by their very constitution individual subjects be pursued according to their own principles, method, and liberty of scientific inquiry, in such a way that an ever deeper understanding in these fields may be obtained and that, as questions that are new and current are raised and investigations carefully made according to the example of the doctors of the

---

[29] Cf. Paul VI's allocution to the International Office of Catholic Education, 25 Feb. 1964: Encyclicals and Discourses of Paul VI, 2, Rome, 1964, p. 232.
[30] Cf. Paul VI's allocution to the Christian Association of Italian Workers, 6 Oct. 1963: Encyclicals and Discourses of Paul VI, 1, Rome, 1964, p. 229.

Church and especially of St. Thomas Aquinas,[31] there may be a deeper realization of the harmony of faith and science. Thus there is accomplished a public, enduring and pervasive influence of the Christian mind in the furtherance of culture and the students of these institutions are moulded into men truly outstanding in their training, ready to undertake weighty responsibilities in society and witness to the faith in the world.[32]

In Catholic universities where there is no faculty of sacred theology there should be established an institute or chair of sacred theology in which there should be lectures suited to lay students. Since science advances by means of the investigations peculiar to higher scientific studies, special attention should be given in Catholic universities and colleges to institutes that serve primarily the development of scientific research.

The sacred synod heartily recommends that Catholic colleges and universities be conveniently located in different parts of the world, but in such a way that they are outstanding not for their numbers but for their pursuit of knowledge. Matriculation should be readily available to students of real promise, even though they be of slender means, especially to students from the newly emerging nations.

Since the destiny of society and of the Church itself is intimately linked with the progress of young people pursuing higher studies,[33] the pastors of the Church are to expend their energies not only on the spiritual life of students who attend Catholic universities, but, solicitous for the spiritual formation of

---

[31] Cf. Paul VI's allocution to the International Thomistic Congress, 10 Sept. 1965: L'Osservatore Romano, 13-14 Sept. 1965.

[32] Cf. Pius XII's allocution to teachers and students of French Institutes of Higher Catholic Education, 21 Sept. 1950: Discourses and Radio Messages, 12, pp. 219-221; letters to the 22nd congress of *Pax Romana*, 12 Aug. 1952: Discourses and Radio Messages, 14, pp. 567-569; John XXIII's allocution to the Federation of Catholic Universities, 1 April 1959: Discourses, Messages and Conversations, 1, Rome, 1960, pp. 226-229; Paul VI's allocution to the Academic Senate of the Catholic University of Milan, 5 April 1964: Encyclicals and Discourses of Paul VI, 2, Rome, 1964, pp. 438-443.

[33] Cf. Pius XII's allocution to the academic senate and students of the University of Rome, 15 June 1952: Discourses and Radio Messages, 14, p. 208: "The direction of today's society principally is placed in the mentality and hearts of the universities of today."

all their children, they must see to it, after consultations between bishops, that even at universities that are not Catholic there should be associations and university centres under Catholic auspices in which priests, religious and laity, carefully selected and prepared, should give abiding spiritual and intellectual assistance to the youth of the university. Whether in Catholic universities or others, young people of greater ability who seem suited for teaching or research should be specially helped and encouraged to undertake a teaching career.

11. *Faculties of Sacred Sciences*   **187**
The Church expects much from the zealous endeavours of the faculties of the sacred sciences.[34] For to them she entrusts the very serious responsibility of preparing her own students not only for the priestly ministry, but especially for teaching in the seats of higher ecclesiastical studies or for promoting learning on their own or for undertaking the work of a more rigorous intellectual apostolate. Likewise it is the role of these very faculties to make more penetrating inquiry into the various aspects of the sacred sciences so that an ever deepening understanding of sacred Revelation is obtained, the legacy of Christian wisdom handed down by our forefathers is more fully developed, the dialogue with our separated brethren and with non-Christians is fostered, and answers are given to questions arising from the development of doctrine.[35]

Therefore ecclesiastical faculties should reappraise their own laws so that they can better promote the sacred sciences and those linked with them and, by employing up-to-date methods and aids, lead their students to more penetrating inquiry.

12. *Coordination to be fostered in scholastic matters*   **188**
Cooperation is the order of the day. It increases more and more to supply the demand on a diocesan, national and international level. Since it is altogether necessary in scholastic matters,

---

[34] Cf. Pius XII's apostolic constitution, *Deus Scientiarum Dominus*, 24 May 1931: A.A.S. 23 (1931) pp. 245-247.
[35] Cf. Pius XII's Encyclical letter, *Humani Generis,* 12 Aug. 1950 A.A.S. 42 (1950) pp. 568 ff. and 578; Paul VI's Encyclical letter, *Ecclesiam Suam*, part III, 6 Aug. 1964; A.A.S. 56 (1964) pp. 637-659; Second Vatican Council's Decree on Eccumenism: A.A.S. 57 (1965) pp. 90-107.

every means should be employed to foster suitable cooperation between Catholic schools, and between these and other schools that collaboration should be developed which the good of all mankind requires.[36] From greater coordination and cooperative endeavour greater fruits will be derived particularly in the area of academic institutions. Therefore in every university let the various faculties work mutually to this end, insofar as their goal will permit. In addition, let the universities also endeavour to work together by promoting international gatherings, by sharing scientific inquiries with one another, by communicating their discoveries to one another, by having exchange of professors for a time and by promoting all else that is conducive to greater assistance.

Conclusion

189   13. The sacred synod earnestly entreats young people themselves to become aware of the importance of the work of education and to prepare themselves to take it up, especially where because of a shortage of teachers the education of youth is in jeopardy. This same sacred synod, while professing its gratitude to priests, Religious men and women, and the laity who by their evangelical self-dedication are devoted to the noble work of education and of schools of every type and level, exhorts them to persevere generously in the work they have undertaken and, imbuing their students with the spirit of Christ, to strive to excel in pedagogy and the pursuit of knowledge in such a way that they not merely advance the internal renewal of the Church but preserve and enhance its beneficent influence upon today's world, especially the intellectual world.

Pope Paul VI

---

[36] Cf. John XXIII's Encyclical letter, *Pacem in Terris*, 11 April 1963: A.A.S. 55 (1963) p. 284 and elsewhere.

THE CATHOLIC SCHOOL
The Sacred Congregation for Catholic Education
19 March 1977

Introduction

1. The Catholic school is receiving more and more attention **190**

in the Church since the Second Vatican Council, with particular emphasis on the Church as she appears in the Constitutions *Lumen Gentium* and *Gaudium et Spes*. In the Council's Declaration *Gravissimum Educationis* it is discussed in the wider sphere of Christian education. The present document develops the idea of this Declaration, limiting itself to a deeper reflection on the Catholic school.

191   2. The Sacred Congregation for Catholic Education is aware of the serious problems which are an integral part of Christian education in a pluralistic society. It regards as a prime duty, therefore, the focusing of any attention on the nature and distinctive characteristics of school which would present itself as Catholic. Yet the diverse situations and legal systems in which the Catholic school has to function in Christian and non-Christian countries demand that local problems be faced and solved by each Church within its own social-cultural context.

192   3. While acknowledging this duty of the local Churches, the Sacred Congregation believes that now is the opportune moment to offer its own contribution by re-emphasising clearly the educational value of the Catholic school. It is in this value that the Catholic school's fundamental reason for existing and the basis of its genuine apostolate is to be found. This document does not pretend to be an exhaustive treatment of the subject; it merely proposes to state the premises that will lead to further fruitful study and implementation.

193   4. To Episcopal Conferences, pastorally concerned for all young Catholics whatever school they attend,[1] the Sacred Congregation for Catholic Education entrusts this present document in order that they may seek to achieve an effective system of education at all levels which corresponds to the total educational needs of young people today in Catholic schools. The Sacred Congregation also addresses itself to all who are responsible for education – parents, teachers, young people and school authorities – and urges them to pool all their resources and the means at their disposal to enable Catholic schools to provide a service which is truly civic and apostolic.

---

[1] Cf. Second Vatican Council, *Declaration on Christian Education GE*, 7.

I. The Catholic School and the Salvific Mission of the Church

The Salvific Mission of the Church

5. In the fulness of time, in His mysterious plan of love, God **194** the Father sent His only Son to begin the Kingdom of God on earth and bring about the spiritual rebirth of mankind. To continue His work of salvation, Jesus Christ founded the Church as a visible organism, living by the power of the Spirit.

6. Moved by the same Spirit, the Church is constantly **195** deepening her awareness of herself and meditating on the mystery of her being and mission.[2] Thus she is ever rediscovering her living relationship with Christ "in order to discover greater light, energy, and joy in fulfilling her mission and determining the best way to ensure that her relationship with humanity is closer and more efficacious"[3] – that humanity of which she is a part and yet so undeniably distinct. Her destiny is to serve humanity until it reaches its fulness in Christ.

7. Evangelisation is, therefore, the mission of the Church; that is **196** she must proclaim the good news of salvation to all, generate new creatures in Christ through Baptism, and train them to live knowingly as children of God.

Means available for the Mission of the Church

8. To carry out her saving mission, the Church uses, above **197** all, the means which Jesus Christ has given her. She also uses other means which at different times and in different cultures have proved effective in achieving and promoting the development of the human person. The Church adapts these means to the changing conditions and emerging needs of mankind.[4] In her encounter with differing cultures and with man's progressive achievements, the Church proclaims the faith and reveals "to all ages the transcendent goal which alone gives life its full meaning".[5] She establishes her own schools because she considers them as a privileged means of promoting the formation of the whole man,

---

[2] Cf. Paul VI, Encyclical Letter *Ecclesiam suam*, 7.

[3] *Ibid.* 13.

[4] Cf Second Vatican Council, Pastoral Constitution on the Church in the Modern World *GS*, 4.

[5] Paul VI, Allocution to Cardinal Gabriel-Marie Garrone, 27 November 1972.

since the school is a centre in which a specific concept of the world, of man, and of history is developed and conveyed.

Contribution of the Catholic school towards the Salvific Mission of the Church

198   9. The Catholic school forms part of the saving mission of the Church, especially for education in the faith. Remembering that "the simultaneous development of man's psychological and moral consciousness is demanded by Christ almost as a pre-condition for the reception of the befitting divine gifts of truth and grace",[6] the Church fulfils her obligation to foster in her children a full awareness of their rebirth to a new life[7]. It is precisely in the Gospel of Christ, taking root in the minds and lives of the faithful, that the Catholic school finds its definition as it comes to terms with the cultural conditions of the times.

The Church's educational involvement and cultural pluralism

199   10. In the course of the centuries "while constantly holding to the fulness of divine truth"[8] the Church has progressively used the sources and the means of culture in order to deepen her understanding of revelation and promote constructive dialogue with the world. Moved by the faith through which she firmly believes herself to be led by the Spirit of the Lord, the Church seeks to discern in the events, needs and hopes of our era[9] the most insistent demands which she must answer if she is to carry out God's plan.

200   11. One such demand is a pressing need to ensure the presence of a Christian mentality in the society of the present day, marked, among other things, by cultural pluralism. For it is Christian thought which constitutes a sound criterion of judgment in the midst of conflicting concepts and behaviour: "Reference to Jesus Christ teaches man to discern the values which ennoble

---

[6] Paul VI, Encyclical Letter *Ecclesiam suam,* 15.
[7] Cf Second Vatican Council, *Declaration on Christian Education GE*, 3.
[8] Second Vatican Council, Dogmatic Constitution on Divine Revelation *Dei Verbum,* 8.
[9] Cf. Second Vatican Council, Pastoral Constitution on the Church in the Modern World *GS*, 11

from those which degrade him"[10].

12. Cultural pluralism, therefore, leads the Church to reaffirm **201**
her mission of education to ensure strong character formation.
Her children, then, will be capable both of resisting the
debilitating influence of relativism and of living up to the
demands made on them by their Baptism. It also stimulates her to
foster truly Christian living and apostolic communities, equipped
to make their own positive contribution, in a spirit of cooperation,
to the building up of the secular society. For this reason the
Church is prompted to mobilise her educational resources in the
face of the materialism, pragmatism and technocracy of contemporary society.

13. The Church upholds the principle of a plurality of school **202**
systems in order to safeguard her objectives in the face of cultural
pluralism. In other words, she encourages the co-existence and, if
possible, the cooperation of diverse educational institutions which
will allow young people to be formed by value judgments based
on a specific view of the world and to be trained to take an active
part in the construction of a community through which the
building of society itself is promoted.

14. Thus, while policies and opportunities differ from place **203**
to place, the Catholic school has its place in any national school
system. By offering such an alternative the Church wishes to
respond to the obvious need for cooperation in a society
characterised by cultural pluralism. Moreover, in this way she
helps to promote that freedom of teaching which champions and
guarantees freedom of conscience and the parental right to choose
the school best suited to parents' educational purpose.[11]

15. Finally, the Church is absolutely convinced that the **204**
educational aims of the Catholic school in the world of today
perform an essential and unique service for the Church herself. It
is, in fact, through the school that she participates in the dialogue
of culture with her own positive contribution to the cause of the
total formation of man. The absence of the Catholic school would

---

[10] Paul VI, Allocution to the Ninth Congress of the Catholic International
Education Office (O.I.E.C.), in *L'Osservatore Romano*, 9 June 1974.
[11] Cf. Second Vatican Council, *Declaration on Christian Education GE*, 8.

be a great loss[12] for civilisation and for the natural and supernatural destiny of man.

II. Present Difficulties over Catholic Schools

205   16. In the light of her mission of salvation, the Church considers that the Catholic school provides a privileged environment for the complete formation of her members, and that it also provides a highly important service to mankind. Nevertheless, she is aware of the many problems that exist and objections that are made against Catholic schools sometimes regarding the very validity of their existence and their functions. The issue is really part of a much wider problem which faces all institutions as such in a society as the present, characterised by rapid and profound change.

Objections raised against Catholic schools

206   17. In the debate about Catholic schools there are some easily identifiable central objections and difficulties. These need to be borne in mind if discussion is to be relevant to the actual situation and if teachers are to make a serious attempt to adapt their work to the needs of the contemporary world.

207   18. In the first place many people, both inside and outside the Church, motivated by a mistaken sense of the lay role in secular society, attack Catholic schools as institutions. They do not admit that, apart from the individual witness of her members, the Church also may offer witness by means of her institutions, e.g. those dedicated to the search for truth or to works of charity.

208   19. Others claim that Catholic schools make use of a human institution for religious and confessional purposes. Christian education can sometimes run into the danger of a so-called proselytism, of imparting a one-sided outlook. This can happen only when Christian educators misunderstand the nature and methods of Christian education. Complete education necessarily includes a religious dimension. Religion is an effective contribution to the development of other aspects of a personality in the measure in which it is integrated into general education.

---

[12] Cf. Paul VI, Allocution to the Ninth Congress of the O.I.E.C., in *L'Osservatore Romano*, 9 June 1974.

20. According to others, Catholic schools have outlived their **209** time – as institutions they were a necessary substitute in the past but have no place at a time when civil authority assumes responsibility for education. In fact, as the State increasingly takes control of education and establishes its own so-called neutral and monolithic system, the survival of those natural communities, based on a shared concept of life, is threatened. Faced with this situation, the Catholic school offers an alternative which is in conformity with the wishes of the members of the community of the Church.

21. In some countries Catholic schools have been obliged to **210** restrict their educational activities to wealthier social classes, thus giving an impression of social and economic discrimination in education. But this occurs only where the State has not weighed the advantages of an alternative presence in their pluralistic society. From such nearsightedness considerable difficulties have arisen for Catholic schools.

22. Allied to these points, objections are raised concerning **211** the educational results of the Catholic school. They are sometimes accused of not knowing how to form convinced, articulate Christians ready to take their place in social and political life. Every educational enterprise, however, involves the risk of failure and one must not be too discouraged by apparent or even real failures, since there are very many formative influences on young people and results often have to be calculated on a long-term basis.

23. Before concluding these comments on the objections **212** raised against Catholic schools, one must remember the context in which contemporary work in the field of education is undertaken, and especially in the Church. The school problem in our rapidly changing society is serious for everyone. The Second Vatican Council has encouraged a more open-minded approach which has sometimes been misrepresented in theory and practice. There are difficulties in the provision of adequate staff and finance. In such a situation should the Church perhaps give up her apostolic mission in Catholic schools, as some people would like her to do, and direct her energy to a more direct work of evangelisation in sectors considered to be of higher priority or more suited to her spiritual mission, or should she make State schools the sole object of her pastoral activity? Such a solution would not only be

contrary to the directives of the Vatican Council, but would also be opposed to the Church's mission and to what is expected of her by Christian people. What follows emphasises this fact.

Some aspects of schools today

213   24. To understand the real nature of the Catholic school one cannot divorce it from wider modern problems concerning schools in general. Apart from the ideas advanced by the promoters of de-schooling – a theory which now seems of minor significance – contemporary society tends to place greater importance than ever on the specific function of the school: its social significance (parental participation, increased democratisation, equality of opportunity); its tendency to coordinate and eventually include the educational work of other institutions; the extension of the statutory duration of attendance at school.

III. The School as a Centre of Human Formation

214   25. To understand fully the specific mission of the Catholic school it is essential to keep in mind the basic concept of what a school is; that which does not reproduce the characteristic features of a school cannot be a Catholic school.

The general purpose of a school

215   26. A close examination of the various definitions of school and of new educational trends at every level, leads one to formulate the concept of school as a place of integral formation by means of a systematic and critical assimilation of culture. A school is, therefore, a privileged place in which, through a living encounter with a cultural inheritance, integral formation occurs.

216   27. This vital approach takes place in the school in the form of personal contacts and commitments which consider absolute values in a life-context and seek to insert them into a life-frame-work. Indeed, culture is only educational when young people can relate their study to real-life situations with which they are familiar. The school must stimulate the pupil to exercise his intelligence through the dynamics of understanding to attain clarity and inventiveness. It must help him spell out the meaning of his experiences and their truths. Any school which neglects this duty and which offers merely pre-cast conclusions hinders the personal development of its pupils.

School and attitudes of life

28. From this it is clear that the school has to review its entire **217** programme of formation, both its content and the methods used, in the light of that vision of the reality from which it draws its inspiration and on which it depends.

29. Either implicit or explicit reference to a determined **218** attitude to life (Weltanschauung) is unavoidable in education because it comes into every decision that is made. It is, therefore, essential, if for no other reason than for a unity in teaching, that each member of the school community, albeit with differing degrees of awareness, adopts a common vision, a common outlook on life, based on adherence to a scale of values in which he believes. This is what gives teachers and adults authority to educate. It must never be forgotten that the purpose of instruction at school is education, that is, the development of man from within, freeing him from that conditioning which would prevent him from becoming a fully integrated human being. The school must begin from the principle that its educational programme is intentionally directed to the growth of the whole person.

30. It is one of the formal tasks of a school, as an institution **219** for education, to draw out the ethical dimension for the precise purpose of arousing the individual's inner spiritual dynamism and to aid his achieving that moral freedom which complements the psychological. Behind this moral freedom, however, stand those absolute values which alone give meaning and value to human life. This has to be said because the tendency to adopt present-day values as a yardstick is not absent even in the educational world. The danger is always to react to passing, superficial ideas and to lose sight of the much deeper needs of the contemporary world.

The school in today's society

31. Precisely because the school endeavours to answer the **220** needs of a society characterised by depersonalisation and a mass production mentality which so easily result from scientific and technological developments, it must develop into an authentically formational school, reducing such risks to a minimum. It must

develop persons who are responsible and inner-directed, capable
of choosing freely in conformity with their conscience. This is
simply another way of saying that the school is an institution
where young people gradually learn to open themselves up to life
as it is, and to create in themselves a definite attitude to life as it
should be.

221   32. When seen in this light, a school is not only a place
where one is given a choice of intellectual values, but a place
where one has presented an array of values which are actively
lived. The school must be a community whose values are
communicated through the interpersonal and sincere relationships
of its members and through both individual and corporative
adherence to the outlook on life that permeates the school.

IV. The Educational Work of the Catholic School

Specific character of the Catholic school

222   33. Having stated the characteristics of the Catholic school
from the point of view of "school" we can now examine its
Catholic quality, namely its reference to a Christian concept of
life centred on Jesus Christ.

223   34. Christ is the foundation of the whole educational
enterprise in a Catholic school. His revelation gives new meaning
to life and helps man to direct his thought, action and will
according to the Gospel, making the beatitudes his norm of life.
The fact that in their own individual ways all members of the
school community share this Christian vision, makes the school
"Catholic"; principles of the Gospel in this manner become the
educational norms since the school then has them as its internal
motivation and final goal.

224   35. The Catholic school is committed thus to the
development of the whole man, since in Christ, the Perfect Man,
all human values find their fulfilment and unity. Herein lies the
specifically Catholic character of the school. Its duty to cultivate
human values in their own legitimate right in accordance with its
particular mission to serve all men has its origin in the figure of
Christ. He is the One Who ennobles man, gives meaning to
human life, and is the Model which the Catholic school offers to
its pupils.

36. If, like every other school, the Catholic school has as its aim the critical communication of human culture and the total formation of the individual, it works towards this goal guided by its Christian vision of reality "through which our cultural heritage acquires its special place in the total vocational life of man"[13]. Mindful of the fact that man has been redeemed by Christ, the Catholic school aims at forming in the Christian those particular virtues which will enable him to live a new life in Christ and help him to play faithfully his part in building up the Kingdom of God[14].

225

37. These premises indicate the duties and the content of the Catholic school. Its task is fundamentally a synthesis of culture and faith, and a synthesis of faith and life: the first is reached by integrating all the different aspects of human knowledge through the subjects taught, in the light of the Gospel; the second, in the growth of the virtues characteristic of the Christian.

226

Integration of faith and culture

38. In helping pupils to achieve through the medium of its teaching an integration of faith and culture, the Catholic school sets out with a deep awareness of the value of knowledge as such. Under no circumstances does it wish to divert the imparting of knowledge from its rightful objective.

227

39. Individual subjects must be taught according to their own particular methods. It would be wrong to consider subjects as mere adjuncts to faith or as a useful means of teaching apologetics. They enable the pupil to assimilate skills, knowledge, intellectual methods and moral and social attitudes, all of which help to develop his personality and lead him to take his place as an active member of the community of man. Their aim is not merely the attainment of knowledge but the acquisition of values and the discovery of truth.

228

40. Since the educative mission of the Catholic school is so wide, the teacher is in an excellent position to guide the pupil to a deepening of his faith and to enrich and enlighten his human

229

---

[13] Second Vatican Council, Pastoral Constitution on the Church in the Modern World *GS*, 57
[14] Cf. Second Vatican Council, *Declaration on Christian Education*, *GE*, 2.

knowledge with the data of the faith. While there are many occasions in teaching when pupils can be stimulated by insights of faith, a Christian education acknowledges the valid contribution which can be made by academic subjects towards the development of a mature Christian. The teacher can form the mind and heart of his pupils and guide them to develop a total commitment to Christ, with their whole personality enriched by human culture.

230 41. The school considers human knowledge as a truth to be discovered. In the measure in which subjects are taught by someone who knowingly and without restraint seeks the truth, they are to that extent Christian. Discovery and awareness of truth leads man to the discovery of Truth itself. A teacher who is full of Christian wisdom, well prepared in his own subject, does more than convey the sense of what he is teaching to his pupils. Over and above what he says, he guides his pupils beyond his mere words to the heart of total Truth.

231 42. The cultural heritage of mankind includes other values apart from the specific ambient of truth. When the Christian teacher helps a pupil to grasp, appreciate and assimilate these values, he is guiding him towards eternal realities. This movement towards the Uncreated Source of all knowledge highlights the importance of teaching for the growth of faith.

232 43. The achievement of this specific aim of the Catholic school depends not so much on subject matter or methodology as on the people who work there. The extent to which the Christian message is transmitted through education depends to a very great extent on the teachers. The integration of culture and faith is mediated by the other integration of faith and life in the person of the teacher. The nobility of the task to which teachers are called demands that, in imitation of Christ, the only Teacher, they reveal the Christian message not only by word but also by every gesture of their behaviour. This is what makes the difference between a school whose education is permeated by the Christian spirit and one in which religion is only regarded as an academic subject like any other.

Integration of faith and life

233 44. The fundamental aim of teaching is the assimilation of objective values, and, when this is undertaken for an apostolic purpose, it does not stop at an integration of faith and culture but leads the pupil on to a personal integration of faith and life.

45. The Catholic school has as its specific duty the complete Christian formation of its pupils, and this task is of special significance today because of the inadequacy of the family and society. It knows that this integration of faith and life is part of a life-long process of conversion until the pupil becomes what God wishes him to be. Young people have to be taught to share their personal lives with God. They are to overcome their individualism and discover, in the light of faith, their specific vocation to live responsibly in a community with others. The very pattern of the Christian life draws them to commit themselves to serve God in their brethren and to make the world a better place for man to live in.

234

46. The Catholic school should teach its pupils to discern in the voice of the universe the Creator Whom it reveals and, in the conquests of science, to know God and man better. In the daily life of the school, the pupil should learn that he is called to be a living witness to God's love for men by the way he acts, and that he is part of that salvation history which has Christ, the Saviour of the world, as its goal.

235

47. Being aware that Baptism by itself does not make a Christian – living and acting in conformity with the Gospel is necessary – the Catholic school tries to create within its walls a climate[15] in which the pupil's faith will gradually mature and enable him to assume the responsibility placed on him by Baptism. It will give pride of place in the education it provides through Christian Doctrine to the gradual formation of conscience in fundamental, permanent virtues – above all the theological virtues, and charity in particular, which is, so to speak, the life-giving spirit which transforms a man of virtue into a man of Christ. Christ, therefore, is the teaching-centre, the Model on Whom the Christian shapes his life. In Him the Catholic school differs from all others which limit themselves to forming men. Its task is to form Christian men, and, by its teaching and witness, show non-Christians something of the mystery of Christ Who

236

---

[15] Cf. Second Vatican Council, *Declaration on Christian Education, GE,* 8.

surpasses all human understanding.[16]

237   48. The Catholic school will work closely with other Christian bodies (the family, the parish and Christian community, youth associations, etc.). But one must not overlook many other spheres of activity in society which are sources of information and in their various ways have an educational influence. Alongside this so-called "parallel school", the school proper is an active force through the systematic formation of the pupils' critical faculties to bring them to a measure of self control[17] and the ability to choose freely and conscientiously in the face of what is offered by the organs of social communication. They must be taught to subject these things to a critical and personal analysis[18], take what is good, and integrate it into their Christian human culture.

Religious teaching

238   49. The specific mission of the school, then, is a critical, systematic transmission of culture in the light of faith and the bringing forth of the power of Christian virtue by the integration of culture with faith and of faith with living.

Consequently, the Catholic school is aware of the importance of the Gospel-teaching as transmitted through the Catholic Church. It is, indeed, the fundamental element in the educative process as it helps the pupil towards his conscious choice of living a responsible and coherent way of life.

239   50. Without entering into the whole problem of teaching religion in schools, it must be emphasised that, while such teaching is not merely confined to "religious classes" within the school curriculum, it must, nevertheless, also be imparted explicitly and in a systematic manner to prevent a distortion in the child's mind between general and religious culture. The fundamental difference between religious and other forms of education is that its aim is not simply intellectual assent to religious truths but also a total commitment of one's whole being to the Person of Christ.

---

[16] Cf. Eph. 3, 18-19.

[17] Cf. Pastoral Instruction *Communio et Progressio*, 67.

[18] Cf. *Ibid.*

51. It is recognised that the proper place for catechesis is the **240** family helped by other Christian communities, especially the local parish. But the importance and need for catechetical instruction in Catholic schools cannot be sufficiently emphasised. Here young people are helped to grow towards maturity in faith.

52. The Catholic school must be alert at all times to **241** developments in the fields of child psychology, pedagogy and particularly catechetics, and should especially keep abreast of directives from competent ecclesiastical authorities. The school must do everything in its power to aid the Church to fulfil its catechetical mission and so must have the best possible qualified teachers of religion.

The Catholic school as the centre of the educative Christian community

53. For all these reasons, Catholic schools must be seen as **242** "meeting places for those who wish to express Christian values in education"[19]. The Catholic school, far more than any other, must be a community whose aim is the transmission of values for living. Its work is seen as promoting a faith-relationship with Christ in Whom all values find fulfilment. But faith is principally assimilated through contact with people whose daily life bears witness to it. Christian faith, in fact, is born and grows inside a community.

54. The community aspect of the Catholic school is necessary **243** because of the nature of the faith and not simply because of the nature of man and the nature of the educational process which is common to every school. No Catholic school can adequately fulfil its educational role on its own. It must continually be fed and stimulated by its Source of life, the Saving Word of Christ as it is expressed in Sacred Scripture, in Tradition, especially liturgical and sacramental tradition, and in the lives of people, past and present, who bear witness to that Word.

55. The Catholic school loses its purpose without constant **244** reference to the Gospel and a frequent encounter with Christ. It derives all the energy necessary for its educational work from

---

[19] Paul VI, Allocution to the Ninth Congress of the O.I.E.C., in *L'Osservatore Romano*, 9 June 1974.

Him and thus "creates in the school community an atmosphere permeated with the Gospel spirit of freedom and love"[20]. In this setting the pupil experiences his dignity as a person before he knows its definition. Faithful, therefore, to the claims of man and of God, the Catholic school makes its own contribution towards man's liberation, making him, in other words, what his destiny implies, one who talks consciously with God, one who is there for God to love.

245   56. "This simple religious doctrine is the cornerstone of the existential, Christian metaphysic."[21] This is the basis of a Catholic school's educational work. Education is not given for the purpose of gaining power but as an aid towards a fuller understanding of, and communion with man, events and things. Knowledge is not to be considered as a means of material prosperity and success, but as a call to serve and to be responsible for others.

Other aspects of the educational process in Catholic schools
246   57. Whether or not the Catholic community forms its young people in the faith by means of a Catholic school, a Catholic school in itself is far from being divisive or presumptuous. It does not exacerbate differences, but rather aids cooperation and contact with others. It opens itself to others and respects their way of thinking and of living. It wants to share their anxieties and their hopes as it, indeed, shares their present and future lot in this world.

247   58. Since it is motivated by the Christian ideal, the Catholic school is particularly sensitive to the call from every part of the world for a more just society, and it tries to make its own contribution towards it. It does not stop at the courageous teaching of the demands of justice even in the face of local opposition, but tries to put these demands into practice in its own community in the daily life of the school. In some countries, because of local laws and economic conditions, the Catholic school runs the risk of giving counter-witness by admitting a majority of children from wealthier families. Schools may have done this

---

[20] Second Vatican Council, *Declaration on Christian Education GE*, 8.
[21] Paul VI, *Valore dell'oblazione nella vita*, in *The Teaching of Pope Paul VI*, vol. 8 (1970), p. 97.

because of their need to be financially self-supporting. This situation is of great concern to those responsible for Catholic education, because first and foremost the Church offers its educational service to "the poor or those who are deprived of family help and affection or those who are far from the faith"[22]. Since education is an important means of improving the social and economic condition of the individual and of peoples, if the Catholic school were to turn its attention exclusively or predominantly to those from the wealthier social classes, it could be contributing towards maintaining their privileged position, and could thereby continue to favour a society which is unjust.

59. It is obvious that in such a demanding educational policy all participants must be committed to it freely. It cannot be imposed, but is offered as a possibility, as good news, and as such can be refused. However, in order to bring it into being and to maintain it, the school must be able to count on the unity of purpose and conviction of all its members. **248**

The participation of the Christian community in the Catholic schools' work

60. From the outset the Catholic school declares its programme and its determination to uphold it. It is a genuine community bent on imparting, over and above an academic education, all the help it can to its members to adopt a Christian way of life. For the Catholic school mutual respect means service to the Person of Christ. Cooperation is between brothers and sisters in Christ. A policy of working for the common good is undertaken seriously as working for the building up of the Kingdom of God. **249**

61. The cooperation required for the realisation of this aim is a duty in conscience for all the members of the community teachers, parents, pupils, administrative personnel. Each has his or her own part to play. Cooperation of all, given in the spirit of the Gospel, is by its very nature a witness not only to Christ as the corner-stone of the community, but also as the light Who shines far beyond it. **250**

---

[22] Second Vatican Council, *Declaration on Christian Education GE, 9.*

The Catholic school as a service to the Church and to society

251   62. The Catholic school community, therefore, is an irreplaceable source of service, not only to the pupils and its other members, but also to society. Today especially one sees a world which clamours for solidarity and yet experiences the rise of new forms of individualism. Society can take note from the Catholic school that it is possible to create true communities out of a common effort for the common good. In the pluralistic society of today the Catholic school, moreover, by maintaining an institutional Christian presence in the academic world, proclaims by its very existence the enriching power of the faith as the answer to the enormous problems which afflict mankind. Above all, it is called to render a humble loving service to the Church by ensuring that she is present in the scholastic field for the benefit of the human family.

252   63. In this way the Catholic school performs "an authentic apostolate"[23]. To work, therefore, in this apostolate "means apostolate performing a unique and invaluable work for the Church"[24].

V. The Responsibility of the Catholic School Today

253   64. The real problem facing the Catholic school is to identify and lay down the conditions necessary for it to fulfil its mission. It is, therefore, a problem requiring clear and positive thinking, courage, perseverance and cooperation to tackle the necessary measures without being overawed by the size of the difficulties from within and without, nor "by persistent and outdated slogans"[25], which in the last analysis aim to abolish Catholic schools[26]. To give into them would be suicidal. To favour in a more or less radical form a merely non-institutional presence of the Church in the scholastic field, is a dangerous illusion[27].

---

[23] Second Vatican Council, *Declaration on Christian Education, GE*, 8.
[24] Paul VI, to Prof. Giuseppe Lazzati, Rector of the University of the Sacred Heart (Milan), in *The Teaching of Pope Paul VI*, vol. 9, p. 1082.
[25] Paul VI, Allocution to the Ninth Congress of the O.I.E.C., in *L'Osservatore Romano*, 9 June 1974..
[26] Cf. above, nn. 18, 20, 23.
[27] Cf. Paul VI, Allocution to the Ninth Congress of the O.I.E.C., in *L'Osservatore Romano*, 9 June 1974.

65. At great cost and sacrifice our forebears were inspired by **254** the teaching of the Church to establish schools which enriched mankind and responded to the needs of time and place. While it recognises its own inadequacies, the Catholic school is conscious of its responsibility to continue this service. Today, as in the past, some scholastic institutions which bear the name Catholic do not appear to correspond fully to the principles of education which should be their distinguishing feature and, therefore, do not fulfil the duties which the Church and the society has every right to expect of them. Without pretending to make an exhaustive enquiry into the factors which may explain the difficulties under which the Catholic school labours, here are a few points in the hope of encouraging some thought as a stimulus to courageous reform.

66. Often what is perhaps fundamentally lacking among **255** Catholics who work in a school is a clear realisation of the identity of a Catholic school and the courage to follow all the consequences of its uniqueness. One must recognise that, more than ever before, a Catholic school's job is infinitely more difficult, more complex, since this is a time when Christianity demands to be clothed in fresh garments, when all manner of changes have been introduced in the Church and in secular life, and, particularly, when a pluralist mentality dominates and the Christian Gospel is increasingly pushed to the side-lines.

67. It is because of this that loyalty to the educational aims of **256** the Catholic school demands constant self-criticism and return to basic principles, to the motives which inspire the Church's involvement in education. They do not provide a quick answer to contemporary problems, but they give a direction which can begin to solve them. Account has to be taken of new pedagogical insights and collaboration with others, irrespective of religious allegiance, who work honestly for the true development of mankind – first and foremost with schools of other Christians – in the interests, even in this field, of Christian unity but also with State schools. In addition to meetings of teachers and mutual research, this collaboration can be extended to the pupils themselves and their families.

68. In conclusion it is only right to repeat what has been said **257**

above[28] about the considerable difficulties arising from legal and economic systems operating in different countries which hinder the activities of the Catholic school, difficulties which prevent them from extending their service to all social and economic classes and compel them to give the false impression of providing schools simply for the rich.

VI. Practical Directions

258   69. After reflecting on the difficulties which the Catholic school encounters, we turn now to the practical possibilities open to those who work in, or are responsible for, these schools. The following more serious questions have been selected for special comment: organisation and planning, ensuring the distinctive Catholic character of the school, the involvement of religious in the school apostolate, the Catholic school in mission countries, pastoral care of teachers, professional associations, the economic question.

The organisation and planning of the Catholic school

259   70. Catholic education is inspired by the general principles enunciated by the Second Vatican Council concerning collaboration between the hierarchy and those who work in the apostolate. In consequence of the principle of participation and co-responsibility, the various groupings which constitute the educational community are, according to their several competencies, to be associated in decision-making concerning the Catholic school and in the application of decisions once taken.[29] It is first and foremost at the stage of planning and of putting into operation an educational project that this principle of the Council is to be applied. The assigning of various responsibilities is governed by the principle of subsidiarity, and, with reference to this principle, ecclesiastical authority respects the competence of the professionals in teaching and education. Indeed, "the right and duty of exercising the apostolate is common to all the faithful,

---

[28] Cf. above, no. 58.

[29] Cf. Second Vatican Council, Pastoral Constitution on the Church in the Modern World *GS*, 43.

clerical and lay, and lay people have their own proper competence in the building up of the Church".[30]

71. This principle enunciated by the Second Vatican Council **260** is particularly applicable to the apostolate of the Catholic school which so closely unites teaching and religious education to a well-defined professional activity. It is here, above all, that the particular mission of the lay person is put into effect, a mission which has become "all the more imperative in view of the fact that many areas of human life have become very largely autonomous. This is as it should be, but it sometimes involves a certain withdrawal from ethical and religious influences and thereby creates a serious danger to Christian life".[31] Moreover, lay involvement in Catholic schools is an invitation "to cooperate more closely with the apostolate of the Bishops",[32] both in the field of religious instruction[33] and in more general religious education which they endeavour to promote by assisting the pupils to a personal integration of culture and faith and of faith and living. The Catholic school in this sense, therefore, receives from the Bishops in some manner the "mandate" of an apostolic undertaking.[34]

72. The essential element of such a mandate is "union with **261** those whom the Holy Spirit has assigned to rule God's Church"[35] and this link is expressed especially in overall pastoral strategy. "In the whole diocese or in given areas of it the coordination and close interconnection of all apostolic works should be fostered under the direction of the Bishop. In this way all undertakings and organisation, whether catechetical, missionary, charitable, social, family, educational, or any other programme serving a pastoral goal will be coordinated. Moreover, the unity of the diocese will thereby be made more evident".[36] This is something which is

---

[30] Second Vatican Council, Decree on the Apostolate of the Laity *Apostolicam Actuositatem*, 25.
[31] Second Vatican Council, Decree on the Apostolate of the Laity *Apostolicam Actuositatem*, 1.
[32] Second Vatican Council, Dogmatic Constitution on the Church, *LG*, 33.
[33] Cf. Second Vatican Council, Decree on the Apostolate of the Laity *Apostolicam Actuositatem*, 10.
[34] *Ibid.*, 24.
[35] *Ibid.*, 23.
[36] Second Vatican Council, Decree on the Bishop's Pastoral Office in the Church *Christus Dominus*, 17.

obviously indispensable for the Catholic school, inasmuch as it involves "apostolic cooperation on the part of both branches of the clergy, as well as of the religious and the laity".[37]

Ensuring the distinctive Catholic character of the school

262   73. This is the framework which guarantees the distinctive Catholic character of the school. While the Bishop's authority is to watch over the orthodoxy of religious instruction and the observance of Christian morals in the Catholic schools, it is the task of the whole educative community to ensure that a distinctive Christian educational environment is maintained in practice. This responsibility applies chiefly to Christian parents who confide their children to the school. Having chosen it does not relieve them of a personal duty to give their children a Christian upbringing. They are bound to cooperate actively with the school – which means supporting the educational efforts of the school and utilising the structures offered for parental involvement, in order to make certain that the school remains faithful to Christian principles of education. An equally important role belongs to the teachers in safeguarding and developing the distinctive mission of the Catholic school, particularly with regard to the Christian atmosphere which should characterise its life and teaching. Where difficulties and conflicts arise about the authentic Christian character of the Catholic school, hierarchical authority can and must intervene.

Involvement of religious in the school apostolate

263   74. Some problems arise from the fact that certain Religious Institutes, founded for the school apostolate, have subsequently abandoned school work because of social or political changes and have involved themselves in other activities. In some cases they have given up their schools as a result of their efforts to adapt their lives and mission to the recommendations of the Second Vatican Council and to the spirit of their original foundation.

264   75. It is necessary, however, to re-assess certain arguments adopted against the teaching apostolate. Some would say they

---

[37] Second Vatican Council, Decree on the Apostolate of the Laity *Apostolicam Actuositatem*, 23.

have chosen a "more direct" apostolat,[38] forgetting the excellence and the apostolic value of educational work in the schoo.[39] Others would appeal to the greater importance of individual over community involvement, of personal over institutional work. The advantages, however, of a community apostolate in the educational field are self evident. Sometimes the abandonment of Catholic schools is justified on the grounds of an apparent failure to gain perceptible results in pursuing certain objectives. If this were true, it would surely be an invitation to undertake a fundamental revision of the whole conduct of the school, reminding everyone who ventures into education of the need for humility and hope and the conviction that his work cannot be assessed by the same rationalistic criteria which apply to other profession.[40]

76. It is the responsibility of competent local ecclesiastical **265** authority to evaluate the advisability and necessity of any change to other forms of apostolic work whenever particular circumstances dictate the need for a re-assessment of the school apostolate, keeping in mind the observations above on overall pastoral strateg.[41]

The Catholic school in mission countries

77. The importance of the Catholic school apostolate is much **266** greater when it is a question of the foreign missions. Where the young Churches still rely on the presence of foreign missionaries, the effectiveness of the Catholic school will largely depend on its ability to adapt to local needs. It must ensure that it is a true expression of the local and national Catholic community and that it contributes to the community's willingness to cooperate. In countries where the Christian community is still at its beginning and incapable of assuming responsibility for its own schools, the Bishops will have to undertake this responsibility themselves for the time being, but must endeavour little by little to fulfil the aims outlined above in connection with the organisation of the Catholic school.[42]

---

[38] Cf. above, 23.
[39] Cf. above, nn. 38-48.
[40] Cf. above, n. 22.
[41] Cf. above, nn. 70-72.
[42] Cf. above, nn. 70-72.

Pastoral care of teachers

267   78. By their witness and their behaviour teachers are of the first importance to impart a distinctive character to Catholic schools. It is, therefore, indispensable to ensure their continuing formation through some form of suitable pastoral provision. This must aim to animate them as witnesses of Christ in the classroom and tackle the problems of their particular apostolate, especially regarding a Christian vision of the world and of education, problems also connected with the art of teaching in accordance with the principles of the Gospel. A huge field is thus opened up for national and international organisations which bring together Catholic teachers and educational institutions at all levels.

268   79. Professional organisations whose aim is to protect the interests of those who work in the educational field cannot themselves be divorced from the specific mission of the Catholic school. The rights of the people who are involved in the school must be safeguarded in strict justice. But, no matter what material interests may be at stake, or what social and moral conditions affect their professional development, the principle of the Second Vatican Council has a special application in this context: "The faithful should learn how to distinguish carefully between those rights and duties which are theirs as members of the Church, and those which they have as members of society. Let them strive to harmonize the two, remembering that in every temporal affair they must be guided by a Christian conscience".[43] Moreover, "even when preoccupied with temporal cares, the laity can and must perform valuable work for the evangelisation of the world".[44] Therefore, the special organisations set up to protect the rights of teachers, parents and pupils must not forget the special mission of the Catholic school to be of service in the Christian education of youth. "The layman is at the same time a believer and a citizen and should be constantly led by Christian conscience alone".[45]

269   80. In the light of what has been said, these associations, while being concerned for the rights of their members, must also

---

[43] Second Vatican Council, Dogmatic Constitution on the Church *LG*, 36.

[44] Second Vatican Council, Dogmatic Constitution on the Church *LG*, 35.

[45] Second Vatican Council, Decree on the Apostolate of the Laity *Apostolicam Actuositatem*, 5.

be alive to the responsibilities which are part and parcel of the specific apostolate of the Catholic school. Catholic teachers who freely accept posts in schools, which have a distinctive character, are obliged to respect that character and give their active support to it under the direction of those responsible.

Economic situation of Catholic schools

81. From the economic point of view the position of very **270** many Catholic schools has improved and in some countries is perfectly acceptable. This is the case where governments have appreciated the advantages and the necessity of a plurality of school systems which offer alternatives to a single State system. While at first Catholic schools received various public grants, often merely conceded, they later began to enter into agreements, conventions, contracts, etc. which guarantee both the preservation of the special status of the Catholic school and its ability to perform its function adequately. Catholic schools are thereby more or less closely associated with the national system and are assured of an economic and juridical status similar to State schools.

82. Such agreements have been reached through the good **271** offices of the respective governments, which have recognised the public service provided by Catholic schools, and through the determination of the Bishops and the Catholic community at the national level. These solutions are an encouragement to those responsible for Catholic schools in countries where the Catholic community must still shoulder a very heavy burden of cost to maintain an often highly important network of Catholic schools. These Catholics need to be assured, as they strive to regularise the frequent injustices in their school situation, that they are not only helping to provide every child with an education that respects his complete development, but they are also defending freedom of teaching and the right of parents to choose an education for their children which conforms to their legitimate requirement.[46]

VII. Courageous and Unified Commitment

83. To commit oneself to working in accordance with the **272**

---

[46] Cf Second Vatican Council, *Declaration on Christian Education GE*, 6.

aims of a Catholic School is to make a great act of faith in the necessity and influence of this apostolate. Only one who has this conviction and accepts Christ's message, who has a love for and understands today's young people, who appreciates what people's real problems and difficulties are, will be led to contribute with courage and even audacity to the progress of this apostolate in building up a Catholic school, which puts its theory into practice, which renews itself according to its ideals and to present needs.

273   84. The validity of the educational results of a Catholic school, however, cannot be measured by immediate efficiency. In the field of Christian education, not only is the freedom-factor of teacher and pupil relationship with each other to be considered, but also the factor of grace. Freedom and grace come to fruition in the spiritual order which defies any merely temporal assessment. When grace infuses human liberty, it makes freedom fully free and raises it to its highest perfection in the freedom of the Spirit. It is when the Catholic school adds its weight, consciously and overtly, to the liberating power of grace, that it becomes the Christian leaven in the world.

274   85. In the certainty that the Spirit is at work in every person, the Catholic school offers itself to all, non-Christians included, with all its distinctive aims and means, acknowledging, preserving and promoting the spiritual and moral qualities, the social and cultural values, which characterise different civilisation.[47]

275   86. Such an outlook overrides any question of the disproportion between resources available and the number of children reached directly by the Catholic school; nothing can stop it from continuing to render its service. The only condition it would make, as is its right, for its continued existence would be remaining faithful to the educational aims of the Catholic school. Loyalty to these aims is, moreover, the basic motive which must inspire any needed reorganisation of the Catholic school institution.

276   87. If all who are responsible for the Catholic school would never lose sight of their mission and the apostolic value of their teaching, the school would enjoy better conditions in which to

---

[47] Cf Second Vatican Council, Declaration on the Relationship of the Church to non-Christian Religions *Nostra Aetate*, 2.

function in the present and would faithfully hand on its mission to future generations. They themselves, moreover, would most surely be filled with a deep conviction, joy and spirit of sacrifice in the knowledge that they are offering innumerable young people the opportunity of growing in faith, of accepting and living its precious principles of truth, charity and hope.

88. The Sacred Congregation for Catholic Education, to **277** foster the full realisation of the aims of the Catholic school, extends once more its warmest and heartfelt encouragement to all who work in these schools. There can be no doubt whatever of the importance of the apostolate of teaching in the total saving mission of the Church.

89. The Church herself in particular looks with confidence **278** and trust to Religious Institutes which have received a special charism of the Holy Spirit and have been most active in the education of the young. May they be faithful to the inspiration of their founders and give their whole-hearted support to the apostolic work of education in Catholic schools and not allow themselves to be diverted from this by attractive invitations to undertake other, often seemingly more effective, apostolates.

90. A little more than ten years after the end of the Second **279** Vatican Council the Sacred Congregation for Catholic Education repeats the final exhortation of the Declaration on Christian Education to the priests, religious and lay people who fulfil their mission in the Catholic school. It reads. "They are urged to persevere generously in their chosen duty, continuing to instil into their pupils the spirit of Christ; let them endeavour to excel in the art of teaching and in the advancement of knowledge. Thus they will not only foster the internal renewal of the Church, but will safeguard and intensify her beneficial presence in the modern world, and above all, in the world of the intellect".[48]

Conclusion

91. This document in no way wishes to minimise the value of **280** the witness and work of the many Catholics who teach in State schools throughout the world. In describing the task confided to the Catholic school it is intended to encourage every effort to

---

[48] Second Vatican Council, *Declaration on Christian Education GE*, Conclusion.

promote the cause of Catholic education, since in the pluralistic world in which we live, the Catholic school is in a unique position to offer, more than ever before, a most valuable and necessary service. With the principles of the Gospel as its abiding point of reference, it offers its collaboration to those who are building a new world – one which is freed from a hedonistic mentality and from the efficiency syndrome of modern consumer society.

281   92. We appeal to each Episcopal Conference to consider and to develop these principles which should inspire the Catholic school and to translate them into concrete programmes which will meet the real needs of the educational systems operating in their countries.

282   93. Realising that the problems are both delicate and highly complex, the Sacred Congregation for Catholic Education also addresses itself to the whole People of God. In the economy of salvation we poor humans must confront problems, suffer their consequences and work, might and main, to solve them. We are certain that in the last analysis success in any venture does not come from trust in our own solutions but from trust in Jesus Who allowed Himself to be called Teacher. May He inspire, guide, support and bring to a safe conclusion all that is undertaken in His name.

Gabriel-Marie Cardinal Garrone, Prefect
Antonio M. Javierre, Secretary, Titular Archbishop of Meta
Rome, 19 March 1977, the Feast of St. Joseph

APOSTOLIC EXHORTATION, *CATECHESI TRADENDAE*
Pope John Paul II, On Catechesis in our Time
16 October 1979

Introduction

Christ's Final Command

1. The Church has always considered catechesis one of her **283** primary tasks, for, before Christ ascended to His Father after His resurrection, He gave the apostles a final command – to make disciples of all nations and to teach them to observe all that He had commanded.[1] He thus entrusted them with the mission and power to proclaim to humanity what they had heard, what they had seen with their eyes, what they had looked upon and touched with their hands, concerning the Word of Life.[2] He also entrusted them with the mission and power to explain with authority what He had taught them, His words and actions, His signs and commandments. And He gave them the Spirit to fulfil this mission.

Very soon the name of catechesis was given to the whole of the efforts within the Church to make disciples, to help people to believe that Jesus is the Son of God, so that believing they might have life in His name,[3] and to educate and instruct them in this life and thus build up the Body of Christ. The Church has not ceased to devote her energy to this task.

Paul VI's Solicitude

2. The most recent Popes gave catechesis a place of **284** eminence in their pastoral solicitude. Through his gestures, his preaching, his authoritative interpretation of the Second Vatican Council (considered by him the great catechism of modern times), and through the whole of his life, my venerated predecessor Paul VI served the Church's catechesis in a particularly exemplary fashion. On 18 March 1971, he approved the General Catechetical Directory prepared by the Sacred Congregation for the Clergy, a directory that is still the basic document for encouraging and guiding catechetical renewal throughout the Church. He set up the

---

[1] Cf. Matt 28:19-20.
[2] Cf. 1 John 1
[3] Cf. John 20:31.

International Council for Catechesis in 1975. He defined in masterly fashion the role and significance of catechesis in the life and mission of the Church when he addressed the participants in the first International Catechetical Congress on 25 September 1971,[4] and he returned explicitly to the subject in his Apostolic Exhortation *Evangelii nuntiandi*.[5] He decided that catechesis, especially that meant for children and young people, should be the theme of the fourth general assembly of the synod of Bishops,[6] which was held in October 1977 and which I myself had the joy of taking part in.

A Fruitful Synod

285   3. At the end of that synod the fathers presented the Pope with a very rich documentation, consisting of the various interventions during the assembly, the conclusions of the working groups, the message that they had with his consent sent to the People of God,[7] and especially the imposing list of "propositions' in which they expressed their views on a very large number of aspects of present-day catechesis.

The Synod worked in an exceptional atmosphere of thanksgiving and hope. It saw in catechetical renewal a precious gift from the Holy Spirit to the Church of today, a gift to which the Christian communities at all levels throughout the world are responding with a generosity and inventive dedication that win admiration. The requisite discernment could then be brought to bear on a reality that is very much alive and it could benefit from great openness among the People of God to the grace of the Lord and the directives of the magisterium.

---

[4] Cf. AAS 63 (1971), pp. 758-764.

[5] Cf.44; cf. also 45-48 and 54: AAS 68 (1976), pp. 34-35; 35-38; 43.

[6] According to the Motu Proprio Apostolica *Sollicitudo* of 15 Sept. 1965, the Synod of Bishops can come together in General Assembly, in extraordinary Assembly or in special assembly. In the present Apostolic Exhortation the words "synod," "synod fathers" and "synod hall" always refer, unless otherwise indicated, to the fourth general assembly of the Synod of Bishops on catechesis, held in Rome in October 1977.

[7] Cf. *Synodus Episcoporum, De catechesi hoc nostro tempore tradenda praesertim pueris atque iuvenibus*, Ad Populum Dei Nuntius, e Civitate Vaticana, 28 October 1977; cf. *L'Osservatore Romano*, 30 October 1977, pp. 3-4.

Purpose of this Exhortation

4. It is in the same climate of faith and hope that I am today **286** addressing this Apostolic Exhortation to you, venerable brothers and dear sons and daughters. The theme is extremely vast and the exhortation will keep to only a few of the most topical and decisive aspects of it, as an affirmation of the happy results of the synod. In essence, the exhortation takes up again the reflections that were prepared by Pope Paul VI, making abundant use of the documents left by the synod. Pope John Paul I, whose zeal and gifts as a catechist amazed us all, had taken them in hand and was preparing to publish them when he was suddenly called to God. To all of us he gave an example of catechesis at once popular and concentrated on the essential, one made up of simple words and actions that were able to touch the heart. I am therefore taking up the inheritance of these two Popes in response to the request which was expressly formulated by the Bishops at the end of the fourth general assembly of the synod and which was welcomed by Pope Paul VI in his closing speech.[8] I am also doing so in order to fulfil one of the chief duties of my apostolic charge. Catechesis has always been a central care in my ministry as a priest and as a Bishop.

I ardently desire that this Apostolic Exhortation to the whole Church should strengthen the solidity of the faith and of Christian living, should give fresh vigour to the initiatives in hand, should stimulate creativity – with the required vigilance – and should help to spread among the communities the joy of bringing the mystery of Christ to the world.

I. We have but One Teacher, Jesus Christ

Putting Into Communion With the Person of Christ

5. The fourth general assembly of the synod of Bishops often **287** stressed the Christocentricity of all authentic catechesis. We can here use the word "Christocentricity" in both its meanings, which are not opposed to each other or mutually exclusive, but each of which rather demands and completes the other.

In the first place, it is intended to stress that at the heart of

---

[8] Cf. AAS 69 (1977), p. 633.

catechesis we find, in essence, a Person, the Person of Jesus of Nazareth, "the only Son from the Father...full of grace and truth,"[9] who suffered and died for us and who now, after rising, is living with us forever. It is Jesus who is "the way, and the truth, and the life,"[10] and Christian living consists in following Christ, the *sequela Christi*.

The primary and essential object of catechesis is, to use an expression dear to St. Paul and also to contemporary theology, "the mystery of Christ." Catechizing is in a way to lead a person to study this mystery in all its dimensions: "to make all men see what is the plan of the mystery...comprehend with all the saints what is the breadth and length and height and depth ...know the love of Christ which surpasses knowledge...(and be filled) with all the fullness of God."[11] It is therefore to reveal in the Person of Christ the whole of God's eternal design reaching fulfilment in that Person. It is to seek to understand the meaning of Christ's actions and words and of the signs worked by Him, for they simultaneously hide and reveal His mystery. Accordingly, the definitive aim of catechesis is to put people not only in touch but in communion, in intimacy, with Jesus Christ: only He can lead us to the love of the Father in the Spirit and make us share in the life of the Holy Trinity.

Transmitting Christ's Teaching

288   6. Christocentricity in catechesis also means the intention to transmit not one's own teaching or that of some other master, but the teaching of Jesus Christ, the Truth that He communicates or, to put it more precisely, the Truth that He is.[12] We must therefore say that in catechesis it is Christ, the Incarnate Word and Son of God, who is taught – everything else is taught with reference to Him – and it is Christ alone who teaches – anyone else teaches to the extent that he is Christ's spokesman, enabling Christ to teach with his lips. Whatever be the level of his responsibility in the Church, every catechist must constantly endeavour to transmit by his teaching and behaviour the teaching and life of Jesus. He will

---

[9] John 1:14.
[10] John 14:6.
[11] Eph. 3:9, 18-19.
[12] Cf. John 14:6.

not seek to keep directed towards himself and his personal opinions and attitudes the attention and the consent of the mind and heart of the person he is catechizing. Above all, he will not try to inculcate his personal opinions and options as if they expressed Christ's teaching and the lessons of His life. Every catechist should be able to apply to himself the mysterious words of Jesus: "My teaching is not mine, but his who sent me."[13] St. Paul did this when he was dealing with a question of prime importance: "I received from the Lord what I also delivered to you."[14] What assiduous study of the word of God transmitted by the Church's magisterium, what profound familiarity with Christ and with the Father, what a spirit of prayer, what detachment from self must a catechist have in order that he can say: "My teaching is not mine!"

Christ the Teacher

7. This teaching is not a body of abstract truths. It is the **289** communication of the living mystery of God. The Person teaching it in the Gospel is altogether superior in excellence to the "masters" in Israel, and the nature of His doctrine surpasses theirs in every way because of the unique link between what He says, what He does and what He is. Nevertheless, the Gospels clearly relate occasions when Jesus "taught." "Jesus began to do and teach"[15] – with these two verbs, placed at the beginning of the book of the Acts, St. Luke links and at the same time distinguishes two poles in Christ's mission.

Jesus taught. It is the witness that He gives of Himself: "Day after day I sat in the temple teaching."[16] It is the admiring observation of the evangelists, surprised to see Him teaching everywhere and at all times, teaching in a manner and with an authority previously unknown: "Crowds gathered to him again;[17] and again,

---

[13] John 7:16. This is a theme dear to the fourth Gospel: cf. John 3:34; 8:28, 12:49-50; 14:24; 17:8,14.

[14] 1 Cor. 11:23: the word "deliver" employed here by St. Paul was frequently repeated in the Apostolic Exhortation *Evangelii Nuntiandi* to describe the evangelizing activity of the Church, for example 4, 15, 78, 79.

[15] Acts 1:1.

[16] Matt 26:55; cf. John 18:20.

[17] Mark 10:1.

as his custom was, he taught them"; "and they were astonished at his teaching, for he taught them as one who had authority."[18] It is also what His enemies note for the purpose of drawing from it grounds for accusation and condemnation: "He stirs up the people, teaching throughout all Judaea, from Galilee even to this place."[19]

The One "Teacher"

290   8. One who teaches in this way has a unique title to the name of "Teacher." Throughout the New Testament, especially in the Gospels, how many times is He given this title of Teacher![20] Of course the Twelve, the other disciples, and the crowds of listeners call Him "Teacher" in tones of admiration, trust and tenderness.[21] Even the Pharisees and the Sadducees, the doctors of the law, and the Jews in general do not refuse Him the title: "Teacher, we wish to see a sign from you"[22]; "Teacher, what shall I do to inherit eternal life?"[23] But above all, Jesus Himself at particularly solemn and highly significant moments calls Himself Teacher: "You call me teacher and Lord; and you are right, for so I am"[24]; and He proclaims the singularity, the uniqueness of His character as teacher: "You have one teacher,"[25] the Christ. One can understand why people of every kind, race and nation have for 2,000 years in all the languages of the earth given Him this title with veneration, repeating in their own ways the exclamation of Nicodemus: "We know that you are a teacher come from God."[26]

This image of Christ the Teacher is at once majestic and familiar, impressive and reassuring. It comes from the pen of the

---

[18] Mark 1:22; cf. Matt 5:2; 11:1; 13:54; 22:16; Mark 2:13; 4:1; 6:2, 6; Luke 5:3, 17; John 7:14; 8:2, etc.

[19] Luke 23:5.

[20] In nearly 50 places in the four Gospels, this title, inherited from the whole Jewish tradition but here given a new meaning that Christ Himself often seeks to emphasize, is attributed to Jesus.

[21] Cf., among others, Matt 8:19; Mark 4:38; 9:38; 10:35; 13:1; John 11:28.

[22] Matt 12:38.

[23] Luke 10:25; cf. Matt 22:16.

[24] John 13:13-14; cf. also Matt 10:25; 26:18 and parallel passages.

[25] Matt 23:8. St. Ignatius of Antioch takes up this affirmation and comments as follows: "We have received the faith; this is why we hold fast, in order to be recognized as disciples of Jesus Christ, our only Teacher" (*Epistola ad Magnesios*, IX, 2; Funk 1, 198).

[26] John 3:2.

evangelists and it has often been evoked subsequently in iconography since earliest Christian times,[27] so captivating is it. And I am pleased to evoke it in my turn at the beginning of these considerations on catechesis in the modern world.

Teaching Through His Life as a Whole

291

9. In doing so, I am not forgetful that the majesty of Christ the Teacher and the unique consistency and persuasiveness of His teaching can only be explained by the fact that His words, His parables and His arguments are never separable from His life and His very being. Accordingly, the whole of Christ's life was a continual teaching: His silences, His miracles, His gestures, His prayer, His love for people, His special affection for the little and the poor, His acceptance of the total sacrifice on the cross for the redemption of the world, and His resurrection are the actualization of His word and the fulfilment of revelation. Hence for Christians the crucifix is one of the most sublime and popular images of Christ the Teacher.

These considerations follow in the wake of the great traditions of the Church and they all strengthen our fervour with regard to Christ, the Teacher who reveals God to man and man to himself, the Teacher who saves, sanctifies and guides, who lives, who speaks, rouses, moves, redresses, judges, forgives, and goes with us day by day on the path of history, the Teacher who comes and will come in glory.

Only in deep communion with Him will catechists find light and strength for an authentic, desirable renewal of catechesis.

II. An Experience as old as the Church

The Mission of the Apostles

292

10. The image of Christ the Teacher was stamped on the spirit of the Twelve and of the first disciples, and the command "Go...and make disciples of all nations"[28] set the course for the

---

[27] The portrayal of Christ as Teacher goes back as far as the Roman Catacombs. It is frequently used in the mosaics of Romano-Byzantine art of the third and fourth centuries. It was to form a predominant artistic motif in the sculptures of the great Romanesque and Gothic cathedrals of the Middle Ages.

[28] Matt 28:19.

whole of their lives. St. John bears witness to this in his Gospel when he reports the words of Jesus: "No longer do I call you servants, for the servant does not know what his master is doing; but I have called you friends, for all that I have heard from my Father I have made known to you."[29] It was not they who chose to follow Jesus; it was Jesus who chose them, kept them with Him, and appointed them even before His Passover, that they should go and bear fruit and that their fruit should remain.[30] For this reason He formally conferred on them after the resurrection the mission of making disciples of all nations.

The whole of the book of the Acts of the Apostles is a witness that they were faithful to their vocation and to the mission they had received. The members of the first Christian community are seen in it as "devoted to the apostles" teaching and fellowship, to the breaking of bread and the prayers."[31] Without any doubt we find in that a lasting image of the Church being born of and continually nourished by the word of the Lord, thanks to the teaching of the apostles, celebrating that word in the Eucharistic Sacrifice and bearing witness to it before the world in the sign of charity.

When those who opposed the apostles took offence at their activity, it was because they were "annoyed because (the apostles) were teaching the people"[32] and the order they gave them was not to teach at all in the name of Jesus.[33] But we know that the apostles considered it right to listen to God rather than to men on this very matter.[34]

293

Catechesis in the Apostolic Age

11. The apostles were not slow to share with others the ministry of apostleship.[35] They transmitted to their successors the task of teaching. They entrusted it also to the deacons from the moment of their institution: Stephen, "full of grace and power,"

---

[29] John 15:15.
[30] Cf. John 15:16.
[31] Acts 2:42
[32] Acts 4:2.
[33] Cf. Acts 4:18; 5:28.
[34] Cf. Acts 4:19.
[35] Cf. Acts 1:25.

taught unceasingly, moved by the wisdom of the Spirit.[36] The apostles associated "many others" with themselves in the task of teaching,[37] and even simple Christians scattered by persecution "went about preaching the word."[38] St. Paul was in a pre-eminent way the herald of this preaching, from Antioch to Rome, where the last picture of him that we have in Acts is that of a person "teaching about the Lord Jesus Christ quite openly."[39] His numerous letters continue and give greater depth to his teaching. The letters of Peter, John, James and Jude are also, in every case, evidence of catechesis in the apostolic age.

Before being written down, the Gospels were the expression of an oral teaching passed on to the Christian communities, and they display with varying degrees of clarity a catechetical structure. St. Matthew's account has indeed been called the catechist's Gospel, and St. Mark's the catechumen's Gospel.

The Fathers of the Church

12. This mission of teaching that belonged to the apostles and **294** their first fellow workers was continued by the Church. Making herself day after day a disciple of the Lord, she earned the title of "Mother and Teacher."[40] From Clement of Rome to Origen,[41] the post-apostolic age saw the birth of remarkable works. Next we see a striking fact: Some of the most impressive Bishops and pastors, especially in the third and fourth centuries considered it an important part of their espiscopal ministry to deliver catechetical instructions and write treatises. It was the age of

---

[36] Cf. Acts 6:8ff.; cf. also Philip catechizing the minister of the Queen of the Ethiopians: Acts 8:26ff.

[37] Cf. Acts 15:35.

[38] Acts 8:4.

[39] Acts 28:31.

[40] Cf. Pope John XXIII, Encyclical *Mater et Magistra* (AAS 53 [1961], p. 401): the Church is "mother" because by baptism she unceasingly begets new children and increases God's family; she is "teacher" because she makes her children grow in the grace of their baptism by nourishing their sensus fidei through instruction in the truths of faith.

[41] Cf., for example the letter of Clement of Rome to the Church of Corinth, the Didache, the *Epistola Apostolorum*, the writings of Irenaeus of Lyons (*Demonstratio Apostolicae Praedicationis* and *Adversus Haereses*), of Tertullian (*De Baptismo*), of Clement of Alexandria (*Paedagogus*), of Cyprian (*Testimonia ad Quirinum*), of Origen (*Contra Celsum*), etc.

Cyril of Jerusalem and John Chrysostom, of Ambrose and Augustine, the age that saw the flowering, from the pen of numerous
Fathers of the Church, of works that are still models for us.

It would be impossible here to recall, even very briefly the
catechesis that gave support to the spread and advance of the
Church in the various periods of history, in every continent, and
in the widest variety of social and cultural contexts. There was
indeed no lack of difficulties. But the word of the Lord completed
its course down the centuries; it sped on and triumphed, to use the
words of the Apostle Paul.[42]

Councils and Missionary Activity

295   13. The ministry of catechesis draws ever fresh energy from
the councils. The Council of Trent is a noteworthy example of
this. It gave catechesis priority in its constitutions and decrees. It
lies at the origin of the Roman Catechism, which is also known
by the name of that council and which is a work of the first rank
as a summary of Christian teaching and traditional theology for
use by priests. It gave rise to a remarkable organization of
catechesis in the Church. It aroused the clergy to their duty of
giving catechetical instruction. Thanks to the work of holy
theologians such as St. Charles Borromeo, St. Robert Bellarmine
and St. Peter Canisius, it involved the publication of catechisms
that were real models for that period. May the Second Vatican
Council stir up in our time a like enthusiasm and similar activity.

The missions are also a special area for the application of
catechesis. The People of God have thus continued for almost
2,000 years to educate themselves in the faith in ways adapted to
the various situations of believers and the many different
circumstances in which the Church finds herself.

Catechesis is intimately bound up with the whole of the
Church's life. Not only her geographical extension and numerical
increase, but even more, her inner growth and correspondence
with God's plan depend essentially on catechesis. It is worthwhile
pointing out some of the many lessons to be drawn from the
experiences in Church history that we have just recalled.

---

[42] Cf. 2 Thes. 3:1.

Catechesis as the Church's Right and Duty

14. To begin with, it is clear that the Church has always **296** looked on catechesis as a sacred duty and an inalienable right. On the one hand, it is certainly a duty springing from a command given by the Lord and resting above all on those who in the new covenant receive the call to the ministry of being pastors. On the other hand, one can likewise speak of a right: from the theological point of view every baptized person, precisely the reason of being baptized, has the right to receive from the Church instruction and education enabling him or her to enter on a truly Christian life; and from the viewpoint of human rights, every human being has the right to seek religious truth and adhere to it freely, that is to say, "without coercion on the part of individuals or of social groups and any human power," in such a way that in this matter of religion, "no one is to be forced to act against his or her conscience or prevented from acting in conformity to it."[43]

That is why catechetical activity should be able to be carried out in favourable circumstances of time and place, and should have access to the mass media and suitable equipment, without discrimination against parents, those receiving catechesis or those imparting it. At present this right is admittedly being given growing recognition, at least on the level of its main principles, as is shown by international declarations and conventions in which, whatever their limitations, one can recognize the desires of the consciences of many people today.[44] But the right is being violated by many States, even to the point that imparting catechesis, having it imparted, and receiving it become punishable offences. I vigorously raise my voice in union with the synod fathers against all discrimination in the field of catechesis, and at the same time I again make a pressing appeal to those in authority to put a complete end to these constraints on human freedom in general and on religious freedom in particular.

---

[43] Second Vatican Council, Declaration on Religious Liberty, *Dignitatis Humanae,* 2: AAS 58 (1966), p. 930.

[44] Cf. The Universal Declaration of Human Rights (UN), 10 December 1948, Art. 18, The International Pact on Civil and Political Rights (UN), 16 December 1966, Art. 4; Final Act of the Conference on European Security and Cooperation, Para. VII.

Priority of this task

297   15. The second lesson concerns the place of catechesis in the Church's pastoral programs. The more the Church, whether on the local or the universal level, gives catechesis priority over other works and undertakings the results of which would be more spectacular, the more she finds in catechesis a strengthening of her internal life as a community of believers and of her external activity as a missionary Church. As the 20th century draws to a close, the Church is bidden by God and by events – each of them a call from Him – to renew her trust in catechetical activity as a prime aspect of her mission. She is bidden to offer catechesis her best resources in people and energy, without sparing effort, toil or material means, in order to organize it better and to train qualified personnel. This is no mere human calculation; it is an attitude of faith. And an attitude of faith always has reference to the faithfulness of God, who never fails to respond.

Shared but differentiated responsibility

298   16. The third lesson is that catechesis always has been and always will be a work for which the whole Church must feel responsible and must wish to be responsible. But the Church's members have different responsibilities, derived from each one's mission. Because of their charge, pastors have, at differing levels, the chief responsibility for fostering, guiding and coordinating catechesis. For his part, the Pope has a lively awareness of the primary responsibility that rests on him in this field: In this he finds reasons for pastoral concern but principally a source of joy and hope. Priests and religious have in catechesis a pre-eminent field for their apostolate. On another level, parents have a unique responsibility. Teachers, the various ministers of the Church, catechists, and also organizers of social communications, all have in various degrees very precise responsibilities in this education of the believing conscience, an education that is important for the life of the Church and affects the life of society as such. It would be one of the best results of the general assembly of the synod that was entirely devoted to catechesis if it stirred up in the Church as a whole and in each sector of the Church a lively and active awareness of this differentiated but shared responsibility.

Continual balanced renewal

17. Finally, catechesis needs to be continually renewed by a **299** certain broadening of its concept, by the revision of its methods, by the search for suitable language, and by the utilization of new means of transmitting the message. Renewal is sometimes unequal in value; the synod fathers realistically recognized, not only an undeniable advance in the vitality of catechetical activity and promising initiatives, but also the limitations or even "deficiencies" in what has been achieved to date.[45] These limitations are particularly serious when they endanger integrity of content. The message to the People of God rightly stressed that "routine, with its refusal to accept any change, and improvisation, with its readiness for any venture, are equally dangerous" for catechesis.[46] Routine leads to stagnation, lethargy and eventual paralysis. Improvisation begets confusion on the part of those being given catechesis and, when these are children, on the part of their parents; it also begets all kinds of deviations, and the fracturing and eventually the complete destruction of unity. It is important for the Church to give proof today, as she has done at other periods of her history, of evangelical wisdom, courage and fidelity in seeking out and putting into operation new methods and new prospects for catechetical instruction.

III. Catechesis in the Church's Pastoral and Missionary Activity

Catechesis as a Stage in Evangelisation

18. Catechesis cannot be dissociated from the Church's **300** pastoral and missionary activity as a whole. Nevertheless it has a specific character which was repeatedly the object of inquiry during the preparatory work and throughout the course of the fourth general assembly of the synod of Bishops. The question also interests the public both within and outside the Church.

This is not the place for giving a rigorous formal definition of

---

[45] Cf. *Synodus Episcoporum, De catechesi hoc nostro tempore tradenda praesertim pueris atque iuvenibus*, Ad Populum Dei Nuntius, 1: loc. cit., pp. 3-4; cf. *L'Osservatore Romano,* 30 October 1977, p. 3.

[46] *Ibid.*, 6: loc. cit., pp. 7-8.

catechesis, which has been sufficiently explained in the General Catechetical Directory.[47] It is for specialists to clarify more and more its concept and divisions.

In view of uncertainties in practice, let us simply recall the essential landmarks – they are already solidly established in Church documents – that are essential for an exact understanding of catechesis and without which there is a risk of failing to grasp its full meaning and import.

All in all, it can be taken here that catechesis is an education of children, young people and adults in the faith, which includes especially the teaching of Christian doctrine imparted, generally speaking, in an organic and systematic way, with a view to initiating the hearers into the fullness of Christian life. Accordingly, while not being formally identified with them, catechesis is built on a certain number of elements of the Church's pastoral mission that have a catechetical aspect, that prepare for catechesis, or that spring from it. These elements are: the initial proclamation of the Gospel or missionary preaching through the *kerygma* to arouse faith, apologetics or examination of the reasons for belief, experience of Christian living, celebration of the sacraments, integration into the ecclesial community, and apostolic and missionary witness.

Let us first of all recall that there is no separation or opposition between catechesis and evangelisation. Nor can the two be simply identified with each other. Instead, they have close links whereby they integrate and complement each other.

The Apostolic Exhortation *Evangelii nuntiandi* of 8 December 1975, on evangelisation in the modern world, rightly stressed that evangelisation – which has the aim of bringing the Good News to the whole of humanity, so that all may live by it – is a rich, complex and dynamic reality, made up of elements, or one could say moments, that are essential and different from each other, and that must all be kept in view simultaneously.[48] Catechesis is one of these moments – a very remarkable one – in the whole process of evangelisation.

---

[47] Sacred Congregation for the Clergy, *Directorium Catechisticum Generale*, 17-35; AAS 64 (1972), pp. 110-118. [See page 28 para 2 – Editor's note].
[48] Cf. 17-24: AAS 68 (1976), pp. 17-22.

Catechesis and the Initial Proclamation of the Gospel

19. The specific character of catechesis, as distinct from the **301** initial conversion – bringing proclamation of the Gospel, has the twofold objective of maturing the initial faith and of educating the true disciple of Christ by means of a deeper and more systematic knowledge of the person and the message of our Lord Jesus Christ.[49]

But in catechetical practice, this model order must allow for the fact that the initial evangelisation has often not taken place. A certain number of children baptized in infancy come for catechesis in the parish without receiving any other initiation into the faith and still without any explicit personal attachment to Jesus Christ; they only have the capacity to believe placed within them by Baptism and the presence of the Holy Spirit; and opposition is quickly created by the prejudices of their non-Christian family background or of the positivist spirit of their education. In addition, there are other children who have not been baptized and whose parents agree only at a later date to religious education: for practical reasons, the catechumenal stage of these children will often be carried out largely in the course of the ordinary catechesis. Again, many pre-adolescents and adolescents who have been baptized and been given a systematic catechesis and the sacraments still remain hesitant for a long time about committing their whole lives to Jesus Christ – if, moreover, they do not attempt to avoid religious education in the name of their freedom. Finally, even adults are not safe from temptations to doubt or to abandon their faith, especially as a result of their unbelieving surroundings. This means that "catechesis" must often concern itself not only with nourishing and teaching the faith, but also with arousing it unceasingly with the help of grace, with opening the heart, with converting, and with preparing total adherence to Jesus Christ on the part of those who are still on the threshold of faith. This concern will in part decide the tone, the language and the method of catechesis.

---

[49] Cf. *Synodus Episcoporum, De catechesi hoc nostro tempore tradenda praesertim pueris atque invenibus, Ad Populum Dei Nuntius*, 1: loc. cit., pp. 3-4, cf. *L'Osservatore Romano*, 30 October 1977, p. 3.

Specific Aim of Catechesis

302   20. Nevertheless, the specific aim of catechesis is to develop, with God's help, an as yet initial faith, and to advance in fullness and to nourish day by day the Christian life of the faithful, young and old. It is in fact a matter of giving growth, at the level of knowledge and in life, to the seed of faith sown by the Holy Spirit with the initial proclamation and effectively transmitted by Baptism.

Catechesis aims therefore at developing understanding of the mystery of Christ in the light of God's word, so that the whole of a person's humanity is impregnated by that word. Changed by the working of grace into a new creature, the Christian thus sets himself to follow Christ and learns more and more within the Church to think like Him, to judge like Him, to act in conformity with His commandments, and to hope as He invites us to.

To put it more precisely: within the whole process of evangelisation, the aim of catechesis is to be the teaching and maturation stage, that is to say, the period in which the Christian, having accepted by faith the person of Jesus Christ as the one Lord and having given Him complete adherence by sincere conversion of heart, endeavours to know better this Jesus to whom he has entrusted himself: to know His "mystery," the kingdom of God proclaimed by Him, the requirements and promises contained in His Gospel message, and the paths that He has laid down for anyone who wishes to follow Him.

It is true that being a Christian means saying "yes" to Jesus Christ, but let us remember that this "yes" has two levels: It consists in surrendering to the word of God and relying on it, but it also means, at a later stage, endeavouring to know better – and better the profound meaning of this word.

Need for Systematic Catechesis

303   21. In his closing speech at the fourth general assembly of the synod, Pope Paul VI rejoiced "to see how everyone drew attention to the absolute need for systematic catechesis, precisely because it is this reflective study of the Christian mystery that fundamentally distinguishes catechesis from all other ways of presenting the word of God."[50]

---

[50] Concluding Address to the Synod, 29 October 1977: AAS 69 (1977), p. 634.

In view of practical difficulties, attention must be drawn to some of the characteristics of this instruction:

- It must be systematic, not improvised but programmed to reach a precise goal;
- It must deal with essentials, without any claim to tackle all disputed questions or to transform itself into theological research or scientific exegesis;
- It must nevertheless be sufficiently complete, not stopping short at the initial proclamation of the Christian mystery such as we have in the *kerygma*;
- It must be an integral Christian initiation, open to all the other factors of Christian life.

I am not forgetting the interest of the many different occasions for catechesis connected with personal, family, social and ecclesial life – these occasions must be utilized and I shall return to them in Chapter VI – but I am stressing the need for organic and systematic Christian instruction, because of the tendency in various quarters to minimize its importance.

Catechesis and Life Experience

22. It is useless to play off orthopraxis against orthodoxy: Christianity is inseparably both. Firm and well-thought – out convictions lead to courageous and upright action, the endeavour to educate the faithful to live as disciples of Christ today calls for and facilitates a discovery in depth of the mystery of Christ in the history of salvation.

304

It is also quite useless to campaign for the abandonment of serious and orderly study of the message of Christ in the name of a method concentrating on life experience. "No one can arrive at the whole truth on the basis solely of some simple private experience, that is to say, without an adequate explanation of the message of Christ, who is 'the way, and the truth, and the life' (Jn. 14:6)."[51]

Nor is any opposition to be set up between a catechesis taking life as its point of departure and a traditional doctrinal and systematic catechesis.[52] Authentic catechesis is always an orderly and systematic initiation into the revelation that God has given of

---

[51] *Ibid.*

[52] *Directorium Catechisticum Generale*, 40 and 46: AAS 64 (1972), pp. 121 and 124-125.

Himself to humanity in Christ Jesus, a revelation stored in the depths of the Church's memory and in Sacred Scripture, and constantly communicated from one generation to the next by a living, active tradition. This revelation is not however isolated from life or artificially juxtaposed to it. It is concerned with the ultimate meaning of life and it illumines the whole of life with the light of the Gospel, to inspire it or to question it.

That is why we can apply to catechists an expression used by the Second Vatican Council with special reference to priests: "Instructors (of the human being and his life) in the faith."[53]

Catechesis and Sacraments

305   23. Catechesis is intrinsically linked with the whole of liturgical and sacramental activity, for it is in the sacraments, especially in the Eucharist, that Christ Jesus works in fulness for the transformation of human beings.

In the early Church, the catechumenate and preparation for the sacraments of Baptism and the Eucharist were the same thing. Although in the countries that have long been Christian the Church has changed her practice in this field, the catechumenate has never been abolished; on the contrary, it is experiencing a renewal in those countries[54] and is abundantly practised in the young missionary Churches. In any case, catechesis always has reference to the sacraments. On the one hand, the catechesis that prepares for the sacraments is an eminent kind, and every form of catechesis necessarily leads to the sacraments of faith. On the other hand, authentic practice of the sacraments is bound to have a catechetical aspect. In other words, sacramental life is impoverished and very soon turns into hollow ritualism if it is not based on serious knowledge of the meaning of the sacraments, and catechesis becomes intellectualized if it fails to come alive in the sacramental practice.

Catechesis and Ecclesial Community

306   24. Finally, catechesis is closely linked with the responsible

---

[53] Cf. Decree on the Ministry and Life of Priests, *Presbyterorum Ordinis*, 6: AAS 58 (1966), p. 999.
[54] Cf. *Ordo Initiationis Christianae Adultorum.*

activity of the Church and of Christians in the world. A person who has given adherence to Jesus Christ by faith and is endeavouring to consolidate that faith by catechesis needs to live in communion with those who have taken the same step. Catechesis runs the risk of becoming barren if no community of faith and Christian life takes the catechumen in at a certain stage of his catechesis. That is why the ecclesial community at all levels has a twofold responsibility with regard to catechesis: it has the responsibility of providing for the training of its members, but it also has the responsibility of welcoming them into an environment where they can live as fully as possible what they have learned.

Catechesis is likewise open to missionary dynamism. If catechesis is done well, Christians will be eager to bear witness to their faith, to hand it on to their children, to make it known to others, and to serve the human community in every way.

Catechesis in the wide sense necessary for maturity and strength of Faith

25. Thus through catechesis the Gospel *kerygma* (the initial **307** ardent proclamation by which a person is one day overwhelmed and brought to the decision to entrust himself to Jesus Christ by faith) is gradually deepened, developed in its implicit consequences, explained in language that includes an appeal to reason, and channelled towards Christian practice in the Church and the world. All this is no less evangelical than the *kerygma*, in spite of what is said by certain people who consider that catechesis necessarily rationalizes, dries up and eventually kills all that is living, spontaneous and vibrant in the *kerygma*. The truths studied in catechesis are the same truths that touched the person's heart when he heard them for the first time. Far from blunting or exhausting them, the fact of knowing them better should make them even more challenging and decisive for one's life.

In the understanding expounded here, catechesis keeps the entirely pastoral perspective with which the synod viewed it. This broad meaning of catechesis in no way contradicts but rather includes and goes beyond a narrow meaning which was once commonly given to catechesis in didactic expositions, namely, the simple teaching of the formulas that express faith.

In the final analysis, catechesis is necessary both for the maturation of the faith of Christians and for their witness in the world: It is aimed at bringing Christians to "attain to the unity of the faith and of the knowledge of the Son of God, to mature manhood, to the measure of the stature of the fulness of Christ"[55]; it is also aimed at making them prepared to make a defence to anyone who calls them to account for the hope that is in them.[56]

IV. The Whole of the Good News drawn from its Source

Content of the Message

308   26. Since catechesis is a moment or aspect of evangelisation, its content cannot be anything else but the content of evangelisation as a whole. The one message – the Good News of salvation – that has been heard once or hundreds of times and has been accepted with the heart, is in catechesis probed unceasingly by reflection and systematic study, by awareness of its repercussions on one's personal life – an awareness calling for ever greater commitment – and by inserting it into an organic and harmonious whole, namely, Christian living in society and the world.

The Source

309   27. Catechesis will always draw its content from the living source of the Word of God transmitted in Tradition and the Scriptures, for "sacred Tradition and Sacred Scripture make up a single sacred deposit of the Word of God, which is entrusted to the Church," as was recalled by the Second Vatican Council, which desired that "the ministry of the word – pastoral preaching, catechetics and all forms of Christian instruction . . . – (should be) healthily nourished and (should) thrive in holiness through the word of Scripture."[57]

To speak of Tradition and Scripture as the source of catechesis is to draw attention to the fact that catechesis must be

---

[55] Eph. 4:13.
[56] Cf. 1 Pt. 3:15.
[57] Dogmatic Constitution on Divine Revelation *Dei Verbum*, 10 and 24: AAS 58 (1966), pp. 822 and 828-829; cf. also Sacred Congregation for the Clergy, *Directorium Catechisticum Generale* 45 (AAS 64 [1972], p. 124), where the principal and complementary sources of catechesis are well set out.

impregnated and penetrated by the thought, the spirit and the outlook of the Bible and the Gospels through assiduous contact with the texts themselves; but it is also a reminder that catechesis will be all the richer and more effective for reading the texts with the intelligence and the heart of the Church and for drawing inspiration from the 2,000 years of the Church's reflection and life.

The Church's teaching, liturgy and life spring from this source and lead back to it, under the guidance of the pastors and, in particular, of the doctrinal magisterium entrusted to them by the Lord.

The Creed, an exceptionally important expression of doctrine

28. An exceptionally important expression of the living **310** heritage placed in the custody of the pastors is found in the Creed or, to put it more concretely, in the Creeds that at crucial moments have summed up the Church's faith in felicitous syntheses. In the course of the centuries an important element of catechesis was constituted by the *traditio Symboli* (transmission of the summary of the faith), followed by the transmission of the Lord's Prayer. This expressive rite has in our time been reintroduced into the initiation of catechumens.[58] Should not greater use be made of an adapted form of it to mark that most important stage at which a new disciple of Jesus Christ accepts with full awareness and courage the content of what will from then on be the object of his earnest study?

In the Creed of the People of God, proclaimed at the close of the 19th centenary of the martyrdom of the Apostles Peter and Paul, my predecessor Paul VI decided to bring together the essential elements of the Catholic Faith, especially those that presented greater difficulty or risked being ignored.[59] This is a sure point of reference for the content of catechesis.

---

[58] Cf. *Ordo Initiationis Christianae Adultorum*, 25-26; 183-187.

[59] Cf. AAS 60 (1968), pp. 436-445. Besides these great professions of faith of the magisterium, note also the popular professions of faith, rooted in the traditional Christian culture of certain countries; cf. what I said to the young people at Gniezno, 3 June 1979, regarding the Bogurodzica song-message: "This is not only a song: it is also a profession of faith, a symbol of the Polish Credo, it is a catechesis and also a document of Christian education. The principal truths of Faith and the principles of morality are contained here. This is not only a historical object. It is a document of life. (It has even been called 'the Polish catechism'" [AAS 71, 1979], p. 754.)

Factors that must not be neglected

311   29. In the third chapter of his Apostolic Exhortation *Evangelii nuntiandi*, the same Pope recalled "the essential content, the living substance" of evangelisation.[60] Catechesis, too, must keep in mind each of these factors and also the living synthesis of which they are part.[61]

I shall therefore limit myself here simply to recalling one or two points.[62] Anyone can see, for instance, how important it is to make the child, the adolescent, the person advancing in faith understand "what can be known about God"[63]; to be able in a way to tell them: "What you worship as unknown, this I proclaim to you"[64]; to set forth briefly for them[65] the mystery of the Word of God become man and accomplishing man's salvation by His Passover, that is to say, through His death and resurrection, but also by His preaching, by the signs worked by Him, and by the sacraments of His permanent presence in our midst. The synod fathers were indeed inspired when they asked that care should be taken not to reduce Christ to His humanity alone or His message to a no more than earthly dimension, but that He should be recognized as the Son of God, the Mediator giving us in the Spirit free access to the Father.[66]

It is important to display before the eyes of the intelligence and of the heart, in the light of faith, the sacrament of Christ's presence constituted by the mystery of the Church, which is an assembly of human beings who are sinners and yet have at the same time been sanctified and who make up the family of God gathered together by the Lord under the guidance of those whom "the Holy Spirit has made...guardians, to feed the Church of God."[67]

---

[60] 25: AAS 68 (1976), p. 23.

[61] *Ibid.*, especially 26-39: loc. cit., pp. 23-25; the "principal elements of the Christian message" are presented in a more systematic fashion in the Directorium Catechisticum Generale, 47-69 (AAS 64 [1972] pp. 125-141), where one also finds the norm for the essential doctrinal content of catechesis.

[62] Consult also on this point the *Directorium Catechisticum Generale*, 37-46 (loc. cit., pp. 120-125).

[63] Rom. 1:19.

[64] Acts 17:23.

[65] Cf. Eph. 3:3.

[66] Cf. Eph. 2:18.

[67] Acts 20:28.

It is important to explain that the history of the human race, marked as it is by grace and sin, greatness and misery, is taken up by God in His Son Jesus, "foreshadowing in some way the age which is to come."[68]

Finally, it is important to reveal frankly the demands – demands that involve self-denial but also joy – made by what the Apostle Paul liked to call "newness of life,"[69] "a new creation,"[70] being in Christ,[71] and "eternal life in Christ Jesus,"[72] which is the same thing as life in the world but lived in accordance with the beatitudes and called to an extension and transfiguration hereafter.

Hence the importance in catechesis of personal moral commitments in keeping with the Gospel and of Christian attitudes, whether heroic or very simple, to life and the world – what we call the Christian or evangelical virtues. Hence also, in its endeavour to educate faith, the concern of catechesis not to omit but to clarify properly realities such as man's activity for his integral liberation,[73] the search for a society with greater solidarity and fraternity, the fight for justice and the building of peace.

Besides, it is not to be thought that this dimension of catechesis is altogether new. As early as the patristic age, St. Ambrose and St. John Chrysostom – to quote only them – gave prominence to the social consequences of the demands made by the Gospel. Close to our own time, the catechism of St. Pius X explicitly listed oppressing the poor and depriving workers of their just wages among the sins that cry to God for vengeance.[74] Since *Rerum novarum* especially, social concern has been actively present in the catechetical teaching of the Popes and the Bishops. Many synod fathers rightly insisted that the rich heritage of the Church's social teaching should, in appropriate forms, find a place in the general catechetical education of the faithful.

---

[68] Second Vatican Council, Pastoral Constitution on the Church in the Modern World *GS*, 39: AAS 58 (1966), pp. 1056-1057.
[69] Rom. 6:4.
[70] 2 Cor. 5:17.
[71] Cf. *Ibid.*
[72] Rom. 6:23.
[73] Cf. Pope Paul VI, Apostolic Exhortation, *Evangelii Nuntiandi*, 30-38: AAS 68 (1976), pp. 25-30.
[74] Cf. *Catechismo Maggiore*, Fifth Part, chap. 6. 965-966.

312 *Integrity of Content*

30. With regard to the content of catechesis, three important points deserve special attention today.

The first point concerns the integrity of the content. In order that the sacrificial offering of his or her faith[75] should be perfect, the person who becomes a disciple of Christ has the right to receive "the word of faith"[76] not in mutilated, falsified or diminished form but whole and entire, in all its rigour and vigour. Unfaithfulness on some point to the integrity of the message means a dangerous weakening of catechesis and putting at risk the results that Christ and the ecclesial community have a right to expect from it. It is certainly not by chance that the final command of Jesus in Matthew's Gospel bears the mark of a certain entireness: "All authority...has been given to me...make disciples of all nations...teaching them to observe all...I am with you always." This is why, when a person first becomes aware of "the surpassing worth of knowing Christ Jesus,"[77] whom he has encountered by faith, and has the perhaps unconscious desire to know Him more extensively and better," hearing about Him and being taught in Him, as the truth is in Jesus,[78] there is no valid pretext for refusing Him any part whatever of that knowledge. What kind of catechesis would it be that failed to give their full place to man's creation and sin; to God's plan of redemption and its long, loving preparation and realization; to the incarnation of the Son of God; to Mary, the Immaculate One, the Mother of God, ever Virgin, raised body and soul to the glory of heaven, and to her role in the mystery of salvation; to the mystery of lawlessness at work in our lives[79] and the power of God freeing us from it; to the need for penance and asceticism; to the sacramental and liturgical actions; to the reality of the Eucharistic Presence; to participation in divine life here and hereafter, and so on? Thus, no true catechist can lawfully, on his own initiative, make a selection of what he considers important in the deposit of faith as opposed to what he considers unimportant, so as to teach the one and reject the other.

---

[75] Cf. Phil. 2:17.
[76] Rom. 10:8.
[77] Phil. 3:8.
[78] Cf. Eph. 4:20-21.
[79] Cf. 2 Thes. 2:7.

By means of suitable pedagogical methods

31. This gives rise to a second remark. It can happen that in **313** the present situation of catechesis reasons of method or pedagogy suggest that the communication of the riches of the content of catechesis should be organized in one way rather than another. Besides, integrity does not dispense from balance and from the organic hierarchical character through which the truths to be taught, the norms to be transmitted, and the ways of Christian life to be indicated will be given the proper importance due to each. It can also happen that a particular sort of language proves preferable for transmitting this content to a particular individual or group. The choice made will be a valid one to the extent that, far from being dictated by more or less subjective theories or prejudices stamped with a certain ideology, it is inspired by the humble concern to stay closer to a content that must remain intact. The method and language used must truly be means for communicating the whole and not just a part of "the words of eternal life"[80] and the "ways of life."[81]

Ecumenical dimension of Catechesis

32. The great movement, one certainly inspired by the Spirit **314** of Jesus, that has for some years been causing the Catholic Church to seek with other Christian Churches or confessions the restoration of the perfect unity willed by the Lord, brings me to the question of the ecumenical character of catechesis. This movement reached its full prominence in the Second Vatican Council[82] and since then has taken on a new extension within the Church, as is shown concretely by the impressive series of events and initiatives with which everyone is now familiar.

Catechesis cannot remain aloof from this ecumenical dimension, since all the faithful are called to share, according to their capacity and place in the Church, in the movement towards unity.[83]

---

[80] John 6:69; cf. Acts 5:20; 7:38

[81] Acts 2:28, quoting Ps. 16:11.

[82] Cf. the entire Decree on *Ecumenism Unitatis Redintegratio*: AAS 57 [1965], pp. 90-112.

[83] Cf. *Ibid.*, 5: loc. cit., p. 96; cf. also Second Vatican Council, Decree on the Missionary Activity of the Church *AG*, 15: AAS 58 (1966), pp. 963-965; Sacred

Catechesis will have an ecumenical dimension if, while not ceasing to teach that the fulness of the revealed truths and of the means of salvation instituted by Christ is found in the Catholic Church,[84] it does so with sincere respect, in words and in deeds, for the ecclesial communities that are not in perfect communion with this Church.

In this context, it is extremely important to give a correct and fair presentation of the other Churches and ecclesial communities that the Spirit of Christ does not refrain from using as means of salvation; "moreover, some, even very many, of the outstanding elements and endowments which together go to build up and give life to the Church herself, can exist outside the visible boundaries of the Catholic Church."[85] Among other things this presentation will help Catholics to have both a deeper understanding of their own faith and a better acquaintance with and esteem for their other Christian brethren, thus facilitating the shared search for the way towards full unity in the whole truth. It should also help non-Catholics to have a better knowledge and appreciation of the Catholic Church and her conviction of being the "universal help toward salvation."

Catechesis will have an ecumenical dimension if, in addition, it creates and fosters a true desire for unity. This will be true all the more if it inspires serious efforts – including the effort of self-purification in the humility and the fervour of the Spirit in order to clear the ways – with a view not to facile irenics made up of omissions and concessions on the level of doctrine, but to perfect unity, when and by what means the Lord will wish.

Finally, catechesis will have an ecumenical dimension if it tries to prepare Catholic children and young people, as well as adults, for living in contact with non-Catholics, affirming their Catholic identity while respecting the faith of others.

Ecumenical Collaboration in the Field of Catechesis

315   33. In situations of religious plurality, the Bishops can

---

Congregation for the Clergy, *Directorium Catechisticum Generale* 27: AAS 64 (1972), p. 115.
[84] Cf. Second Vatican Counci, Decree on Ecumenism, *Unitatis Redintegratio*, 3-4: AAS 57 (1965), pp. 92-96.
[85] *Ibid.*, 3: loc. cit., p. 93.

consider it opportune or even necessary to have certain experiences of collaboration in the field of catechesis between Catholics and other Christians, complementing the normal catechesis that must in any case be given to Catholics. Such experiences have a theological foundation in the elements shared by all Christians.[86] But the communion of faith between Catholics and other Christians is not complete and perfect; in certain cases there are even profound divergences. Consequently, this ecumenical collaboration is by its very nature limited: it must never mean a "reduction" to a common minimum. Furthermore, catechesis does not consist merely in the teaching of doctrine: it also means initiating into the whole of Christian life, bringing full participation in the sacraments of the Church. Therefore, where there is an experience of ecumenical collaboration in the field of catechesis, care must be taken that the education of Catholics in the Catholic Church should be well ensured in matters of doctrine and of Christian living.

During the synod, a certain number of Bishops drew attention to what they referred to as the increasingly frequent cases in which the civil authority or other circumstances impose on the schools in some countries a common instruction in the Christian religion, with common textbooks, class periods, etc., for Catholics and non-Catholics alike. Needless to say, this is not true catechesis. But this teaching also has ecumenical importance when it presents Christian doctrine fairly and honestly. In cases where circumstances impose it, it is important that in addition a specifically Catholic catechesis should be ensured with all the greater care.

The Question of Textbooks Dealing with the Various Religions

34. At this point another observation must be made on the same lines but from a different point of view. State schools sometimes provide their pupils with books that for cultural reasons (history, morals or literature) present the various religions, including the Catholic religion. An objective presentation of historical events, of the different religions and of the various Christian confessions can make a contribution here to

316

---

[86] Cf. *Ibid.*; cf. also Dogmatic Constitution on the Church *LG* 15: AAS 57 (1965), p. 19.

better mutual understanding. Care will then be taken that every effort is made to ensure that the presentation is truly objective and free from the distorting influence of ideological and political systems or of prejudices with claims to be scientific. In any case, such schoolbooks can obviously not be considered catechetical works: they lack both the witness of believers stating their faith to other believers and an understanding of the Christian mysteries and of what is specific about Catholicism, as these are understood within the faith.

V. Everybody needs to be Catechized

The Importance of Children and the Young

317   35. The theme designated by my predecessor Paul VI for the fourth general assembly of the synod of Bishops was: "Catechesis in our time, with special reference to the catechesis of children and young people." The increase in the number of young people is without doubt a fact charged with hope and at the same time with anxiety for a large part of the contemporary world. In certain countries, especially those of the Third World, more than half of the population is under 25 or 30 years of age. This means millions and millions of children and young people preparing for their adult future. And there is more than just the factor of numbers: recent events, as well as the daily news, tell us that, although this countless multitude of young people is here and there dominated by uncertainty and fear, seduced by the escapism of indifference or drugs, or tempted by nihilism and violence, nevertheless it constitutes in its major part the great force that amid many hazards is set on building the civilization of the future.

In our pastoral care we ask ourselves: How are we to reveal Jesus Christ, God made man, to this multitude of children and young people, reveal Him not just in the fascination of a first fleeting encounter but through an acquaintance, growing deeper and clearer daily, with Him, His message, the plan of God that He has revealed, the call He addresses to each person, and the kingdom that He wishes to establish in this world with the "little flock"[87] of those who believe in Him, a kingdom that will be

---

[87] Luke 12:32.

complete only in eternity? How are we to enable them to know the meaning, the import, the fundamental requirements, the law of love, the promises and the hopes of this kingdom?

There are many observations that could be made about the special characteristics that catechesis assumes at the different stages of life.

Infants

36. One moment that is often decisive is the one at which the **318** very young child receives the first elements of catechesis from its parents and the family surroundings. These elements will perhaps be no more than a simple revelation of a good and provident Father in heaven to whom the child learns to turn its heart. The very short prayers that the child learns to lisp will be the start of a loving dialogue with this hidden God whose word it will then begin to hear. I cannot insist too strongly on this early initiation by Christian parents in which the child's faculties are integrated into a living relationship with God. It is a work of prime importance. It demands great love and profound respect for the child who has a right to a simple and true presentation of the Christian faith.

Children

37. For the child there comes soon, at school and in Church, **319** in institutions connected with the parish or with the spiritual care of the Catholic or state school not only an introduction into a wider social circle, but also the moment for a catechesis aimed at inserting him or her organically into the life of the Church, a moment that includes an immediate preparation for the celebration of the sacraments. This catechesis is didactic in character, but is directed towards the giving of witness in the faith. It is an initial catechesis but not a fragmentary one, since it will have to reveal, although in an elementary way, all the principal mysteries of faith and their effects on the child's moral and religious life. It is a catechesis that gives meaning to the sacraments, but at the same time it receives from the experience of the sacraments a living dimension that keeps it from remaining merely doctrinal, and it communicates to the child the joy of being a witness to Christ in ordinary life.

Adolescents

320   38. Next comes puberty and adolescence, with all the greatness and dangers which that age brings. It is the time of discovering oneself and one's own inner world, the time of generous plans, the time when the feeling of love awakens, with the biological impulses of sexuality, the time of the desire to be together, the time of a particularly intense joy connected with the exhilarating discovery of life. But often it is also the age of deeper questioning, of anguished or even frustrating searching, of a certain mistrust of others and dangerous introspection, and the age sometimes of the first experiences of setbacks and of disappointments. Catechesis cannot ignore these changeable aspects of this delicate period of life. A catechesis capable of leading the adolescent to re-examine his or her life and to engage in dialogue, a catechesis that does not ignore the adolescent's great questions – self-giving, belief, love and the means of expressing it constituted by sexuality – such a catechesis can be decisive. The revelation of Jesus Christ as a Friend, Guide and Model, capable of being admired but also imitated; the revelation of this message which provides an answer to the fundamental questions, the revelation of the loving plan of Christ the Saviour as the incarnation of the only authentic love and as the possibility of uniting the human race – all this can provide the basis for genuine education in faith. Above all, the mysteries of the passion and death of Jesus, through which, according to St. Paul, he merited His glorious resurrection, can speak eloquently to the adolescent's conscience and heart and cast light on his first sufferings and on the suffering of the world that he is discovering.

The Young

321   39. With youth comes the moment of the first great decisions. Although the young may enjoy the support of the members of their family and their friends, they have to rely on themselves and their own conscience and must ever more frequently and decisively assume responsibility for their destiny. Good and evil, grace and sin, life and death will more and more confront one another within them, not just as moral categories but chiefly as fundamental options which they must accept or reject lucidly, conscious of their own responsibility. It is obvious that a catechesis which denounces selfishness in the name of generosity, and which without any illusory over-simplification presents the Christian meaning of work, of the common good, of justice and charity, a catechesis on international peace and on the advancement of human dignity, on development, and on liberation, as these are presented in recent documents of the Church,[88] fittingly completes in the minds of the young the good catechesis on strictly religious realities which is never to be neglected. Catechesis then takes on considerable importance, since it is the time when the Gospel can be presented, understood and accepted as capable of giving meaning to life and thus of inspiring attitudes that would have no other explanation, such as self-sacrifice, detachment, forbearance, justice, commitment, reconciliation, a sense of the Absolute and the unseen. All these are traits that distinguish a young person from his or her companions as a disciple of Jesus Christ.

Catechesis thus prepares for the important Christian commitments of adult life. For example, it is certain that many vocations to the priesthood and religious life have their origin during a well-imparted catechesis in infancy and adolescence.

From infancy until the threshold of maturity, catechesis is thus a permanent school of the faith and follows the major stages of life, like a beacon lighting the path of the child, the adolescent and the young person.

The Adaptation of Catechesis for Young People

40. It is reassuring to note that, during the fourth general assembly of the synod and the following years, the Church has widely shared in concern about how to impart catechesis to children and young people. God grant that the attention thus aroused will long endure in the Church's consciousness. In this way the synod has been valuable for the whole Church by seeking to trace with the greatest possible precision the complex characteristics of present-day youth; by showing that these young

322

---

[88] Cf. for example, Second Vatican Council, Pastoral Constitution on the Church in the Modern World *GS*, AAS 58 (1966), pp. 1025-1120; Pope Paul VI, Encyclical *Populorum Progressio*: AAS 59 (1967), pp. 257-299; Apostolic Letter *Octogesima Adveniens*: AAS 63 (1971), pp. 401-441; Apostolic Exhortation *Evangelii Nuntiandi*: AAS 68 (1976), pp. 5-76.

persons speak a language into which the message of Jesus must be translated with patience and wisdom and without betrayal; by demonstrating that, in spite of appearances, these young people have within them, even though often in a confused way, not just a readiness or openness, but rather a real desire to know "Jesus...who is called Christ"[89]; and by indicating that if the work of catechesis is to be carried out rigorously and seriously, it is today more difficult and tiring than ever before, because of the obstacles and difficulties of all kinds that it meets; but it is also more consoling, because of the depth of the response it receives from children and young people. This is a treasure which the Church can and should count on in the years ahead.

The Handicapped

323   41. Children and young people who are physically or mentally handicapped come first to mind. They have a right, like others of their age, to know "the mystery of faith." The greater difficulties that they encounter give greater merit to their efforts and to those of their teachers. It is pleasant to see that Catholic organizations especially dedicated to young handicapped people contributed to the synod a renewed desire to deal better with this important problem. They deserve to be given warm encouragement in this endeavour.

Young People without religious support

324   42. My thoughts turn next to the ever increasing number of children and young people born and brought up in a non-Christian or at least non-practising home but who wish to know the Christian faith. They must be ensured a catechesis attuned to them, so that they will be able to grow in faith and live by it more and more, in spite of the lack of support or even the opposition they meet in their surroundings.

Adults

325   43. To continue the series of receivers of catechesis, I cannot fail to emphasize now one of the most constant concerns of the synod fathers, a concern imposed with vigour and urgency by

---

[89] Matt 1:16.

present experiences throughout the world: I am referring to the
central problem of the catechesis of adults. This is the principal
form of catechesis, because it is addressed to persons who have
the greatest responsibilities and the capacity to live the Christian
message in its fully developed form.[90] The Christian community
cannot carry out a permanent catechesis without the direct and
skilled participation of adults, whether as receivers or as
promoters of catechetical activity. The world, in which the young
are called to live and to give witness to the faith which catechesis
seeks to deepen and strengthen, is governed by adults. The faith
of these adults too should continually be enlightened, stimulated
and renewed, so that it may pervade the temporal realities in their
charge. Thus, for catechesis to be effective, it must be permanent,
and it would be quite useless if it stopped short at the threshold of
maturity, since catechesis, admittedly under another form, proves
no less necessary for adults.

Quasi-Catechumens

44. Among the adults who need catechesis, our pastoral **326**
missionary concern is directed to those who were born and reared
in areas not yet Christianized, and who have never been able to
study deeply the Christian teaching that the circumstances of life
have at a certain moment caused them to come across. It is also
directed to those who in childhood received a catechesis suited to
their age but who later drifted away from all religious practice
and as adults find themselves with religious knowledge of a rather
childish kind. It is likewise directed to those who feel the effects
of a catechesis received early in life but badly imparted or badly
assimilated. It is directed to those who, although they were born
in a Christian country or in sociologically Christian surroundings,
have never been educated in their faith and, as adult are really
catechumens.

---

[90] Cf. Second Vatican Council, Decree on the Bishop's Pastoral Office in the
Church *Christus Dominus*, 14: AAS 58 (1966), p. 679; Decree on the
Missionary Activity of the Church *AG*, 14: AAS 58 (1966), pp. 962-963; Sacred
Congregation for the Clergy, *Directorium Catechisticum Generale* 20: AAS 64
(1972), p. 112; cf. also *Ordo Initiationis Christianae Adultorum*.

Diversified and Complementary Forms of Catechesis

327   45. Catechesis is therefore for adults of every age, including the elderly – persons who deserve particular attention in view of their experience and their problems – no less than for children, adolescents and the young. We should also mention migrants, those who are by-passed by modern developments, those who live in areas of large cities which are often without churches, buildings and suitable organization, and other such groups. It is desirable that initiatives meant to give all these groups a Christian formation, with appropriate means (audio-visual aids, booklets, discussions, lectures), should increase in number, enabling many adults to fill the gap left by an insufficient or deficient catechesis, to complete harmoniously at a higher level their childhood catechesis, or even to prepare themselves enough in this field to be able to help others in a more serious way.

It is important also that the catechesis of children and young people, permanent catechesis, and the catechesis of adults should not be separate watertight compartments. It is even more important that there should be no break between them. On the contrary, their perfect complementarity must be fostered: adults have much to give to young people and children in the field of catechesis, but they can also receive much from them for the growth of their own Christian lives.

It must be restated that nobody in the Church of Jesus Christ should feel excused from receiving catechesis. This is true even of young seminarians and young religious, and of all those called to the task of being pastors and catechists. They will fulfil this task all the better if they are humble pupils of the Church, the great giver as well as the great receiver of catechesis.

VI. Some Ways and Means of Catechesis

Communications Media

328   46. From the oral teaching by the apostles and the letters circulating among the churches down to the most modern means, catechesis has not ceased to look for the most suitable ways and means for its mission, with the active participation of the communities and at the urging of the pastors. This effort must continue.

I think immediately of the great possibilities offered by the means of social communication and the means of group communication: television, radio, the press, records, tape recordings – the whole series of audio-visual means. The achievements in these spheres are such as to encourage the greatest hope. Experience shows, for example, the effect had by instruction given on radio or television, when it combines a high aesthetic level and rigorous fidelity to the magisterium. The Church now has many opportunities for considering these questions – as, for instance, on Social Communications Days – and it is not necessary to speak of them at length here, in spite of their prime importance.

Utilization of Various Places, Occasions and Gatherings

47. I am also thinking of various occasions of special value which are exactly suitable for catechesis: for example, diocesan, regional or national pilgrimages, which gain from being centred on some judiciously chosen theme based on the life of Christ, of the Blessed Virgin or of the saints. Then there are the traditional missions, often too hastily dropped but irreplaceable for the periodic and vigorous renewal of Christian life – they should be revived and brought up to date. Again there are Bible-study groups, which ought to go beyond exegesis and lead their members to live by the Word of God. Yet other instances are the meetings of ecclesial basic communities, in so far as they correspond to the criteria laid down in the Apostolic Exhortation *Evangelii nuntiandi*.[91] I may also mention the youth groups that, under varying names and forms but always with the purpose of making Jesus Christ known and of living by the Gospel, are in some areas multiplying and flourishing in a sort of springtime that is very comforting for the Church. These include Catholic action groups, charitable groups, prayer groups and Christian meditation groups. These groups are a source of great hope for the Church of tomorrow. But, in the name of Jesus, I exhort the young people who belong to them, their leaders, and the priests who devote the best part of their ministry to them: no matter what it costs, do not allow these groups – which are exceptional occasions for meeting others, and which are blessed with such riches of friendship and

329

---

[91] Cf. 58: AAS 68 (1976), pp. 46-49.

solidarity among the young, of joy and enthusiasm, of reflection
on events and facts – do not allow them to lack serious study of
Christian doctrine. If they do, they will be in danger – a danger
that has unfortunately proved only too real – of disappointing
their members and also the Church.

The catechetical endeavour that is possible in these various
surroundings, and in many others besides, will have all the greater
chance of being accepted and bearing fruit if it respects their
individual nature. By becoming part of them in the right way, it
will achieve the diversity and complementarity of approach that
will enable it to develop all the riches of its concept, with its three
dimensions of word, memorial and witness-doctrine, celebration
and commitment in living – which the synod Message to the
People of God emphasized.[92]

The Homily

330   48. This remark is even more valid for the catechesis given in
the setting of the liturgy, especially at the Eucharistic assembly.
Respecting the specific nature and proper cadence of this setting,
the homily takes up again the journey of faith put forward by
catechesis, and brings it to its natural fulfilment. At the same time
it encourages the Lord's disciples to begin anew each day their
spiritual journey in truth, adoration and thanksgiving. Accordingly, one can say that catechetical teaching too finds its source and
its fulfilment in the Eucharist, within the whole circle of the
liturgical year. Preaching, centred upon the Bible texts, must then
in its own way make it possible to familiarize the faithful with the
whole of the mysteries of the faith and with the norms of
Christian living. Much attention must be given to the homily: it
should be neither too long nor too short; it should always be
carefully prepared, rich in substance and adapted to the hearers,
and reserved to ordained ministers. The homily should have its
place not only in every Sunday and feast-day Eucharist, but also
in the celebration of baptisms, penitential liturgies, marriages and
funerals. This is one of the benefits of the liturgical renewal.

---

[92] Cf. *Synodus Episcoporum, De catechesi hoc nostro tempore tradenda praesertim pueris atque iuvenibus, Ad Populum Dei Nuntius,* 7-10: loc. cit., pp. 9-12; cf. *L'Osservatore Romano,* 30 October 1977, p. 3.

Catechetical Literature

49. Among these various ways and means – all the Church's **331** activities have a catechetical dimension – catechetical works, far from losing their essential importance, acquire fresh significance. One of the major features of the renewal of catechetics today is the rewriting and multiplication of catechetical books taking place in many parts of the Church. Numerous very successful works have been produced and are a real treasure in the service of catechetical instruction. But it must be humbly and honestly recognized that this rich flowering has brought with it articles and publications which are ambiguous and harmful to young people and to the life of the Church. In certain places, the desire to find the best forms of expression or to keep up with fashions in pedagogical methods has often enough resulted in certain catechetical works which bewilder the young and even adults, either by deliberately or unconsciously omitting elements essential to the Church's faith, or by attributing excessive importance to certain themes at the expense of others, or, chiefly, by a rather horizontalist overall view out of keeping with the teaching of the Church's magisterium.

Therefore, it is not enough to multiply catechetical works. In order that these works may correspond with their aim, several conditions are essential:

a) they must be linked with the real life of the generation to which they are addressed, showing close acquaintance with its anxieties and questionings, struggles and hopes;

b) they must try to speak a language comprehensible to the generation in question;

c) they must make a point of giving the whole message of Christ and His Church, without neglecting or distorting anything, and in expounding it they will follow a line and structure that highlights what is essential;

d) they must really aim to give to those who use them a better knowledge of the mysteries of Christ, aimed at true conversion and a life more in conformity with God's will.

Catechisms

50. All those who take on the heavy task of preparing these **332** catechetical tools, especially catechism texts, can do so only with

the approval of the pastors who have the authority to give it, and taking their inspiration as closely as possible from the General Catechetical Directory, which remains the standard of reference.[93]

In this regard, I must warmly encourage episcopal conferences of the whole world to undertake, patiently but resolutely, the considerable work to be accomplished in agreement with the Apostolic See in order to prepare genuine catechisms which will be faithful to the essential content of revelation and up to date in method, and which will be capable of educating the Christian generations of the future to a sturdy faith.

This brief mention of ways and means of modern catechetics does not exhaust the wealth of suggestions worked out by the synod fathers. It is comforting to think that at the present time every country is seeing valuable collaboration for a more organic and more secure renewal of these aspects of catechetics. There can be no doubt that the Church will find the experts and the right means for responding, with God's grace, to the complex requirements of communicating with the people of today.

VII. How to impart Catechesis

Diversity of Methods

333   51. The age and the intellectual development of Christians, their degree of ecclesial and spiritual maturity and many other personal circumstances demand that catechesis should adopt widely differing methods for the attainment of its specific aim: education in the faith. On a more general level, this variety is also demanded by the social and cultural surrounding in which the Church carries out her catechetical work.

The variety in the methods used is a sign of life and a resource. That is how it was considered by the fathers of the fourth general assembly of the synod, although they also drew attention to the conditions necessary for that variety to be useful and not harmful to the unity of the teaching of the one Faith.

---

[93] Cf. Sacred Congregation for the Clergy, *Directorium Catechisticum Generale*, 119-121; 134: AAS 64 (1972), pp. 166-167; 172. [Editor's Note: This was replaced by *The General Directory for Catechesis* in 1997, included in this volume; see page 28 para 2.]

At the Service of Revelation and Conversion   **334**

52. The first question of a general kind that presents itself here concerns the danger and the temptation to mix catechetical teaching unduly with overt or masked ideological views, especially political and social ones, or with personal political options. When such views get the better of the central message to be transmitted, to the point of obscuring it and putting it in second place or even using it to further their own ends, catechesis then becomes radically distorted. The synod rightly insisted on the need for catechesis to remain above one-sided divergent trends – to avoid "dichotomies" – even in the field of theological interpretation of such questions. It is on the basis of revelation that catechesis will try to set its course, revelation as transmitted by the universal magisterium of the Church, in its solemn or ordinary form. This revelation tells of a creating and redeeming God, Whose Son has come among us in our flesh and enters not only into each individual's personal history but into human history itself, becoming its centre. Accordingly, this revelation tells of the radical chance of man and the universe, of all that makes up the web of human life under the influence of the Good News of Jesus Christ. If conceived in this way, catechesis goes beyond every form of formalistic moralism, although it will include true Christian moral teaching. Chiefly, it goes beyond any kind of temporal, social or political "messianism." It seeks to arrive at man's innermost being.

The Message embodied in cultures

53. Now a second question. As I said recently to the   **335**
members of the Biblical Commission: "The term 'acculturation' or 'inculturation' may be a neologism, but it expresses very well one factor of the great mystery of the Incarnation."[94] We can say of catechesis, as well as of evangelisation in general, that it is called to bring the power of the Gospel into the very heart of culture and cultures. For this purpose, catechesis will seek to know these cultures and their essential components; it will learn their most significant expressions; it will respect their particular values and riches. In this manner it will be able to offer these

---

[94] Cf. AAS 71 (1979), p. 607.

cultures the knowledge of the hidden mystery[95] and help them to bring forth from their own living tradition original expressions of Christian life, celebration and thought. Two things must however be kept in mind.

On the one hand the Gospel message cannot be purely and simply isolated from the culture in which it was first inserted (the biblical world or, more concretely, the cultural milieu in which Jesus of Nazareth lived), nor, without serious loss, from the cultures in which it has already been expressed down the centuries; it does not spring spontaneously from any cultural soil; it has always been transmitted by means of an apostolic dialogue which inevitably becomes part of a certain dialogue of cultures.

On the other hand, the power of the Gospel everywhere transforms and regenerates. When that power enters into a culture, it is no surprise that it rectifies many of its elements. There would be no catechesis if it were the Gospel that had to change when it came into contact with the cultures.

To forget this would simply amount to what St. Paul very forcefully calls "emptying the cross of Christ of its power."[96]

It is a different matter to take, with wise discernment, certain elements, religious or otherwise, that form part of the cultural heritage of a human group and use them to help its members to understand better the whole of the Christian mystery. Genuine catechists know that catechesis "takes flesh" in the various cultures and milieux: one has only to think of the peoples with their great differences, of modern youth, of the great variety of circumstances in which people find themselves today. But they refuse to accept an impoverishment of catechesis through a renunciation or obscuring of its message, by adaptations, even in language, that would endanger the "precious deposit" of the faith,[97] or by concessions in matters of faith or morals. They are convinced that true catechesis eventually enriches these cultures by helping them to go beyond the defective or even inhuman features in them, and by communicating to their legitimate values the fulness of Christ.[98]

---

[95]Cf. Rom. 16:25; Eph. 3:5.

[96] 1 Cor. 1:17.

[97] Cf. 2 Tm. 1:14.

[98] Cf. John 1:16; Eph. 1:10.

The contribution of popular devotion

54. Another question of method concerns the utilization in **336** catechetical instruction of valid elements in popular piety. I have in mind devotions practised by the faithful in certain regions with moving fervour and purity of intention, even if the faith underlying them needs to be purified or rectified in many aspects. I have in mind certain easily understood prayers that many simple people are fond of repeating. I have in mind certain acts of piety practised with a sincere desire to do penance or to please the Lord. Underlying most of these prayers and practices, besides elements that should be discarded, there are other elements which, if they were properly used, could serve very well to help people advance towards knowledge of the mystery of Christ and of His message: the love and mercy of God, the Incarnation of Christ, His redeeming cross and resurrection, the activity of the Spirit in each Christian and in the Church, the mystery of the hereafter, the evangelical virtues to be practised, the presence of the Christian in the world, etc. And why should we appeal to non-Christian or even anti-Christian elements refusing to build on elements which, even if they need to be revised or improved, have something Christian at their root?

Memorization

55. The final methodological question, the importance of **337** which should at least be referred to – one that was debated several times in the synod – is that of memorization. In the beginnings of Christian catechesis, which coincided with a civilization that was mainly oral, recourse was had very freely to memorization. Catechesis has since then known a long tradition of learning the principal truths by memorizing. We are all aware that this method can present certain disadvantages, not the least of which is that it lends itself to insufficient or at times almost non-existent assimilation, reducing all knowledge to formulas that are repeated without being properly understood. These disadvantages and the different characteristics of our own civilization have in some places led to the almost complete suppression – according to some, alas, the definitive suppression – of memorization in catechesis. And yet certain very authoritative voices made themselves heard on the occasion of the fourth general assembly

of the synod, calling for the restoration of a judicious balance between reflection and spontaneity, between dialogue and silence, between written work and memory work. Moreover certain cultures still set great value on memorization.

At a time when, in non-religious teaching in certain countries, more and more complaints are being made about the unfortunate consequences of disregarding the human faculty of memory, should we not attempt to put this faculty back into use in an intelligent and even an original way in catechesis, all the more since the celebration or "memorial" of the great events of the history of salvation require a precise knowledge of them? A certain memorization of the words of Jesus, of important Bible passages, of the Ten Commandments, of the formulas of profession of the faith, of the liturgical texts, of the essential prayers, of key doctrinal ideas, etc., far from being opposed to the dignity of young Christians, or constituting an obstacle to personal dialogue with the Lord, is a real need, as the synod fathers forcefully recalled. We must be realists. The blossoms, if we may call them that, of faith and piety do not grow in the desert places of a memory-less catechesis. What is essential is that the texts that are memorized must at the same time be taken in and gradually understood in depth, in order to become a source of Christian life on the personal level and the community level.

The plurality of methods in contemporary catechesis can be a sign of vitality and ingenuity. In any case, the method chosen must ultimately be referred to a law that is fundamental for the whole of the Church's life: the law of fidelity to God and of fidelity to man in a single loving attitude.

VII. The Joy of Faith in a Troubled World

Affirming Christian Identity

338   56. We live in a difficult world in which the anguish of seeing the best creations of man slip away from him and turn against him creates a climate of uncertainty.[99] In this world catechesis should help Christians to be, for their own joy and the

---

[99] Cf. Encyclical *Redemptor Hominis*, 15-16: AAS 71 (1979), pp. 286-295.

service of all, "light" and "salt."[100] Undoubtedly this demands that catechesis should strengthen them in their identity and that it should continually separate itself from the surrounding atmosphere of hesitation, uncertainty and insipidity. Among the many difficulties, each of them a challenge for faith, I shall indicate a few in order to assist catechesis in overcoming them.

In an Indifferent World

57. A few years ago, there was much talk of the secularized world, the post-Christian era. Fashion changes, but a profound reality remains. Christians today must be formed to live in a world which largely ignores God or which, in religious matters, in place of an exacting and fraternal dialogue, stimulating for all, too often flounders in a debasing indifferentism, if it does not remain in a scornful attitude of "suspicion" in the name of the progress it has made in the field of scientific "explanations." To "hold on" in this world, to offer to all a "dialogue of salvation"[101] in which each person feels respected in his or her most basic dignity, the dignity of one who is seeking God, we need a catechesis which trains the young people and adults of our communities to remain clear and consistent in their faith, to affirm serenely their Christian and Catholic identity, to "see him who is invisible"[102] and to adhere so firmly to the absoluteness of God that they can be witnesses to Him in a materialistic civilization that denies Him.

339

With the Original Pedagogy of the Faith

58. The irreducible originality of Christian identity has for corollary and condition no less original a pedagogy of the faith. Among the many prestigious sciences of man that are nowadays making immense advances, pedagogy is certainly one of the most important. The attainments of the other sciences – biology, psychology, sociology – are providing it with valuable elements. The science of education and the art of teaching are continually being subjected to review, with a view to making them better adapted or more effective, with varying degrees of success.

340

---

[100] Cf. Matt 5:13-16.
[101] Cf. Pope Paul VI, Encyclical *Ecclesiam Suam*, Part Three, AAS 56 (1964), pp. 637-659.
[102] Cf. Heb. 11:27.

There is also a pedagogy of faith, and the good that it can do for catechesis cannot be overstated. In fact, it is natural that techniques perfected and tested for education in general should be adapted for the service of education in the faith. However, account must always be taken of the absolute originality of faith. Pedagogy of faith is not a question of transmitting human knowledge, even of the highest kind; it is a question of communicating God's revelation in its entirety. Throughout sacred history, especially in the Gospel, God Himself used a pedagogy that must continue to be a model for the pedagogy of faith. A technique is of value in catechesis only to the extent that it serves the faith that is to be transmitted and learned; otherwise it is of no value.

Language Suited to the Service of the Credo

341   59. A problem very close to the preceding one is that of language. This is obviously a burning question today. It is paradoxical to see that, while modern studies, for instance in the field of communication, semantics and symbology, attribute extraordinary importance to language, nevertheless language is being misused today for ideological mystification, for mass conformity in thought and for reducing man to the level of an object.

All this has extensive influence in the field of catechesis. For catechesis has a pressing obligation to speak a language suited to today's children and young people in general and to many other categories of people – the language of students, intellectuals and scientists; the language of the illiterate or of people of simple culture; the language of the handicapped, and so on. St. Augustine encountered this same problem and contributed to its solution for his own time with his well known work *De Catechizandis Rudibus*. In catechesis as in theology, there is no doubt that the question of language is of the first order. But there is good reason for recalling here that catechesis cannot admit any language that would result in altering the substance of the content of the Creed, under any pretext whatever, even a pretended scientific one. Deceitful or beguiling language is no better. On the contrary, the supreme rule is that the great advances in the science of language must be capable of being placed at the service of catechesis so as to enable it really to "tell" or "communicate" to the child, the adolescent, the young people and adults of today the whole content of doctrine without distortion.

Research and Certainty of Faith

60. A more subtle challenge occasionally comes from the very way of conceiving faith. Certain contemporary philosophical schools, which seem to be exercising a strong influence on some theological currents and, through them, on pastoral practice, like to emphasize that the fundamental human attitude is that of seeking the infinite, a seeking that never attains its object. In theology, this view of things will state very categorically that faith is not certainty but questioning, not clarity but a leap in the dark.

These currents of thought certainly have the advantage of reminding us that faith concerns things not yet in our possession, since they are hoped for; that as yet we see only "in a mirror dimly"[103]; and that God dwells always in inaccessible light.[104] They help us to make the Christian faith not the attitude of one who has already arrived, but a journey forward as with Abraham. For all the more reason one must avoid presenting as certain things which are not.

However, we must not fall into the opposite extreme, as too often happens. The Letter to the Hebrews says that "faith is the assurance of things hoped for, the conviction of things not seen."[105] Although we are not in full possession, we do have an assurance and a conviction. When educating children, adolescents and young people, let us not give them too negative an idea of faith – as if it were absolute non-knowing, a kind of blindness, a world of darkness – but let us show them that the humble yet courageous seeking of the believer, far from having its starting point in nothingness, in plain self-deception, in fallible opinions or in uncertainty, is based on the Word of God who cannot deceive or be deceived, and is unceasingly built on the immovable rock of this Word. It is the search of the Magi under the guidance of a star,[106] the search of which Pascal, taking up a phrase of St. Augustine, wrote so profoundly: "You would not be

---

[103] 1 Cor. 13:12.
[104] Cf. 1 Tm. 6:16.
[105] Heb. 11:1.
[106] Cf. Matt 2: 1ff.

342

searching for me, if you had not found me."[107]

It is also one of the aims of catechesis to give young catechumens the simple but solid certainties that will help them to seek to know the Lord more and better.

Catechesis and Theology

343   61. In this context, it seems important to me that the connection between catechesis and theology should be well understood.

Obviously this connection is profound and vital for those who understand the irreplaceable mission of theology in the service of Faith. Thus it is no surprise that every stirring in the field of theology also has repercussions in that of catechesis. In this period immediately after the Council, the Church is living through an important but hazardous time of theological research. The same must be said of hermeneutics with respect to exegesis.

Synod fathers from all continents dealt with this question in very frank terms: they spoke of the danger of an "unstable balance" passing from theology to catechesis and they stressed the need to do something about this difficulty. Pope Paul VI himself had dealt with the problem in no less frank terms in the introduction to his Solemn Profession of Faith[108] and in the Apostolic Exhortation marking the fifth anniversary of the close of the Second Vatican Council.[109]

This point must again be insisted on. Aware of the influence that their research and their statements have on catechetical instruction, theologians and exegetes have a duty to take great care that people do not take for a certainty what on the contrary belongs to the area of questions of opinion or of discussion among experts. Catechists for their part must have the wisdom to pick from the field of theological research those points that can provide light for their own reflection and their teaching, drawing, like the theologians, from the true sources, in the light of the magisterium. They must refuse to trouble the minds of the children and young people, at this stage of their catechesis, with outlandish theories, useless questions and unproductive discuss-

---

[107] Blaise Pascal, *Le mystere de Jesus: Pensees* 553.
[108] Pope Paul VI, *Sollemnis Professio Fidei*, 4: AAS 60 (1968), p. 434.
[109] Pope Paul VI, Apostolic Exhortation *Quinque Iam Anni*: AAS 63 (1971), p. 99.

ions, things that St. Paul often condemned in his pastoral letters.[110]

The most valuable gift that the Church can offer to the bewildered and restless world of our time is to form within it Christians who are confirmed in what is essential and who are humbly joyful in their faith. Catechesis will teach this to them, and it will itself be the first to benefit from it: "The man who wishes to understand himself thoroughly – and not just in accordance with immediate, partial, often superficial, and even illusory standards and measures of his being – must come to Christ with his unrest and uncertainty, and even his weakness and sinfulness, his life and death. He must, so to speak, enter into Christ with all his own self, he must 'appropriate' Christ and assimilate the whole of the reality of the Incarnation and redemption in order to find himself."[111]

IX. The Task concerns us all

Encouragement to All Responsible for Catechesis

62. Now, beloved brothers and sons and daughters, I would like my words, which are intended as a serious and heartfelt exhortation from me in my ministry as pastor of the universal Church, to set your hearts aflame, like the letters of St. Paul to his companions in the Gospel, Titus and Timothy, or like St. Augustine writing for the deacon Deogratias, when the latter lost heart before his task as a catechist, a real little treatise on the joy of catechizing.[112] Yes, I wish to sow courage, hope and enthusiasm abundantly in the hearts of all those many diverse people who are in charge of religious instruction and training for life in keeping with the Gospel. **344**

Bishops

63. To begin with, I turn to my brother Bishops: The Second Vatican Council has already explicitly reminded you of your task **345**

---

[110] Cf. 1 Tim. 1:3ff.; 4:1ff.; 2 Tim. 2:14ff.; 4:1-5; Tit. 1:10-12; cf. also Apostolic Exhortation, *Evangelii Nuntiandi*, 78: AAS 68 (1976), p. 70.
[111] Encyclical *Redemptor Hominis*, 10: AAS 71 (1979), p. 274.
[112] *De Catechizandis Rudibus*, PL 40, 310-347.

in the catechetical area,[113] and the fathers of the fourth general assembly of the synod have also strongly underlined it.

Dearly beloved brothers, you have here a special mission within your Churches: You are beyond all others the ones primarily responsible for catechesis, the catechists par excellence. Together with the Pope, in the spirit of episcopal collegiality, you too have charge of catechesis throughout the Church. Accept therefore what I say to you from my heart.

I know that your ministry as Bishops is growing daily more complex and overwhelming. A thousand duties call you: from the training of new priests to being actively present within the lay communities, from the living, worthy celebration of the sacraments and acts of worship to concern for human advancement and the defence of human rights. But let the concern to foster active and effective catechesis yield to no other care whatever in any way. This concern will lead you to transmit personally to your faithful the doctrine of life. But it should also lead you to take on in your diocese, in accordance with the plans of the episcopal conference to which you belong, the chief management of catechesis, while at the same time surrounding yourselves with competent and trustworthy assistants. Your principal role will be to bring about and maintain in your Churches a real passion for catechesis, a passion embodied in a pertinent and effective organization, putting into operation the necessary personnel, means and equipment, and also financial resources. You can be sure that if catechesis is done well in your local Churches, everything else will be easier to do. And needless to say, although your zeal must sometimes impose upon you the thankless task of denouncing deviations and correcting errors, it will much more often win for you the joy and consolation of seeing your Churches flourishing because catechesis is given in them as the Lord wishes.

Priests

346   64. For your part, priests, here you have a field in which you are the immediate assistants of your Bishops. The Council has

---

[113] Cf. Decree on the Bishop's Pastoral Office in the Church *Christus Dominus*, 14: AAS 58 (1966), p. 679.

called you "instructors in the faith"[114]; there is no better way for you to be such instructors than by devoting your best efforts to the growth of your communities in the faith. Whether you are in charge of a parish, or are chaplains to primary or secondary schools or universities, or have responsibility for pastoral activity at any level, or are leaders of large or small communities, especially youth groups, the Church expects you to neglect nothing with a view to a well-organized and well-oriented catechetical effort. The deacons and other ministers that you may have the good fortune to have with you are your natural assistants in this. All believers have a right to catechesis; all pastors have the duty to provide it. I shall always ask civil leaders to respect the freedom of catechetical teaching; but with all my strength I beg you, ministers of Jesus Christ: Do not, for lack of zeal or because of some unfortunate preconceived idea, leave the faithful without catechesis. Let it not be said that "the children beg for food, but no one gives to them."[115]

Men and Women Religious

65. Many religious institutes for men and women came into being for the purpose of giving Christian education to children and young people, especially the most abandoned. Throughout history, men and women religious have been deeply committed to the Church's catechetical activity, doing particularly apposite and effective work. At a time when it is desired that the links between religious and pastors should be accentuated and consequently the active presence of religious communities and their members in the pastoral projects of the local Churches, I wholeheartedly exhort you, whose religious consecration should make you even more readily available for the Church's service, to prepare as well as possible for the task of catechesis according to the differing vocations of your institutes and the missions entrusted to you, and to carry this concern everywhere. Let the communities dedicate as much as possible of what ability and means they have to the specific work of catechesis.

347

---

[114] Decree on the Ministry and Life of Priests, *Presbyterorum Ordinis*, 6: AAS 58 (1966), p. 999.
[115] Lam. 4:4.

Lay Catechists

348   66. I am anxious to give thanks in the Church's name to all of
you, lay teachers of catechesis in the parishes, the men and the still
more numerous women throughout the world who are devoting
yourselves to the religious education of many generations. Your
work is often lowly and hidden but it is carried out with ardent and
generous zeal, and it is an eminent form of the lay apostolate, a
form that is particularly important where for various reasons children and young people do not receive suitable religious training in
the home. How many of us have received from people like you our
first notions of catechism and our preparation for the sacrament of
Penance, for our first Communion and Confirmation! The fourth
general assembly of the synod did not forget you. I join with it in
encouraging you to continue your collaboration for the life of the
Church.

But the term "catechists" belongs above all to the catechists
in mission lands. Born of families that are already Christian or
converted at some time to Christianity and instructed by
missionaries or by another catechist, they then consecrate their
lives, year after year, to catechizing children and adults in their
own country. Churches that are flourishing today would not have
been built up without them. I rejoice at the efforts made by the
Sacred Congregation for the Evangelisation of Peoples to
improve more and more the training of these catechists. I
gratefully recall the memory of those whom the Lord has already
called to Himself. I beg the intercession of those whom my
predecessors have raised to the glory of the altars. I wholeheartedly encourage those engaged in the work. I express the wish
that many others may succeed them and that they may increase in
numbers for a task so necessary for the missions.

In the Parish

349   67. I now wish to speak of the actual setting in which all
these catechists normally work. I am returning this time, taking a
more overall view, to the "places" for catechesis, some of which
have already been mentioned in chapter VI: the parish, the family,
the school, organizations.

It is true that catechesis can be given anywhere, but I wish to
stress, in accordance with the desire of very many Bishops, that

the parish community must continue to be the prime mover and pre- eminent place for catechesis. Admittedly, in many countries the parish has been as it were shaken by the phenomenon of urbanization. Perhaps some have too easily accepted that the parish should be considered old-fashioned, if not doomed to disappear, in favour of more pertinent and effective small communities. Whatever one may think, the parish is still a major point of reference for the Christian people, even for the non-practising. Accordingly, realism and wisdom demand that we continue along the path aiming to restore to the parish, as needed, more adequate structures and, above all a new impetus through the increasing integration into it of qualified, responsible and generous members. This being said and taking into account the necessary diversity of places for catechesis (the parish as such, families taking in children and adolescents, chaplaincies for State schools, Catholic educational establishments, apostolic move-ments that give periods of catechesis, clubs open to youth in general, spiritual formation weekends, etc.), it is supremely important that all these catechetical channels should really con-verge on the same confession of faith, on the same membership of the Church, and on commitments in society lived in the same Gospel spirit: "one Lord, one faith, one baptism, one God and Father."[116] That is why every big parish or every group of parishes with small numbers has the serious duty to train people completely dedicated to providing catechetical leadership (priests, men and women religious, and lay people), to provide the equip-ment needed for catechesis under all aspects, to increase and adapt the places for catechesis to the extent that it is possible and useful to do so, and to be watchful about the quality of the religious formation of the various groups and their integration into the ecclesial community.

In short, without monopolizing or enforcing uniformity, the parish remains, as I have said, the pre-eminent place for catechesis. It must rediscover its vocation, which is to be a fraternal and welcoming family home, where those who have been baptized and confirmed become aware of forming the People of God. In that home, the bread of good doctrine and the Eucharistic Bread are

---

[116] Eph. 4:5-6.

broken for them in abundance, in the setting of the one act of worship;[117] from that home they are sent out day by day to their apostolic mission in all the centres of activity of the life of the world.

In the Family

350   68. The family's catechetical activity has a special character, which is in a sense irreplaceable. This special character has been rightly stressed by the Church, particularly by the Second Vatican Council.[118] Education in the faith by parents, which should begin from the children's tenderest age,[119] is already being given when the members of a family help each other to grow in faith through the witness of their Christian lives, a witness that is often without words but which perseveres throughout a day-to-day life lived in accordance with the Gospel. This catechesis is more incisive when, in the course of family events (such as the reception of the sacraments, the celebration of great liturgical feasts, the birth of a child, a bereavement) care is taken to explain in the home the Christian or religious content of these events. But that is not enough: Christian parents must strive to follow and repeat, within the setting of family life, the more methodical teaching received elsewhere. The fact that these truths about the main questions of

---

[117] Cf. Second Vatican Council, Constitution on the Sacred Liturgy *Sacrosanctum Concilium*, 35, 52: AAS 56 (1964), pp. 109, 114; cf. also *Institutio Generalis Misalis Romani*, promulgated by a Decree of the Sacred Congregation of Rites on 6 April 1969, 33, and what has been said above in Chapter VI concerning the homily.

[118] Since the High Middle Ages, provincial councils have insisted on the responsibility of parents in regard to education in the faith: cf. Sixth Council of Arles, Canon 19, Council of Mainz, Canons 45, 47; Sixth Council of Paris, Book 1, Ch 7: Mansi, *Sacrorum Conciliorum Nova et Amplissima Collectio*, XIV, 62, 74, 542. Among the more recent documents of the Magisterium, note the Encyclical *Divini illius Magistri* of Pius XI, 31 December 1929: AAS 22 (1930), pp. 49-86; the many discourses and messages of Pius XII; and above all the texts of the Second Vatican Council: the Dogmatic Constitution on the Church *LG*, 11, 35: AAS 57 (1965), pp. 15, 40; the Decree on the Apostolate of the Laity *Apostolicam Actuositatem*, 11, 30: AAS 58 (1966), pp. 847, 860; the Pastoral Constitution on the Church in the Modern World *GS*, 52: AAS 58 (1966) p. 1073; and especially the *Declaration on Christian Education GE*, 3: AAS 58 (1966), p. 731.

[119] Cf. Second Vatican Council, *Declaration on Christian Education GE*, 3: AAS 58 (1966), p. 731.

faith and Christian living are thus repeated within a family setting impregnated with love and respect will often make it possible to influence the children in a decisive way for life. The parents themselves profit from the effort that this demands of them, for in a catechetical dialogue of this sort each individual both receives and gives.

Family catechesis therefore precedes, accompanies and enriches all other forms of catechesis. Furthermore, in places where anti-religious legislation endeavours even to prevent education in the faith, and in places where widespread unbelief or invasive secularism makes real religious growth practically impossible, "the church of the home"[120] remains the one place where children and young people can receive an authentic catechesis. Thus there cannot be too great an effort on the part of Christian parents to prepare for this ministry of being their own children's catechists and to carry it out with tireless zeal. Encouragement must also be given to the individuals or institutions that, through person-to-person contacts, through meetings, and through all kinds of pedagogical means, help parents to perform their task: The service they are doing to catechesis is beyond price.

At School

351

69. Together with and in connection with the family, the school provides catechesis with possibilities that are not to be neglected. In the unfortunately decreasing number of countries in which it is possible to give education in the faith within the school framework, the Church has the duty to do so as well as possible. This of course concerns first and foremost the Catholic school: it would no longer deserve this title if, no matter how much it shone for its high level of teaching in non-religious matters, there were justification for reproaching it for negligence or deviation in strictly religious education. Let it not be said that such education will always be given implicitly and indirectly. The special character of the Catholic school, the underlying reason for it, the reason why Catholic parents should prefer it, is precisely

---

[120] Second Vatican Council, Dogmatic Constitution on the Church *LG*, 11: AAS 57 (1965), p. 16; cf. Decree on the Apostolate of the Laity *Apostolicam Actuositatem*, 11: AAS 58 (1966), p. 848

the quality of the religious instruction integrated into the education of the pupils. While Catholic establishments should respect freedom of conscience, that is to say, avoid burdening consciences from without by exerting physical or moral pressure, especially in the case of the religious activity of adolescents, they still have a grave duty to offer a religious training suited to the often widely varying religious situations of the pupils. They also have a duty to make them understand that, although God's call to serve Him in spirit and truth, in accordance with the Commandments of God and the precepts of the Church, does not apply constraint, it is nevertheless binding in conscience.

But I am also thinking of non-confessional and public schools. I express the fervent wish that, in response to a very clear right of the human person and of the family, and out of respect for everyone's religious freedom, all Catholic pupils may be enabled to advance in their spiritual formation with the aid of a religious instruction dependent on the Church, but which, according to the circumstances of different countries, can be offered either by the school or in the setting of the school, or again within the framework of an agreement with the public authorities regarding school timetables, if catechesis takes place only in the parish or in another pastoral centre. In fact, even in places where objective difficulties exist, it should be possible to arrange school timetables in such a way as to enable the Catholics to deepen their faith and religious experience, with qualified teachers, whether priests or lay people.

Admittedly, apart from the school, many other elements of life help in influencing the mentality of the young, for instance, recreation, social background and work surroundings. But those who study are bound to bear the stamp of their studies, to be introduced to cultural or moral values within the atmosphere of the establishment in which they are taught, and to be faced with many ideas met with in school. It is important for catechesis to take full account of this effect of the school on the pupils, if it is to keep in touch with the other elements of the pupil's knowledge and education; thus the Gospel will impregnate the mentality of the pupils in the field of their learning, and the harmonization of their culture will be achieved in the light of faith. Accordingly, I give encouragement to the priests, religious and lay people who are devoting themselves to sustaining these pupils' faith. This is

moreover an occasion for me to reaffirm my firm conviction that
to show respect for the Catholic faith of the young to the extent of
facilitating its education, its implantation, its consolidation, its
free profession and practice would certainly be to the honour of
any government, whatever be the system on which it is based or
the ideology from which it draws its inspiration.

Within Organizations

70. Lastly, encouragement must be given to the lay **352**
associations, movements and groups, whether their aim is the
practice of piety, the direct apostolate, charity and relief work, or
a Christian presence in temporal matters. They will all
accomplish their objectives better, and serve the Church better, if
they give an important place in their internal organization and
their method of action to the serious religious training of their
members. In this way every association of the faithful in the
Church has by definition the duty to educate in the faith.

This makes more evident the role given to the laity in catechesis today, always under the pastoral direction of their Bishops, as
the propositions left by the synod stressed several times.

Training Institutes

71. We must be grateful to the Lord for this contribution by **353**
the laity, but it is also a challenge to our responsibility as pastors,
since these lay catechists must be carefully prepared for what is,
if not a formally instituted ministry, at the very least a function of
great importance in the Church. Their preparation calls on us to
organize special centres and institutes, which are to be given
assiduous attention by the Bishops. This is a field in which
diocesan, interdiocesan or national cooperation proves fertile and
fruitful. Here also the material aid provided by the richer
Churches to their poor sisters can show the greatest effectiveness,
for what better assistance can one Church give to another than to
help it to grow as a Church with its own strength?

I would like to recall to all those who are working generously
in the service of the Gospel, and to whom I have expressed here
my lively encouragement, the instruction given by my venerated
predecessor Paul VI: "As evangelizers, we must offer... the
image of people who are mature in faith and capable of finding a

meeting-point beyond the real tensions, thanks to a shared, sincere and disinterested search for truth. Yes, the destiny of evangelisation is certainly bound up with the witness of unity given by the Church. This is a source of responsibility and also of comfort."[121]

Conclusion

The Holy Spirit, the Teacher Within

354   72. At the end of this Apostolic Exhortation, the gaze of my heart turns to Him who is the principle inspiring all catechetical work and all who do this work – the Spirit of the Father and of the Son, the Holy Spirit.

In describing the mission that this Spirit would have in the Church, Christ used the significant words: "He will teach you all things, and bring to your remembrance all that I have said to you."[122] And He added: "When the Spirit of truth comes, he will guide you into all the truth...he will declare to you the things that are to come."[123]

The Spirit is thus promised to the Church and to each Christian as a teacher within, who, in the secret of the conscience and the heart, makes one understand what one has heard but was not capable of grasping: "Even now the Holy Spirit teaches the faithful," said St. Augustine in this regard, "in accordance with each one's spiritual capacity. And he sets their hearts aflame with greater desire according as each one progresses in the charity that makes him love what he already knows and desire what he has yet to know."[124]

Furthermore, the Spirit's mission is also to transform the disciples into witnesses to Christ: "He will bear witness to me; and you also are witnesses."[125]

But this is not all. For St. Paul, who on this matter synthesizes a theology that is latent throughout the New Testament, it is the whole of one's "being a Christian," the whole of the Christian life, the new life of the children of God, that constitutes a life in accordance with the Spirit.[126] Only the Spirit enables us to say to

---

[121] Apostolic Exhortation *Evangelii Nuntiandi*, 77: AAS 68 (1976), p. 69.
[122] John 14:26.
[123] John 16:13.
[124] *In Ioannis Evangelium Tractatus*, 97, 1: PL 35, 1877.
[125] John 15:26-27.
[126] Cf. Rom. 8:14-17; Gal. 4:6.

God: "Abba, Father."[127] Without the Spirit we cannot say: "Jesus is Lord."[128] From the Spirit come all the charisms that build up the Church, the community of Christians.[129]

In keeping with this, St. Paul gives each disciple of Christ the instruction: "Be filled with the Spirit."[130] St. Augustine is very explicit: "Both (our believing and our doing good) are ours because of the choice of our will, and yet both are gifts from the Spirit of faith and charity."[131]

Catechesis, which is growth in faith and the maturing of Christian life towards its fulness, is consequently a work of the Holy Spirit, a work that He alone can initiate and sustain in the Church.

This realization, based on the text quoted above and on many other passages of the New Testament, convinces us of two things.

To begin with, it is clear that, when carrying out her mission of giving catechesis, the Church – and also every individual Christian devoting himself to that mission within the Church and in her name – must be very much aware of acting as a living, pliant instrument of the Holy Spirit. To invoke this Spirit constantly, to be in communion with Him, to endeavour to know His authentic inspirations must be the attitude of the teaching Church and of every catechist.

Secondly, the deep desire to understand better the Spirit's action and to entrust oneself to Him more fully – at a time when "in the Church we are living an exceptionally favourable season of the Spirit," as my predecessor Paul VI remarked in his Apostolic Exhortation *Evangelii nuntiandi*[132] – must bring about a catechetical awakening. For "renewal in the Spirit" will be authentic and will have real fruitfulness in the Church, not so much according as it gives rise to extraordinary charisms, but according as it leads the greatest possible number of the faithful, as they travel their daily paths, to make a humble, patient and persevering effort to know the mystery of Christ better and better, and to bear witness to it.

---

[127] Rom. 8:15
[128] 1 Cor 12:3.
[129] Cf. 1 Cor. 12:4-11.
[130] Eph. 5:18.
[131] *Retractationum Liber I*, 23, 2: PL 32, 621.
[132] 75: AAS 68 (1976), p. 66.

I invoke on the catechizing Church this Spirit of the Father and the Son, and I beg Him to renew catechetical dynamism in the Church.

Mary, Mother and Model of the Disciple

355   73. May the Virgin of Pentecost obtain this for us through her intercession. By a unique vocation, she saw her Son Jesus "increase in wisdom and in stature, and in favour."[133] As He sat on her lap and later as He listened to her throughout the hidden life at Nazareth, this Son, who was "the only Son from the Father," "full of grace and truth," was formed by her in human knowledge of the Scriptures and of the history of God's plan for His people, and in adoration of the Father.[134] She in turn was the first of His disciples. She was the first in time, because even when she found her adolescent Son in the temple she received from Him lessons that she kept in her heart.[135] She was the first disciple above all else because no one has been "taught by God"[136] to such depth. She was "both mother and disciple," as St. Augustine said of her, venturing to add that her discipleship was more important for her than her motherhood.[137] There are good grounds for the statement made in the synod hall that Mary is "a living catechism" and "the mother and model of catechists."

May the presence of the Holy Spirit, through the prayers of Mary, grant the Church unprecedented enthusiasm in the catechetical work that is essential for her. Thus will she effectively carry out, at this moment of grace, her inalienable and universal mission, the mission given her by her Teacher: "Go therefore and make disciples of all nations."[138]

With my apostolic blessing.

Given in Rome, at St. Peter's, on 16 October 1979, the second year of my pontificate.

                                                        John Paul II

---

[133] Cf. Luke 2:52.
[134] Cf. John 1:14; Heb. 10:5; S. Th., III, Q. 12, a. 2; a. 3, ad 3.
[135] Cf. Luke 2:51.
[136] Cf. John 6:45.
[137] Cf. Sermo 25, 7: PL 46, 937-938.
[138] Matt 28:19.

The Sacred Congregation for Catholic Education
15 October 1982

Introduction

1. Lay Catholics, both men and women, who devote their lives to teaching in primary and secondary schools, have become

356

more and more vitally important in recent years.[1] Whether we look at schools in general, or Catholic schools in particular, the importance is deserved.

For it is the lay teachers, and indeed all lay persons, believers or not, who will substantially determine whether or not a school realizes its aims and accomplishes its objectives.[2] In the Second Vatican Council, and specifically in the Declaration on Christian Education, the Church recognized the role and the responsibility that this situation confers on all those lay Catholics who work in any type of elementary and secondary schools, whether as teachers, directors, administrators, or auxiliary staff. The Declaration invites us to expand on its contents and deepen them; in doing this, it is not our intention to ignore or minimize the significant accomplishments of Christians who belong to other Churches, or of non-Christians, in the field of education.

357   2. The most basic reason for this new role for Catholic laity, a role which the Church regards as positive and enriching, is theological. Especially in the course of the last century, the authentic image of the laity within the People of God has become increasingly clear; it has now been set down in two documents of the Second Vatican Council, which give profound expression to the richness and uniqueness of the lay vocation: The Dogmatic Constitution on the Church, and the Decree on the Apostolate of the Laity.

358   3. Theological development has been reinforced by the social, economic, and political developments of recent years. The cultural level has progressively risen; because this is closely tied to advances in science and technology, every profession requires a more extensive preparation. To this must be added a more general awareness of the fact that every person has a right to an integral education, an education which responds to all of the needs of the human person. These two advances in human life have required, and in part have created, an extensive development of school systems everywhere in the world, together with an extraordinary increase in the number of people who are

---

[1] Second Vatican Council: Const. *LG*, 31: "The term laity is here understood to mean all the faithful except those in holy orders and those in a religious state sanctioned by the Church."
[2] Cf. Second Vatican Council: Decl. *GE*, 8.

professionally trained in education. As a result, there is a corresponding growth in the number of Catholic laity who work in the field.

This process has coincided with a notable decrease in the number of priests and Religious, both men and women, dedicated to teaching. The decrease is due to a lack of vocations, to the urgent call of other apostolic needs, and – at times – to the erroneous opinion that a school is no longer an appropriate place for the Church's pastoral activity.[3] The efficacious work that so many different Religious Congregations have traditionally accomplished through teaching activities is greatly esteemed by the Church; and so she can do no less than regret the decline in Religious personnel which has had such a profound effect on Catholic schools, especially in some countries. The Church believes that, for an integral education of children and young people, both Religious and lay Catholics are needed in the schools.

4. This Sacred Congregation sees a genuine "sign of the times" for schools in the various facts and causes described above; it is an invitation to give special attention to the role of lay Catholics, as witnesses to the faith in what can only be described as a privileged environment for human formation. Without claiming to be exhaustive, but after serious and prolonged reflection on the importance of the theme, it desires to offer some considerations which will complete what has already been said in the document "The Catholic School", and which will be of help to all those interested in the problem, inspiring them to undertake further and more extended developments of the same.

359

I. The Identity of the Lay Catholic in a School

5. It seems necessary to begin by trying to delineate the identity of the lay Catholics who work in a school; the way in which they bear witness to the faith will depend on this specific identity, in the Church and in this particular field of labour. In trying to contribute to the investigation, it is the intention of this

360

---

[3] Cf. Sacred Congregation for Catholic Education: *The Catholic School*, 19 March 1979, 18-22.

Sacred Congregation to offer a service to lay Catholics who work in schools (and who should have a clear idea of the specific character of their vocation), and also to the People of God (who need to have a true picture of the laity as an active element, accomplishing an important task for the entire Church through their labour).

The laity in the Church

361   6. The lay Catholic working in a school is, along with every Christian, a member of the People of God. As such, united to Christ through Baptism, he or she shares in the basic dignity that is common to all members. For, "they share a common dignity from their rebirth in Christ. They have the same filial grace and the same vocation to perfection. They possess in common one salvation, one hope, and one undivided charity".[4] Although it is true that, in the Church, "by the will of Christ, some are made teachers, dispensers of mysteries and shepherds on behalf of others, yet all share a true equality with regard to the dignity and to the activity common to all the faithful for the building up of the Body of Christ".[5]

Every Christian, and therefore also every lay person, has been made a sharer in "the priestly, prophetic, and kingly functions of Christ",[6] and their apostolate "is a participation in the saving mission of the Church itself ... All are commissioned to that apostolate by the Lord Himself".[7]

362   7. This call to personal holiness and to apostolic mission is common to all believers; but there are many cases in which the life of a lay person takes on specific characteristics which transform this life into a specific "wonderful" vocation within the Church. The laity "seeks the kingdom of God by engaging in temporal affairs and by ordering them according to the plan of God".[8] They live in the midst of the world's activities and professions, and in the ordinary circumstances of family and social life; and there they are called by God so that by exercising

---

[4] Second Vatican Council: Const. *LG*, 32.
[5] *Ibid.*
[6] *Ibid.*, 31.
[7] *Ibid.*, 33.
[8] *Ibid.*, 31.

their proper function and being led by the spirit of the Gospel they can work for the sanctification of the world from within, in the manner of leaven. In this way they can make Christ known to others, especially by the testimony of a life resplendent in faith, hope, and charity".[9]

363

8. The renewal of the temporal order, giving it a Christian inspiration, is the special role of the laity; this should encourage them to heal "the institutions and conditions of the world"[10] when it is seen that these can be inducements to sin. In this way, human reality is raised up, and conformed to the Gospel as far as this is possible; and "the world is permeated by the Spirit of Christ, and more effectively achieves its purpose in justice, charity, and peace".[11] "Therefore, by their competence in secular fields, and by their personal activity, elevated from within by the grace of Christ, let them labour vigorously so that, by human labour, technical skill, and civic culture, created goods may be perfected for the benefit of every last person ... and be more suitably distributed among them".[12]

364

9. The evangelisation of the world involves an encounter with such. a wide variety and complexity of different situations that very frequently, in concrete circumstances and for most people, only the laity can be effective witnesses of the Gospel. Therefore, "the laity are called in a special way to make the Church present and operative in those places and circumstances where only through them can she become the salt of the earth".[13] In order to achieve this presence of the whole Church, and of the Saviour whom she proclaims, lay people must be ready to proclaim the message through their words, and witness to it in what they do.

365

10. Because of the experiences that lay people acquire in their lives, and through their presence in all of the various spheres of human activity, they will be especially capable of recognizing and clarifying the signs of the times that characterize the present

---

[9] *Ibid.*

[10] Second Vatican Council: Const. *LG*, 36; Cf. Decl. *Apostolicam actuositatem*, 7.

[11] Second Vatican Council: Const. *LG*, 36.

[12] *Ibid.*

[13] *Ibid.*, 33.

historical period of the People of God. Therefore, as a proper part of their vocation, they should contribute their initiative, their creativity, and their competent, conscious, and enthusiastic labour to this task. In this way, the whole People of God will be able to distinguish more precisely those elements of the signs that are Gospel values, or values contrary to the Gospel.

Lay Catholics in the schools

366   11. All those elements proper to the lay vocation in the Church are, surely, also true of those lay people who live their vocation in a school. But the fact that lay people can concretize their specific vocation in a variety of different sectors and areas of human life would seem to imply that the one common vocation will receive different specific characteristics from the different situations and states of life in which it is lived.

If, then, we are to have a better understanding of the school vocation of the lay Catholic, we must first look more precisely at the school.

The School

367   12. While it is true that parents are the first and foremost educators of their children[14] and that the rights and duties that they have in this regard are "original and primary with respect to the educational role of others",[15] it is also true that among the means which will assist and complement the exercise of the educational rights and duties of the family, the school has a value and an importance that are fundamental. In virtue of its mission, then, the school must be concerned with constant and careful attention to cultivating in students the intellectual, creative, and aesthetic faculties of the human person; to develop in them the ability to make correct use of their judgement, will, and affectivity; to promote in them a sense of values; to encourage just attitudes and prudent behaviour; to introduce them to the cultural patrimony handed down from previous generations; to prepare them for professional life, and to encourage the friendly

---

[14] Cf. Second Vatican Council: Decl. *GE*, 3.
[15] John Paul II, Apostolic Exhortation *Familiaris consortio*, 22 Nov. 1981, AAS, 74 (1982) 36.

interchange among students of diverse cultures and backgrounds that will lead to mutual understanding.[16] For all of these reasons, the school enters into the specific mission of the Church.

13. The function exercised by the school in society has no **368** substitute; it is the most important institution that society has so far developed to respond to the right of each individual to an education and, therefore, to full personal development; it is one of the decisive elements in the structuring and the life of society itself. In today's world, social interchange and mass media grow in importance (and their influence is sometimes harmful or counter-productive); the cultural milieu continues to expand; preparation for professional life is becoming ever more complex, more varied, and more specialized. The family, on its own, is less and less able to confront all of these serious problems; the presence of the school, then, becomes more and more necessary.

14. If the school is such an important educational instrument, **369** then the individual being educated has the right to choose the system of education – and therefore the type of school – that he or she prefers.[17] (When a person does not yet have the capacity to do this, then the parents, who have the primary rights in the education of their children,[18] have the right to make this choice). From this it clearly follows that, in principle, a State monopoly of education is not permissible,[19] and that only a pluralism of school systems will respect the fundamental right and the freedom of individuals – although the exercise of this right may be conditioned by a multiplicity of factors, according to the social realities of each country. The Church offers the Catholic school as a specific and enriching contribution to this variety of school possibilities. The lay Catholic, however, exercises the role of evangelisation in all the different schools, not only in the Catholic school, to the extent that this is possible in the diverse socio-political contexts of the present world.

The Lay Catholic as an Educator

15. The Second Vatican Council gives specific attention to **370**

---

[16] Cf. Second Vatican Council: Decl. *GE*, 5.
[17] *Ibid.*, 3.
[18] *Ibid.*, 6; Universal Declaration on Human Rights, art. 26, 3.
[19] Cf. Second Vatican Council: Decl. *GE*, 6.

the vocation of an educator, a vocation which is as proper to the laity[20] as to those who follow other states of life in the Church.

Every person who contributes to integral human formation is an educator; but teachers have made integral human formation their very profession. When, then, we discuss the school, teachers deserve special consideration: because of their number, but also because of the institutional purpose of the school. But everyone who has a share in this formation is also to be included in the discussion: especially those who are responsible for the direction of the school, or are counsellors, tutors or coordinators; also those who complement and complete the educational activities of the teacher or help in administrative and auxiliary positions. While the present analysis of the lay Catholic as an educator will concentrate on the role of the teacher, the analysis is applicable to all of the other roles, each according to their own proper activity. The material can be a basis for deep personal reflection.

371   16. The teacher under discussion here is not simply a professional person who systematically transmits a body of knowledge in the context of a school; "teacher" is to be understood as "educator" – one who helps to form human persons. The task of a teacher goes well beyond transmission of knowledge, although that is not excluded. Therefore, if adequate professional preparation is required in order to transmit knowledge, then adequate professional preparation is even more necessary in order to fulfil the role of a genuine teacher. It is an indispensable human formation, and without it, it would be foolish to undertake any educational work.

One specific characteristic of the educational profession assumes its most profound significance in the Catholic educator: the communication of truth. For the Catholic educator, whatever is true is a participation in Him who is the Truth; the communication of truth, therefore, as a professional activity, is thus fundament-ally transformed into a unique participation in the prophetic mission of Christ, carried on through one's teaching.

372   17. The integral formation of the human person, which is the purpose of education, includes the development of all the human

---

[20] *Ibid.*, 5; Cf. Paul VI, Apostolic Exhortation *Evangelii nuntiandi*, 8 December 1975, AAS 68 (1976) 70, pp. 59-60.

faculties of the students, together with preparation for professional life, formation of ethical and social awareness, becoming aware
of the transcendental, and religious education. Every school, and
every educator in the school, ought to be striving "to form strong
and responsible individuals, who are capable of making free and
correct choices", thus preparing young people "to open themselves more and more to reality, and to form in themselves a clear
idea of the meaning of life".[21]

18. Each type of education, moreover, is influenced by a **373**
particular concept of what it means to be a human person. In
today's pluralistic world, the Catholic educator must consciously
inspire his or her activity with the Christian concept of the person,
in communion with the Magisterium of the Church. It is a concept
which includes a defence of human rights, but also attributes to
the human person the dignity of a child of God; it attributes the
fullest liberty, freed from sin itself by Christ, the most exalted
destiny, which is the definitive and total possession of God Himself, through love. It establishes the strictest possible relationship
of solidarity among all persons; through mutual love and an
ecclesial community. It calls for the fullest development of all
that is human, because we have been made masters of the world
by its Creator. Finally, it proposes Christ, Incarnate Son of God
and perfect Man, as both model and means; to imitate Him, is, for
all men and women, the inexhaustible source of personal and
communal perfection. Thus, Catholic educators can be certain
that they make human beings more human.[22] Moreover, the
special task of those educators who are lay persons is to offer to
their students a concrete example of the fact that people deeply
immersed in the world, living fully the same secular life as the
vast majority of the human family, possess this same exalted
dignity.

19. The vocation of every Catholic educator includes the **374**
work of ongoing social development: to form men and women
who will be ready to take their place in society, preparing them in
such a way that they will make the kind of social commitment

---

[21] Sacred Congregation for Catholic Education: *The Catholic School*, 31.
[22] Cf. Paul VI, Encyclical Letter *Populorum progressio*; 26 March 1967, AAS
59 (1967), 19, pp. 267-268; cf. John Paul II, *Discourse to UNESCO*, 2 June
1980, AAS 72 (1980) 11, p. 742.

which will enable them to work for the improvement of social structures, making these structures more conformed to the principles of the Gospel. Thus, they will form human beings who will make human society more peaceful, fraternal, and communitarian. Today's world has tremendous problems: hunger, illiteracy and human exploitation; sharp contrasts in the standard of living of individuals and of countries; aggression and violence, a growing drug problem, legalization of abortion, along with many other examples of the degradation of human life. All of this demands that Catholic educators develop in themselves, and cultivate in their students, a keen social awareness and a profound sense of civic and political responsibility. The Catholic educator, in other words, must be committed to the task of forming men and women who will make the "civilization of love"[23] a reality.

But lay educators must bring the experience of their own lives to this social development and social awareness, so that students can be prepared to take their place in society with an appreciation of the specific role of the lay person – for this is the life that nearly all of the students will be called to live.

375   20. A school uses its own specific means for the integral formation of the human person: the communication of culture. It is extremely important, then, that the Catholic educator reflect on the profound relationship that exists between culture and the Church. For the Church not only influences culture and is, in turn, conditioned by culture; the Church embraces everything in human culture which is compatible with Revelation and which it needs in order to proclaim the message of Christ and express it more adequately according to the cultural characteristics of each people and each age. The close relationship between culture and the life of the Church is an especially clear manifestation of the unity that exists between creation and redemption.

For this reason, if the communication of culture is to be a genuine educational activity, it must not only be organic, but also critical and evaluative, historical and dynamic. Faith will provide Catholic educators with some essential principles for critique and evaluation; faith will help them to see all of human history as a

---

[23] Paul VI, *Discourse on Christmas Night*, 25 December 1976, AAS 68 (1976) p. 145.

history of salvation which culminates in the fulness of the Kingdom. This puts culture into a creative context, constantly being perfected.

Here too, in the communication of culture, lay educators have a special role to play. They are the authors of, and the sharers in, the more lay aspects of culture; their mission, then, is to help the students come to understand, from a lay point of view, the global character that is proper to culture, the synthesis which will join together the lay and the religious aspects of culture, and the personal contribution which those in the lay state can be expected to make to culture.

21. The communication of culture in an educational context **376** involves a methodology, whose principles and techniques are collected together into a consistent pedagogy. A variety of pedagogical theories exist; the choice of the Catholic educator, based on a Christian concept of the human person, should be the practice of a pedagogy which gives special emphasis to direct and personal contact with the students. If the teacher undertakes this contact with the conviction that students are already in possession of fundamentally positive values, the relationship will allow for an openness and a dialogue which will facilitate an understanding of the witness to faith that is revealed through the behaviour of the teacher.

22. Everything that the Catholic educator does in a school **377** takes place within the structure of an educational community, made up of the contacts and the collaboration among all of the various groups – students, parents, teachers, directors, non-teaching staff – that together are responsible for making the school an instrument for integral formation. Although it is not exhaustive, this concept of the scholarly institution as an educational community, together with a more widespread awareness of this concept, is one of the most enriching developments for the contemporary school. The Catholic educator exercises his or her profession as a member of one of the constitutive elements of this community. The professional structure itself offers an excellent opportunity to live – and bring to life in the students the communitarian dimension of the human person. Every human being is called to live in a community, as a social being, and as a member of the People of God.

Therefore, the educational community of a school is itself a "school". It teaches one how to be a member of the wider social communities; and when the educational community is at the same time a Christian community – and this is what the educational community of a Catholic school must always be striving toward – then it offers a great opportunity for the teachers to provide the students with a living example of what it means to be a member of that great community which is the Church.

378   23. The communitarian structure of the school brings the Catholic educator into contact with a wide and rich assortment of people; not only the students, who are the reason why the school and the teaching profession exist, but also with one's colleagues in the work of education, with parents, with other personnel in the school, with the school directors. The Catholic educator must be a source of spiritual inspiration for each of these groups, as well as for each of the scholastic and cultural organizations that the school comes in contact with, for the local Church and the parishes, for the entire human ambience in which he or she is inserted and, in a variety of ways, should have an effect on. In this way, the Catholic educator is called to display that kind of spiritual inspiration which will manifest different forms of evangelisation.

379   24. To summarize: The Lay Catholic educator is a person who exercises a specific mission within the Church by living, in faith, a secular vocation in the communitarian structure of the school: with the best possible professional qualifications, with an apostolic intention inspired by faith, for the integral formation of the human person, in a communication of culture, in an exercise of that pedagogy which will give emphasis to direct and personal contact with students, giving spiritual inspiration to the educational community of which he or she is a member, as well as to all the different persons related to the educational community. To this lay person, as a member of this community, the family and the Church entrust the school's educational endeavour. Lay teachers must be profoundly convinced that they share in the sanctifying, and therefore educational mission of the Church; they cannot regard themselves as cut off from the ecclesial complex.

II. How to live one's Personal Identity

25. The human person is called to be a worker; work is one **380** of the characteristics which distinguish human beings from the rest of creatures.[24] From this it is evident that it is not enough to possess a vocational identity, an identity which involves the whole person; it must be lived. More concretely, if, through their work, human beings must contribute "above all to elevating unceasingly the cultural and moral level of society",[25] then the educator who does not educate can no longer truly be called an educator. And if there is no trace of Catholic identity in the education, the educator can hardly be called a Catholic educator. Some of the aspects of this living out of one's identity are common and essential; they must be present no matter what the school is in which the lay educator exercises his or her vocation. Others will differ according to the diverse nature of various types of schools.

Common elements of an identity that is being lived: Realism combined with hope

26. The identity of the lay Catholic educator is, of necessity, **381** an ideal; innumerable obstacles stand in the way of its accomplishment. Some are the result of one's own personal situation; others are due to deficiencies in the school and in society; all of them have their strongest effect on children and young people. Identity crisis, loss of trust in social structures, the resulting insecurity and loss of any personal convictions, the contagion of a progressive secularization of society, loss of the proper concept of authority and lack of a proper use of freedom – these are only a few of the multitude of difficulties which, in varying degrees, according to the diverse cultures and the different countries, the adolescents and young people of today bring to the Catholic educator. Moreover, the lay state in which the teacher lives is itself seriously threatened by crises in the family and in the world of labour.

---

[24] Cf. John Paul II, Encyclical Letter *Laborem exercens*, 14. Sept. 1981, AAS 73 (1981), Foreword, p. 578.
[25] John Paul II, Encyclical Letter *Laborem exercens, Ibid.* p. 577.

These present difficulties should be realistically recognized. But they should, at the same time, be viewed and confronted with a healthy optimism, and with the forceful courage that Christian hope and a sharing in the mystery of the Cross demand of all believers. Therefore, the first indispensable necessity in one who is going to live the identity of a lay Catholic educator is to sincerely share in, and make one's own, the statements that the Church, illuminated by Divine Revelation, has made about the identity of an educator. The strength needed to do this should be found through a personal identification with Christ.

Professionalism. A Christian Concept of Humanity and of Life

382   27. Professionalism is one of the most important character-istics in the identity of every lay Catholic. The first requirement, then, for a lay educator who wishes to live out his or her ecclesial vocation, is the acquisition of a solid professional formation. In the case of an educator, this includes competency in a wide range of cultural, psychological, and pedagogical areas.[26] However, it is not enough that the initial training be at a good level; this must be maintained and deepened, always bringing it up to date. This can be very difficult for a lay teacher, and to ignore this fact is to ignore reality: salaries are often inadequate, and supplementary employment is often a necessity. Such a situation is incompatible with professional development, either because of the time required for other work, or because of the fatigue that results. In many countries, especially in those less developed, the problem is insoluble at the present time.

Even so, educators must realize that poor teaching, resulting from insufficient preparation of classes or outdated pedagogical methods, is going to hinder them severely in their call to contribute to an integral formation of the students; it will also obscure the life witness that they must present.

383   28. The entire effort of the Catholic teacher is oriented toward an integral formation of each student. New horizons will be opened to students through the responses that Christian revelation brings to questions about the ultimate meaning of the human person, of human life, of history, and of the world. These

---

[26] Cf. above, 16.

must be offered to the students as responses which flow out of the profound faith of the educator, but at the same time with the greatest sensitive respect for the conscience of each student. Students will surely have many different levels of faith response; the Christian vision of existence must be presented in such a way that it meets all of these levels, ranging from the most elementary evangelisation all the way to communion in the same faith. And whatever the situation, the presentation must always be in the nature of a gift: though offered insistently and urgently, it cannot be imposed.

On the other hand, the gift cannot be offered coldly and abstractly. It must be seen as a vital reality, one which deserves the commitment of the entire person, something which is to become a part of one's own life.

Synthesis of Faith, Culture and Life

29. For the accomplishment of this vast undertaking, many **384** different educational elements must converge; in each of them, the lay Catholic must appear as a witness to faith. An organic, critical, and value-oriented communication of culture[27] clearly includes the communication of truth and knowledge; while doing this, a Catholic teacher should always be alert for opportunities to initiate the appropriate dialogue between culture and faith – two things which are intimately related – in order to bring the interior synthesis of the student to this deeper level. It is, of course, a synthesis which should already exist in the teacher.

30. Critical transmission also involves the presentation of a **385** set of values and counter-values. These must be judged within the context of an appropriate concept of life and of the – human person. The Catholic teacher, therefore, cannot be content simply to present Christian values as a set of abstract objectives to be admired, even if this be done positively and with imagination; they must be presented as values which generate human attitudes, and these attitudes must be encouraged in the students. Examples of such attitudes would be these: a freedom which includes respect for others; conscientious responsibility; a sincere and constant search for truth; a calm and peaceful critical spirit; a

---

[27] Cf. above, 20.

spirit of solidarity with and service toward all other persons; a sensitivity for justice; a special awareness of being called to be positive agents of change in a society that is undergoing continuous transformation.

Since Catholic teachers frequently have to exercise their mission within a general atmosphere of secularization and unbelief, it is important that they not be limited to a mentality that is merely experimental and critical; thus, they will be able to bring the students to an awareness of the transcendental, and dispose them to welcome revealed truth.

386   31. In the process of developing attitudes such as these, the teacher can more easily show the positive nature of the behaviour that flows from such attitudes. Ideally, attitudes and behaviour will gradually be motivated by, and flow out of, the interior faith of the individual student. In this way, the fulness of faith will be achieved; it will then extend to such things as filial prayer, sacramental life, love for one another, and a following of Jesus Christ – all of the elements that form a part of the specific heritage of the faithful. Knowledge, values, attitudes, and behaviour fully integrated, with faith will result in the student's personal synthesis of life and faith. Very few Catholics, then, have the opportunity that the educator has to accomplish the very purpose of evangelisation: the incarnation of the Christian message in the lives of men and women.

Personal Life Witness. Direct and Personal Contact with Students

387   32. Conduct is always much more important than speech; this fact becomes especially important in the formation period of students. The more completely an educator can give concrete witness to the model of the ideal person that is being presented to the students, the more this ideal will be believed and imitated. For it will then be seen as something reasonable and worthy of being lived, something concrete and realizable. It is in this context that the faith witness of the lay teacher becomes especially important. Students should see in their teachers the Christian attitude and behaviour that is often so conspicuously absent from the secular atmosphere in which they live. Without this witness, living in such an atmosphere, they may begin to regard Christian behaviour as an impossible ideal. It must never be forgotten that, in the crises "which have their greatest effect on the younger generations ", the most important element in the educational endeavour is "always the individual person: the person, and the moral dignity of that person which is the result of his or her principles, and the conformity of actions with those principles".[28]

33. In this context, what was said above about direct and personal contact between teachers and students[29] becomes especially significant: it is a privileged opportunity for giving witness. A personal relationship is always a dialogue rather than a monologue, and the teacher must be convinced that the enrichment in the relationship is mutual. But the mission must never be lost sight of: the educator can never forget that students need a companion and guide during their period of growth; they need help from others in order to overcome doubts and dis-orientation. Also, rapport with the students ought to be a prudent combination of familiarity and distance; and this must be adapted to the need of each individual student. Familiarity will make a personal relationship easier, but a certain distance is also needed: students need to learn how to express their own personality without being pre-conditioned; they need to be freed from inhibitions in the responsible exercise of their freedom.

388

It is good to remember here that a responsible use of freedom also involves the choice of one's own state of life. In contacts with those students who are believers, Catholic teachers should not be hesitant to discuss the question of one's personal vocation in the Church. They should try to discover and cultivate vocations to the priesthood or to Religious life, or the call to live a private commitment in a Secular Institute or Catholic apostolic organization; these latter possibilities are areas which are often neglected. And they should also help students to discern a vocation to marriage or to celibacy, including consecrated celibacy, within the lay state. This direct and personal contact is not just a methodology by which the teacher can help in the formation of the students; it is also the means by which teachers learn what they need to know about the students in order to guide them adequately. The

---

[28] John Paul II, *Discourse to UNESCO*, 2 June 1980, AAS 72 (1980) 11, p. 742.
[29] Cf. above, 21.

difference in generation is deeper, and the time between generations is shorter, today more than ever before; direct contact, then, is more necessary than ever.

Communitarian aspects

389 34. Along with a proper development of their individual personalities, and as an integral part of this process, students should be guided by their Catholic teachers toward the development of an attitude of sociability: toward others in the educational community, in the other communities that they may belong to, and with the entire human community. Lay Catholic educators are also members of the educational community; they influence, and are influenced by, the social ambience of the school. Therefore, close relationship should be established with one's colleagues; they should work together as a team. And teachers should establish close relationships with the other groups that make up the educational community, and be willing to contribute their share to all of the diverse activities that make up the common educational endeavour of a scholastic institution.

The family is "the first and fundamental school of social living"[30] therefore, there is a special duty to accept willingly and even to encourage opportunities for contact with the parents of students. These contacts are very necessary, because the educational task of the family and that of the school complement one another in many concrete areas; and they will facilitate the "serious duty" that parents have "to commit themselves totally to a cordial and active relationship with the teachers and the school authorities".[31] Finally, such contacts will offer to many families the assistance they need in order to educate their own children properly; and thus fulfil the "irreplaceable and inalienable"[32] function that is theirs.

390 35. A teacher must also be constantly attentive to the socio-cultural, economic, and political environment of the school: in the immediate area that the school is located in, and also in the region and the nation. Given today's means of communication, the

---

[30] John Paul II, Apostolic Exhortation *Familiaris consortio*, AAS, 74 (1982) 37, p. 127.
[31] *Ibid.*, 40.
[32] *Ibid.*, 36.

national scene exerts a great influence on the local situation. Only close attention to the global reality – local, national, and international – will provide the data needed to give the kind of formation that students need now, and to prepare them for the future that can now be predicted.

36. While it is only natural to expect lay Catholic educators to give preference to Catholic professional associations, it is not foreign to their educational role to participate in and collaborate with all educational groups and associations, along with other groups that are connected with education. They should also lend support to the struggle for an adequate national educational policy, in whatever ways such support is possible. Their involvement may also include Trade Union activity, though always mindful of human rights and Christian educational principles.[33] Lay teachers should be reminded that professional life can sometimes be very remote from the activities of associations; they should realize that if they are never involved in or even aware of these activities, this absence could be seriously harmful to important educational issues.

It is true that there is often no reward for such activities; success or failure depends on the generosity of those who participate. But when there are issues at stake so vital that the Catholic teacher cannot ignore them, then generosity is urgently needed.

391

A Vocation, rather than a Profession

37. The work of a lay educator has an undeniably professional aspect; but it cannot be reduced to professionalism alone. Professionalism is marked by, and raised to, a supernatural Christian vocation. The life of the Catholic teacher must be marked by the exercise of a personal vocation in the Church, and not simply by the exercise of a profession. In a lay vocation, detachment and generosity are joined to legitimate defence of personal rights; but it is still a vocation, with the fulness of life and the personal commitment that the word implies. It offers ample opportunity for a life filled with enthusiasm.

392

---

[33] Cf. John Paul II, Encyclical Letter *Laborem exercens*, 14 September 1981, AAS 73 (1981) 20, pp. 629-632.

It is, therefore, very desirable that every lay Catholic educator become fully aware of the importance, the richness, and the responsibility of this vocation. They should fully respond to all of its demands, secure in the knowledge that their response is vital for the construction and ongoing renewal of the earthly city, and for the evangelisation of the world.

Elements of the Catholic educational vocation which are specific to different types of schools
In the Catholic School

393

38. The distinctive feature of the Catholic school is "to create for the school community an atmosphere enlivened by the gospel spirit of freedom and charity. It aims to help the adolescent in such a way that the development of his or her own personality will be matched by the growth of that new creation which he or she becomes by baptism. It strives to relate all human culture eventually to the news of salvation, so that the light of faith will illumine the knowledge which students gradually gain of the world, of life and of the human race".[34] From all this, it is obvious that the Catholic school "fully enters into the salvific mission of the Church, especially in the need for education in the faith",[35] and involves a sincere adherence to the Magisterium of the Church, a presentation of Christ as the supreme model of the human person, and a special care for the quality of the religious education in the school.

The lay Catholic who works in a Catholic school should be aware of the ideals and specific objectives which constitute the general educational philosophy of the institution, and realize that it is because of this educational philosophy that the Catholic school is the school in which the vocation of a lay Catholic teacher can be lived most freely and most completely. It is the model for the apostolic activity of lay Catholics in all other schools, according to the possibilities that each one of them offers. This realization will inspire lay Catholics in Catholic schools to commit themselves sincerely and personally to share in

---

[34] Second Vatican Council, Decl. *GE*, 8; cf. Sacred Congregation for Catholic Education: *The Catholic School* 34.
[35] Sacred Congregation for Catholic Education: *The Catholic School*, 9.

the responsibility for the attainment of these ideals and objectives. This is not to deny that difficulties exist; among them we mention, because of the great consequences that it has, the great heterogeneity of both students and teachers within the Catholic schools of many countries today.

39. Certain elements will be characteristic of all Catholic schools. But these can be expressed in a variety of ways; often enough, the concrete expression will correspond to the specific charism of the Religious Institute that founded the school and continues to direct it. Whatever be its origin – diocesan, Religious, or lay – each Catholic school can preserve its own specific character, spelled out in an educational philosophy, rationale, or in its own pedagogy. Lay Catholics should try to understand the special characteristics of the school they are working in, and the reasons that have inspired them. They should try to so identify themselves with these characteristics that their own work will help toward realizing the specific nature of the school. **394**

40. As a visible manifestation of the faith they profess and the life witness they are supposed to manifest,[36] it is important that lay Catholics who work in a Catholic school participate simply and actively in the liturgical and sacramental life of the school. Students will share in this life more readily when they have concrete examples: when they see the importance that this life has for believers. In today's secularized world, students will see many lay people who call themselves Catholics, but who never take part in liturgy or sacraments. It is very important that they also have the example of lay adults who take such things seriously, who find in them a source and nourishment for Christian living. **395**

41. The educational community of a Catholic school should be trying to become a Christian community: a genuine community of faith. This will not take place, it will not even begin to happen, unless there is a sharing of the Christian commitment among at least a portion of each of the principal groups that make up the educational community: parents, teachers, and students. It is highly desirable that every lay Catholic, especially the educator, be ready to participate actively in groups of pastoral **396**

---

[36] Cf. above, 29 and 32.

inspiration, or in other groups capable of nourishing a life lived according to the Gospel.

397   42. At times there are students in Catholic schools who do not profess the Catholic faith, or perhaps are without any religious faith at all. Faith does not admit of violence; it is a free response of the human person to God as He reveals Himself. Therefore, while Catholic educators will teach doctrine in conformity with their own religious convictions and in accord with the identity of the school, they must at the same time have the greatest respect for those students who are not Catholics. They should be open at all times to authentic dialogue, convinced that in these circumstances the best testimony that they can give of their own faith is a warm and sincere appreciation for anyone who is honestly seeking God according to his or her own conscience.[37]

398   43. Education in the faith is a part of the finality of a Catholic school. The more fully the educational community represents the richness of the ecclesial community, the more capable it will be of fulfilling this mission. When priests, men and women Religious, and lay people are all present together in a school, they will present students with a living image of this richness, which can lead to a better understanding of the reality of the Church. Lay Catholics should reflect on the importance of their presence, from this point of view, alongside the priests and Religious. For each of these types of ecclesial vocation presents to the students its own distinct incarnational model: lay Catholics, the intimate dependence of earthly realities on God in Christ, the lay professional as one who disposes the world toward God; the priest, the multiple sources of grace offered by Christ to all believers through the sacraments, the revealing light of the Word, and the character of service which clothes the hierarchical structure of the Church; Religious, the radical spirit of Beatitudes, the continuous call of the Kingdom as the single definitive reality, the love of Christ, and the love of all men and women in Christ.

399   44. If each vocation has its own distinct characteristics, then all should be aware of the fact that a mutual and complementary presence will be a great help in ensuring the character of the Catholic school. This means that each one should be dedicated to

---

[37] Cf. Second Vatican Council, Decl. *Dignitatis humanae*, 3.

the search for unity and coordination. Furthermore, the attitude of the lay people should be one which will help to insert the Catholic school into pastoral activities, in union with the local Church – a perspective which must never be forgotten – in ways that are complementary to the activities of parish ministry. The initiatives and experiences of lay people should also help to bring about more effective relationships and closer collaboration among Catholic schools, as well as between Catholic schools and other schools – especially those which share a Christian orientation – and with society as a whole.

45. Lay Catholic educators must be very aware of the real **400** impoverishment which will result if priests and Religious disappear from the Catholic schools, or noticeably decline in number. This is to be avoided as far as is possible; and yet, the laity must prepare themselves in such a way that they will be able to maintain Catholic schools on their own whenever this becomes necessary or at least more desirable, in the present or in the future. Historical forces at work in the schools of today lead to the conclusion that, at least for the immediate future, continued existence of Catholic schools in many traditionally Catholic countries is going to depend largely on the laity, just as that existence has depended and does depend, with great fruit, on lay people – in so many of the young Churches. This responsibility cannot be assumed with passive attitudes of fear and regret; it is a responsibility that offers a challenge to firm and effective action. And this action should even now look to and plan for the future with the help of the Religious Institutes who see their possibilities diminishing in the days immediately ahead.

46. There are times in which the Bishops will take advantage **401** of the availability of competent lay persons who wish to give clear Christian witness in the field of education, and will entrust them with complete direction of Catholic schools, thus incorporating them more closely into the apostolic mission of the Church.[38]

Given the ever greater expansion of the field of education, the Church needs to take advantage of every available resource for the Christian education of youth. To increase the participation of

---

[38] Cf. *Apostolicam actuositatem*, 2.

lay Catholic educators is not meant to diminish the importance of those schools directed by Religious Congregations in any way. The unique kind of witness that men and women Religious give in their own teaching centres, whether as individuals or as a community, surely implies that these schools are more necessary than ever in a secularized world.

Few situations are as apt as their own schools for the members of a Religious community to give this kind of witness. For in the schools, Religious men and women establish an immediate and lasting contact with young people, in a context in which the truths of faith frequently come up spontaneously as a means to illuminate the varied dimensions of existence. This contact has a special importance at a time of life in which ideas and experiences leave such a lasting impression on the personality of the students.

However, the call of the Church to lay Catholic educators, to commit themselves to an active apostolate in education, is not a call limited to the Church's own schools. It is a call that extends to the entire vast teaching field, to the extent in which it may be possible to give Christian witness in teaching.

In Schools that have different educational philosophies

402   47. We now consider all those schools, public or private, whose educational philosophy is different from that of the Catholic school, but is not essentially incompatible with the Christian concept of the human person and of life. Schools of this type form the vast majority of the schools that exist in the world. Their educational philosophy may be developed by means of a well-defined concept of the human person and of life; more simply and narrowly, they may have a determined ideology;[39] or the school may admit the coexistence of a variety of philosophies and ideologies among the teachers, within the framework of some general principles. "Coexistence" should be understood here as a manifestation of pluralism: in such schools, each of the educators gives lessons, explains principles, and promotes values according to his or her own concept of the human person, and specific

---

[39] The concept here is a more ample one: a system of ideas joined to social, economic, and/or political structures.

ideology. We do not speak here about the so-called neutral school because, in practice, such a school does not exist.

48. In today's pluralistic and secularized world, it will frequently happen that the presence of lay Catholics in these schools is the only way in which the Church is present. This is a concrete example of what was said above: that the Church can only reach out to certain situations or institutions through the laity.[40] A clear awareness of this fact will be a great help to encourage lay Catholics to assume the responsibility that is theirs.

49. Lay Catholic teachers should be influenced by a Christian faith vision in the way they teach their course, to the extent that this is consistent with the subject matter, and the circumstances of the student body and the school. In doing this, they will help students to discover true human values; and even though they must work within the limitations proper to a school that makes no attempt to educate in the faith, in which many factors will actually work directly against faith education, they will still be able to contribute to the beginnings of a dialogue between faith and culture. It is a dialogue which may, one day, lead to the students' genuine synthesis of the two. This effort can be especially fruitful for those students who are Catholics; it can be a form of evangelisation for those who are not.

50. In a pluralistic school, living according to one's faith must be joined to careful respect for the ideological convictions and the work of the other educators, assuming always that they do not violate the human rights of the students. Mutual respect should lead to constructive dialogue, especially with other Christians, but with all men and women of good will. In this way it can become clearly evident that religious and human freedom, the logical fruit of a pluralistic society, is not only defended in theory by Christian faith, but also concretely practised.

51. Active participation in the activities of colleagues, in relationships with other members of the educational community; and especially in relationships with parents of the students, is extremely important. In this way the objectives, programs, and teaching methods of the school in which the lay Catholic is

403

404

405

406

---

[40] Cf. above 9.

working can be gradually impregnated with the spirit of the Gospel.

407   52. Professional commitment; support of truth, justice and freedom; openness to the point of view of others, combined with an habitual attitude of service; personal commitment to the students, and fraternal solidarity with everyone; a life that is integrally moral in all its aspects. The lay Catholic who brings all of this to his or her work in a pluralist school becomes a living mirror, in whom every individual in the educational community will see reflected an image of one inspired by the Gospel.

In other schools

408   53. Here we consider more specifically the situation in schools of what are called mission countries, or countries where the practice of Christianity has almost totally disappeared. The lay Catholic may be the only presence of the Church, not only in the school, but also in the place in which he or she is living. The call of faith makes this situation especially compelling: the lay Catholic teacher may be the only voice that proclaims the message of the Gospel: to students, to other members of the educational community, to everyone that he or she comes in contact with, as an educator or simply as a person.[41] Everything that has been said above about awareness of responsibility, a Christian perspective in teaching (and in education more generally), respect for the convictions of others, constructive dialogue with other Christians as well as with those who do not believe in Christianity, active participation in various school groups, and, most important of all, personal life witness all of these things become crucially important in this type of school situation.

409   54. Finally, we cannot forget those lay Catholics who work in schools in countries where the Church is persecuted, where one who is known to be a Christian is forbidden to function as an educator. The orientation of the school is atheist; laity who work in them must conceal the fact that they are believers. In this difficult situation simple presence, if it is the silent but vital presence of a person inspired by the Gospel, is already an efficacious

---

[41] Cf. Second Vatican Council, Decl. *AG*, 21.

proclamation of the message of Christ. It is a counterbalance to the pernicious intentions of those who promote an atheistic education in the school. And this witness, when joined to personal contact with the students, can, in spite of the difficulties, lead to opportunities for more explicit evangelisation. Although forced to live his or her Catholicism anonymously, the lay educator can still be (because of regrettable human and religious motives) the only way that many of the young people in these countries can come to some genuine knowledge of the Gospel and of the Church, which are distorted and attacked in the school.

55. In every kind of school, the Catholic educator will not infrequently come in contact with non-Catholic students, especially in some countries. The attitude should not only be one of respect, but also welcoming, and open to dialogue motivated by a universal Christian love. Furthermore, they should always remember that true education is not limited to the imparting of knowledge; it promotes human dignity and genuine human relationships, and prepares the way for opening oneself to the Truth that is Christ. **410**

The Lay Catholic Educator as a Teacher of Religion

56. Religious instruction is appropriate in every school, for the purpose of the school is human formation in all of its fundamental dimensions, and the religious dimension is an integral part of this formation. Religious education is actually a right – with the corresponding duties – of the student and of the parents. It is also, at least in the case of the Catholic religion, an extremely important instrument for attaining the adequate synthesis of faith and culture that has been insisted on so often. **411**

Therefore, the teaching of the Catholic religion, distinct from and at the same time complementary to catechesis properly so-called,[42] ought to form a part of the curriculum of every school.

57. The teaching of religion is, along with catechesis, "an eminent form of the lay apostolate".[43] Because of this, and **412**

---

[42] Cf. John Paul II, *Discourse to the Clerics of Rome Concerning the Teaching of Religion and Catechesis*, 5 March 1981, *Insegnamenti di Giovanni Paolo II*, 1981, IV, I, 3, p. 630.
[43] John Paul II, Apostolic Exhortation *Catechesi tradendae*, 16 October 1979, AAS 71 66, p. 1331.

because of the number of religion teachers needed for today's vast school systems, lay people will have the responsibility for religious education in the majority of cases, especially at the level of basic education.

413   58. Lay Catholics, therefore, in different places and according to different circumstances, should become aware of the great role that is offered to them in this field of religious education. Without their generous collaboration, the number of religious teachers will not be adequate to meet the need that exists; this is already the situation in some countries. In this respect, as in so many others, the Church depends on lay collaboration. The need can be especially urgent in young Churches.

414   59. The role of the religion teacher is of first importance; for "what is asked for is not that one impart one's own doctrine, or that of some other teacher, but the teaching of Jesus Christ Himself".[44] In their teaching, therefore, taking into account the nature of the group being taught, teachers of religion (and also catechists) "should take advantage of every opportunity to profit from the fruits of theological research, which can shed light on their own reflections and also on their teaching, always taking care ... to be faithful to the genuine sources, and to the light of the Magisterium", on which they depend for the proper fulfilment of their role; and 'they should refrain from upsetting the minds of children and young people ... with outlandish theories".[45] The norms of the local bishop should be faithfully followed in everything that has to do with their own theological and pedagogical formation, and also in the course syllabi; and they should remember that, in this area above all, life witness and an intensely lived spirituality have an especially great importance.

III. The Formation that is needed if Lay Catholics are to give Witness to the Faith in a School

415   60. The concrete living out of a vocation as rich and profound as that of the lay Catholic in a school requires an appropriate formation, both on the professional plane and on the

---

[44] *Ibid.*, 6.
[45] *Ibid.*, 61.

religious plane. Most especially, it requires the educator to have a mature spiritual personality, expressed in a profound Christian life. "This calling" says the Second Vatican Council, speaking about educators, requires "extremely careful preparation".[46] "(Teachers) should therefore be trained with particular care, so that they may be enriched with both secular and religious knowledge, appropriately certified, and may be equipped with an educational skill which reflects modern day findings."[47] The need for an adequate formation is often felt most acutely in religious and spiritual areas; all too frequently, lay Catholics have not had a religious formation that is equal to their general, cultural, and, most especially, professional formation.

Awareness and Stimulation

61. Generally speaking, lay Catholics preparing themselves **416** for work in a school have a genuine human vocation; they are very aware of the good professional formation that they need in order to become educators. But an awareness that is limited only to the professional level is not what ought to characterize a lay Catholic, whose educational work is the basic instrument for personal sanctification and the exercise of an apostolic mission. What is being asked of lay Catholics who work in schools is precisely an awareness that what they are doing is exercising a vocation. To what extent they actually do have such an awareness is something that these lay people should be asking themselves.

62. The need for religious formation is related to this specific **417** awareness that is being asked of lay Catholics; religious formation must be broadened and be kept up to date, on the same level as, and in harmony with, human formation as a whole. Lay Catholics need to be keenly aware of the need for this kind of religious formation; it is not only the exercise of an apostolate that depends on it, but even an appropriate professional competence, especially when the competence is in the field of education.

63. The purpose of these reflections is to help awaken such a **418** consciousness, and to help each individual to consider his or her

---

[46] Second Vatican Council: Decl. *GE*, 5.
[47] *Ibid.*, 8.

own personal situation in an area which is so fundamental for the full exercise of the lay vocation of a Catholic educator. What is at stake is so essential that simply to become aware of it should be a major stimulus toward putting forth the effort needed: to acquire whatever may have been lacking in formation, and to maintain at an adequate level all that has been already acquired. Lay Catholic educators also have a right to expect that, within the ecclesial community, bishops, priests, and Religious, especially those dedicated to the apostolate of education, and also various groups and associations of lay Catholic educators, will help to awaken them to their personal needs in the area of formation, and will find the means to stimulate them so that they can give themselves more totally to the social commitment that such a formation requires.

Professional and religious formation

419   64. It may be worth noting that centres of teacher formation will differ in their ability to provide the kind of professional training that will best help Catholic educators to fulfil their educational mission. The reason for this is the close relationship that exists between the way a discipline (especially in the humanities) is taught, and the teacher's basic concept of the human person, of life, and of the world. If the ideological orientation of a centre for teacher formation is pluralist, it can easily happen that the future Catholic educator will have to do supplementary work in order to make a personal synthesis of faith and culture in the different disciplines that are being studied. It must never be forgotten, during the days of formation, that the role of a teacher is to present the class materials in such a way that students can easily discover a dialogue between faith and culture, and gradually be led to a personal synthesis of these. If we take all of this into account, it follows that it would be better to attend a centre for teacher formation under the direction of the Church where one exists, and to create such centres, if possible, where they do not yet exist.

420   65. For the Catholic educator, religious formation does not come to an end with the completion of basic education; it must be a part of and a complement to one's professional formation, and so be proportionate to adult faith, human culture, and the specific lay vocation. This means that religious formation must be oriented toward both personal sanctification and apostolic mission, for these are two inseparable elements in a Christian vocation. "Formation for apostolic mission means a certain human and well-rounded formation, adapted to the natural abilities and circumstances of each person" and requires "in addition to spiritual formation, ... solid doctrinal instruction ... in theology, ethics and philosophy".[48] Nor can we forget, in the case of an educator, adequate formation in the social teachings of the Church, which are "an integral part of the Christian concept of life",[49] and help to keep intensely alive the kind of social sensitivity that is needed.[50]

With regard to the doctrinal plane, and speaking more specifically of teachers, it may be worth recalling that the Second Vatican Council speaks of the need for religious knowledge guaranteed by appropriate certification.[51] It is highly recommended, therefore, that all Catholics who work in schools, and most especially those who are educators, obtain the necessary qualifications by pursuing programs of religious formation in Ecclesiastical Faculties or in Institutes of Religious Science that are suitable for this purpose, wherever this is possible.

66. With appropriate degrees, and with an adequate **421** preparation in religious pedagogy, they will have the basic training needed for the teaching of religion. Bishops will promote and provide for the necessary training, both for teachers of religion and for catechists; at the same time, they will not neglect the kind of dialogue with the corps of teachers being formed that can be mutually enlightening.

Updating. Permanent formation

67. Recent years have witnessed an extraordinary growth in **422** science and technology; every object, situation, or value is subjected to a constant critical analysis. One effect is that our age is characterized by change; change that is constant and accelerated,

---

[48] Second Vatican Council: Decree *Apostolicam actuositatem*, 29.
[49] John Paul II, *Discourse on the Occasion of the 90th Anniversary of Rerum Novarum*, 13 May 1981 (not delivered), *L'Osservatore Romano*, 15 May 1981.
[50] Cf. *Ibid.*
[51] Cf. Second Vatican Council: Decl. *GE*, 8.

that affects every last aspect of the human person and the society that he or she lives in. Because of change, knowledge that has been acquired, and structures that have been established, are quickly outdated; the need for new attitudes and new methods is constant.

423 68. Faced with this reality, which lay people are the first to experience, the Catholic educator has an obvious and constant need for updating: in personal attitudes, in the content of the subjects, that are taught, in the pedagogical methods that are used. Recall that the vocation of an educator requires "a constant readiness to begin anew and to adapt".[52] If the need for updating is constant, then the formation must be permanent. This need is not limited to professional formation; it includes religious formation and, in general, the enrichment of the whole person. In this way, the Church will constantly adapt its pastoral mission to the circumstances of the men and women of each age, so that the message of Jesus Christ can be brought to them in a way that is understandable and adapted to their condition.

424 69. Permanent formation involves a wide variety of different elements; a constant search for ways to bring it about is therefore required of both individuals and the community. Among the variety of means for permanent formation, some have become ordinary and virtually indispensable instruments: reading periodicals and pertinent books, attending conferences and seminars, participating in workshops, assemblies and congresses, making appropriate use of periods of free time for formation. All lay Catholics who work in schools should make these a habitual part of their own human, professional, and religious life.

425 70. No one can deny that permanent formation, as the name itself suggests, is a difficult task; not everyone succeeds in doing it. This becomes especially true in the face of the growing complexity of contemporary life and the difficult nature of the educational mission, combined with the economic insecurity that so often accompanies it. But in spite of all these factors, no lay Catholic who works in a school can ignore this present-day need. To do so would be to remain locked up in outdated knowledge, criteria, and attitudes. To reject a formation that is permanent and

---

[52] Second Vatican Council, Decl. *GE*, 5.

that involves the whole person – human, professional, and religious – is to isolate oneself from that very world that has to be brought closer to the Gospel.

IV. The Support that the Church offers to Lay Catholics working in Schools

71. The different circumstances in which lay Catholics have to carry out their work in schools can often create feelings of isolation or misunderstanding, and as a result lead to depression, or even to the giving up of teaching responsibilities. In order to find help in overcoming such difficulties; in order, more generally, to be helped to fulfil the vocation to which they are called, lay Catholics who work in schools should always be able to count on the support and aid of the entire Church.

426

Support in the faith, in the word, and in sacramental life

72. Above all else, lay Catholics will find support in their own faith. Faith is the unfailing source of the humility, the hope, and the charity needed for perseverance in their vocation.[53] For every educator is in need of humility in order to recognize one's own limitations, one's mistakes, along with the need for constant growth, and the realization that the ideal being pursued is always beyond one's grasp. Every educator needs a firm hope, because the teacher is never the one who truly reaps the fruits of the labour expended on the students. And, finally, every educator is in need of a permanent and growing charity, in order to love each of the students as an individual created in the image and likeness of God, raised to the status of a child of God by the redemption of Jesus Christ.

427

This humble faith, this hope, and this charity are supported by the Church through the Word, the life of the Sacraments, and the prayer of the entire People of God.

For the Word will speak to educators, and remind them of the tremendous greatness of their identity and of their task; Sacramental life will give them the strength they need to live this career, and bring support when they fail; the prayer of the whole

---

[53] Cf. Sacred Congregation for Catholic Education, *The Catholic School*, 75.

Church will present to God, with them and for them, with the assured response that Jesus Christ has promised, all that the human heart desires and pleads for, and even the things that it does not dare to desire or plead for.

Community support

428   73. The work of education is arduous, and very important; for that reason, its realization is delicate and complex. It requires calm, interior peace, freedom from an excessive amount of work, continuous cultural and religious enrichment. In today's society, it is seldom that conditions can all be met simultaneously. The nature of the educational vocation of lay Catholics should be publicized more frequently and more profoundly among the People of God by those in the Church most capable of doing it. The theme of education, with all that is implied in this term, should be developed more insistently; for education is one of the great opportunities for the salvific mission of the Church.

429   74. From this knowledge will logically flow understanding and proper esteem. All of the faithful should be conscious of the fact that, without lay Catholics as educators, the Church's education in the faith would lack one of its important basic elements. As far as they can, therefore, all believers should actively collaborate in the work of helping educators to reach the social status and the economic level that is their due, together with the stability and the security that they must have if they are to accomplish their task. No members of the Church can be considered exempt from the struggle to ensure that, in each of their countries, both the legislation of educational policy and the practical carrying out of this legislation reflect, as far as possible, Christian educational principles.

430   75. Contemporary world conditions should be an inducement for the hierarchy, along with those Religious Institutes that have a commitment to education, to give their support to existing groups, movements, and Catholic Associations of lay believers engaged in education; and also to create other, new groups, always searching for the type of association that will best respond to the needs of the times and the different situations in different countries. The vocation of the lay Catholic educator requires the fulfilment of many educational objectives, along with the social and religious objectives that flow from them. These will be virtually impossible to bring into reality without the united strength of strong associations.

The support of the educational institutions themselves. The Catholic school and the laity

76. The importance of the Catholic school suggests that we **431** reflect specifically on this case; it can serve as a concrete example of how other Catholic institutions should support the lay people who work in them. In speaking about lay people, this Sacred Congregation has declared without hesitation that "by their witness and behaviour, teachers are of the first importance to impart a distinctive character to Catholic schools".[54]

77. Before all else, lay people should find in a Catholic **432** school an atmosphere of sincere respect and cordiality; it should be a place in which authentic human relationships can be formed among all of the educators. Priests, men and women Religious, and lay persons, each preserving their specific vocational identity,[55] should be integrated fully into one educational community; and each one should be treated as a fully equal member of that community.

78. If the directors of the school and the lay people who work **433** in the school are to live according to the same ideals, two things are essential. First, lay people must receive an adequate salary, guaranteed by a well defined contract, for the work they do in the school: a salary that will permit them to live in dignity, without excessive work or a need for additional employment that will interfere with the duties of an educator. This may not be immediately possible without putting an enormous financial burden on the families, or making the school so expensive that it becomes a school for a small elite group; but so long as a truly adequate salary is not being paid, the laity should see in the school directors a genuine preoccupation to find the resources necessary to achieve this end. Secondly, laity should participate authentically in the responsibility for the school; this assumes that they have the ability that is needed in all areas, and are sincerely

---

[54] Sacred Congregation for Catholic Education, *The Catholic School*, 78.
[55] Cf above, 43

committed to the educational objectives which characterize a
Catholic school. And the school should use every means possible
to encourage this kind of commitment; without it, the objectives
of the school can never be fully realized. It must never be
forgotten that the school itself is always in the process of being
created, due to the labour brought to fruition by all those who
have a role to play in it, and most especially by those who are
teachers.[56] To achieve the kind of participation that is desirable,
several conditions are indispensable: genuine esteem of the lay
vocation, sharing the information that is necessary, deep
confidence, and, finally, when it should become necessary,
turning over the distinct responsibilities for teaching,
administration, and government of the school, to the laity.

434   79. As a part of its mission, an element proper to the school
is solicitous care for the permanent professional and religious
formation of its lay members. Lay people should be able to look
to the school for the orientation and the assistance that they need,
including the willingness to make time available when this is
needed. Formation is indispensable; without it, the school will
wander further and further away from its objectives. Often
enough, if it will join forces with other educational centres and
with Catholic professional organizations, a Catholic school will
not find it too difficult to organize conferences, seminars, and
other meetings which will provide the needed formation.
According to circumstances, these could be expanded to include
other lay Catholic educators who do not work in Catholic schools;
these people would thus be offered an opportunity they are
frequently in need of, and do not easily find elsewhere.

435   80. The ongoing improvement of the Catholic school, and the
assistance which the school, joined to other educational
institutions of the Church, can offer to lay Catholic educators,
depend heavily on the support that Catholic families offer to the
school – families in general, and most especially those that send
their children to these schools. Families should recognize the
level of their responsibility for a support that extends to all
aspects of the school: interest, esteem, collaboration, and

---

[56] Cf. John Paul II, Encyclical Letter *Laborem Exercens*, AAS, 73, (1981) 14, p.
614.

economic assistance. Not everyone can collaborate to the same degree or in the same way; nonetheless, each one should be ready to be as generous as possible, according to the resources that are available. Collaboration of the families should extend to a share in accomplishing the objectives of the school, and also sharing in responsibility for the school. And the school should keep the families informed about the ways in which the educational philosophy is being applied or improved on, about formation, about administration, and, in certain cases, about the management.

Conclusion

81. Lay Catholic educators in schools, whether teachers, **436** directors, administrators, or auxiliary staff, must never have any doubts about the fact that they constitute an element of great hope for the Church. The Church puts its trust in them entrusting them with the task of gradually bringing about an integration of temporal reality with the Gospel, so that the Gospel can thus reach into the lives of all men and women. More particularly, it has entrusted them with the integral human formation and the faith education of young people. These young people are the ones who will determine whether the world of tomorrow is more closely or more loosely bound to Christ.

82. This Sacred Congregation for Catholic Education echoes **437** the same hope. When it considers the tremendous evangelical resource embodied in the millions of lay Catholics who devote their lives to schools, it recalls the words with which the Second Vatican Council ended its Decree on the Apostolate of the Laity, and "earnestly entreats in the Lord that all lay persons give a glad, generous, and prompt response to the voice of Christ, who is giving them an especially urgent invitation at this moment; ... they should respond to it eagerly and magnanimously ... and, recognizing that what is His is also their own (*Phil* 2, 5), to associate themselves with Him in His saving mission ... Thus they can show that they are His co-workers in the various forms and methods of the Church's one apostolate, which must be constantly adapted to the new needs of the times. May they

always abound in the works of God, knowing that they will not labour in vain when their labour is for Him (Cf. 1 *Cor* 15:58)".[57]

William Cardinal Baum
Prefect
Antonio M. Javierre, Secretary
Titular Archbishop of Meta
Rome, 15 October 1982, Feast of St. Teresa of Avila,
in the Fourth Centenary of her death

---

[57] Second Vatican Council, Decree *Apostolicam actuositatem*, 33.

THE RELIGIOUS DIMENSION OF EDUCATION IN A CATHOLIC
SCHOOL: GUIDELINES FOR REFLECTION AND RENEWAL
Congregation for Catholic Education, 7 April 1988

Introduction

1. On 28 October 1965, the Second Vatican Council promul- **438**
gated the Declaration on Christian Education *Gravissimum
educationis*. The document describes the distinguishing characteristic of a Catholic school in this way; "The Catholic school
pursues cultural goals and the natural development of youth to the
same degree as any other school. What makes the Catholic school
distinctive is its attempt to generate a community climate in the
school that is permeated by the Gospel spirit of freedom and love.

It tries to guide the adolescents in such a way that personality development goes hand in hand with the development of the "new creature" that each one has become through baptism. It tries to relate all of human culture to the good news of salvation so that the light of faith will illumine everything that the students will gradually come to learn about the world, about life, and about the human person".[1]

The Council, therefore, declared that what makes the Catholic school distinctive is its religious dimension, and that this is to be found in *a*) the educational climate, *b*) the personal development of each student, *c*) the relationship established between culture and the Gospel, *d*) the illumination of all knowledge with the light of faith.

439   2. More than twenty years have passed since this declaration of the Council. In response to suggestions received from many parts of the world, the Congregation for Catholic Education warmly invites local ordinaries and the superiors of Religious Congregations dedicated to the education of young people to examine whether or not the words of the Council have become a reality. The Second Extraordinary General Assembly of the Synod of Bishops of 1985 said that this opportunity should not be missed! The reflection should lead to concrete decisions about what can and should be done to make Catholic schools more effective in meeting the expectations of the Church, expectations shared by many families and students.

440   3. In order to be of assistance in implementing the Council's declaration, the Congregation for Catholic Education has already published several papers dealing with questions of concern to Catholic schools. *The Catholic School*[2] develops a basic outline of the specific identity and mission of the school in today's world. *Lay Catholics in Schools: Witnesses to the Faith*[3] emphasizes the contributions of lay people, who complement the valuable service offered in the past and still offered today by so many Religious Congregations of men and women. This present document is closely linked to the preceding ones; it is based on the same

---

[1] Second Vatican Council, Decl. *GE*, 8.

[2] 19 March 1977.

[3] 15 October 1982.

sources, appropriately applied to the world of today.[4]

4 The present document restricts its attention to Catholic **441** schools: that is, educational institutions of whatever type, devoted to the formation of young people at all pre-university levels, dependent on ecclesiastical authority, and therefore falling within the competence of this Dicastery. This clearly leaves many other questions untouched, but it is better to concentrate our attention on one area rather than try to deal with several different issues at once. We are confident that attention will be given to the other questions at some appropriate time.[5]

5. The pages which follow contain guidelines which are **442** rather general. Different regions, different schools, and even different classes within the same school will have their own distinct history, ambience, and personal characteristics. The Congregation asks bishops, Religious superiors and those in charge of the schools to study these general guidelines and adapt them to their own local situations.

6. Not all students in Catholic schools are members of the **443** Catholic Church; not all are Christians. There are, in fact, countries in which the vast majority of the students are not Catholics – a reality which the Council called attention to.[6] The religious freedom and the personal conscience of individual students and

---

[4] From Vatican Council II: *Declaration on Christian Education GE*; Dogmatic Constitution on the Church *LG*; Pastoral Constitution on the Church in the Modern World *GS*; Dogmatic Constitution on Divine Revelation *Dei verbum*; Constitution on the Liturgy *Sacrosanctum Concilium*; Decree on the Apostolate of the Laity *Apostolicam actuositatem*; Decree on Missionary Activity *AG divinitus*; Declaration on Non-Christian Religions *Nostra aetate*; Decree on Ecumenism *Unitatis redintegratio*; Declaration on Religious Liberty *Dignitatis humanae*. From Paul VI, the Apostolic Exhortation *Evangelii nuntiandi* of 8 December 1975. From John Paul II, the Apostolic Exhortation *Catechesi tradendae* of 16 October 1979; in addition, a number of his talks given to educators and to young people will be cited below. From the Congregation for Clergy, the *Directorium catechisticum generale* of 11 April 1971. All of these documents will be cited by their Latin titles. In a few places, pastoral letters of bishops will be quoted.

[5] Note that the Congregation has also published *Educational Guidance in Human Love: Outlines for Sex Education*, 1 November 1983. This theme, therefore, will receive only brief and passing mention in the present document.

[6] *GE*, 9: "It is clear that the Church has a deep respect for those Catholic schools, especially in countries where the Church is young, which have large numbers of students who are not Catholics".

their families must be respected, and this freedom is explicitly recognized by the Church.[7] On the other hand, a Catholic school cannot relinquish its own freedom to proclaim the Gospel and to offer a formation based on the values to be found in a Christian education; this is its right and its duty. To proclaim or to offer is not to impose, however; the latter suggests a moral violence which is strictly forbidden, both by the Gospel and by Church law.[8]

I. The Religious Dimension in the lives of Today's Youth

1. *Youth in a changing world*

444   7. The Council provided a realistic analysis of the religious condition in the world today,[9] and paid explicit attention to the special situation of young people;[10] educators must do the same. Whatever methods they employ to do this, they should be attentive to the results of research with youth done at the local level, and they should be mindful of the fact that the young today are, in some respects, different from those that the Council had in mind.

445   8. Many Catholic schools are located in countries which are undergoing radical changes in outlook and in life-style: these countries are becoming urbanized and industrialized, and are moving into the so-called "tertiary" economy, characterized by a high standard of living, a wide choice of educational opportunities, and complex communication systems. Young people in these countries are familiar with the media from their infancy; they have been exposed to a wide variety of opinions on every possible topic, and are surprisingly well-informed even when they are still very young.

446   9. These young people absorb a wide and varied assortment of knowledge from all kinds of sources, including the school. But they are not yet capable of ordering or prioritizing what they have learned. Often enough, they do not yet have the critical ability needed to distinguish the true and good from their opposites; they

---

[7] Cf. *Dignitatis humanae*, 2; 9; 10; 12 *et passim*.

[8] C.I.C., canon 748 § 2: "Homines ad amplectendam fidem catholicam contra ipsorum conscientiam per coactionem adducere nemini umquam fas est."

[9] Cf *GS*, 4-10.

[10] *Ibid.*, 7: "The change of mentality and of structures often call into question traditional values, especially among the young ...".

have not yet acquired the necessary religious and moral criteria that will enable them to remain objective and independent when faced with the prevailing attitudes and habits of society. Concepts such as truth, beauty and goodness have become so vague today that young people do not know where to turn to find help; even when they are able to hold on to certain values, they do not yet have the capacity to develop these values into a way of life; all too often they are more inclined simply to go their own way, accepting whatever is popular at the moment.

Changes occur in different ways and at different rates. Each school will have to look carefully at the religious behaviour of the young people "in loco" in order to discover their thought processes, their life-style, their reaction to change. Depending on the situation, the change may be profound, it may be only beginning, or the local culture may be resistant to change. Even a culture resistant to change is being influenced by the all-pervasive mass media!

2. *Some common characteristics of the young*

10. Although local situations create great diversity, there are **447** characteristics that today's young people have in common, and educators need to be aware of them.

Many young people find themselves in a condition of radical instability. On the one hand they live in a one-dimensional universe in which the only criterion is practical utility and the only value is economic and technological progress. On the other hand, these same young people seem to be progressing to a stage beyond this narrow universe; nearly everywhere, evidence can be found of a desire to be released from it.

11. Others live in an environment devoid of truly human **448** relationships; as a result, they suffer from loneliness and a lack of affection. This is a widespread phenomenon that seems to be independent of life-style: it is found in oppressive regimes, among the homeless, and in the cold and impersonal dwellings of the rich. Young people today are notably more depressed than in the past; this is surely a sign of the poverty of human relationships in families and in society today.

12. Large numbers of today's youth are very worried about **449** an uncertain future. They have been influenced by a world in which human values are in chaos because these values are no

longer rooted in God; the result is that these young people are very much afraid when they think about the appalling problems in the world: the threat of nuclear annihilation, vast unemployment, the high number of marriages that end in separation or divorce, widespread poverty, etc. Their worry and insecurity become an almost irresistible urge to focus in on themselves, and this can lead to violence when young people are together – a violence that is not always limited to words.

450   13. Not a few young people, unable to find any meaning in life or trying to find an escape from loneliness, turn to alcohol drugs, the erotic, the exotic etc. Christian education is faced with the huge challenge of helping these young people discover something of value in their lives.

451   14. The normal instability of youth is accentuated by the times they are living in. Their decisions are not solidly based: today's "yes" easily becomes tomorrow's "no".

Finally, a vague sort of generosity is characteristic of many young people. Filled with enthusiasm, they are eager to join in popular causes. Too often, however, these movements are without any specific orientation or inner coherence. It is important to channel this potential for good and, when possible, give it the orientation that comes from the light of faith.

452   15. In some parts of the world it might be profitable to pay particular attention to the reasons why young people abandon their faith. Often enough, this begins by giving up religious practices. As time goes on, it can develop into a hostility toward Church structures and a crisis of conscience regarding the truths of faith and their accompanying moral values. This can be especially true in those countries where education in general is secular or even imbued with atheism. The crisis seems to occur more frequently in places where there is high economic development and rapid social and cultural change. Sometimes the phenomenon is not recent; it is something that the parents went through, and they are now passing their own attitudes along to the new generation. When this is the case, it is no longer a personal crisis, but one that has become religious and social. It has been called a "split between the Gospel and culture".[11]

---

[11] Cf *Evangelii nuntiandi*, 20.

16. A break with the faith often takes the form of total religious indifference. Experts suggest that certain patterns of behaviour found among young people are actually attempts to fill the religious void with some sort of a substitute: the pagan cult of the body, drug escape, or even those massive "youth events" which sometimes deteriorate into fanaticism and total alienation from reality. **453**

17. Educators cannot be content with merely observing these behaviour patterns; they have to search for the causes. It may be some lack at the start, some problem in the family background. Or it may be that parish and Church organizations are deficient. Christian formation given in childhood and early adolescence is not always proof against the influence of the environment. Perhaps there are cases in which the fault lies with the Catholic school itself. **454**

18. There are also a number of positive signs, which give grounds for encouragement. In a Catholic school, as in any school, one can find young people who are outstanding in every way – in religious attitude, moral behaviour, and academic achievement. When we look for the cause, we often discover an excellent family background reinforced by both Church and school. There is always a combination of factors, open to the interior workings of grace. **455**

Some young people are searching for a deeper understanding of their religion; as they reflect on the real meaning of life they begin to find answers to their questions in the Gospel. Others have already passed through the crisis of indifference and doubt, and are now ready to commit themselves – or recommit themselves – to a Christian way of life. These positive signs give us reason to hope that a sense of religion can develop in more of today's young people, and that it can be more deeply rooted in them.

19. For some of today's youth, the years spent in a Catholic school seem to have scarcely any effect. They seem to have a negative attitude toward all the various ways in which a Christian life is expressed – prayer, participation in the Mass, or frequenting of the Sacraments. Some even reject these expressions outright, especially those associated with an institutional Church. If a school is excellent as an academic institution, but does not witness to authentic values, then both good pedagogy and a **456**

concern for pastoral care make it obvious that renewal is called for – not only in the content and methodology of religious instruction, but in the overall school planning which governs the whole process of formation of the students.

457   20. The religious questioning of young people today needs to be better understood. Many of them are asking about the value of science and technology when everything could end in a nuclear holocaust; they look at how modern civilization floods the world with material goods, beautiful and useful as these may be, and they wonder whether the purpose of life is really to possess many "things" or whether there may not be something far more valuable; they are deeply disturbed by the injustice which divides the free and the rich from the poor and the oppressed.

458   21. For many young people, a critical look at the world they are living in leads to crucial questions on the religious plane. They ask whether religion can provide any answers to the pressing problems afflicting humanity. Large numbers of them sincerely want to know how to deepen their faith and live a meaningful life. Then there is the further practical question of how to translate responsible commitment into effective action. Future historians will have to evaluate the "youth group" phenomenon, along with the movements founded for spiritual growth, apostolic work, or service of others. But these are signs that words are not enough for the young people of today. They want to be active – to do something worthwhile for themselves and for others.

459   22. Catholic schools are spread throughout the world and enrol literally millions of students.[12] These students are children of their own race, nationality, traditions, and family. They are also the children of our age. Each student has a distinct origin and is a unique individual. A Catholic school is not simply a place where lessons are taught; it is a centre that has an operative educational philosophy, attentive to the needs of today's youth and illumined by the Gospel message. A thorough and exact knowledge of the real situation will suggest the best educational methods.

460   23. We must be ready to repeat the basic essentials over and

---

[12] Cf the *Annuario Statistico della Chiesa* published by the Central Statistical Office of the Church, an office within the Secretariate of State for Vatican City. By way of example, on 31 December 1985, there were 154,126 Catholic schools with 38,243,304 students.

over again, so long as the need is present. We need to integrate what has already been learned, and respond to the questions which come from the restless and critical minds of the young. We need to break through the wall of indifference, and at the same time be ready to help those who are doing well to discover a "better way", offering them a knowledge that also embraces Christian wisdom.[13] The specific methods and the steps used to accomplish the educational philosophy of the school will, therefore, be conditioned and guided by an intimate knowledge of each student's unique situation.[14]

II. The Religious Dimension of the School Climate

1. *What is a Christian school climate?*

24. In pedagogical circles, today as in the past, great stress is **461** put on the climate of a school: the sum total of the different components at work in the school which interact with one another in such a way as to create favourable conditions for a formation process. Education always takes place within certain specific conditions of space and time, through the activities of a group of individuals who are active and also interactive among themselves. They follow a programme of studies which is logically ordered and freely accepted. Therefore, the elements to be considered in developing an organic vision of a school climate are: persons, space, time, relationships, teaching, study, and various other activities.

25. From the first moment that a student sets foot in a Catholic **462** school, he or she ought to have the impression of entering a new environment, one illumined by the light of faith, and having its own unique characteristics. The Council summed this up by speaking of an environment permeated with the Gospel spirit of love and freedom.[15] In a Catholic school, everyone should be aware of the

---

[13] Cf 1 Cor 12:31.

[14] Various aspects of the religious attitudes of young people developed in this section have been the object of recent statements of the Holy Father. A handy compilation of these numerous talks can be found in a book edited by the Pontifical Council for the Laity, *The Holy Father Speaks to Youth*: 1980-1985. The book is published in several languages.

[15] Cf *GE*, 8. For the Gospel spirit of love and freedom, cf *GS*, 38: "[The Lord Jesus] reveals to us that God is love (1 John 4:8), and at the same time teaches us that the fundamental rule for human perfection, and therefore also for the

living presence of Jesus the "Master" who, today as always, is with us in our journey through life as the one genuine "Teacher", the perfect Man in whom all human values find their fullest perfection. The inspiration of Jesus must be translated from the ideal into the real. The Gospel spirit should be evident in a Christian way of thought and life which permeates all facets of the educational climate. Having crucifixes in the school will remind everyone, teachers and students alike, of this familiar and moving presence of Jesus, the "Master" who gave his most complete and sublime teaching from the cross.

463 26. Prime responsibility for creating this unique Christian school climate rests with the teachers, as individuals and as a community. The religious dimension of the school climate is expressed through the celebration of Christian values in Word and Sacrament, in individual behaviour, in friendly and harmonious interpersonal relationships, and in a ready availability. Through this daily witness, the students will come to appreciate the uniqueness of the environment to which their youth has been entrusted. If it is not present, then there is little left which can make the school Catholic.

2. The physical environment of a Catholic school

464 27. Many of the students will attend a Catholic school – often the same school – from the time they are very young children until they are nearly adults. It is only natural that they should come to think of the school as an extension of their own homes, and therefore a "school-home" ought to have some of the amenities which can create a pleasant and happy family atmosphere. When this is missing from the home, the school can often do a great deal to make up for it.

465 28. The first thing that will help to create a pleasant environment is an adequate physical facility: one that includes sufficient space for classrooms, sports and recreation, and also such things as a staff room and rooms for parent-teacher meetings, group work, etc. The possibilities for this vary from place to place; we have to be honest enough to admit that some school buildings are

---

transformation of the world, is the new commandment of love". See also 2 Cor 3:17: "Where the Spirit of the Lord is present, there is freedom".

unsuitable and unpleasant. But students can be made to feel "at home" even when the surroundings are modest, if the climate is humanly and spiritually rich.

29. A Catholic school should be an example of simplicity and evangelical poverty, but this is not inconsistent with having the **466** materials needed to educate properly. Because of rapid technological progress, a school today must have access to equipment that, at times, is complex and expensive. This is not a luxury; it is simply what a school needs to carry out its role as an educational institution. Catholic schools, therefore, have a right to expect the help from others that will make the purchase of modern educational materials possible.[16] Both individuals and public bodies have a duty to provide this support.

Students should feel a responsibility for their "school home"; they should take care of it and help to keep it as clean and neat as possible. Concern for the environment is part of a formation in ecological awareness, the need for which is becoming increasingly apparent.

An awareness of Mary's presence can be a great help toward making the school into a "home". Mary, Mother and Teacher of the Church, accompanied her Son as he grew in wisdom and grace; from its earliest days, she has accompanied the Church in its mission of salvation.

30. The physical proximity of the school to a church can **467** contribute a great deal toward achieving the educational aims. A church should not be seen as something extraneous, but as a familiar and intimate place where those young people who are believers can find the presence of the Lord: "Behold, I am with you all days"[17] Liturgy planning should be especially careful to bring the school community and the local Church together.

3. *The ecclesial and educational climate of the school*

31. The declaration *Gravissimum educationis*[18] notes an **468** important advance in the way a Catholic school is thought of: the transition from the school as an institution to the school as a

---

[16] This question was treated in *The Catholic School*, 81-82.
[17] Matt 28:20.
[18] No. 6.

community. This community dimension is, perhaps, one result of the new awareness of the Church's nature as developed by the Council. In the Council texts, the community dimension is primarily a theological concept rather than a sociological category; this is the sense in which it is used in the second chapter of *Lumen gentium*, where the Church is described as the People of God.

As it reflects on the mission entrusted to it by the Lord, the Church gradually develops its pastoral instruments so that they may become ever more effective in proclaiming the Gospel and promoting total human formation. The Catholic school is one of these pastoral instruments; its specific pastoral service consists in mediating between faith and culture: being faithful to the newness of the Gospel while at the same time respecting the autonomy and the methods proper to human knowledge.

469   32. Everyone directly involved in the school is a part of the school community: teachers, directors, administrative and auxiliary staff. Parents are central figures, since they are the natural and irreplaceable agents in the education of their children. And the community also includes the students, since they must be active agents in their own education.[19]

470   33. At least since the time of the Council, therefore, the Catholic school has had a clear identity, not only as a presence of the Church in society, but also as a genuine and proper instrument of the Church. It is a place of evangelisation, of authentic apostolate and of pastoral action – not through complementary or parallel or extracurricular activity, but of its very nature: its work of educating the Christian person. The words of the present Holy Father make this abundantly clear: "the Catholic school is not a marginal or secondary element in the pastoral mission of the bishop. Its function is not merely to be an instrument with which to combat the education given in a State school".[20]

471   34. The Catholic school finds its true justification in the

---

[19] Cf the address of John Paul II to the parents, teachers and students from the Catholic schools of the Italian Province of Lazio, 9 March 1985, *Insegnamenti*, VIII/1, p. 620. Address of John Paul II to the bishops of Lombardy, Italy, on the occasion of their "Ad limina" visit, 15 January 1982, *Insegnamenti*, V/1, 1982, p. 105.

[20] Address of John Paul II to the bishops of Lombardy, Italy, on the occasion of their "Ad limina" visit, 15 January 1982, *Insegnamenti*, V/1, 1982, p. 105.

mission of the Church; it is based on an educational philosophy in which faith, culture and life are brought into harmony. Through it, the local Church evangelizes, educates, and contributes to the formation of a healthy and morally sound life-style among its members. The Holy Father affirms that "the need for the Catholic school becomes evidently clear when we consider what it contributes to the development of the mission of the People of God, to the dialogue between Church and the human community, to the safeguarding of freedom of conscience ...". Above all, according to the Holy Father, the Catholic school helps in achieving a double objective: "of its nature it guides men and women to human and Christian perfection, and at the same time helps them to become mature in their faith. For those who believe in Christ, these are two facets of a single reality".[21]

35. Most Catholic schools are under the direction of Reli- **472** gious Congregations, whose consecrated members enrich the educational climate by bringing to it the values of their own Religious communities. These men and women have dedicated themselves to the service of the students without thought of personal gain, because they are convinced that it is really the Lord whom they are serving.[22]

Through the prayer, work and love that make up their life in community, they express in a visible way the life of the Church. Each Congregation brings the richness of its own educational tradition to the school, found in its original charism; its members each bring the careful professional preparation that is required by the call to be an educator. The strength and gentleness of their total dedication to God enlightens their work, and students gradually come to appreciate the value of this witness. They come to love these educators who seem to have the gift of eternal spiritual youth, and it is an affection which endures long after students leave the school.

36. The Church offers encouragement to these men and **473** women who have dedicated their lives to the fulfilment of an

---

[21] *Insegnamenti*, VIII/1, pp. 618f.

[22] Matt 25:40: "For indeed I tell you, as often as you have done these things to one of these least of my brothers, you have done it to me".

educational charism.[23] It urges those in education not to give up this work, even in situations where it involves suffering and persecution. In fact, the Church hopes that many others will be called to this special vocation. When afflicted by doubts and uncertainty, when difficulties are multiplied, these Religious men and women should recall the nature of their consecration, which is a type of holocaust[24] – a holocaust which is offered "in the perfection of love, which is the scope of the consecrated life".[25] Their merit is the greater because their offering is made on behalf of young people, who are the hope of the Church.

474 37. At the side of the priests and Religious, lay teachers contribute their competence and their faith witness to the Catholic school. Ideally, this lay witness is a concrete example of the lay vocation that most of the students will be called to. The Congregation has devoted a specific document to lay teachers,[26] meant to remind lay people of their apostolic responsibility in the field of education and to summon them to participate in a common mission, whose point of convergence is found in the unity of the Church. For all are active members of one Church and cooperate in its one mission, even though the fields of labour and the states of life are different because of the personal call each one receives from God.

475 38. The Church, therefore, is willing to give lay people charge of the schools that it has established, and the laity themselves establish schools. The recognition of the school as a Catholic school is, however, always reserved to the competent ecclesiastical authority[27] When lay people do establish schools, they should be especially concerned with the creation of a

---

[23] Cf *Perfectae caritatis*, 8: "There are in the Church a great number of institutes, clerical or lay, dedicated to various aspects of the apostolate, which have different gifts according to the grace that has been given to each: 'some exercise a ministry of service; some teach' (cf Rom 12:5-8)". Also see *AG divinitus*, 40.

[24] *Summa Theol.* II-II, q. 186, a. 1: "By antonomasis those are called 'religious' who dedicate themselves to the service of God as if they were offering themselves as a holocaust to the Lord".

[25] *Ibid.*, a. 2.

[26] *Lay Catholics in Schools: Witnesses to the Faith*.

[27] The norms of the Church in this respect are to be found in canons 800-803 of the Code of Canon Law.

community climate permeated by the Gospel spirit of freedom and love, and they should witness to this in their own lives.

39. The more the members of the educational community develop a real willingness to collaborate among themselves, the more fruitful their work will be. Achieving the educational aims of the school should be an equal priority for teachers, students and families alike, each one according to his or her own role, always in the Gospel spirit of freedom and love. Therefore channels of communication should be open among all those concerned with the school. Frequent meetings will help to make this possible, and a willingness to discuss common problems candidly will enrich this communication.   **476**

The daily problems of school life are sometimes aggravated by misunderstandings and various tensions. A determination to collaborate in achieving common educational goals can help to overcome these difficulties and reconcile different points of view. A willingness to collaborate helps to facilitate decisions that need to be made about the ways to achieve these goals and, while preserving proper respect for school authorities, even makes it possible to conduct a critical evaluation of the school – a process in which teachers, students and families can all take part because of their common concern to work for the good of all.

40. Considering the special age group they are working with, primary schools should try to create a community school climate that reproduces, as far as possible, the warm and intimate atmosphere of family life. Those responsible for these schools will, therefore, do everything they can to promote a common spirit of trust and spontaneity. In addition, they will take great care to promote close and constant collaboration with the parents of these pupils. An integration of school and home is an essential condition for the birth and development of all of the potential which these children manifest in one or the other of these two situations – including their openness to religion with all that this implies.   **477**

41. The Congregation wishes to express its appreciation to all those dioceses which have worked to establish primary schools in their parishes; these deserve the strong support of all Catholics. It also wishes to thank the Religious Congregations helping to sustain these primary schools, often at great sacrifice. Moreover, the Congregation offers enthusiastic encouragement to those   **478**

dioceses and Religious Congregations who wish to establish new schools. Such things as film clubs and sports groups are not enough; not even classes in catechism instruction are sufficient. What is needed is a school. This is a goal which, in some countries, was the starting point. There are countries in which the Church began with schools and only later was able to construct Churches and to establish a new Christian community.[28]

4. *The Catholic school as an open community*

479   42. Partnership between a Catholic school and the families of the students must continue and be strengthened: not simply to be able to deal with academic problems that may arise, but rather so that the educational goals of the school can be achieved. Close cooperation with the family is especially important when treating sensitive issues such as religious, moral, or sexual education, orientation toward a profession, or a choice of one's vocation in life. It is not a question of convenience, but a partnership based on faith. Catholic tradition teaches that God has bestowed on the family its own specific and unique educational mission.

480   43. The first and primary educators of children are their parents.[29] The school is aware of this fact but, unfortunately, the same is not always true of the families themselves; it is the school's responsibility to give them this awareness, Every school should initiate meetings and other programmes which will make the parents more conscious of their role, and help to establish a partnership; it is impossible to do too much along these lines. It often happens that a meeting called to talk about the children becomes an opportunity to raise the consciousness of the parents. In addition, the school should try to involve the family as much as possible in the educational aims of the school – both in helping to plan these goals and in helping to achieve them. Experience shows that parents who were once totally unaware of their role can be transformed into excellent partners.

481   44. "The involvement of the Church in the field of education

---

[28] Cf the address of Pope Paul VI to the National Congress of Diocesan Directors of the Teachers' Organizations of Catholic Action, *Insegnamenti*, I, 1963, p. 594.
[29] Cf *GE*, 3

is demonstrated especially by the Catholic school".[30] This affirmation of the Council has both historical and practical importance. Church schools first appeared centuries ago, growing up alongside monasteries, cathedrals and parish churches. The Church has always had a love for its schools, because this is where its children receive their formation. These schools have continued to flourish with the help of bishops, countless Religious Congregations, and laity; the Church has never ceased to support the schools in their difficulties and to defend them against governments seeking to close or confiscate them.

Just as the Church is present in the school, so the school is present in the Church; this is a logical consequence of their reciprocal commitment. The Church, through which the Redemption of Christ is revealed and made operative, is where the Catholic school receives its spirit. It recognizes the Holy Father as the centre and the measure of unity in the entire Christian community. Love for and fidelity to the Church is the organizing principle and the source of strength of a Catholic school.

Teachers find the light and the courage for authentic Religious education in their unity among themselves and their generous and humble communion with the Holy Father. Concretely, the educational goals of the school include a concern for the life and the problems of the Church, both local and universal. These goals are attentive to the Magisterium, and include cooperation with Church authorities. Catholic students are helped to become active members of the parish and diocesan communities. They have opportunities to join Church associations and Church youth groups, and they are taught to collaborate in local Church projects.

Mutual esteem and reciprocal collaboration will be established between the Catholic school and the bishop and other Church authorities through direct contacts. We are pleased to note that a concern for Catholic schools is becoming more of a priority of local Churches in many parts of the world.[31]

45. A Christian education must promote respect for the State   **482**

---

[30] *GE*, 8

[31] A number of recent documents from national Episcopal Conferences and from individual local ordinaries have had the Catholic school as their theme. These documents should be known and put into practice.

and its representatives, the observance of just laws, and a search for the common good. Therefore, traditional civic values such as freedom, justice, the nobility of work and the need to pursue social progress are all included among the school goals, and the life of the school gives witness to them. The national anniversaries and other important civic events are commemorated and celebrated in appropriate ways in the schools of each country.

The school life should also reflect an awareness of international society. Christian education sees all of humanity as one large family, divided perhaps by historical and political events, but always one in God who is Father of all. Therefore a Catholic school should be sensitive to and help to promulgate Church appeals for peace, justice, freedom, progress for all peoples and assistance for countries in need. And it should not ignore similar appeals coming from recognized international organizations such as UNESCO and the United Nations.

483   46. That Catholic schools help to form good citizens is a fact apparent to everyone. Both government policy and public opinion should, therefore, recognize the work these schools do as a real service to society. It is unjust to accept the service and ignore or fight against its source. Fortunately, a good number of countries seem to have a growing understanding of and sympathy for the Catholic school.[32] A recent survey conducted by the Congregation demonstrates that a new age may be dawning.

III. The Religious Dimension of School Life and Work

1. The religious dimension of school life

484   47. Students spend a large share of each day and the greater part of their youth either at school or doing activities that are related to school. "School" is often identified with "teaching"; actually, classes and lessons are only a small part of school life. Along with the lessons that a teacher gives, there is the active participation of the students individually or as a group: study, research, exercises, para-curricular activities, examinations,

---

[32] See, for example, the Resolution of the European Parliament on freedom of education in the European Community, approved by a large majority on 14 March 1984.

relationships with teachers and with one another, group activities, class meetings, school assemblies. While the Catholic school is like any other school in this complex variety of events that make up the life of the school, there is one essential difference: it draws its inspiration and its strength from the Gospel in which it is rooted. The principle that no human act is morally indifferent to one's conscience or before God has clear applications to school life: examples of it are school work accepted as a duty and done with good will; courage and perseverance when difficulties come; respect for teachers; loyalty toward and love for fellow students; sincerity, tolerance, and goodness in all relationships.

48. The educational process is not simply a human activity; it is a genuine Christian journey toward perfection. Students who are sensitive to the religious dimension of life realize that the will of God is found in the work and the human relationships of each day. They learn to follow the example of the Master, who spent his youth working and who did good to all.[33] Those students who are unaware of this religious dimension are deprived of its benefits and they run the risk of living the best years of their lives at a shallow level. **485**

49. Within the overall process of education, special mention must be made of the intellectual work done by students. Although Christian life consists in loving God and doing his will, intellectual work is intimately involved. The light of Christian faith stimulates a desire to know the universe as God's creation. It enkindles a love for the truth that will not be satisfied with superficiality in knowledge or judgment. It awakens a critical sense which examines statements rather than accepting them blindly. It impels the mind to learn with careful order and precise methods, and to work with a sense of responsibility. It provides the strength needed to accept the sacrifices and the perseverance required by intellectual labour. When fatigued, the Christian student remembers the command of Genesis[34] and the invitation of the Lord.[35] **486**

---

[33] Cf Mark 6: 3; Acts 10: 35. Useful applications of the ethics of work to the work done in school can be found in the 14 September 1981 Encyclical *Laborem exercens* of John Paul II, especially in Part Five.

[34] Gen 3: 19: "By the sweat on your face shall you get bread to eat".

[35] Luke 9: 23: "...let him take up his cross each day".

487   50. The religious dimension enhances intellectual efforts in a variety of ways: interest in academic work is stimulated by the presence of new perspectives; Christian formation is strengthened; supernatural grace is given. How sad it would be if the young people in Catholic schools were to have no knowledge of this reality in the midst of all the difficult and tiring work they have to do!

2. *The religious dimension of the school culture*

488   51. Intellectual development and growth as a Christian go forward hand in hand. As students move up from one class into the next it becomes increasingly imperative that a Catholic school help them become aware that a relationship exists between faith and human culture.[36] Human culture remains human, and must be taught with scientific objectivity. But the lessons of the teacher and the reception of those students who are believers will not divorce faith from this culture;[37] this would be a major spiritual loss. The world of human culture and the world of religion are not like two parallel lines that never meet; points of contact are established within the human person. For a believer is both human and a person of faith, the protagonist of culture and the subject of religion. Anyone who searches for the contact points will be able to find them.[38] Helping in the search is not solely the task of religion teachers; their time is quite limited, while other teachers have many hours at their disposal every day. Everyone should work together, each one developing his or her own subject area with professional competence, but sensitive to those opportunities in which they can help students to see beyond the limited horizon of human reality. In a Catholic school, and analogously in every school, God cannot be the Great Absent One or the unwelcome intruder. The Creator does not put obstacles in

---

[36] *GE*, 8: among the elements characteristic of the Catholic school, there is that of "developing the relationship between human culture and the message of salvation, so that the knowledge of the world, of life and of the human person which the students are gradually acquiring is illuminated by faith".

[37] For a description of culture and of the relationship between culture and faith, see *GS*, 54 ff.

[38] Cf Dz-Sch. 3016-3017 for the traditional doctrine on the rapport between reason and faith, as defined by Vatican Council I.

the path of someone trying to learn more about the universe he created, a universe which is given new significance when seen with the eyes of faith.

52. A Catholic secondary school will give special attention to the "challenges" that human culture poses for faith. Students will be helped to attain that synthesis of faith and culture which is necessary for faith to be mature. But a mature faith is also able to recognize and reject cultural counter-values which threaten human dignity and are therefore contrary to the Gospel.[39] No one should think that all of the problems of religion and of faith will be completely solved by academic studies; nevertheless, we are convinced that a school is a privileged place for finding adequate ways to deal with these problems. The declaration *Gravissimum educationis*,[40] echoing *Gaudium et spes*,[41] indicates that one of the characteristics of a Catholic school is that it interpret and give order to human culture in the light of faith.

489

53. As the Council points out, giving order to human culture in the light of the message of salvation cannot mean a lack of respect for the autonomy of the different academic disciplines and the methodology proper to them; nor can it mean that these disciplines are to be seen merely as subservient to faith. On the other hand, it is necessary to point out that a proper autonomy of culture has to be distinguished from a vision of the human person or of the world as totally autonomous, implying that one can negate spiritual values or prescind from them. We must always remember that, while faith is not to be identified with any one culture and is independent of all cultures, it must inspire every culture: "Faith which does not become culture is faith which is not received fully, not assimilated entirely, not lived faithfully".[42]

490

54. In a number of countries, renewal in school programming has given increased attention to science and technology. Those

491

---

[39] Cf the address of Pope John Paul II to the teachers and students of Catholic schools in Melbourne, Australia, on the occasion of his pastoral journey to East Asia and Oceania: *Insegnamenti* 28 November 1986; IX/2, 1986, pp. 1710 ff.
[40] Cf 8.
[41] Cf 53-62.
[42] Pope John Paul II, speaking at the National Congress of Catholic Cultural Organizations: *Insegnamenti*, V/1, 1982, p. 131. See also John Paul II, *Epistula qua Pontificium Consilium pro hominum Cultura instituitur*: AAS 74 (1982), p. 685.

teaching these subject areas must not ignore the religious dimension. They should help their students to understand that positive science, and the technology allied to it, is a part of the universe created by God. Understanding this can help encourage an interest in research: the whole of creation, from the distant celestial bodies and the immeasurable cosmic forces down to the infinitesimal particles and waves of matter and energy, all bear the imprint of the Creator's wisdom and power, The wonder that past ages felt when contemplating this universe, recorded by the Biblical authors,[43] is still valid for the students of today; the only difference is that we have a knowledge that is much more vast and profound. There can be no conflict between faith and true scientific knowledge; both find their source in God.

The student who is able to discover the harmony between faith and science will, in future professional life, be better able to put science and technology to the service of men and women, and to the service of God. It is a way of giving back to God what he has first given to us.[44]

492   55. A Catholic school must be committed to the development of a programme which will overcome the problems of a fragmented and insufficient curriculum. Teachers dealing with areas such as anthropology, biology, psychology, sociology and philosophy all have the opportunity to present a complete picture of the human person, including the religious dimension. Students should be helped to see the human person as a living creature having both a physical and a spiritual nature; each of us has an immortal soul, and we are in need of redemption. The older students can gradually come to a more mature understanding of all that is implied in the concept of "person": intelligence and will, freedom and feelings, the capacity to be an active and creative agent; a being endowed with both rights and duties, capable of interpersonal relationships, called to a specific mission in the world.

493   56. The religious dimension makes a true understanding of the human person possible. A human being has a dignity and a

---

[43] Wis 13:5: "Through the grandeur and beauty of the creatures we may, by analogy, contemplate their Author". Ps 18: 2ff.: "The heavens tell of the glory of God...".

[44] Cf Matt 25:14-30.

greatness exceeding that of all other creatures: a work of God that has been elevated to the supernatural order as a child of God, and therefore having both a divine origin and an eternal destiny which transcend this physical universe.[45] Religion teachers will find the way already prepared for an organic presentation of Christian anthropology.

57. Every society has its own heritage of accumulated wisdom. Many people find inspiration in these philosophical and religious concepts which have endured for millennia. The systematic genius of classical Greek and European thought has, over the centuries, generated countless different doctrinal systems, but it has also given us a set of truths which we can recognize as a part of our permanent philosophical heritage. A Catholic school conforms to the generally accepted school programming of today, but implements these programmes within an overall religious perspective. This perspective includes criteria such as the following:

Respect for those who seek the truth, who raise fundamental questions about human existence.[46] Confidence in our ability to attain truth, at least in a limited way – a confidence based not on feeling but on faith. God created us "in his own image and likeness" and will not deprive us of the truth necessary to orient our lives.[47] The ability to make judgments about what is true and what is false; and to make choices based on these judgments.[48] Making use of a systematic framework, such as that offered by our philosophical heritage, with which to find the best possible human responses to questions regarding the human person, the world, and God.[49] Lively dialogue between culture and the Gospel message.[50] The fulness of truth contained in the Gospel message itself, which embraces and integrates the wisdom of all

494

---

[45] Cf *GS*, 12; 14; 17; 22.

[46] Cf *GS*, 10.

[47] Cf Dz.-Sch. 3004 for the ability to know God through human reason, and 3005 for the ability to know other truths.

[48] 1 Thes 5: 21: "Examine all things, hold on to what is good". Phil 4: 8: "Everything that is true, noble, or just ... let all this be the object of your thoughts".

[49] Cf *GS*, 61, on the need to hold on to certain fundamental concepts.

[50] *Ibid.*, 44: "At the same time there should be a vital exchange between the Church and the diverse cultures of peoples".

cultures, and enriches them with the divine mysteries known only to God but which, out of love, he has chosen to reveal to us.[51] With such criteria as a basis, the student's careful and reflective study of philosophy will bring human wisdom into an encounter with divine wisdom.

495   58. Teachers should guide the students' work in such a way that they will be able to discover a religious dimension in the world of human history. As a preliminary, they should be encouraged to develop a taste for historical truth, and therefore to realize the need to look critically at texts and curricula which, at times, are imposed by a government or distorted by the ideology of the author. The next step is to help students see history as something real: the drama of human grandeur and human misery.[52] The protagonist of history is the human person, who projects onto the world, on a larger scale, the good and the evil that is within each individual. History is, then, a monumental struggle between these two fundamental realities,[53] and is subject to moral judgments. But such judgments must always be made with understanding.

496   59. To this end, the teacher should help students to see history as a whole. Looking at the grand picture, they will see the development of civilizations, and learn about progress in such things as economic development, human freedom, and international cooperation. Realizing this can help to offset the disgust that comes from learning about the darker side of human history. But even this is not the whole story. When they are ready to appreciate it, students can be invited to reflect on the fact that this human struggle takes place within the divine history universal salvation, At this moment, the religious dimension of history begins to shine forth in all its luminous grandeur.[54]

497   60. The increased attention given to science and technology must not lead to a neglect of the humanities: philosophy, history, literature and art. Since earliest times, each society has developed

---

[51] Cf *Dei verbum* 2.
[52] Cf Blaise Pascal, *Pensées*, fr. 397.
[53] *GS*, 37: "The whole of human history is permeated with the gigantic struggle against the powers of darkness
[54] Invaluable material for presenting the divine history of salvation can be found in *LG* and *Dei verbum*.

and handed on its artistic and literary heritage, and our human patrimony is nothing more than the sum total of this cultural wealth. Thus, while teachers are helping students to develop an aesthetic sense, they can bring them to a deeper awareness of all peoples as one great human family. The simplest way to uncover the religious dimension of the artistic and literary world is to start with its concrete expressions: in every human culture, art and literature have been closely linked to religious beliefs. The artistic and literary patrimony of Christianity, is vast and gives visible testimony to a faith that has been handed down through centuries.

61. Literary and artistic works depict the struggles of societies, of families, and of individuals. They spring from the depths of the human heart, revealing its lights and its shadows, its hope and its despair. The Christian perspective goes beyond the merely human, and offers more penetrating criteria for understanding the human struggle and the mysteries of the human spirit.[55] Furthermore, an adequate religious formation has been the starting point for the vocation of a number of Christian artists and art critics. In the upper grades, a teacher can bring students to: an even more profound appreciation of artistic works: as a reflection of the divine beauty in tangible form. Both the Fathers of the Church and the masters of Christian philosophy teach this in their writings on aesthetics – St. Augustine invites us to go beyond the intention of the artists in order to find the eternal order of God in the work of art; St. Thomas sees the presence of the Divine Word in art.[56]

498

62. A Catholic school is often attentive to issues having to do with educational methods, and this can be of great service both to civil society and to the Church. Government requirements for teacher preparation usually require historical and systematic courses in pedagogy, psychology and teaching methods. In more recent times, educational science has been subdivided into a number of areas of specialization and has been subjected to a variety of different philosophies and political ideologies; those preparing to become teachers may feel that the whole field is

499

---

[55] Cf *GS*, 62.
[56] Cf St. Augustine, *De libero arbitrio*, II, 16, 42. PL 32, 1264. St. Thomas, *Contra gentiles*, IV, 42.

confused and fragmented. Teachers of pedagogical science can help these students in their bewilderment, and guide them in the formulation of a carefully thought out synthesis, whose elaboration begins with the premise that every pedagogical current of thought contains things which are true and useful. But then one must begin to reflect, judge, and choose.

500   63. Future teachers should be helped to realize that any genuine educational philosophy has to be based on the nature of the human person, and therefore must take into account all of the physical and spiritual powers of each individual, along with the call of each one to be an active and creative agent in service to society. And this philosophy must be open to a religious dimension. Human beings are fundamentally free; they are not the property of the state or of any human organization. The entire process of education, therefore, is a service to the individual students, helping each one to achieve the most complete formation possible.

The Christian model, based on the person of Christ, is then linked to this human concept of the person – that is, the model begins with an educational framework based on the person as human, and then enriches it with supernatural gifts, virtues, and values – and a supernatural call. It is indeed possible to speak about Christian education; the Conciliar declaration provides us with a clear synthesis of it.[57] Proper pedagogical formation, finally, will guide these students to a self-formation that is both human and Christian, because this is the best possible preparation for one who is preparing to educate others.

501   64. Interdisciplinary work has been introduced into Catholic schools with positive results, for there are questions and topics that are not easily treated within the limitations of a single subject area. Religious themes should be included; they arise naturally when dealing with topics such as the human person, the family, society, or history. Teachers should be adequately prepared to deal with such questions and be ready to give them the attention they deserve.

502   65. Religion teachers are not excluded. While their primary mission must be the systematic presentation of religion, they can

---

[57] Cf *GE*, 1-2.

also be invited – within the limitations of what is concretely possible – to assist in clarifying religious questions that come up in other classes. Conversely, they may wish to invite one of their colleagues to attend a religion class, in order to have the help of an expert when dealing with some specific issue. Whenever this happens, students will be favourably impressed by the cooperative spirit among the teachers: the one purpose all of them have in mind is to help these students grow in knowledge and in commitment.

IV. Religious Instruction in the Classroom and the Religious Dimension of Formation

1. *The nature of religious instruction*

66. The mission of the Church is to evangelize, for the interior transformation and the renewal of humanity[58] For young people, the school is one of the ways for this evangelisation to take place.[59] It may be profitable to recall what the Magisterium has said: "Together with and in collaboration with the family, schools provide possibilities for catechesis that must not be neglected ... This refers especially to the Catholic school, of course: it would no longer deserve the title if, no matter how good its reputation for teaching in other areas there were just grounds for a reproach of negligence or deviation in religious education properly so-called. It is not true that such education is always given implicitly or indirectly. The special character of the Catholic school and the underlying reason for its existence, the reason why Catholic parents should prefer it, is precisely the quality of the religious instruction integrated into the overall education of the students"[60]

67. Sometimes there is an uncertainty, a difference of opinion, or an uneasiness about the underlying principles

503

504

---

[58] *Evangelii nuntiandi*, 18: "For the Church to evangelize is to bring the Good News to all aspects of humanity and, through its influence, to transform it from within, making humanity itself into some thing new".

[59] *Ibid.*, 44: "The effort to evangelize will bring great profit, through catechetical instruction given at Church, in schools wherever this is possible, and always within the Christian family".

[60] *Catechesi tradendae*, 69.

governing religious formation in a Catholic school, and therefore about the concrete approach to be taken in religious instruction. On the one hand, a Catholic school is a "civic institution"; its aim, methods and characteristics are the same as those of every other school. On the other hand, it is a "Christian community", whose educational goals are rooted in Christ and his Gospel. It is not always easy to bring these two aspects into harmony; the task requires constant attention, so that the tension between a serious effort to transmit culture and a forceful witness to the Gospel does not turn into a conflict harmful to both.

505   68. There is a close connection, and at the same time a clear distinction, between religious instruction and catechesis, or the handing on of the Gospel message.[61] The close connection makes it possible for a school to remain a school and still integrate culture with the message of Christianity. The distinction comes from the fact that, unlike religious instruction, catechesis presupposes that the hearer is receiving the Christian message as a salvific reality. Moreover, catechesis takes place within a community living out its faith at a level of space and time not available to a school: a whole lifetime.

506   69. The aim of catechesis, or handing on the Gospel message, is maturity: spiritual, liturgical, sacramental and apostolic; this happens most especially in a local Church community. The aim of the school however, is knowledge. While it uses the same elements of the Gospel message, it tries to convey a sense of the nature of Christianity, and of how Christians are trying to live their lives. It is evident, of course, that religious instruction cannot help but strengthen the faith of a believing student, just as catechesis cannot help but increase one's knowledge of the Christian message.

The distinction between religious instruction and catechesis does not change the fact that a school can and must play its specific role in the work of catechesis. Since its educational goals are rooted in Christian principles, the school as a whole is inserted into the evangelical function of the Church. It assists in and promotes faith education.

---

[61] Cf The address of Paul VI at the Wednesday audience of 31 May 1967, *Insegnamenti*, V, 1967, p. 788.

70. Recent Church teaching has added an essential note: "The basic principle which must guide us in our commitment to this sensitive area of pastoral activity is that religious instruction and catechesis are at the same time distinct and complementary. A school has as its purpose the students' integral formation. Religious instruction, therefore, should be integrated into the objectives and criteria which characterize a modern school".[62] School directors should keep this directive of the Magisterium in mind, and they should respect the distinctive characteristics of religious instruction. It should have a place in the weekly order alongside the other classes, for example; it should have its own syllabus, approved by those in authority; it should seek appropriate interdisciplinary links with other course material so that there is a coordination between human learning and religious awareness. Like other course work, it should promote culture, and it should make use of the best educational methods available to schools today. In some countries, the results of examinations in religious knowledge are included within the overall measure of student progress.

507

Finally, religious instruction in the school needs to be coordinated with the catechesis offered in parishes, in the family, and in youth associations.

2. Some basic presuppositions about religious instruction

71. It should be no surprise that young people bring with them into the classroom what they see and hear in the world around them, along with the impressions gained from the "world" of mass media. Perhaps some have become indifferent or insensitive. The school curriculum as such does not take these attitudes into account, but teachers must be very aware of them. With kindness and understanding, they will accept the students as they are, helping them to see that doubt and indifference are common phenomena, and that the reasons for this are readily understandable. But they will invite students in a friendly manner to seek and discover together the message of the Gospel, the source of joy and peace.

508

---

[62] Address of John Paul II to the priests of the diocese of Rome, 5 March 1981, *Insegnamenti*, IV/1, pp. 629 f.

The teachers' attitudes and behaviour should be those of one preparing the soil.[63] They then add their own spiritual lives, and the prayers they offer for the students entrusted to them.[64]

509   72. An excellent way to establish rapport with students is simply to talk to them – and to let them talk. Once a warm and trusting atmosphere has been established, various questions will come up naturally. These obviously depend on age and living situation, but many of the questions seem to be common among all of today's youth; and they tend to raise them at a younger age.[65] These questions are serious ones for young people, and they make a calm study of the Christian faith very difficult. Teachers should respond with patience and humility, and should avoid the type of peremptory statements that can be so easily contradicted:

Experts in history and science could be invited to class. One's own experiences and study should be used to help the students. Inspiration can be found in the numerous and carefully worked out responses which Vatican II gives to these kinds of questions. In theory at least, this patient work of clarification should take place at the beginning of each year, since it is almost certain that new questions and new difficulties will have come up during the vacation period. And experience suggests that every other opportune occasion should be taken advantage of.

510   73. It is not easy to develop a course syllabus for religious instruction classes which will present the Christian faith systematically and in a way suited to the young people of today.

The Second Extraordinary General Assembly of the Synod of Bishops in 1985 suggested that a new catechism be developed for the universal Church, and the Holy Father immediately created a commission to begin the preparatory work on this project.* When

---

[63] Cf Matt 3: 1-3 on the mission of the Precursor.

[64] Cf John 17: 9, the prayer of the Lord for those entrusted to him.

[65] Apart from strictly local concerns, these questions are generally the ones treated in university "apologetics" manuals, and are about the "preambles to the faith". But the questions acquire a specific nuance for today's students, because of the material they are studying and the world they are living in. Typical questions have to do with atheism, non-Christian religions, divisions among Christians, events in the life of the Church; the violence and injustice of supposedly Christian nations, etc.

* The *Catechism of the Catholic Church* is the result of this project – Editor's Note.

the catechism becomes available, adaptations will be necessary in order to develop course outlines that conform to the requirements of education authorities and respond to the concrete situations that depend on local circumstances of time and place.

While we await the new synthesis of Christian doctrine – the completion of the work mandated by the Synod we present by way of example an outline which is the fruit of experience. It is complete in content, faithful to the Gospel message, organic in form, and is developed according to a methodology based on the words and deeds of the Lord.

3. An outline for an organic presentation of the Christian event and the Christian message

74. As expressed by Vatican II, the task of the teacher is to summarize Christology and present it in everyday language. Depending on the level of the class, this should be preceded by a presentation of some basic ideas about Sacred Scripture, especially those having to do with the Gospels, Divine Revelation, and the Tradition that is alive in the Church.[66] With this as a base, the class begins to learn about the Lord Jesus. His person, his message, his deeds, and the historical fact of his resurrection lead to the mystery of his divinity: "You are the Christ, the Son of the living God".[67] For more mature students, this study can be expanded to include Jesus as Saviour, Priest, Teacher, and Lord of the universe. At his side is Mary his Mother, who cooperates in his mission.[68]

511

The discovery process is an important pedagogical method. The person of Jesus will come alive for the students. They will see again the example of his life, listen to his words, hear his invitation as addressed to them: "Come to me, all of you ...".[69] Faith is thus based on knowing Jesus and following him; its growth depends on each one's good will and cooperation with grace.

75. The teacher has a reliable way to bring young people

512

---

[66] Revelation, Scripture, Tradition and Christology are themes developed in *Dei verbum*, *LG*, and *GS*. Study of the Gospels should be extended to include a study of these documents.

[67] Matt 16:16.

[68] Concerning the Blessed Virgin Mary in the life of the Pilgrim Church, cf the Encyclical *Redemptoris Mater* of Pope John Paul II, no. 39.

[69] Matt 11:28.

closer to the mystery of the revealed God, to the extent that this can ever be humanly possible.[70] It is the way indicated by the Saviour: "Whoever has seen me, has seen the Father".[71] Through his person and his message we learn about God: we examine what he has said about the Father, and what he has done in the name of the Father. Through the Lord Jesus, therefore, we come to the mystery of God the Father, who created the universe and who sent his Son into the world so that all men and women might be saved.[72] Through Christ we come to the mystery of the Holy Spirit, sent into the world to bring the mission of the Son to fulfilment.[73] And thus we approach the supreme mystery of the Holy Trinity, in itself and as operative in the world. It is this mystery that the Church venerates and proclaims whenever it recites the Creed, repeating the words of the first Christian communities.

The process has great educational value. Its successful completion will help to strengthen the virtues of faith and of Christian religion, both of which have God as their object: Father, Son and Holy Spirit; known, loved and served in this life as we await an eternal life in union with them.

513   76. Students learn many things about the human person by studying science; but science has nothing to say about mystery. Teachers should help students begin to discover the mystery within the human person, just as Paul tried to help the people of Athens discover the "Unknown God". The text of John already cited[74] demonstrates that, in and through Christ, a close relationship has been established between God and each human being. The relationship has its beginning in the love of the Father; it is expressed in the love of Jesus, which led to the ultimate sacrifice of himself: "No one has greater love than this: to lay down one's life for one's friends".[75] A crowd of people constantly surrounded Jesus; they were of all types, as if representing all of humanity. As the students see this, they will begin to ask

---

[70] Cf Dz.-Sch. 2854: one cannot speak about God in the same way that one speaks about the objects of human knowledge.
[71] John 14: 9.
[72] Cf Luke 12: 24-28; John 3: 16 f.
[73] Cf John 16: 13.
[74] Cf John 3: 16 f.
[75] John 15: 13.

themselves why Jesus loves everyone, why he offers an invitation to all, why he gives his life for us all. And they will be forced to conclude that each person must be a very privileged creature of God, to be the object of so much love. This is the point at which students will begin to discover another mystery – that human history unfolds within a divine history of salvation: from creation, through the first sin, the covenant with the ancient people of God, the long period of waiting until finally Jesus our Saviour came, so that now we are the new People of God, pilgrims on earth journeying toward our eternal home.[76]

The educational value of Christian anthropology is obvious. Here is where students discover the true value of the human person: loved by God, with a mission on earth and a destiny that is immortal. As a result, they learn the virtues of self-respect and self-love, and of love for others – a love that is universal. In addition, each student will develop a willingness to embrace life, and also his or her own unique vocation, as a fulfilment of God's will.

77. The history of salvation continues in the Church, an **514** historical reality that is visible to the students. They should be encouraged to discover its origins in the Gospels, in Acts, and in the Apostolic Letters; as they study these works they will see the Church at its birth, and then as it begins to grow and take its place in the world. From the way it comes into being, from its miraculous growth, and from its fidelity to the Gospel message the transition is made to the Church as a mystery. The teacher will help students to discover the Church as the People of God, composed of women and men just like ourselves, bringing salvation to all of humanity. The Church is guided by Jesus the Eternal Shepherd; guided by his Spirit, which sustains it and is forever renewing it; guided visibly by the pastors he has ordained: the Holy Father and the bishops, assisted by priests and the deacons who are their collaborators in priesthood and in ministry. The Church, called by God to be holy in all its members, continues to be at work in the world. This is the mystery of the One, Holy, Catholic, and Apostolic Church that we celebrate in the Creed.[77]

---

[76] From the point of view of Christian anthropology, it is essential that the history of salvation presented in *LG* and *GS* be a part of what is studied in class.

[77] Important and valuable material for teaching about the Church can be found in *LG*.

Ecclesiology has an extremely important educational value: the ideal of a universal human family is realized in the Church. As young people come to a better knowledge of the Church they belong to, they will learn to love it with a filial affection; this has obvious consequences for life, for apostolate, and for a Christian vision of the world.

515

78. As they get older, many young people stop receiving the Sacraments; this may be a sign that their meaning has not been grasped. Perhaps they are seen as devotional, practices for children, or a popular devotion joined to a secular feast. Teachers are familiar with this phenomenon and its dangers. They will, therefore, help students to discover the real value of the Sacraments: they accompany the believer on his or her journey through life. This journey takes place within the Church, and therefore becomes more comprehensible as students grow in an understanding of what it means to be a member of the Church. The essential point for students to understand is that Jesus Christ is always truly present in the Sacraments which he has instituted,[78] and his presence makes them efficacious means of grace. The moment of closest encounter with the Lord Jesus occurs in the Eucharist, which is both Sacrifice and Sacrament. In the Eucharist, two supreme acts of love are united: Our Lord renews his sacrifice of salvation for us, and he truly gives himself to us.

516

79. An understanding of the sacramental journey has profound educational implications. Students become aware that being a member of the Church is something dynamic, responding to every person's need to continue growing all through life. When we meet the Lord in the Sacraments, we are never left unchanged. Through the Spirit, he causes us to grow in the Church, offering us "grace upon grace";[79] the only thing he asks is our cooperation. The educational consequences of this touch on our relationship with God, our witness as a Christian, and our choice of a personal vocation.[80]

517

80. Young people today are assaulted by distractions; the circumstances are not ideal for reflecting on the last things. An

---

[78] *Sacrosanctum Concilium*, 7: "Christ is present in the Sacraments with his own authority, so that when one baptizes it is Christ himself who baptizes ...".

[79] John 1: 16.

[80] The content and the methods for teaching about the Sacraments can be enriched through studying parts of *LG* and *Sacrosanctum Concilium*.

effective way to approach this mystery of faith is, however, available to the teacher: the Lord proposes it in his own unique way. In the story of Lazarus, he calls himself "the resurrection and the life"[81] In the parable of the rich man he helps us to understand that a personal judgement awaits each one of us.[82] In the impressive drama of the last judgment he points to an eternal destiny which each of us merits through our own works.[83] The good or evil done to each human being is as if done to him.[84]

81. Then, using the Creed as a pattern, the teacher can help students to learn about the Kingdom of Heaven: that it consists of those who have believed in him and spent their lives in his service. The Church calls them "saints" even if not all are formally venerated under that title. First among them is Mary, the Mother of Jesus, living a glorified life at the side of her Son. Those who have died are not separated from us. They, with us, form the one Church, the People of God, united in the "communion of saints". Those dear to us who have left us are alive and are in communion with us.[85]

518

These truths of faith contribute to human and Christian maturity in several important areas. They provide a sense of the dignity of the person, as destined to immortality. Christian hope offers comfort in life's difficulties. We are personally responsible in everything we do, because we must render an account to God.

4. *An outline for a systematic presentation of the Christian life*

82. As we have seen, each truth of faith has educational and ethical implications, and students should be helped to learn about these from the time when they first begin the study of religion. But a systematic presentation of Christian ethics is also needed; to assist in this task, we present here a sample outline.

519

As an introduction to a study of the relationship between faith and life through religious ethics it can be helpful to reflect on the first Christian communities, where the Gospel message

---

[81] John 11: 25-27.

[82] Cf Luke 16: 19-31.

[83] Cf Matt 25: 31-46.

[84] Cf *Ibid.* 25: 40.

[85] Cf *LG*, Chapter VII on the eschatological nature of the pilgrim Church and its union with the heavenly Church.

was accompanied by prayer and the celebration of the Sacraments.[86] This has permanent value. Students will begin to understand the meaning of the virtue of faith: helped by grace, to give complete, free, personal and affective loyalty to the God who reveals himself through his Son.

This commitment is not automatic; it is itself a gift of God. We must ask for it and wait for it patiently. And students must be given time to grow and to mature.

520 83. The life of faith is expressed in acts of religion. The teacher will assist students to open their hearts in confidence to Father, Son, and Holy Spirit through personal and liturgical prayer. The latter is not just another way of praying; it is the official prayer of the Church, which makes the mystery of Christ present in our lives – especially through the Eucharist, Sacrifice and Sacrament, and through the Sacrament of Reconciliation. Religious experiences are then seen, not as something externally imposed, but as a free and loving response to the God who first loved us.[87] The virtues of faith and religion, thus rooted and cultivated, are enabled to develop during childhood, youth, and in all the years that follow.

521 84. The human person is present in all the truths of faith: created in "the image and likeness" of God; elevated by God to the dignity of a child of God; unfaithful to God in original sin, but redeemed by Christ; a temple of the Holy Spirit; a member of the Church; destined to eternal life.

Students may well object that we are a long way from this ideal. The teacher must listen to these pessimistic responses, but point out that they are also found in the Gospel.[88] Students may need to be convinced that it is better to know the positive picture of personal Christian ethics rather than to get lost in an analysis of human misery. In practice, this means respect for oneself and for others. We must cultivate intelligence and the other spiritual gifts, especially through scholastic work. We must learn to care for our

---

[86] Cf Eph 1: 1-14 and Col 1: 13-20 for doxologies which witness to the faith of the early communities. Acts 10 speaks of evangelisation, conversion, faith, and the gift of the Spirit in the house of the Roman official Cornelius. Acts 20: 7-12 describes evangelisation and the Eucharist in a house at Troas.

[87] 1 John 4:10: "It is not we who have loved God, but God who first loved us ... ."

[88] Cf Matt 15: 19 f.

body and its health, and this includes physical activity and sports. And we must be careful of our sexual integrity through the virtue of chastity, because sexual energies are also a gift of God, contributing to the perfection of the person and having a providential function for the life of society and of the Church.[89] Thus, gradually, the teacher will guide students to the idea, and then to the realization, of a process of total formation.

85. Christian love is neither sentimentalism nor humanitarianism; it is a new reality, born of faith. Teachers must remember that the love of God governs the divine plan of universal salvation. The Lord Jesus came to live among us in order to show us the Father's love. His ultimate sacrifice testifies to his love for his friends. And the Lord's new commandment is at the centre of our faith: "This is my commandment: that you love one another as I have loved you".[90] The "as" is the model and the measure of Christian love.

522

86. Students will raise the standard objections: violence in the world, racial hatred, daily crime, both young and old concerned only with themselves and what they can get for themselves. Teachers cannot avoid discussing these issues, but they should insist that the commandment of Christ is new and revolutionary, and that it stands in opposition to all that is evil and to every form of egoism. The new Christian ethic needs to be understood and put into practice.

523

87. It begins at the level of family and school: affection, respect, obedience, gratitude, gentleness, goodness, helpfulness, service and good example. All manifestations of egoism, rebellion, antipathy, jealousy, hatred or revenge must be rooted out. At the broader level of Church: a love for all that excludes no one because of religion, nationality or race; prayer for all, so that all may know the Lord; labouring together in apostolic works and in efforts to relieve human suffering; a preferential option for the less fortunate, the sick, the poor, the handicapped, the lonely, As love grows in the Church, more young people may choose a life of service in it, responding to a call to the priesthood or to Religious life.

524

---

[89] Cf the document of the Congregation for Catholic Education already referred to – Educational Guidance in Human Love: Outlines for Sex Education.
[90] John 15:12.

As they begin to prepare for marriage: rejecting anything that would hint at a desecration of love; discovering the newness and the depth of Christian love between man and woman, including the mutuality and reserve with which it is expressed and the sincere tenderness by which it is preserved. Young people should experience love in this way from their first friendships, gradually leading to the possibility of a commitment, until finally love is consecrated for the whole of life in the Sacrament of Matrimony.

525 88. Christian. social ethics must always be founded on faith. From this starting point it can shed light on related disciplines such as law, economics and political science, all of which study the human situation,[91] and this is an obvious area for fruitful interdisciplinary study. But it is important to remind ourselves that God has put the world at the service of the human family.[92] As our Lord pointed out,[93] violence and injustice in society come from men and women, and they are contrary to the will of God. But in saving us, God also saves our works: a renewed world flows from a renewed heart. The works of the new Christian order of humanity are love, justice, freedom and grace.[94]

526 89. These, then, are the basic elements of a Christian social ethic: the human person, the central focus of the social order; justice, the recognition of the rights of each individual; honesty, the basic condition for all human relationships; freedom, the basic right of each individual and of society. World peace must then be founded on good order and the justice to which all men and women have a right as children of God; national and international well-being depend on the fact that the goods of the earth are gifts of God, and are not the privilege of some individuals or groups while others are deprived of them. Misery and hunger weigh on the conscience of humanity and cry out to God for justice.

527 90. This is an area which can open up broad possibilities. Students will be enriched by the principles and values they learn, and their service of society will be more effective. The Church supports and enlightens them with a social doctrine which is

---

[91] Cf *GS*, 63-66 and related applications.
[92] Cf Gen 1: 27 f.
[93] Again cf Matt 15: 19 f.
[94] Cf *GS*, 93. Students should become aware of at least some of the Church's major social documents.

waiting to be put into practice by courageous and generous men and women of faith.[95]

91. The guidelines developed up to this point seem excess- **528** ively optimistic. While the presentation of the Christian message as "good news" is pedagogically sound,[96] the realism of revelation, history and daily experience all require that students have a clear awareness of the evil that is at work in the world and in the human person. The Lord spoke about the "power of darkness".[97] Men and women wander far away from God, and rebel against the Gospel message; they continue to poison the world with war, violence, injustice and crime.

92. A teacher can invite the students to examine their own **529** consciences. Which one of us can honestly claim to be without sin?[98] Thus they will acquire a sense of sin: the great sin of humanity as a whole and the personal sin which all of us discover within ourselves. Sin drives us away from God, rejects the message of Christ, and transgresses the law of love; sin betrays conscience, abuses the gift of freedom, offends the other children of God, and harms the Church of which we are all members.

93. But we are not in a hopeless situation. The teacher should **530** help students to see, in the light of faith, that this reality has another side to it. On the world scale, the Gospel message continues to "die" as the "seed" in the soil of the earth only to blossom and bear fruit in due season.[99] At the personal level, the Lord waits for us in the Sacrament of Reconciliation. It is not just a devotional practice, but rather a personal encounter with him, through the mediation of his minister. After this celebration we can resume our journey with renewed strength and joy.

---

[95] Students should become aware of at least some of the Church's major social documents.

[96] Luke 2: 10: "I bring you news of great joy...".

[97] Luke 22: 53: "But this is your hour; this is the reign of darkness". Evidence of this is easily found in various abuses, acts of injustice, attacks on freedom, the overwhelming weight of misery that leads to sickness, decline and death, the scandalous inequality between rich and poor, the lack of any equity or sense of solidarity in international relations. (Cf Some Aspects of the "Theology of Liberation", published by the Congregation for the Doctrine of the Faith, Introduction and Part I).

[98] John 8: 7: "Let the one who is without sin cast the first stone ...".

[99] Cf Luke 8: 4.15.

531   94. These truths can lead to a new and more mature understanding of Christianity. The Lord calls us to an endless struggle:
to resist the forces of evil and, with his help, to have the courage
to overpower it. This is a Christianity which is alive and healthy,
at work in history and within the life of each individual.[100]

The call to be a Christian involves a call to help liberate the
human family from its radical slavery to sin and, therefore, from
the effects of sin in the cultural, economic, social and political
orders. Ultimately, these effects all result from sin; they are
obstacles which prevent men and women from living according to
the dignity which is theirs.[101]

532   95. Perfection is a theme which must be part of this
systematic presentation of the Christian message. To pass over it
would be disloyal: to the Lord, who calls us to limitless perfection;[102] to the Church, which invites us all to perfection;[103] and to
the young people themselves, who have the right to know what
the Lord and the Church expect of them. The teacher will begin
by reminding believing students that, through their baptism, they
have become members of the Church. The Christian perfection to
which we are all called is a gift of Jesus through the mediation of
the Spirit; but the gift requires our cooperation. Our apostolic
witness must make this perfection visible in the world, today and
in the future.

Once they get beyond feeling that too much is being asked of
them, students will realize that perfection is actually within their
grasp. The only thing they have to do is live their lives as students
as well as they can:[104] do their best in study and work; put into
practice the virtues they already know in theory – especially love,
which must be lived in the classroom, at home, and among
friends; accept difficulties with courage; help those in need; give
good example. In addition, they must find the inspiration for their

---

[100] Cf Eph 6: 10-17, a characteristically vigorous Pauline description.
[101] Cf the Introduction to Some Aspects of the "Theology of Liberation"
published by the Congregation for the Doctrine of the Faith, 6 August 1984.
[102] Matt 5: 48: "You must be perfect as your heavenly Father is perfect".
[103] *LG*, 42: "All the faithful are invited and called to holiness and to perfection
within their own state of live".
[104] *Ibid.*, 39: "This holiness of the Church... is expressed in various forms
according to each individual, who in their lives and their activities join
perfection to love".

daily lives in the words and the example of Jesus. They must converse with him in prayer and receive him in the Eucharist. No student can say that these are impossible demands.

The ideal would be for each student to have an opportunity for spiritual guidance, to help in interior formation. It is the best way of giving orientation and completion to the religious instruction given in the classroom and, at the same time, of integrating this instruction into the personal experiences of each individual.

5. *The religion teacher*

96. The fruits of an organic presentation of the faith and of **533** Christian ethics depend in great part on the religion teachers: who they are and what they do.

The religion teacher is the key, the vital component, if the educational goals of the school are to be achieved. But the effectiveness of religious instruction is closely tied to the personal witness given by the teacher; this witness is what brings the content of the lessons to life. Teachers of religion, therefore, must be men and women endowed with many gifts, both natural and supernatural, who are also capable of giving witness to these gifts; they must have a thorough cultural, professional, and pedagogical training, and they must be capable of genuine dialogue.

Most of all, students should be able to recognize authentic human qualities in their teachers. They are teachers of the faith; however, like Christ, they must also be teachers of what it means to be human. This includes culture, but it also includes such things as affection, tact, understanding, serenity of spirit, a balanced judgment, patience in listening to others and prudence in the way they respond, and, finally, availability for personal meetings and conversations with the students. A teacher who has a clear vision of the Christian milieu and lives in accord with it will be able to help young people develop a similar vision, and will give them the inspiration they need to put it into practice.

97. In this area, especially, an unprepared teacher can do a **534** great deal of harm. Everything possible must be done to ensure that Catholic schools have adequately trained religion teachers; it is a vital necessity and a legitimate expectation. In Catholic schools today, these teachers tend more and more to be lay people, and they should have the opportunity of receiving the

specific experiential knowledge of the mystery of Christ and of the Church that priests and Religious automatically acquire in the course of their formation. We need to look to the future and promote the establishment of formation centres for these teachers; ecclesiastical universities and faculties should do what they can to develop appropriate programs so that the teachers of tomorrow will be able to carry out their task with the competence and efficacy that is expected of them.[105]

V: A General Summary: The Religious Dimension of the Formation Process as a whole

1. *What is a Christian formation process?*

535

98. The declaration of the Council insists on the dynamic nature of integral human formation,[106] but it adds immediately that, from a Christian point of view, human development by itself is not sufficient. Education "does not merely strive to foster in the human person the maturity already described. Rather, its principal aims are these: that as the baptized person is gradually introduced into a knowledge of the mystery of salvation, he or she may daily grow more conscious of the gift of faith which has been received ...".[107] What characterizes a Catholic school, therefore, is that it guide students in such a way "that the development of each one's own personality will be matched by the growth of that new creation which he or she became by baptism".[108] We need to think of Christian education as a movement or a growth process, directed toward an ideal goal which goes beyond the limitations of any-thing human.[109] At the same time the process must be harmonious, so that Christian formation takes place within and in the course of human formation. The two are not separate and parallel paths; they are complementary forms of education which become one in

---

[105] Some aspects of this are treated in the documents already referred to: The Catholic School, 78-80; Lay Catholics in Schools: Witnesses to the Faith, especially 56-59. What is said there does not apply only to the lay teachers.

[106] *GE*, 1; "Children and young people should be assisted in the harmonious development of their physical, moral and intellectual gifts ... They should be helped to acquire gradually a more mature sense of responsibility ... ."

[107] *Ibid.*, 2.

[108] *Ibid.*, 8.

[109] Cf Matt 5: 48.

the goals of the teacher and the willing reception of the students. The Gospel notes this harmonious growth in the child Jesus.[110]

99. A Christian formation process might therefore be described as an organic set of elements with a single purpose: the gradual development of every capability of every student, enabling each one to attain an integral formation within a context that includes the Christian religious dimension and recognizes the help of grace. But what really matters is not the terminology but the reality, and this reality will be assured only if all the teachers unite their educational efforts in the pursuit of a common goal. Sporadic, partial, or uncoordinated efforts, or a situation in which there is a conflict of opinion among the teachers, will interfere with rather than assist in the students' personal development.

536

2. Educational goals

100. The responsibility of a Catholic school is enormous and complex. It must respect and obey the laws that define methods, programmes, structure, etc., and at the same time it must fulfil its own educational goals by blending human culture with the message of salvation into a coordinated programme; it must help each of the students to actually become the "new creature" that each one is potentially, and at the same time prepare them for the responsibilities of an adult member of society. This means that a Catholic school needs to have a set of educational goals which are "distinctive" in the sense that the school has a specific objective in mind, and all of the goals are related to this objective. Concretely, the educational goals provide a frame of reference which:

537

- defines the school's identity: in particular, the Gospel values which are its inspiration must be explicitly mentioned;
- gives a precise description of the pedagogical, educational and cultural aims of the school;
- presents the course content, along with the values that are to be transmitted through these courses;
- describes the organization and the management of the school;

---

[110] Luke 2:40: "The child grew and became strong, filled with wisdom; and the favour of God was upon him". Luke 2:52: "And Jesus grew in wisdom and in stature, and in favour with God and with men".

• determines which policy decisions are to be reserved to professional staff (governors and teachers), which policies are to be developed with the help of parents and students, and which activities are to be left to the free initiative of teachers, parents, or students;

• indicates the ways in which student progress is to be tested and evaluated.

538   101. In addition, careful attention must be given to the development of general criteria which will enable each aspect of school activity to assist in the attainment of the educational objective, so that the cultural, pedagogical, social, civil and political aspects of school life are all integrated:

a) Fidelity to the Gospel as proclaimed by the Church. The activity of a Catholic school is, above all else, an activity that shares in the evangelizing mission of the Church; it is a part of the particular local Church of the country in which it is situated, and shares in the life and work of the local Christian community.

b) Careful rigour in the study of culture and the development of a critical sense, maintaining a respect for the autonomy of human knowledge and for the rules and methods proper to each of the disciplines, and at the same time orienting the whole process toward the integral formation of the person.

c) Adapting the educational process in a way that respects the particular circumstances of individual students and their families.

d) Sharing responsibility with the Church. While school authorities are the ones primarily responsible for the educational and cultural activities of the school, the local Church should also be involved in appropriate ways; the educational goals should be the result of dialogue with this ecclesial community.

It is clear, then, that the set of educational goals is something quite distinct from internal school regulations or teaching methods; and it is not just a description of vague intentions.

539   102. The educational goals should be revised each year on the basis of experience and need. They will be achieved through a formation process which takes place in stages; it has a starting point, various intermediate points, and a conclusion, At each stage, teachers, students and families should determine the degree of success in achieving these goals; where there is insufficient progress they should look for the reasons and find suitable remedies. It is essential that this evaluation be seen as a common responsibility, and that it be carried out faithfully.

The end of each school year is one appropriate time for such an evaluation. From a Christian perspective, it is not enough to say that this is the time for examinations. The academic programme is only one part of the process, and the end of the school year is also the time for a serious and intelligent examination of which educational goals have been achieved and which have not. A much more decisive time comes at the completion of a student's years in the school, because this is the moment when students should have reached the maximum level of an education that integrates the human and the Christian.[111]

103. The religious dimension of the school climate **540** strengthens the quality of the formation process, so long as certain conditions are verified – conditions that depend both on teachers and students. It is worth noting, once again, that the students are not spectators; they help to determine the quality of this climate.

Some of the conditions for creating a positive and supportive climate are the following: that everyone agree with the educational goals and cooperate in achieving them; that interpersonal relationships be based on love and Christian freedom; that each individual, in daily life, be a witness to Gospel values; that every student be challenged to strive for the highest possible level of formation, both human and Christian. In addition, the climate must be one in which families are welcomed, the local Church is an active participant, and civil society – local, national, and international – is included. If all share a common faith, this can be an added advantage.

104. Strong determination is needed to do everything **541** possible to eliminate conditions which threaten the health of the school climate. Some examples of potential problems are these: the educational goals are either not defined or are defined badly; those responsible for the school are not sufficiently trained; concern for academic achievement is excessive; relations between teachers and students are cold and impersonal; teachers are antagonistic toward one another; discipline is imposed from on high without any participation or cooperation from the students;

---

[111] Cf once again *GE*, 1-2.

relationships with families are formal or even strained, and families are not involved in helping to determine the educational goals; some within the school community are giving a negative witness; individuals are unwilling to work together for the common good; the school is isolated from the local Church; there is no interest in or concern for the problems of society; religious instruction is "routine". Whenever some combination of these symptoms is present, the religious dimension of the school is seriously threatened. Religious instruction can become empty words falling on deaf ears, because the authentically Christian witness that reinforces it is absent from the school climate. All symptoms of ill health have to be faced honestly and directly, remembering that the Gospel calls us to a continuous process of conversion.

542   105. A school exerts a great deal of effort in trying to obtain the students' active cooperation. Since they are active agents in their own formation process, this cooperation is essential. To be human is to be endowed with intelligence and freedom; it is impossible for education to be genuine without the active involvement of the one being educated. Students must act and react; with their intelligence, freedom, will, and the whole complex range of human emotions. The formation process comes to a halt when students are uninvolved and unmoved. Experienced teachers are familiar with the causes of such "blocks" in young people; the roots are both psychological and theological, and original sin is not excluded.

543   106. There are many ways to encourage students to become active participants in their own formation. Those with sufficient knowledge and maturity can be asked to help in the development of educational goals. While they are clearly not yet able to determine the final objective, they can help in determining the concrete means which will help to attain this objective. When students are trusted and given responsibility, when they are invited to contribute their own ideas and efforts for the common good, their gratitude rules out indifference and inertia. The more that students can be helped to realize that a school and all its activities have only one purpose – to help them in their growth toward maturity – the more those students will be willing to become actively involved.

Even students who are very young can sense whether the atmosphere in the school is pleasant or not. They are more willing to cooperate when they feel respected, trusted and loved. And their willingness to cooperate will be reinforced by a school climate which is warm and friendly, when teachers are ready to help, and when they find it easy to get along with the other students.

107. One important result of religious instruction is the development of religious values and religious motivation; these can be a great help in obtaining the willing participation of the students. But we must remember that religious values and motivation are cultivated in all subject areas and, indeed, in all of the various activities going on in the school, One way that teachers can encourage an understanding of and commitment to religious values is by frequent references to God. Teachers learn through experience how to help the students understand and appreciate the religious truths they are being taught, and this appreciation can easily develop into love, a truth which is loved by the teacher, and communicated in such a way that it is seen to be something valuable in itself, then becomes valuable to the student. One advantage of the Christological approach to religious instruction is that it can develop this love more easily in young people. The approach we have suggested concentrates on the person of Jesus. It is possible to love a person; it is rather difficult to love a formula. This love for Christ is then transferred to his message which, because it is loved, has value. **544**

But every true educator knows that a further step is necessary: values must lead to action; they are the motivation for action. Finally, truth becomes fully alive through the supernatural dynamism of grace, which enlightens and leads to faith, to love, to action that is in accord with the will of God, through the Lord Jesus, in the Holy Spirit. The Christian process of formation is, therefore, the result of a constant interaction involving the expert labour of the teachers, the free cooperation of the students, and the help of grace.

108. We have already referred to the fact that, in many parts of the world, the student body in a Catholic school includes increasing numbers of young people from different faiths and different ideological backgrounds. In these situations it is essential to clarify the relationship between religious development **545**

and cultural growth. It is a question which must not be ignored, and dealing with it is the responsibility of each Christian member of the educational community.

In these situations, however, evangelisation is not easy – it may not even be possible. We should look to pre-evangelisation: to the development of a religious sense of life. In order to do this, the process of formation must constantly raise questions about the "how" and the "why" and the "what" and then point out and deepen the positive results of this investigation.

The transmission of a culture ought to be especially attentive to the practical effects of that culture, and strengthen those aspects of it which will make a person more human. In particular, it ought to pay attention to the religious dimension of the culture and the emerging ethical requirements to be found in it.

There can be unity in the midst of pluralism, and we need to exercise a wise discernment in order to distinguish between what is essential and what is accidental. Prudent use of the "why" and the "what" and the "how" will lead to integral human development in the formation process, and this is what we mean by a genuine pre-evangelisation. It is fertile ground which may, at some future time, be able to bear fruit.

546   109. In order to describe the formation process, we have had to proceed by an analysis of its various elements; this, of course, is not the way things happen in the real world. The Catholic school is a centre of life, and life is synthetic, In this vital centre, the formation process is a constant interplay of action and reaction. The interplay has both a horizontal and a vertical dimension, and it is this qualification that makes the Catholic school distinctive from those other schools whose educational objectives are not inspired by Christianity.

547   110. The teachers love their students, and they show this love in the way they interact with them. They take advantage of every opportunity to encourage and strengthen them in those areas which will help to achieve the goals of the educational process. Their words, their witness, their encouragement and help, their advice and friendly correction are all important in achieving these goals, which must always be understood to include academic achievement, moral behaviour, and a religious dimension.

When students feel loved, they will love in return. Their

questioning, their trust, their critical observations and suggestions for improvement in the classroom and the school milieu will enrich the teachers and also help to facilitate a shared commitment to the formation process.

111. In a Catholic school, even this is not enough. There is **548** also a continuous vertical interaction, through prayer; this is the fullest and most complete expression of the religious dimension.

Each of the students has his or her own life, family and social background, and these are not always happy situations. They feel the unrest of the child or adolescent, which grows more intense as they face the problems and worries of a young person approaching maturity. Teachers will pray for each of them, that the grace present in the Catholic school's milieu may permeate their whole person, enlightening them and helping them to respond adequately to all that is demanded of them in order to live Christian lives.

And the students will learn that they must pray for their teachers. As they get older, they will come to appreciate the pain and the difficulties that teaching involves. They will pray that the educational gifts of their teachers may be more effective, that they may be comforted by success in their work, that grace may sustain their dedication and bring them peace in their work.

112. Thus a relationship is built up which is both human and **549** divine; there is a flow of love, and also of grace. And this will make the Catholic school truly authentic. As the years go by, students will have the joy of seeing themselves nearing maturity; not only physically, but also intellectually and spiritually. When they look back, they will realize that, with their cooperation, the educational objectives of the school have become a reality. And as they look forward, they will feel free and secure, because they will be able to face the new, and now proximate, life commitments.

Conclusion

113. The Congregation for Catholic Education asks local **550** ordinaries and superiors of Religious Congregations dedicated to the education of youth to bring these reflections to the attention of all teachers and directors of Catholic schools, At the same time, the Congregation wishes to affirm once again that it is fully

conscious of the important service they offer – to youth and to the Church.

551   114. Therefore the Congregation extends warm thanks to all those engaged in this work: for all they have done, and for all that they continue to do in spite of political, economic, and practical difficulties. For many, to continue in this mission involves great sacrifice. The Church is deeply grateful to everyone dedicated to the educational mission in a Catholic school; it is confident that, with the help of God, many others will be called to join in this mission and will respond generously.

552   115. The Congregation would like to suggest that further study, research, and experimentation be done in all areas that affect the religious dimension of education in Catholic schools. Much has been done, but many people are asking for even more. This is surely possible in every school whose freedom is sufficiently protected by civil law. It may be difficult in those countries which allow the Catholic school as an academic institution, but where the religious dimension leads to constant conflict. Local experience must be the determining factor in such situations; however, to the extent that it is possible, a religious dimension should always be present – either in the school or outside its walls. There has never been a shortage of families and students, of different faiths and religions, who choose a Catholic school because they appreciate the value of an education where instruction is enhanced by a religious dimension.

Educators will know the best way to respond to their expectations, knowing that, in a world of cultural pluralism, dialogue always gives grounds for hope.

Rome, 7 April 1988, Feast of Saint John Baptist de La Salle, Principal Patron of teachers.

William Cardinal Baum
Prefect
Antonio M. Javierre Ortas
Titular Archbishop of Meta
Secretary

Congregation for the Clergy, 11 August 1997

Preface

553   1. The Second Vatican Council prescribed that a "Directory for the catechetical instruction of the Christian people"[1] be drawn up. The Congregation for the Clergy, in execution of this conciliar mandate, availed itself of a special commission of experts, and consulted the various Episcopal Conferences, throughout the world, which made numerous suggestions and observations on the subject. The text prepared was revised by an *ad hoc* theological Commission and by the Congregation for the Doctrine of the Faith. The *General Catechetical Directory* was definitively approved by Pope Paul VI on 18 March 1971 and promulgated on 11 April 1971.

554   2. The thirty-year period between the conclusion of the Second Vatican Council and the threshold of the third millennium is without doubt most providential for the orientation and pro-motion of catechesis. It has been a time in which the evangelizing vigour of the original ecclesial community has in some ways re-emerged. It has also seen a renewal of interest in the teaching of the Fathers and has made possible a return to the catechumenate.

---

[1] CD 44.

Since 1971, the General Catechetical Directory has oriented the particular Churches in their renewal of catechesis and has acted as a point of reference for content and pedagogy, as well as for methodology.

The course of catechesis during this same period has been characterized everywhere by generous dedication, worthy initiatives and by positive results for the education and growth in the faith of children, young people and adults. At the same time, however, there have been crises, doctrinal inadequacies, influences from the evolution of global culture and ecclesial questions derived from outside the field of catechesis which have often impoverished its quality.

3. The Magisterium of the Church, throughout these years, **555** has never ceased to exercise its pastoral solicitude for catechesis. Numerous Bishops and Episcopal Conferences in all parts of the world have devoted considerable attention to catechesis by means of catechisms and pastoral guidelines, by promoting the formation of their priests and by encouraging catechetical research. Efforts such as these have proved fruitful and have contributed much to catechetical praxis in the particular Churches. *The Rite of Christian Initiation of Adults*, published by the Congregation for Divine Worship on 6 January 1972, has proved especially useful for catechetical renewal.

Mention must also be made in a particular way of the ministry of Pope Paul VI, who shepherded the Church in the immediate post-conciliar period. In his regard, Pope John Paul II has said: "... through his gestures, his preaching, his authoritative interpretation of the Second Vatican Council – considered by him to have been the great catechism of modern times – and through the whole of his life, my venerable predecessor Paul VI served the Church's catechesis in a particularly exemplary fashion".[2]

4. The reflections of the General Assembly of the Synod of **556** Bishops of October 1974 on the theme of Evangelisation in the Contemporary World constitute a decisive milestone for catechesis. The propositions subsequently drawn up by the Synod were presented to Pope Paul VI, who promulgated the post-synodal Apostolic Exhortation *Evangelii Nuntiandi* of 8 December 1975.

---

[2] CT 2.

This document enunciates, amongst other things, a particularly important principle, namely, that of catechesis as a work of evangelisation in the context of the mission of the Church. Henceforth catechesis would be considered as one of the enduring concerns of the Church's missionary mandate for our times.

The final General Assembly of the Synod of Bishops, convoked by Pope Paul VI in October 1977, proposed catechesis to its participants as the theme for analysis and reflection. This Synod saw "in catechetical renewal a precious gift of the Holy Spirit to the contemporary Church".[3]

557   5. Taking up this catechetical heritage in 1978, Pope John Paul II set out his first orientations for catechesis in the Apostolic Exhortation *Catechesi Tradendae* of 16 October 1979. This Exhortation forms a cohesive unity with *Evangelii Nuntiandi* and fully locates catechesis within the context of evangelisation.

Throughout his entire pontificate, Pope John Paul II has continually proposed a constant magisterium of the highest catechetical value. From amongst his discourses, his letters, his written teaching, particular emphasis must be given to the twelve Encyclicals, from *Redemptor Hominis* to *Ut Unum Sint.* These Encyclicals constitute in themselves a synthetic corpus of coherent doctrine with regard to the renewal of ecclesial life desired by the Second Vatican Council.

Of particular catechetical value, amongst these documents of the Petrine ministry of Pope John Paul II, the following are of special importance: *Redemptor Hominis* (4 March 1979), *Dives in Misericordia* (30 November 1980), *Dominum et Vivificantem* (18 May 1986) and *Redemptoris Missio* (7 December 1990), in which last, the permanent validity of the Church's missionary mandate is re-affirmed.

558   6. On the other hand the General Assemblies of the Synod of Bishops, both ordinary and extraordinary, have been particularly important for catechesis. In this respect mention must be made of the Synods of 1980 and 1987 which dealt with the mission of the family and the vocation of the laity. Following the work of these Synods, Pope John Paul II promulgated the respective Apostolic Exhortations *Familiaris Consortio* (22 November 1981) and

---

[3] CT 3.

Christifideles Laici (30 December 1987). The Extraordinary Synod of Bishops of 1985 was also of decisive importance for the catechesis of our times and for the future. On that occasion, following a review of the previous twenty years of the application of the Second Vatican Council the Synodal Fathers proposed to the Holy Father a universal catechism for the Catholic Church. The proposal was most favourably received and made his own by Pope John Paul II. After a long and complex process of elaboration the *Catechism of the Catholic Church* was presented to the bishops and the Particular Churches by the Apostolic Constitution *Fidei Depositum* of the 11 October 1992.

559 7. The publication of the Catechism together with the aforementioned interventions of the Magisterium necessitated a revision of the *General Catechetical Directory* so as to adapt this valuable theologico-pastoral instrument to new situations and needs. It is in service of the entire Church that the Holy See now seeks to collate this heritage and to organize it systematically in order to make it available for catechetical purposes.

The work of revising the *General Catechetical Directory* undertaken by the Congregation for the Clergy, was conducted by a group of Bishops and experts in theology and catechesis. In the revision of the General Directory, its original inspiration and content were respected. Episcopal Conferences and several experts were consulted as were the principal catechetical institutes and centres.

In its present form the *General Directory for Catechesis* seeks to arrive at a balance between two principal requirements:
– on the one hand the contextualization of catechesis in evangelisation as envisaged by *Evangelii Nuntiandi;*
– on the other the appropriation of the content of the faith as presented in the *Catechism of the Catholic Church.*

560 8. The *General Directory for Catechesis*, while retaining the basic structure of that of 1971, is divided as follows:
– The *Introduction* takes its starting point from faith and trust in the power of the Gospel seed, and proposes guidelines for interpreting and understanding human and ecclesial conditions. These are intended to assist mission.

    – *Part One*[4] has three chapters and roots catechesis above all in the conciliar Constitution *Dei Verbum,* placing it in the context of evangelisation as seen in *Evangelii Nuntiandi* and *Catechesi Tradendae,* and proposes, moreover, to clarify the nature of catechesis;

    – *Part Two*[5] contains two chapters, the first of which, under the title *Norms and Criteria for presenting the Gospel message in Catechesis,* puts forward afresh the entire content of the corresponding chapter of the previous text from a new and enriched perspective; the second chapter, which is completely new, serves to present the *Catechism of the Catholic Church* as a reference point for the transmission of the faith in catechesis and for the preparation of catechisms at local level; this chapter also outlines those fundamental principles to be employed in the redaction of catechisms in particular and local Churches;

    – *Part Three*[6] has also been revised to formulate the main elements of a pedagogy of the faith inspired by divine pedagogy; while this question is primarily a theological one, it also involves the human sciences;

    – *Part Four*[7] is entitled *Those to be catechized*; in five short chapters attention is given to the diverse situations and contexts of those to whom catechesis is directed, to matters arising from socio-religious situations, and in particular, to the question of inculturation;

    – *Part Five*[8] focuses on the centrality of the particular Church and on its primordial duty to promote, organize, oversee and co-ordinate all catechetical activities; of particular significance is the description of the roles proper to the various agents involved in catechesis (who, of course, are always dependent on the Pastors

---

[4] Corresponds to Part II of the DCG.

[5] It has the same objectives of Part III to the DCG.

[6] Corresponds to Part IV of the DCG.

[7] Corresponds to Part V of the DCG of 1971. While several significant reasons would suggest that this section should preceed that on pedagogy, however, given the new form of Part Three it is preferred to maintain the same order as that in the 1971 text. This underlines that attention to those to whom catechesis is directed is a partipation in and a consequence of this same divine pedagogy, this Acondescenion of God in the history of Salvation (DV 13) of his self adaptation in revelation to the human condition.

[8] Assumes all the elements of Paul VI of the DCG.

of the particular Churches) and of the requirements necessary for their respective formation;

– The *Conclusion* advocates an intensification of catechetical activity in our times, and concludes with an appeal to faith in the action of the Holy Spirit and in the efficacy of the word of God sown in love.

9. The object of this Directory is clearly the same as that **561** pursued by the 1971 Directory. It attempts to provide those fundamental theologico-pastoral principles drawn from the Church's Magisterium, particularly those inspired by the Second Vatican Council, which are capable of better orienting and coordinating the pastoral activity of the ministry of the word and, concretely, catechesis.[9] The basic intention of the Directory was (and remains) that of offering reflections and principles, rather than immediate applications or practical directives. This method has been adopted principally for the reason that defects and errors in catechetical material can be avoided only if the nature and end of catechesis, as well as the truths and values which must be transmitted, are correctly understood from the outset.[10]

The concrete application of these principles and pronouncements by means of guidelines, national, regional or diocesan directories, catechisms and other ways deemed suitable for the effective promotion of catechesis is something which pertains to the specific competence of the various Episcopates.

10. It is evident that not all parts of the Directory have the same **562** importance. Those dealing with Divine Revelation, the nature of catechesis, the criteria governing the proclamation of the Gospel message are universally valid. Those, however, referring to present circumstances, to methodology and to the manner of adapting catechesis to diverse age groups and cultural contexts are to be understood rather as indications or guidelines.[11]

11. The Directory is addressed principally to the Bishops, **563** Episcopal Conferences and, in a general way, in accordance with their competence, to those who have responsibility for catechesis. Clearly it will be of use in forming those preparing for ordination

---

[9] Cf. DCG (1971), Introduction.

[10] Cf. *ibidem.*

[11] Cf. ibidem.

to the Priesthood, in the continuing formation of priests and in the formation of catechists.

The immediate end of the Directory is to assist in the composition of catechetical directories and catechisms. Numerous notes and references have been included in this Directory, at the suggestion of many Bishops, which may be useful in drawing up such catechetical aids.

564   12. Since the Directory is intended for the use of particular Churches, whose pastoral needs vary greatly, it is obvious that only common or intermediate concerns could be taken into account. This is true also of the sections dealing with the organization of catechesis at different levels. Due note should be made of this observation while using the Directory. As has been already noted in the 1971 Directory, what may appear insufficient in areas where catechesis and catechetical resources have reached a high standard, may perhaps seem excessive in areas where catechesis has not yet undergone such development.

565   13. It is hoped that the publication of this document, testimony of the Apostolic See's solicitude for catechetical ministry, will be received and carefully studied in the context of the pastoral needs of each particular Church. It is to be hoped that it will promote future study and deepen research so as to respond to the needs of catechesis and the norms and directives of the Church's Magisterium.

Finally, brethren, pray for us, that the word of the Lord may speed on, and triumph as it did among you (2 Thess 3:1).

From the Vatican, 15 August 1997
Solemnity of the Assumption of the Blessed Virgin Mary

Darío Castrillón Hoyos
Archbishop Emeritus of Bucamaramga, Pro-Prefect
Crescenzio Sepe
Titular Archbishop of Grado, Secretary

Introduction

Preaching the Gospel in the contemporary world

"Behold! A sower went out to sow. As he sowed some seed fell along the path, and the birds came and devoured it. Other seed fell on rocky ground, where it had not much soil, and immediately it sprang up, since it had no depth of soil; and when the sun rose it was scorched, and since it had no root it withered away. Other seed fell among thorns which grew up and choked it, and it yielded no grain. And other seeds fell into good soil and brought forth grain, growing up and increasing, and yielding thirty fold, sixty fold, and a hundred fold" (Mk 4:3-8).

14. The purpose of this Introduction is to foster in pastors and **566** catechists a greater consciousness of the necessity to keep in mind the field in which the seed is sown, and to do so with the perspective of faith and mercy. The interpretation of the contemporary world presented here is obviously dependent on contingent historical circumstances.

"Behold! A sower going out to sow" (Mark 4:3)

15. The parable of the sower going out to sow is the source of **567** inspiration for evangelisation. The seed is the word of God (Luke 8:11). The sower is Jesus Christ. Two thousand years ago he proclaimed the Gospel in Palestine and sent the disciples to sow the Gospel in the world. Today, Jesus Christ, present in the Church through his Spirit, continues to scatter the word of the Father ever more widely in the field of the world. The conditions of the soil into which it falls vary greatly. The Gospel "falls by the wayside" (Luke 4:4) when it is not really heard; it falls on "stony soil" without taking root; it falls "amongst the thorns" (Luke 4:2) where it is quickly choked by the cares and troubles that weigh upon the hearts of men. Nonetheless, some seed falls "on good soil" (Mark 4:8) that is among men and women who are open to a personal relationship with God and who are in solidarity with their neighbour. This seed brings forth fruit in great abundance. Jesus, in the parable of the sower, proclaims the Good News that the Kingdom of God is near, notwithstanding the problems in the soil, the tensions, conflicts and difficulties of the world. The Gospel seed makes fertile the history of mankind and

promises a rich harvest. Jesus also cautions, however, that the
word of God grows only in a well disposed heart.

Looking at the world from the standpoint of faith

568   16. The Church continues to sow the Gospel in God's field.
Christians, in the most diverse social situations, perceive the
world with the same eyes with which Jesus contemplated the
society of his time. The disciple of Jesus Christ deeply shares the
"joys and hopes, the sadness and the anxieties of the men today".[1]
He gazes upon human history and participates in it, not only from
the standpoint of reason but also from that of faith. In the light of
faith the world appears at once "created and sustained by the love
of the Creator, which has been freed from the slavery of sin by
Christ, who was crucified and rose".[2] The Christian knows that
every human event – indeed all reality – is marked by the creative
activity of God which communicates goodness to all beings; the
power of sin which limits and numbs man; and the dynamism
which bursts forth from the Resurrection of Christ, the seed renewing believers is the hope of a definitive "fulfilment".[3] A
world-view not incorporating these three elements cannot be
authentically Christian. Hence the importance of a catechesis
capable of initiating catechumens and those to be catechized into
a "theological reading of modern problems".[4]

The field that is the world

569   17. The Church, Mother of mankind, above all, sees with
profound sorrow "an innumerable multitude of men and women,
children, adults and old people and unique human beings, who
suffer misery".[5]

By means of catechesis, in which due emphasis is given to
her social teaching, the Church[6] desires to stir Christian hearts "to

---

[1] GS 1.
[2] GS 2.
[3] GS 2.
[4] SRS 35.
[5] SRS 13b; cf. EN 30.
[6] Cf. CT 29.

the cause of justice"[7] and to a "preferential option or love for the poor",[8] so that her presence may really be light that shines and salt that cures.

Human rights

18. The Church, in her analysis of the soil of the world, is **570** acutely conscious of everything that injures the dignity of the human person. She is aware that all human rights[9] spring from this dignity, the constant object of Christian concern and commitment. For this reason, she looks beyond mere "social and economic indices"[10] to embrace also cultural and religious factors. What interests the Church is above all the integral development of the human person and of all peoples.[11] She notes with joy that "a beneficial trend is advancing and permeating peoples of the earth, making them ever more aware of the dignity of the individual".[12] Her vigorous insistence on respect for human rights and her decisive rejection of all their violations are clear expressions of that consciousness. The right to life, work, education, the foundation of a family, participation in public life, and to religious liberty are, today, demanded more than ever.

19. In many places, however, human rights are clearly **571** violated,[13] in apparent contradiction of the dignity proper to the human person. Such violations feed other forms of poverty beyond the material level: they contribute to a cultural and religious impoverishment which equally concerns the Church. The negation or restriction of human rights impoverishes the human person and entire peoples at least as much as, if not more

---

[7] SRS 41, cf. 1971 Documents of The Synod of Bishops, II: *"Justice in the world"* (30 Nov. 1971), III, *"The struggle for justice"*: AAS 43 (1971), pp. 935-937; and LC 77.

[8] SRS 41. Cf. ChL 42; TMA 51; CCC 2444-2448.

[9] Cf. John XXIII. *Pacem in Terris*, Encyclical Letter (11 April 1963), 9-27: AAS 55 (1963). pp. 261-270. Here are pointed out for the Church those more fundamental human rights. In numbers 28-34 (AAS 55 (1963), pp. 270-273) are indicated the principal "human rights". Catechesis should pay attention to both of these perspectives.

[10] Cf. SRS 15a.

[11] Cf. PP 14; CA 29.

[12] ChL 5; cf. SRS 26b; VS 31c.

[13] Cf. ChL 5a. The Extraordinary Synod of 1985, II, D, 1.

than, material privation itself.[14] The evangelizing activity of the Church in this field of human rights has, as its undeniable objective, the task of revealing the inviolable dignity of every human person. In a certain sense, "it is the central and unifying task of service which the Church, and the lay faithful in her, are called to render to the human family".[15] Catechesis must prepare them for this task.

Culture and cultures

572   20. The sower knows that the seed falls on specific soils and that it must absorb all the elements that enable it to bear fruit.[16] He also knows that some of these elements can prejudice the germination of the seed and indeed the very harvest itself.

The Constitution *Gaudium et Spes* underlines the importance of science and technology for the birth and development of modern culture. The scientific mentality, which derives from them, profoundly modifies "culture and ways of thinking",[17] with consequent human and religious repercussions. Modern man is deeply influenced by this scientific and experimental method.

Nevertheless, there is today a growing realization that such a mentality is incapable of explaining everything. Scientists themselves acknowledge that the rigour of experimental method must be complemented by some other method of knowing, if a profound understanding of the human being is ever to be attained. Linguistic theory, for example, shows that symbolic thought affords an approach to the mystery of the human person which would otherwise remain inaccessible. A rationalism which does not dichotomize man but which integrates his affective dimension, unifies him and gives fuller meaning to his life, is thus indispensable.

573   21. Together with this "more universal form of culture",[18] there is a growing desire to esteem a new autochthonous cultures. The question posed by the Second Vatican Council is still valid: "What is to be done to prevent increased exchange between cultures (which ought to lead to genuine and fruitful dialogue

---

[14] Cf. SRS 15e; CCC 2444; CA 57b.
[15] ChL 37. Cf. CA 47.
[16] AG 22a.
[17] GS 5.
[18] GS 54

between groups and nations) from disturbing the life of communities, overthrowing traditional wisdom and endangering the character proper to each people".[19]

– In many places there is an acute awareness that traditional cultures are being assailed by powerful external forces and by alien imitations of imported life-styles, with the result that the identity and values proper to peoples are thus being gradually eroded.

– Similarly acknowledged is the widespread influence of the communications media, which out of economic or ideological interest, often imposes a vision of life which does not respect the cultural distinctiveness of the peoples whom they address.

Thus, with inculturation, evangelisation encounters one of its greatest challenges. In the light of the Gospel, the Church must appropriate all the positive values of culture and of cultures[20] and reject those elements which impede development of the true potential of persons and peoples.

Religious and moral factors

22. Among the elements which make up the cultural heritage of a people, religious and moral factors are of particular interest to the sower. There is in contemporary culture a persistent spread of religious indifference: "Many however of our contemporaries ... either do not at all perceive, or else explicitly reject, this intimate and vital bond of man to God".[21]

Atheism, understood as a negation of God, "must therefore be regarded as one of the most serious problems of our time".[22] While it can take various forms, it often appears today under the guise of secularism, which consists in an excessively autonomous view of man and of the world "according to which it is entirely self-explanatory without any reference to God".[23] In the specifically religious sphere there are signs of "a return to the sacred",[24] of a new thirst for transcendent reality and for the divine. The

574

---

[19] GS 56c.
[20] Cf. EN 20; CT 53.
[21] GS 19.
[22] *Ibid.*
[23] EN 55; cf. LC 41 and GS 19.
[24] Synod, II, A 1.

contemporary world acknowledges in a more comprehensive and vital way "the renewed interest in religious research".[25] Certainly this phenomenon "is not without ambiguity".[26] The widespread growth of sects and new religious movements and the revival of "fundamentalism"[27] are factors of serious concern for the Church and require careful analysis

575   23. The moral situation of today is on a par with its religious situation. There is an evident obscuring of the ontological truth of the human person – as though the denial of God meant an interior breakdown of the aspirations of the human being.[28] In many places this contributes to the rise of an "ethical relativism which would remove any sure moral reference point from political and social life".[29] Evangelisation encounters a privileged field of activity in the religious and moral sphere. Indeed the primordial mission of the Church is to proclaim God and to be his witness before the world. This involves making known the true face of God and his loving plan of salvation for man, as it has been revealed in Jesus Christ. To prepare such witnesses, it is necessary for the Church to develop a profoundly religious catechesis, nourished on the Gospel, which will deepen man's encounter with God and forge a bond of permanent communion with Him.

The Church in the world

The faith of Christians

576   24. The disciples of Jesus are scattered in the world as leaven but, as in every age, they are not immune from the influences of human situations. It is therefore necessary to enquire into the current situation of the faith of Christians. Catechetical renewal, developed in the Church over the last decades, continues to bear very welcome fruit.[30] The catechesis of children, of young people

---

[25] ChL 4.

[26] Cf. RM 38.

[27] CA 29 and 46c.

[28] Cf. GS 36. John Paul II, in the Encyclical letter *Dominum et vivificantem* (18 May 1986), 38: AAS 78 (1986), pp. 851-852, also establishes this connection: "The ideology of the 'death of God' easily demonstrates in its effects that on the 'theoretical and practical' levels it is the ideology of the 'death of man'".

[29] VS 101; cf. EV 19, 20.

[30] CT 3; cf. MPD 4.

and of adults has given rise to a type of Christian who is conscious of his faith and who acts consistently with it in his life. In such Christians this catechesis has encouraged:

– a new and vital experience of God as merciful Father;

– a more profound rediscovery of Jesus Christ, not only in his divinity but also in his humanity;

– a sense of co-responsibility on the part of all for the mission of the Church in the world;

– and a raising of consciousness with regard to the social obligations of the faith.

25. Nonetheless, in considering today's religious situation, the Church is also obliged to take into account the extent to which Christians "have been shaped by the climate of secularism and ethical relativism?"[31] A prime category requiring examination is that of the "many people who have been baptized but lead lives entirely divorced from Christianity".[32] This in fact constitutes a mass of "non-practising Christians"[33] even though in many hearts religious feeling has not been completely lost. Re-awakening these to the faith is a real challenge for the Church. Then there are "the simple people"[34] who express themselves, at times with sincere religious feeling and deep rooted "popular devotion".[35] They possess a certain faith, "but know little even of its fundamental principles".[36] There are, moreover, numerous other Christians, often highly educated, whose religious formation amounts solely to that which they received in childhood. These also need to re-examine and develop their faith "from a different standpoint".[37]

577

26. There is also a certain number of baptized Christians who, desiring to promote dialogue with various cultures and other religious confessions, or on account of a certain reticence on their part to live in contemporary society as believers, fail to give explicit and courageous witness in their lives to the faith of Jesus

578

---

[31] TMA 36b; GS 19c.
[32] EN 52. Cf. CT 19 and 42.
[33] EN 56.
[34] EN 52.
[35] EN 48; cr. CT 54; ChL 34b; 1985 Synod, II, A, 4; DCG (1971), 6.
[36] EN 52.
[37] Cf. EN 52; CT 44.

Christ. These concrete situations of the Christian faith call urgently on the sower to develop *a new evangelisation,*[38] especially in those Churches of long-standing Christian tradition where secularism has made greater inroads. In this new context of evangelisation, missionary proclamation and catechesis, especially of the young and of adults, is an evident priority.

The internal life of the ecclesial community

579   27. It is important to consider also the very life of the ecclesial community which is its innermost quality. Firstly, it is necessary to see how the Second Vatican Council has been accepted in the Church, and how it has borne fruit. The great conciliar documents have not remained a dead letter: their effects are widely acknowledged. The four constitutions (*Sacrosanctum Concilium, Lumen Gentium, Dei Verbum* and *Gaudium et Spes*) have indeed enriched the Church. In fact:

– liturgical life is more profoundly understood as the source and summit of ecclesial life;

– the people of God has acquired a keener awareness of the "common priesthood"[39] founded on Baptism, and is rediscovering evermore the universal call to holiness and a livelier sense of mutual service in charity;

– the ecclesial community has acquired a livelier sense of the word of God. Sacred Scripture, for example, is read, savoured and meditated upon more intensely;

– the mission of the Church in the world is perceived in a new way: on the basis of interior renewal, the Second Vatican Council has opened Catholics to the demands of evangelisation as necessarily linked to dialogue with the world, to human development, to different cultures and religions as well as to the urgent quest for Christian unity.

580   28. It must be recognized, however, that in the midst of this richness there also occur "difficulties about the acceptance of the Council".[40] Despite so comprehensive and profound an ecclesiology, the sense of belonging to the Church has weakened and "a

---

[38] ChL, 34b; 33d.
[39] LG 10.
[40] Synod, 1985, I, 3.

certain disaffection towards the Church is frequently noted".[41] Thus the Church is often regarded in a one-dimensional way as a mere institution and deprived of her mystery. In some instances tendentious positions have been adopted and set in opposition to the interpretation and application of the renewal sought in the Church by the Second Vatican Council. Such ideologies and conduct have led to divisions which damage that witness of communion indispensable to evangelisation. The evangelizing activity of the Church, catechesis included, must tend all the more decisively toward solid ecclesial cohesion. To this end it is urgent that an authentic ecclesiology of communion,[42] be promoted and deepened in order to arouse in Christians a deep ecclesial spirituality.

The situation of catechesis: its vitality and difficulties
29. The vitality of catechesis in recent years has been amply **581** demonstrated by many positive aspects. Amongst others the following must be highlighted:
– the great number of priests, religious and laity who devote themselves with enthusiasm to catechesis, one of the most important ecclesial activities.
– the missionary character of contemporary catechesis and its ability to secure adherence to the faith on the part of catechumens and those to be catechized in a world in which religious sense is obscured must also be underlined: in this dynamic there is an acute awareness that catechesis must have a catechumenal style, as of integral formation rather than mere information; it must act in reality as a means of arousing true conversion;[43]
– consonant with what has been said, concerning the expanding role of adult catechesis[44] the catechetical programmes of many particular Churches assume extraordinary importance. This option appears to be a priority in the pastoral planning of many dioceses, and also plays a central role in many ecclesial groups and movements;
– promoted no doubt by recent directions of the Magisterium,

---

[41] *Ibid.*
[42] Congregation for the Doctrine of the Faith, Letter *Communionis notio* (28 May 1992), 1, AAS 85 (1993), p. 838; cf. TMA 36e.
[43] Cf. CT 19b.
[44] Cf. CT 43.

catechetical thought, has gained much in our times in terms of quality and profundity. In this sense many local Churches already have at their disposal suitable and opportune pastoral programmes.

582
30. It is necessary, however, to examine with particular attention some problems so as to identify their solutions:

– the first concerns the conception of catechesis as a school of faith, an initiation and apprenticeship in the entire Christian life of which catechists do not yet have a full understanding.

– with regard to the fundamental direction of catechesis, catechetical activity is still usually impregnated with the idea of 'Revelation': however, the conciliar concept of 'Tradition' is much less influential as an inspiration for catechesis: in much catechesis, indeed, reference to Sacred Scripture is virtually exclusive and unaccompanied by sufficient reference to the Church's long experience and reflection,[45] acquired in the course of her two-thousand-year history. The ecclesial nature of catechesis, in this case, appears less clearly; the inter-relation of Sacred Scripture, Tradition and the Magisterium, each according to "its proper mode"[46] does not yet harmoniously enrich a catechetical trans-mission of the faith;

– Concerning the object of catechesis, which always seeks to promote communion with Jesus Christ, it is necessary to arrive at a more balanced presentation of the entire truth of the mystery of Christ. Often, emphasis is given only to his humanity without any explicit reference to his divinity; at other times, less frequently today, emphasis is so exclusively placed on his divinity that the reality of the mystery of the Incarnate Word is no longer evident;[47]

– Various problems exist with regard to the content of catechesis: there are certain doctrinal *lacunae* concerning the truth about God and man; about sin and grace and about eschatology; there is a need for a more solid moral formation; presentations of the history of the Church are inadequate; and too little importance is given to her social teaching; in some regions there has been a proliferation of catechisms and texts, the products of particular

---

[45] Cf. CT 27b.
[46] DV 10c.
[47] Cf. CT 29b.

initiatives whose selective tendencies and emphases are so differing as to damage that convergence necessary for the unity of the faith;[48]

– "Catechesis is intrinsically bound to every liturgical and sacramental action"[49] Frequently however, the practice of catechetics testifies to a weak and fragmentary link with the liturgy: limited attention to liturgical symbols and rites, scant use of the liturgical fonts, catechetical courses with little or no connection with the liturgical year; the marginalization of liturgical celebrations in catechetical programs;

– Concerning pedagogy, after a period in which excessive insistence on the value of method and techniques was promoted by some, sufficient attention is still not given to the demands and to the originality of that pedagogy which is proper to the faith. It remains easy to fall into a 'content-method' dualism, with resultant reductionism to one or other extreme; with regard to the pedagogical dimension the requisite theological discernment has not always been exercised;[50]

– Regarding differences between cultures in the service of the faith, it is difficult to know how to transmit the Gospel within the cultural horizons of the peoples to whom it is proclaimed, in such a way that it can be really perceived as Good News for the lives of people and of society;[51]

– Formation for the apostolate and for mission is one of the fundamental tasks of catechesis. Nevertheless while there is a new sensitivity to the formation of the laity for Christian witness, for inter-religious dialogue, and for their secular obligations, education for missionary activity "ad gentes" still seems weak and inadequate. Frequently, ordinary catechesis gives only marginal and inconsistent attention to the missions.

The sowing of the Gospel

31. Having tested the ground, the sower sends out his work-ers to proclaim the Gospel through all the world and to that end shares with them the power of his Spirit. At the same time he

583

---

[48] Cf. CT 30.
[49] CT 23.
[50] Cf. CT 58.
[51] EN 63.

shows them how to read the signs of the times and asks of them that special preparation which is necessary to carry out the sowing.

How to read the signs of the times

584   32. The voice of the Spirit, which Jesus, on behalf of the Father, has communicated to his disciples "resounds in the very events of history".[52] Behind the changing data of present situations and in the deep motives of evangelisation, it is necessary to discover "what may be genuine signs of the presence or the purpose of God".[53]

Such analysis, however, must always be done in the light of faith. Availing herself of the human sciences,[54] which are always necessary, the Church seeks to discover the meaning of the present situation within the perspective of the history of salvation. Her judgements on reality are always a diagnosis of the need for mission.

Some challenges for catechesis

585   33. In order to express its vitality and to be efficacious, catechesis today needs to undertake the following challenges and directions:

– Above all it needs to present itself as a valid service to evangelisation of the Church with an accent on missionary character;

– It should address itself to those who have been and continue to be its privileged recipients: children, adolescents, young people and adults;

– Based on the example of catechesis in the patristic era, it needs to form the personality of the believer and therefore be a true and proper school of Christian pedagogy;

– It needs to announce the essential mysteries of Christianity, promoting the trinitarian experience of life in Christ as the centre of the life of faith;

– It needs to consider as its primary task the preparation and formation of catechists in the deep riches of the faith.

---

[52] FC 4b; cf. ChL 3e.
[53] GS 11; cf. GS 4.
[54] Cf. GS 62; FC 5.

Part One: Catechesis in the Church's Mission of Evangelisation

Catechesis in the Church's mission of evangelisation
"Go into all the world; and preach the Gospel to the whole creation" (Mark 16:15).

"Go, therefore make disciples of all nations; baptizing them in the name of the Father, and of the Son and of the Holy Spirit, teaching them to observe all that I have commanded you" (Matt 28:19-20). "You are witnesses of these things" (Luke 24:48); "But you shall receive power when the Holy Spirit has come upon you, and you shall be my witnesses... to the end of the earth" (Acts 1:8).

The missionary mandate of Jesus
34. Jesus Christ, after his Resurrection together with the **586** Father sent the Holy Spirit in order that he might accomplish from within the work of salvation and that he might animate his disciples to continue the mission to the whole world.

He was the first and supreme evangelizer. He proclaimed the Kingdom of God,[55] as the urgent and definitive intervention of God in history, and defined this proclamation *"the Gospel"*, that is, the Good News. To this Gospel, Jesus devoted his entire earthly life: he made known the joy of belonging to the Kingdom,[56] its demands, its *magna carta*,[57] the mysteries which it embraces,[58] the life of fraternal charity of those who enter it[59] and its future fulfilment.[60]

The meaning and purpose of Part One
35. This first part intends to define the proper character of **587** catechesis. Its first chapter, with regard to theology, recalls briefly the concept of Revelation as set forth in the conciliar constitution *Dei Verbum.* It determines in a specific manner the way in which the ministry of the word is to be conceived. The concepts *word of*

---

[55] Cf. *Mark* 1:15 and parallels. RM 12-20; CCC 541-560.
[56] Cf. *Matt* 5:3-12.
[57] Cf. *Matt* 5:1-7:29.
[58] Cf. *Matt* 13:11.
[59] Cf. *Matt* 18:1-35.
[60] Cf. *Matt* 24:1-25, 46.

God, Gospel, Kingdom of God, and Tradition, in this dogmatic constitution, are fundamental to the meaning of catechesis. Together with these, the concept of evangelisation is an indispensable point of reference for catechesis. The same dynamic is presented with new and profound precision in the Apostolic Exhortation *Evangelii Nuntiandi.*

The second chapter situates catechesis within the context of evangelisation and relates it to other forms of the ministry of the word of God. Thanks to this rapport one more easily discovers the proper character of catechesis.

The third chapter presents a more direct analysis of catechesis in itself: its ecclesial nature, its binding objective of communion with Jesus Christ, its tasks and the catechumenal idea by which it is inspired.

The term catechesis has undergone a semantic evolution during the twenty centuries of the Church's history. In this Directory the concept of catechesis takes its inspiration from the post-conciliar Magisterial documents, principally from *Evangelii Nuntiandi, Catechesi Tradendae and Redemptoris Missio.*

The concept of catechesis which one has, profoundly conditions the selection and organization of its contents *(cognitive, experiential, behavioural),* identifies those to whom it is addressed and defines the pedagogy to be employed in accomplishing its objectives.

Chapter One: Revelation and its transmission through evangelisation

"Blessed be the God and Father of Our Lord Jesus Christ, who has blessed us in Christ with every spiritual blessing in the heavenly places... for he has made known to us in all wisdom and insight the mystery of his will, according to his purpose which he set forth in Christ as a plan for the fulness of time, to unite all things in him, things in heaven and things on earth" (Eph 1:3-10).

The revelation of God's providential plan

588 36. "God who creates and conserves all things by his Word, offers to men a constant evidence of himself in created things".[61]

---

[61] DV 3.

Man, who by his nature and his vocation is capable of knowing God, when he listens to this message of creation is able to arrive at the certainty of the existence of God, as the cause and end of all things and as the one who is able to reveal himself to man.

The Constitution *Dei Verbum* of the Second Vatican Council describes Revelation as that act by which God manifests himself personally to man. God truly reveals himself as one who desires to communicate himself, making the human person a participant in his divine nature.[62] In this way God accomplishes his plan of love.

"It pleased God, in his goodness and wisdom, to reveal himself and to make known the mystery of his will [to men]...in order to invite and receive them into communion with himself".[63]

37. The "providential plan"[64] of the Father, fully revealed in Jesus Christ, is realized by the power of the Holy Spirit. This implies:

– the Revelation of God, of his "innermost truth",[65] of his "secret",[66] of the true vocation and dignity of the human person;[67]

– the offer of salvation to all men, as a gift of God's grace and mercy,[68] which implies freedom from evil, sin and death;[69]

– the definitive call to gather into the family of God all of his scattered children, thus realizing a fraternal union amongst men.[70]

589

Revelation: deeds and words

38. God, in his greatness, uses a pedagogy[71] to reveal himself to the human person: he uses human events and words to communicate his plan; he does so progressively and in stages,[72] so as to draw even closer to man. God, in fact, operates in such a manner that man comes to knowledge of his salvific plan by

590

---

[62] Cf. *2 Pet* 1:4; CCC 51-52.
[63] 2 DV 2.
[64] 2 *Eph* 1:9.
[65] 2 DV 2.
[66] 2 EN 11.
[67] Cf. GS 22a.
[68] Cf. *Eph* 2:8; EN 27.
[69] Cf. EN 9.
[70] Cf. *Gen* 11:52; AG 2b and 3a.
[71] Cf. St Irenaeus of Lyons, *"Adversus haereses"* III, 20, 2. SCh 211, 389-393. DV 15; CT 58; ChL 61; CCC 53 and 122; and also Part III, chap. 1.
[72] CCC 54-64

means of the events of salvation history and the inspired words which accompany and explain them.

"This economy of Revelation is realized by deeds and words, which are intrinsically bound up with each other. As a result,

– the works performed by God in the history of Salvation show forth and bear out the doctrine and realities signified by the words,

– the words, for their part, proclaim the works, and bring to light the mystery they contain".[73]

591   39. Evangelisation too which transmits Revelation to the world, is also brought about in words and deeds. It is at once testimony and proclamation, word and sacrament, teaching and task. Catechesis, for its part, transmits the words and deeds of Revelation; it is obliged to proclaim and narrate them and, at the same time, to make clear the profound mysteries they contain. Moreover, since Revelation is a source of light for the human person, catechesis not only recalls the marvels worked by God in the past, but also, in the light of the same Revelation, it interprets the signs of the times and the present life of man, since it is in these that the plan of God for the salvation of the world is realized.[74]

Jesus Christ: mediator and fulness of Revelation

592   40. God revealed himself progressively to man, through the prophets and through salvific events, until he brought to completion his self-revelation by sending his own Son:[75]

"[Jesus Christ] completed and perfected Revelation, he did this by way of his presence and self manifestation – by words and works, signs and miracles, but above all by his death and glorious resurrection from the dead, and finally by sending the Spirit of truth".[76]

Jesus Christ is not merely the greatest of the prophets but is the eternal Son of God, made man. He is, therefore, the final event towards which all the events of salvation history converge.[77] He is indeed "the Father's one, perfect and

---

[73] DV 2.
[74] Cf. DCG (1971) 11b.
[75] Cf. *Heb* 1:1-2.
[76] DV 4.
[77] Cf. *Luke* 24:27.

unsurpassable Word".[78]

41. The ministry of the word must always give prominence to **593** this wonderful characteristic, proper to the economy of Revelation: the Son of God enters human history, assumes human life and death, and brings about the new and definitive covenant between God and man. It is the task of catechesis to show who Jesus Christ is, his life and ministry, and to present the Christian faith as the following of his person.[79] Consequently, it must base itself constantly on the Gospels, which "are the heart of all the Scriptures 'because they are our principal source for the life and teaching of the Incarnate Word, our Saviour'".[80]

The fact that Jesus Christ is the fulness of Revelation is the foundation for the "Christocentricity"[81] of catechesis: the mystery of Christ, in the revealed message, is not another element alongside others, it is rather the centre from which all other elements are structured and illuminated.

The transmission of Revelation by the Church, the work of the Holy Spirit

42. The Revelation of God, culminating in Jesus Christ, is **594** destined for all mankind: "He (God) desires all men to be saved and to come to the knowledge of the truth" (1 Tim 2:4)[82] In virtue of his universal salvific will, God has ordained that Revelation should be transmitted to all peoples and to all generations and should remain always in its entirety.

43. To fulfil this divine plan, Jesus Christ founded the **595** Church, built on the Apostles. He gave them the Holy Spirit from the Father and sent them to preach the Gospel to the whole world. The Apostles, by words, deeds and writings, faithfully discharged this task.[83]

---

[78] CCC 65; St John of the Cross puts it as follows: "He has told us everything at once in this one Word" (*"The Ascent of Mount Carmel"* 2,22; cf. The Liturgy of Hours, I, Office of Readings for Monday of the Second week of Advent).

[79] Cf. CT 5; CCC 520 and 2053.

[80] CCC 125, which refers to DV 18.

[81] CT 5. The Theme of Christocentrism, is explained in "The object of catechesis: communion with Jesus Christ" (Part I Chapter 3) and in "The Christocentricity of the Gospel Message (Part II, Chapter 1).

[82] Cf.DV 7.

[83] Cf. DV 7a.

This Apostolic Tradition is perpetuated in the Church by means of the Church herself. The entire Church, pastors and faithful, is responsible for its conservation and transmission. The Gospel is conserved whole and entire in the Church: the disciples of Jesus Christ contemplate it and meditate upon it unceasingly; they live it out in their everyday lives; they proclaim it in their missionary activity. As the Church lives the Gospel she is continually made fruitful by the Holy Spirit. The Spirit causes her to grow constantly in her understanding of the Gospel, prompts her and sustains the task of proclaiming the Gospel in every corner of the world.[84]

596   44. The integral conservation of Revelation, the word of God contained in Tradition and Scripture, as well as its continuous transmission, are guaranteed in their authenticity. The Magisterium of the Church, sustained by the Holy Spirit and endowed with "the sure charism of truth",[85] exercises the function of "authentically interpreting the word of God".[86]

597   45. The Church, "universal sacrament of salvation", born of the Holy Spirit, transmits Revelation through evangelisation; she announces the Good News of the salvific plan of the Father and in the sacraments, communicates his Diving gifts.

To God who reveals himself is due this obedience of faith by which man adheres to the "Gospel of the grace of God" (Acts 20:24) with full assent of the intellect and of the will. Guided by faith, by means of the gift of the Spirit, man succeeds in attaining to contemplate and to delight in the God of love, who in Christ has revealed the riches of his glory.[87]

Evangelisation[88]

598   46. The Church "exists in order to evangelize"[89] that is "the

---

[84] Cf. DV 8 and CCC 75-79.

[85] DV 10b; cf CCC 85-87.

[86] LG 448; AG 1; GS 45; cf. CCC 774-776.

[87] Cf. Col 1:26.

[88] Dei Verbum and the Catechism of the Catholic Church (nn. 150-175) speak of faith as a response to Revelation. In this context, for catechetical pastoral motivation, it is preferred to associate faith more with Evangelisation than with Revelation in so far as the latter, in fact, reaches man normally by way of the evangelical mission of the Church.

[89] EN 14.

carrying forth of the Good News to every sector of the human race so that by its strength it may enter into the hearts of men and renew the human race".[90]

The missionary mandate of Jesus to evangelize has various aspects, all of which, however, are closely connected with each other: "proclaim", (Mark 16:15) *"make disciples and teach"*,[91] *"be my witnesses"*,[92] *"baptize"*,[93] *"do this in memory of me"*, (Luke 22:19) *"love one another"* (John 15:12). Proclamation, witness, teaching, sacraments, love of neighbour: all of these aspects are the means by which the one Gospel is transmitted and they constitute the essential elements of evangelisation itself.

Indeed they are so important that, at times, there is a tendency to identify them with the action of evangelisation. However, "no such definition can be accepted for that complex, rich and dynamic reality which is called evangelisation".[94] There is the risk of impoverishing it or even of distorting it. Evangelisation, on the contrary, must develop its "totality"[95] and completely incorporate its intrinsic bipolarity: witness and proclamation,[96] word and sacrament,[97] interior change and social transformation.[98] Those who evangelize have a "global vision"[99] of evangelisation and identify with the overall mission of the Church.[100]

The process of evangelisation

599

47. The Church, while ever containing in herself the fulness of the means of salvation, always operates "by slow stages".[101] The conciliar decree *Ad Gentes* clarifies well the dynamic of the process of evangelisation: Christian witness, dialogue and

---

[90] EN 18.
[91] Cf. Matt 28:19-20.
[92] Acts 1:8.
[93] Matt 28:19.
[94] EN 17.
[95] EN 28.
[96] Cf. EN 22a.
[97] Cf. EN 47b.
[98] Cf. EN 18.
[99] EN 24d.
[100] Cf. EN 14.
[101] AG 6b.

presence in charity (11-12), the proclamation of the Gospel and the call to conversion, the catechumenate and Christian Initiation, the formation of the Christian communities through and by means of the sacraments and their ministers (1518).[102] This is the dynamic for establishing and building up the Church.

600   48. Accordingly, in conformity with this, evangelisation must be viewed as the process by which the Church, moved by the Spirit, proclaims and spreads the Gospel throughout the entire world. Evangelisation:

– is urged by *charity,* impregnating and transforming the whole temporal order, appropriating and renewing all cultures;[103]

– bears *witness*[104] amongst peoples of the new way of being and living which characterizes Christians;

– *proclaims   explicitly   the   Gospel,*   through   "first proclamation",[105] calling to conversion.[106]

– *initiates into the faith and the Christian life,* by means of "catechesis"[107] and the "sacraments of Christian initiation",[108] those who convert to Jesus Christ or those who take up again the path of following him, incorporating both into the Christian community;[109]

– constantly nourishes the gift of *communion*[110] amongst the faithful by means of continuous education in the faith (homilies and other forms of catechesis), the sacraments and the practice of charity;

– continuously arouses *mission,*[111] sending all the disciples of Christ to proclaim the Gospel, by word and deed throughout the whole world.

---

[102] In the dynamism of evangelisation a distinction must be made between "initial situations" (*initia*), "gradual developments" (*gradus*) and situations of maturity: "appropriate acts must correspond to condition and state" (AG 6).

[103] EN 18-20 and RM 52-54; cf. AG 11-12 and 22.

[104] EN 21 and 41; RM 42-43; AG 11.

[105] EN 51,52,53. cf. CT 18, 19, 21, 25; RM 44.

[106] AG 13; EN 10 and 23; CT 19; RM 46.

[107] EN 22 and 24; CT 18; cf. AG 14 and RM 47.

[108] AG 14; CCC 1212; cf. CCC 1229-1233.

[109] EN 23; CT 24; RM 48-49; cf. AG 15.

[110] ChL 18.

[111] ChL 32, which demonstrates the close connection between "communion" and "mission".

49. The process of evangelisation,[112] consequently, is structured in stages or "essential moments":[113] missionary activity directed toward non-believers and those who live in religious indifference; initial catechetical activity for those who choose the Gospel and for those who need to complete or modify their initiation; pastoral activity directed toward the Christian faithful of mature faith in the bosom of the Christian community.[114] These moments, however, are not unique: they may be repeated, if necessary, as they give evangelical nourishment in proportion to the spiritual growth of each person or of the entire community.

601

The ministry of the word in evangelisation
50. The ministry of the word[115] is a fundamental element of evangelisation. The presence of Christianity amongst different human groups and its living witness must be explained and justified by the explicit proclamation of Jesus Christ the Lord. "There is no true evangelisation if the name, the teaching, the life, the promises, the Kingdom and the mystery of Jesus of Nazareth, the Son of God, are not proclaimed".[116] Those who are already disciples of Jesus Christ also require to be constantly nourished by the word of God so that they may grow in their Christian life.[117]

602

---

[112] Cf. EN 24.

[113] Cf. CT 18.

[114] Cf. AG 6f; RM 33 and 48.

[115] Cf. *Acts* 6:4. The Ministry of the Word of God is fostered in the Church by:
– the ordained ministers (cf. CIC 756-757);
– members of institutes of consecrated life in light of their consecration to God (cf. CIC 758);
– the lay faithful in light of their baptism and confirmation (cf. CIC 759). In regard to the term *ministry* (*servitium*), it is necessary that all reference be made to the uniqueness and to the source of all ministry which is the *ministry of Christ.* To a certain extent this applies also without ambiguity to the non-ordained faithful. In the original meaning, it expresses the work with which the members of the Church carry on the mission of Christ, both within the Church and throughout the world. However, when the term is distinguished from and compared with the various *munera and officia,* then it should be clearly noted that only in virtue of sacred ordination does the word obtain that full, univocal meaning that tradition has attributed to it (cf. John Paul II, Allocution at the Symposium on "The Participation of the Lay Faithul in the Priestly Ministry" 4, *L'Osservatore Romano,* English Edition, 11 May 1994.)

[116] EN 22; cf. EN 51-53.

[117] Cf. EN 42-45, 54, 57.

The ministry of the word, within the context of evangelisation, transmits Revelation, through the Church, by using human words. These, however, always refer to works: to those which God has done and continues to do, especially in the liturgy; to the witness of Christians; to the transforming action which these Christians achieve, together with so many men of good will, throughout the world. This human word of the Church is the means used by the Holy Spirit to continue dialogue with humanity. He is, in fact, the principal agent of the ministry of the word, the one through whom "the living voice of the Gospel rings out in the Church – and through her in the world".[118]

The ministry of the word is exercised in "different forms".[119] The Church, since apostolic times,[120] in her desire to offer the word of God in the most appropriate manner, has realized this ministry in the most varied of ways.[121] All of these, however, perform the essential and fundamental functions of the ministry of the word itself.

Functions and forms of the ministry of the word

603   51. The following are the principal functions of the ministry of the word:

– Called together and called to faith

This function is the most immediate expression of the missionary mandate of Jesus. It is realized through "the primary proclamation", directed to non-believers; those who have chosen unbelief, those Christians who live on the margins of Christian life, those who follow other religions.[122] The religious awakening of the children of Christian families, is also an eminent form of this function.

---

[118] DV 8c.

[119] PO 4b; cf. CD 13c.

[120] Many diverse forms of this single ministry appear in the New Testament: "Proclamation, teaching, exhortation, prophecy, witness... this richness of expression is notable.

[121] The forms through which the ministry of the word is filtered are not in reality intrinsic to the Christian message as though to imply that diversity of form connotes different messages. These are, rather, accentuations or tones more or less explicitated and adapted to the situation of faith of each person or group of persons in their concrete situations.

[122] EN 51-53.

– Initiation

Those who are moved by grace to decide to follow Jesus are "introduced into the life of faith, of the liturgy and of the charity of the People of God".[123] The Church achieves this function fundamentally by catechesis, in close relation with the sacraments of initiation, whether these are about to be received or have already been received. Important forms include: the catechesis of non-baptized adults in the catechumenate, the catechesis of baptized adults who wish to return to the faith, or of those who need to complete their initiation; the catechesis of children and of the young, which of itself has the character of initiation. Christian education in families and religious instruction in schools also have an initiatory function.

– Continuous education in the faith: In many regions this is also called "permanent catechesis".[124]

It is intended for those Christians who have been initiated in the basic elements of the Christian faith, but who need constantly to nourish and deepen their faith throughout their lives. This function is accomplished through a great variety of forms: "systematic and occasional, individual and community, organized and spontaneous".[125]

– The liturgical function: The ministry of the word also has a liturgical function since, when realized within the context of a sacred action, it is an integral part of that action.[126] It takes different forms but amongst them the most important is the homily. Other forms in the liturgical context include celebrations of the word and instruction received during the administration of

---

[123] AG 14.

[124] There are different reasons for using such expressions as "continuing education in the faith" or "continuing catechesis". They may not however, relativise the prior, basic, structural and specific character of catechesis understood as basic initiation. The expression "continuing education in the faith" has been widely used in catechetical praxis since the Second Vatican Council. It denotes a second grade of catechesis which is subject to initiatory catechesis. It does not denote the totality of catechetical activity. The distinction between basic formation and permanent formation is used in reference to priestly formation in the Apostolic Exhortation, *Pastores dabo vobis* of John Paul II, chapters five and six, especially in 71: AAS 84 (1992), pp. 729 ff; 778 ff; 782-783.

[125] DCG (1971) 19d.

[126] Cf. SC 35; CCC 1154.

the sacraments. On the other hand, mention must also be made of the immediate preparation for reception of the different sacraments, the celebration of sacramentals and above all of the participation of the faithful in the Eucharist, as a primary means of education in the faith.

– The theological function: This seeks to develop understanding of the faith and is to be situated in the dynamic of *"fides quaerens intellectum"*, that is, of belief which seeks to understand.[127] Theology, in order to fulfil this function, needs to confront philosophical forms of thought, various forms of humanism and the human sciences, and dialogue with them. It is articulated whenever: "the systematic treatment and the scientific investigation of the truths of the Faith"[128] are promoted.

604   52. The important forms of the ministry of the Word are: the first announcement or missionary preaching, pre and post baptismal catechesis, the liturgical forms and the theological forms. Then, it often happens, for pastoral reasons, that important forms of the ministry of the word must assume more than one function. Catechesis, for example, together with its initiatory forms, has frequently to discharge tasks of mission. The same homily, depending on circumstances, can take on both the functions of convocation and of integral initiation.

Conversion and faith

605   53. In proclaiming the Good News of Revelation to the world, evangelisation invites men and women to conversion and faith.[129] The call of Jesus, "Repent and believe in the Gospel", (Mark 1:15) continues to resound today by means of the Church's work of evangelisation. The Christian faith is, above all, conversion to Jesus Christ,[130] full and sincere adherence to his person and the decision to walk in his footsteps.[131] Faith is a personal encounter with Jesus Christ making, of oneself a disciple

---

[127] Cf. Congregation for the Doctrine of the Faith, *Instruction on the ecclesial vocation of the theologian, Donum veritatis* (24 May 1990), 6: AAS 82 (1990), p. 1552

[128] DCG (1971) 17; cf. GS 62g.

[129] Cf. Rm 10:17; LG 16 and AG 7; cf. CCC 846-848.

[130] Cf. AG 13a.

[131] Cf. CT 5b.

of him. This demands a permanent commitment to think like him, to judge like him and to live as he lived.[132] In this way the believer unites himself to the community of disciples and appropriates the faith of the Church.[133]

54. This "Yes" to Jesus Christ, who is the fulness of the **606** revelation of the Father is twofold: a trustful abandonment to God and a loving assent to all that he has revealed to us. This is possible only by means of the action of the Holy Spirit.[134]

"By faith man freely commits his entire self completely to God, making the full submission of his intellect and will to God who reveals, and willingly assenting to the Revelation given by him".[135]

"To believe has thus a double reference: to the person and to the truth; to the truth, by trust in the person who bears witness to it".[136]

55. Faith involves a change of life, a *"metanoia"*,[137] that is a **607** profound transformation of mind and heart; it causes the believer to live that conversion.[138] This transformation of life manifests itself at all levels of the Christian's existence: in his interior life of adoration and acceptance of the divine will, in his action, participation in the mission of the Church, in his married and family life; in his professional life; in fulfilling economic and social responsibilities.

Faith and conversion arise from the *"heart"*, that is, they arise from the depth of the human person and they involve all that he is. By meeting Jesus Christ and by adhering to him the human being sees all of his deepest aspirations completely fulfilled. He finds what he had always been seeking and he finds it superabundantly.[139] Faith responds to that *"waiting"*,[140] often unconscious and always limited in its knowledge of the truth about God, about man himself and about the destiny that awaits him. It is like pure water[141] which refreshes the journey of man,

---

[132] Cf. CT 20b.
[133] Cf. CCC 166-167.
[134] Cf. CCC 150 and 176.
[135] DV 5.
[136] CCC 177.
[137] Cf. EN 10; AG 13b; CCC 1430-1431.
[138] EN 23.
[139] Cf. AG 13.
[140] Cf. RM 45c.
[141] Cf. RM 46d.

wandering in search of his home. Faith is a gift from God. It can only be born in the intimacy of Man's heart as a fruit of that "grace [which] moves and assists him",[142] and as a completely free response to the promptings of the Holy Spirit who moves the heart and turns it toward God, and who "makes it easy for all to accept and believe the truth".[143] The Blessed Virgin Mary lived these dimensions of faith in the most perfect way. The Church "venerates in Mary the purest realization of faith".[144]

The process of continuing conversion

608 56. Faith is a gift destined to grow in the hearts of believers.[145] Adhering to Jesus Christ, in fact, sets in motion a process of continuing conversion, which lasts for the whole of life.[146] He who comes to faith is like a new born child,[147] who, little by little, will grow and change into an adult, tending towards the state of the "perfect man",[148] and to maturity in the fulness of Christ. From a theological viewpoint, several important moments can be identified in the process of faith and conversion:

a) *Interest in the Gospel.* The first moment is one in which, in the heart of the non-believer or of the indifferent or of those who practise other religions, there is born, as a result of its first proclamation, an interest in the Gospel, yet without any firm decision. This first movement of the human spirit towards faith, which is already a fruit of grace, is identified by different terms: "propensity for the faith",[149] "evangelic preparation",[150] inclination to believe, "religious quest".[151] The Church calls those who show such concern "sympathizers".[152]

---

[142] DV 5; cf. CCC 153.
[143] *Ibidem.*
[144] CCC 149.
[145] CT 20a: "It is in fact a matter of giving growth, at the level of knowledge and in life, to the seed of faith sown by the Holy Spirit with the initial proclamation".
[146] Cf. RM 46b.
[147] Cf. *1 Pet* 2:2; *Heb* 5:13.
[148] *Eph* 4:13.
[149] RCIA 12.
[150] Cf. Eusebius of Caesrea, *"Praeparatio evangelica",* I, 1; SCh 206, 6; LG 16; AG 3a.
[151] ChL 4c.
[152] RCIA 12 and 111.

b) Conversion. This first moment of interest in the Gospel requires a period of searching[153] to be transformed into a firm option. The option for faith must be a considered and mature one. Such searching, guided by the Holy Spirit and the proclamation of the *Kerygma,* prepares the way for conversion which is certainly "initial",[154] but brings with it adherence to Christ and the will to walk in his footsteps. This "fundamental option" is the basis for the whole Christian life of the Lord's disciple.[155]

c) Profession of faith. Abandonment of self to Jesus Christ arouses in believers a desire to know him more profoundly and to identify with him. Catechesis initiates them in knowledge of faith and apprenticeship in the Christian life, thereby promoting a spiritual journey which brings about a "progressive change in outlook and morals".[156] This is achieved in sacrifices and in challenges, as well as in the joys which God gives in abundance. The disciple of Jesus Christ is then ready to make an explicit, living and fruitful profession of faith.[157]

d) Journeying towards perfection. The basic maturity which gives rise to the profession of faith is not the final point in the process of continuing conversion. The profession of baptismal faith is but the foundation of a spiritual building which is destined to grow. The baptized, moved always by the Spirit, nourished by the sacraments, by prayer and by the practice of charity, and assisted by multiple forms of ongoing education in the faith, seeks to realize the desire of Christ: "Be perfect as your heavenly Father is perfect".[158] This is the call to the fulness of perfection which is addressed to all the baptized.

57. The ministry of the word is at the service of this process **609** of full conversion. The first proclamation of the Gospel is characterized by the call to faith; catechesis by giving a foundation to conversion and providing Christian life with a basic structure; while ongoing education in the faith, in which the place of the homily must be underlined, is characterized by being the

---

[153] Cf. RCIA 6 and 7.
[154] AG 13b.
[155] Cf. AG 13; EN 10; RM 46; VS 66; RCIA 10.
[156] AG 13b.
[157] Cf. MPD 8b; CCC 187-189.
[158] *Matt* 5:48; cf. LG 11, 40b, 42e.

necessary nourishment of which every baptized adult has need in order to live.[159]

Socio-religious situations and evangelisation

610 58. The evangelisation of the world finds itself placed in a very diversified and changing religious panorama, in which it is possible to distinguish three basic situations[160] requiring particular and precise responses.

a) The situation of those "peoples, groups and socio-cultural contexts in which Christ and his Gospel are not known, or which lack Christian communities sufficiently mature to be able to incarnate the faith in their own environment and proclaim it to other groups".[161] This situation requires a "mission *ad gentes*",[162] where missionary activity is concentrated preferably toward young people and adults. Its particular characteristic consists in the fact that it is directed to non-Christians and invites them to conversion. In this context catechesis is usually developed within the baptismal catechumenate.

b) There are, moreover, situations in which, in a definite socio-cultural context, "there are Christian communities with adequate and solid ecclesial structures. They are fervent in their faith and in Christian living. They bear witness to the Gospel in their surroundings and have a sense of commitment to the Universal mission".[163] These communities demand an intense "pastoral action of the Church" since they are made up of people and families of profound Christian outlook. In such contexts it is vital that catechesis for children, adolescents and young people develop various processes of well articulated Christian initiation which permit these to arrive at adulthood with mature faith which

---

[159] Cf. DV 24; EN 45.

[160] Cf. RM 33.

[161] RM 33b.

[162] RM 33b. It is important to be cognisant of the parameters (*fines*) that RM assigns to the "mission *AG*". This is not restricted solely to territorial parameters (RM 37) but also to new social environments and phenomena (RM 37) such as large cities, youth, migration and to cultural areas and modern fora (RM 37) such as modern communications, science and ecology. In virtue of this a particular Church already rooted in a particular territory carries on a *missio AG* not only *ad extra* but also *ad intra*.

[163] RM 33c.

makes evangelizers of those who have been evagelized. Also in these situations adults are also in need of different types of Christian formation.

c) In many countries of established Christian tradition and sometimes in younger Churches there exists "an intermediate situation",[164] where "entire groups of the baptized have lost a living sense of the faith, or even no longer consider themselves members of the Church and live a life far removed from Christ and his Gospel".[165] Such situations require "a new evangelisation". The peculiar nature of this situation is found in the fact that missionary activity is directed towards the baptized of all ages, who live in a religious context in which Christian points of reference are perceived purely exteriorly. Here primary proclamation and basic catechesis are priorities.

The mutual connection between the activities of evangelisation which correspond to these socio-religious situations.

611

59. These socio-religious situations obviously differ from each other and it is wrong to regard them as equal. Such diversity, which has always existed in the Church's mission, acquires in today's changing world a new significance. Indeed, increasingly different situations oftentimes co-exist in the same territory. In many of the great cities, for example, a situation requiring *"missio ad gentes"* can co-exist along with one which requires "new evangelisation". Together with these there can be present in a dynamic way Christian missionary communities sustained by "comprehensive pastoral activity". Very often today, local Churches are obliged to address the entire panorama of these religious situations. "The boundaries between pastoral care of the faithful, new evangelisation and specific missionary activity are not clearly definable, and it is unthinkable to create barriers between them or to put them into water-tight compartments".[166] In fact, "each of them influences, stimulates and assists the others".[167]

---

[164] RM 33d.
[165] *Ibidem.*
[166] RM 34b.
[167] RM 34c. The text also speaks of the mutual enrichment between the mission ad *intra* and the mission ad *extra*. In RM 59c, in the same way, it is shown how the mission *AG* encourages people towards development, while "new evangelisation"

In order, therefore, to arrive at a mutual enrichment between the various activities of evangelisation which can co-exist, it is useful to remember that:

– Mission *ad gentes,* regardless of the zone or context in which it is realized, is the missionary responsibility most specifically entrusted to the Church by Jesus and thus the exemplary model for all her missionary activity. New evangelisation cannot supplant or be substituted for 'the mission *ad gentes*,' which continues to be the paradigm and primary task of missionary activity.[168]

– "The model for all catechesis is the baptismal catechumenate when, by specific formation, an adult converted to belief is brought to explicit profession of baptismal faith during the Paschal Vigil".[169] This catechumenal formation should inspire the other forms of catechesis in both their objectives and in their dynamism.

– "Catechesis for adults, since it deals with persons who are capable of an adherence that is fully responsible, must be considered the chief form of catechesis. All the other forms, which are indeed always necessary, are in some way oriented to it".[170] This implies that the catechesis of other age groups should have it for a point of reference and should be expressed in conjunction with it, in a coherent catechetical programme suitable to meet the pastoral needs of dioceses.

In this way catechesis, situated in the context of the Church's mission of evangelisation and seen as an essential moment of that mission, receives from evangelisation a missionary dynamic which deeply enriches it and defines its own identity. The ministry of catechesis appears, then, as a fundamental ecclesial service for the realization of the missionary mandate of Jesus.

Chapter Two: Catechesis in the process of evangelisation

"Things what we have heard and known, that our fathers

---

in the more developed nations brings about a clear sense of solidarity towards others.

[168] Cf. RM 31,34.

[169] 1977 Synod, MPD 8.

[170] DCG (1971) 20; CT 43; cf. Part Four, chap. 2.

have told us. We will not hide them from their children, but tell to the coming generation, the glorious deeds of the Lord, and his might, and the wonders he has wrought" (Ps 78:3-4).

"He (Apollos) had been instructed in the Way of the Lord and being fervent in spirit he spoke and taught accurately in the things concerning Jesus" (Acts 18:25).

60. In this chapter the relationship of catechesis with the **612** other elements of evangelisation, of which it is itself an integral part, is demonstrated. Thus, firstly, the relationship of catechesis with the primary proclamation, which is realized in mission, is described. There follows an examination of the close connection between catechesis and the sacraments of Christian initiation. Then is perceived the fundamental role of catechesis in the ordinary life of the Church and its role as continuing teacher in the faith. Special consideration is given to the relationship between catechesis and the teaching of religion in schools, since both activities are profoundly inter-connected, and, together with education in the Christian home, are basic to the formation of children and young people.

Primary or first proclamation and catechesis

61. Primary proclamation is addressed to non-believers and **613** those living in religious indifference. Its functions are to proclaim the Gospel and to call to conversion. Catechesis, "distinct from the primary proclamation of the Gospel",[171] promotes and matures initial conversion, educates the convert in the faith and incorporates him into the Christian community. The relationship between these two forms of the ministry of the word is, therefore, a relationship of complementary distinction. Primary proclamation, which every Christian is called to perform, is part of that *"Go"*[172] which Jesus imposes on his disciples: it implies, therefore, a going-out, a haste, a message. Catechesis, however, starts with the condition indicated by Jesus himself: "whosoever believes",[173] whosoever converts, whosoever decides. Both activities are essential and mutually complementary: go and welcome,

---

[171] CT 19.

[172] *Mark* 16:15 and *Matt* 28:19.

[173] *Mark* 16:16.

proclaim and educate, call and incorporate.

614   62. Nevertheless in pastoral practice it is not always easy to define the boundaries of these activities. Frequently, many who present themselves for catechesis truly require genuine conversion. Because of this the Church usually desires that the first stage in the catechetical process be dedicated to ensuring conversion.[174] In the *missio ad gentes*, this task is normally accomplished during the 'pre-catechumenate'.[175] In the context of "new evangelisation" it is effected by means of a *"kerygmatic catechesis"*, sometimes called "pre-catechesis",[176] because it is based on the pre-catechumenate and is proposed by the Gospel and directed towards a solid option of faith. Only by starting with conversion, and therefore by making allowance for the interior disposition of "whoever believes", can catechesis, strictly speaking, fulfil its proper task of education in the faith.[177]

The fact that catechesis, at least initially, assumes a missionary objective, does not dispense a particular Church from promoting an institutionalized programme of primary proclamation to execute more directly Jesus' missionary command. Catechetical renewal should be based thus on prior missionary evangelisation.

Catechesis, an essential "moment" in the process of evangelisation

615   63. The Apostolic Exhortation *Catechesi Tradendae* places catechesis firmly within the Church's mission and notes that evangelisation is a rich, complex and dynamic reality which comprises essential but different "moments". "Catechesis", it adds, "is one of these moments – a very remarkable one – in the whole process of evangelisation".[178] This is to say that there are activities which "prepare"[179] for catechesis and activities which "derive" from it[180] The "moment" of catechesis is that which

---

[174] Cf. CT 19; DCG (1971) 18.

[175] RCIA 9-13. cf. CIC 788.

[176] In the present directory it is supposed that those to whom *kerygmatic catechesis* or *pre-catechesis* is addressed will be interested in the Gospel. In situations where they have no such interest then primary proclamation is called for.

[177] Cf. RCIA 9,10,50; CT 19.

[178] CT 18; cf CT 20c.

[179] CT 18.

[180] *Ibidem.*

corresponds to the period in which conversion to Jesus Christ is formalized, and provides a basis for first adhering to him. Converts, by means of "a period of formation, an apprenticeship in the whole Christian life",[181] are initiated into the mystery of salvation and an evangelical style of life. This means "initiating the hearers into the fulness of Christian life".[182]

64. In discharging in different ways the initiatory function of the ministry of the word, catechesis lays the foundation for the building of the faith.[183] Other functions of the same ministry will continue to build, at different levels, on that foundation. **616**

Initiatory catechesis is thus the necessary link between missionary activity which calls to faith and pastoral activity which continually nourishes the Christian community. This is not, therefore, an optional activity, but basic and fundamental for building up the personality of the individual disciple, as it is for the whole Christian community. Without it, missionary activity lacks continuity and is sterile, while pastoral activity lacks roots and becomes superficial and confused: any misfortune could cause the collapse of the entire building.[184]

In truth, "the inner growth [of the Church] and her correspondence with God's plan depend essentially on catechesis".[185] In this sense catechesis must always be considered a priority in evangelisation.

Catechesis, at the service of Christian initiation

65. Faith, by means of which man responds to the proclamation of the Gospel, requires Baptism. The close connection between the two realities is rooted in the will of Christ himself, who commanded his apostles to make disciples of all nations and to baptize them. "The mission to baptize, and so the sacramental mission, is implied in the mission to evangelize".[186] **617**

Those who have converted to Jesus Christ and who have been educated in the faith by means of catechesis, by receiving

---

[181] AG 14.
[182] CT 18.
[183] St Cyril of Jerusalem, *Catecheses illuminandorum*, I, 11; PG. 33, 351-352.
[184] Cf. *Matt* 7:24-27.
[185] CT 13; cf. CT 15.
[186] CCC 1122.

the sacraments of Christian initiation (Baptism, Confirmation and Eucharist) "are delivered from the powers of darkness through the sacraments of Christian initiation and having died, been buried, and risen with Christ, they receive the Spirit of adoption as children and celebrate with the whole people of God the memorial of the Lord's death and resurrection".[187]

618   66. Catechesis, is thus, a fundamental element of Christian initiation and is closely connected with the sacraments of initiation, especially with Baptism, "the sacrament of faith".[188] The link uniting catechesis and Baptism is true profession of faith, which is at once an element inherent in this sacrament and the goal of catechesis. The aim of catechetical activity consists in precisely this: to encourage a living, explicit and fruitful profession of faith.[189] The Church, in order to achieve this, transmits to catechumens and those to be catechized, her living experience of the Gospel, her faith, so that they may appropriate and profess it. Hence, "authentic catechesis is always an orderly and systematic initiation into the revelation that God has given of himself to humanity in Christ Jesus, a revelation stored in the depths of the Church's memory and in Sacred Scripture, and constantly communicated from one generation to the next by a living active *traditio*".[190]

Fundamental characteristics of initiatory catechesis

619   67. Catechesis acquires certain characteristics in virtue of being an "essential moment" in the process of evangelisation, in the service of Christian initiation.[191] It is:

– a comprehensive and systematic formation in the faith. The Synod of 1977 underscored the need for a "comprehensive and

---

[187] AG 14. Cf. CCC 1212, 1229.

[188] CCC 1253. In the baptismal catechumenate of adults in the mission *AG* catechesis precedes Baptism. In the catechesis of the baptized, formation is subsequent to Baptism. However, also in this case a function of catechesis is to help to discover and bring to life the immense richness of Baptism already received. CCC 1231 uses the expression *post-baptismal catechumenate*. ChL 61 calls it post-baptismal catechesis.

[189] Cf. CCC 1229; CD 14.

[190] CT 22. Cf. CT 21b, 18d.

[191] Cf. CT 21.

structured"[192] catechesis, since catechesis is principally distinguished from other forms of presenting the word of God by its comprehensive and vital deepening of the mystery of Christ;

– this comprehensive formation includes more than instruction: it is an apprenticeship of the entire Christian life, it is a "complete Christian initiation",[193] which promotes an authentic following of Christ, focused on his Person; it implies education in knowledge of the faith and in the life of faith, in such a manner that the entire person, at his deepest levels, feels enriched by the word of God; it helps the disciple of Christ to transform the old man in order to assume his baptismal responsibilities and to profess the faith from the "heart";[194]

– a basic and essential formation,[195] centred on what constitutes the nucleus of Christian experience, the most fundamental certainties of the faith and the most essential evangelical values; it lays the foundation of the spiritual edifice of the Christian, nurtures the roots of his faith life and enables him to receive more solid nourishment in the ordinary life of the Christian community.

620

68. In summary, initiatory catechesis, being comprehensive and systematic, cannot be reduced to the circumstantial or the occasional.[196] As it is formation for the Christian life it comprises but surpasses mere instruction.[197] Being essential, it looks to what is "common" for the Christian, without entering into disputed questions nor transforming itself into a form of theological investigation. Finally, being initiatory, it incorporates into the community, which lives, celebrates and bears witness to the faith. It fulfils, at once, initiatory, educational and instructional

---

[192] Two things need to be underlined in this synodal contribution taken from *Catechesi Tradendae:* the preoccupation to take into account a pastoral problem ("I insist on the necessity of an organic and systematic Christian education because for diverse reasons there has been a tendency to minimize its importance"), and the fact of considering the organic nature of catechesis as the *principal characteristic* connoting it.

[193] CT 21.

[194] Cf. CT 20; St Augustine, *De catechizandis rudibus,* I, chap. 4, 8; CCL 46, 128-129.

[195] Cf. CT 21b.

[196] Cf. CT 21c.

[197] Cf. CT 33 and CCC 1231; AG 14.

functions.[198] This inherent richness in the Catechumenate of non-baptized adults should serve to inspire other forms of catechesis.

Catechesis at the service of ongoing formation in the faith:
Continuing education in faith within the Christian community

621   69. Continuing or on-going education in the faith follows upon basic education and presupposes it. Both fulfil two distinct but complementary functions of the ministry of the word while serving the process of continuing conversion. Initiatory catechesis lays the basis for the Christian life of the followers of Jesus. The process of continuing conversion goes beyond what is provided by basic catechesis. In order to encourage this process, it is necessary to have a Christian community which welcomes the initiated, sustains them and forms them in the faith: "Catechesis runs the risk of becoming barren if no community of faith and Christian life welcomes the catechumen at a certain stage of his catechesis".[199] The accompaniment which a community gives to the initiated is eventually transformed into their being totally integrated by the same community.

622   70. In the Christian community the disciples of Jesus Christ are nourished at a twofold table; "that of the word of God and that of the Body of Christ".[200] The Gospel and the Eucharist are the constant food for the journey to the Father's House. The action of the Holy Spirit operates so that the gift of "communion" and the task of "mission" are deepened and lived in an increasingly intense way.

Continuing formation in the faith is directed not only to the individual Christian, to accompany them in their journey towards holiness, but also to the Christian community as such so that it may mature also in its interior life of love of God and of the brethren as well as in its openness to the world as a missionary community. The desire of Jesus and his prayer to the Father are an unceasing appeal: "May they all be one; even as thou, Father, art in me, and I in thee, that they may also be in us, so that the world may believe that thou hast sent me".[201] Approaching this

---

[198] Cf. DCG (1971) 31.
[199] CT 24.
[200] DV 21.
[201] *John* 17:21.

ideal, little by little, demands of the community a great fidelity to the action of the Holy Spirit, the constant nourishment of the Body and Blood of Christ and continuing education in the faith, listening all the time to the word.

At this table of the word of God, the homily occupies a privileged position, since it "takes up again the journey of faith put forward by catechesis and brings it to its natural fulfilment, at the same time it encourages the Lord's disciples to begin anew each day their spiritual journey in truth, adoration and thanksgiving".[202]

Various forms of continuing catechesis   **623**

71. For continuing education in the faith, the ministry of the word uses many forms of catechesis. Among these the following may be highlighted:

– The study and exploration of Sacred Scripture, read not only in the Church but with the Church and her living faith, which helps to discover divine truth, which it contains, in such a way as to arouse a response of faith.[203] The *"lectio divina"* is an eminent form of this vital study of Scripture.

– A Christian reading of events, which is required of the missionary vocation of the Christian community. In this respect the study of the social teaching of the Church is indispensable, since "its main aim is to interpret these realities, determining their conformity with or divergence from the lines of the Gospel teaching".[204]

– Liturgical catechesis, prepares for the sacraments by promoting a deeper understanding and experience of the liturgy. This explains the contents of the prayers, the meaning of the signs and gestures, educates to active participation, contemplation and silence. It must be regarded as an "eminent kind of catechesis".[205]

– Occasional catechesis which seeks to interpret determined

---

[202] Cf. CT 48; cf. SC 52; DV 24; DCG (1971) 17; *Missale Romanum, Ordo Lectionum Missae*, 24 Editio Typica Altera, Libreria Editrice Vaticana 1981.

[203] Cf. DV 21-25; Pontifical Biblical Commission, *The interpretation of the Bible in the Church* (21 September 1993), especially in IV, see 2 and 3, Città del Vaticano 1993.

[204] SRS 41; cf. CA 5, 53-62. Congregation for Catholic Education, *Guidelines for the study and teaching of the Social Doctrine of the Church in the formation of priests* (30 December, 1988), Rome 1988.

[205] CT 23. Cf. SC 35 ad 3; CIC 777, 1 and 2

circumstances of personal, family, ecclesial or social life and to help live them in the prospect of faith.[206]

– Initiatives of spiritual formation which seek to reinforce conviction, open new perspectives and encourage perseverance in prayer and in the duties of following Christ.

– A systematic deepening of the Christian message by means of theological instruction, so as truly to educate in the faith, encourage growth in understanding of it and to equip the Christian for giving the reason for his hope in the present world.[207] In a certain sense, it is appropriate to call such instruction "perfective catechesis".

624   72. It is fundamentally important that initiatory catechesis for adults, whether baptized or not, initiatory catechesis for children and young people and continuing catechesis are closely linked with the catechetical endeavour of the Christian community, so that the particular Church may grow harmoniously and that its evangelizing activity may spring from authentic sources. "It is important also that the catechesis of children and young people, permanent catechesis and the catechesis of adults should not be separate watertight compartments... it is important that their perfect complementarity be fostered".[208]

Catechesis and religious instruction in schools: The proper character of religious instruction in schools

625   73. Within the ministry of the word, the character proper to religious instruction in schools and its relationship with the catech-esis of children and of young people merit special consideration.

The relationship between religious instruction in schools and catechesis is one of distinction and complementarity: "there is an absolute necessity to distinguish clearly between religious instruction and catechesis".[209]

---

[206] Cf. CT 21c and 47; DCG (1971) 96 c, d, e, f.

[207] Cf. 1 Pet 3:15 Congregation for the Doctrine of the Faith, Instruction *Dominum veritatis,* 6b *l.c.* 1552. Confer also what is indicated in CT 61, about the correlation between catechesis and theology.

[208] CT 45c.

[209] Congregation for Catholic Education, "The Religious Dimension of Education in the Catholic School" (7 April 1988), 68; Tipografia Poliglotta Vaticana, Roma 1988 cf. John Paul II, *Allocution* to the priests of the diocese of Rome (5 March 1981). *Insegnamenti di Giovanni Paolo II,* IV 1 pp. 629-630, CD 13c CIC 761.

What confers on religious instruction in schools its proper evangelizing character is the fact that it is called to penetrate a particular area of culture and to relate with other areas of knowledge. As an original form of the ministry of the word, it makes present the Gospel in a personal process of cultural, systematic and critical assimilation.[210]

In the cultural universe, which is assimilated by students and which is defined by knowledge and values offered by other scholastic disciplines, religious instruction in schools sows the dynamic seed of the Gospel and seeks to "keep in touch with the other elements of the student's knowledge and education; thus the Gospel will impregnate the mentality of the students in the field of their learning, and the harmonization of their culture will be achieved in the light of faith".[211]

It is necessary, therefore, that religious instruction in schools appear as a scholastic discipline with the same systematic demands and the same rigour as other disciplines. It must present the Christian message and the Christian event with the same seriousness and the same depth with which other disciplines present their knowledge. It should not be an accessory alongside of these disciplines, but rather it should engage in a necessary inter-disciplinary dialogue. This dialogue should take place above all at that level at which every discipline forms the personality of students. In this way the presentation of the Christian message influences the way in which the origins of the world, the sense of history, the basis of ethical values, the function of religion in culture, the destiny of man and his relationship with nature, are understood. Through inter-disciplinary dialogue religious instruction in schools underpins, activates, develops and completes the educational activity of the school.[212]

---

[210] Sacred Congregation for Catholic Education, Document, *The Catholic School* (19 March 1977) 26.

[211] CT 69. Note also as per CT 69 the originality of religious instruction in schools does not consist solely in rendering possible dialogue with culture in general since this pertains to all the forms of ministry of the word. Religious instruction in schools seeks in a more immediate way to promote this dialogue in a personal process of systematic and critical initiation and by encounter with the cultural patrimony promoted by the school.

[212] Cf. Congregation for Catholic Education, *"The religious dimension of education in the Catholic school"*, l.c. 70.

The school context and those to whom religious instruction in schools is directed

626   74. Religious instruction in schools is developed in diverse scholastic contexts, while always maintaining its proper character, to acquire different emphases. These depend on legal and organizational circumstances, educational theories, personal outlook of individual teachers and students as well as the relationship between religious instruction in the schools and family or parish catechesis.

It is not possible to reduce the various forms of religious instruction in schools, which have developed as a result of accords between individual states and Episcopal Conferences. It is, however, necessary that efforts be made so that religious instruction in schools respond to its objectives and its own characteristics.[213]

Students "have the right to learn with truth and certainty the religion to which they belong. This right to know Christ, and the salvific message proclaimed by Him cannot be neglected. The confessional character of religious instruction in schools, in its various focuses, given by the Church in different countries is an indispensable guarantee offered to families and students who choose such education".[214]

When given in the context of the Catholic school, religious instruction is part of and completed by other forms of the ministry of the word (catechesis, homilies, liturgical celebration, etc.). It is indispensable to their pedagogical function and the basis for their existence.[215]

In the context of state schools or non-confessional schools where the civil authorities or other circumstances impose the teaching of religion common to both Catholics and non-Catholics[216] it will have a more ecumenical character and have a

---

[213]Cf. John Paul II, *Allocution* on the Symposium of the Council of the Episcopal Conference on the Teaching of the Catholic Religion in the public school (15 April 1991): *Teachings of John Paul II,* XIV1, pp. 780s.

[214] *Ibid.*

[215] Cf. CT 69, Congregation for Catholic Education, *The religious dimension of education in the Catholic school,* 66: l.c.

[216] Cf. CT 33.

more inter-religious awareness.

In other circumstances religious instruction will have an extensively cultural character and teach a knowledge of religions including the Catholic religion. In this case too and especially if presented by teachers with a sincere respect for the Christian religion, religious instruction maintains a true dimension of "evangelic preparation".[217]

627 75. The life and faith of students who receive religious instruction in school are characterized by continuous change. Religious instruction should be cognizant of that fact if it is to accomplish its own ends. In the case of students who are believers, religious instruction assists them to understand better the Christian message, by relating it to the great existential concerns common to all religions and to every human being, to the various visions of life particularly evident in culture and to those major moral questions which confront humanity today.

Those students who are searching, or who have religious doubts, can also find in religious instruction the possibility of discovering what exactly faith in Jesus Christ is, what response the Church makes to their questions, and gives them the opportunity to examine their own choice more deeply.

In the case of students who are non-believers, religious instruction assumes the character of a missionary proclamation of the Gospel and is ordered to a decision of faith, which catechesis, in its turn, will nurture and mature.

Education in the Christian family, catechesis and religious instruction at the service of education in the faith

628 76. Christian education in the family, catechesis and religious instruction in schools are, each in its own way, closely interrelated with the service of Christian education of children, adolescents, and young people. In practice, however, different factors must be taken into consideration in order to proceed realistically and with pastoral prudence in the application of general guidelines.

It is for each diocese or pastoral region to discern the diverse circumstances which arise with regard to the existence or not of Christian initiation of children in the context of the family, and

---

[217] Cf. CT 34.

with regard to the formative duties which are traditionally exercised by the parish, the school etc. Consequently the particular Church and the Episcopal Conference shall establish proper guidelines for various situations and foster distinct but complementary activities.

Chapter Three: The nature, object and the duties of catechesis

"And every tongue confess that Jesus Christ is Lord, to the glory of God the Father" (Phil 2:11).

629   77. Having outlined the place of catechesis in the Church's mission of evangelisation, its relationship with the various elements of evangelisation, and with other forms of the ministry of the word, this chapter examines catechesis particularly in relation to:

– the ecclesial nature of catechesis, that is to say, the agent of catechesis, the Church animated by the Holy Spirit;

– the fundamental object of catechesis;

– the tasks whereby this objective is achieved and which constitute its more immediate objectives;

– the gradual nature of the catechetical process and its catechumenal inspiration.

Moreover, in this chapter, the proper character of catechesis – already described in the preceding chapter – is examined through the analysis of its relationship with other ecclesial activities.

Catechesis: activity of an ecclesial nature

630   78. Catechesis is an essentially ecclesial act.[218] The true subject of catechesis is the Church which, continuing the mission of Jesus the Master and, therefore animated by the Holy Spirit, is sent to be the teacher of the faith. The Church imitates the Mother of the Lord in treasuring the Gospel in her heart.[219] She proclaims it, celebrates it, lives it, and she transmits it in catechesis to all those who have decided to follow Jesus Christ. This transmission

---

[218] As has been stated in chapter I of this part in "The transmission of Revelation by the Church, the work of the Holy Spirit" and in part II, chapter I in "The ecclesial nature of the Gospel message". Cf. EN 60 which speaks of the ecclesial nature of any evangelizing activity.

[219] Cf. LG 64; DV 10a.

of the Gospel is a living act of ecclesial tradition:[220]

– The Church transmits the faith which she herself lives: her understanding of the mystery of God and his salvific plan, her vision of man's highest vocation, the style of evangelic life which communicates the joy of the Kingdom, the hope which pervades her and the love which she has for mankind and all God's creatures.

– The Church transmits the faith in an active way; she sows it in the hearts of catechumens and those to be catechized so as to nourish their profoundest experience of life.[221] The profession of faith received by the Church (*traditio*), which germinates and grows during the catechetical process, is given back (*redditio*), enriched by the values of different cultures.[222] The catechumenate is thus transformed into a centre of deepening catholicity and a ferment of ecclesial renewal.

79. In transmitting faith and new life, the Church acts as a **631** mother for mankind who begets children conceived by the power of the Spirit and born of God.[223] Precisely "because she is a mother, she is also the educator of our faith";[224] she is at the same time mother and teacher. Through catechesis she feeds her children with her own faith and incorporates them as members into the ecclesial family. As a good mother she gives them the Gospel in all its authenticity and purity as apposite food, culturally enriched and a response to the deepest aspirations of the human heart.

---

[220] Cf. DCG (1971) 13.

[221] Cf. AG 22a.

[222] Cf. CT 28, RCIA 25 and 183-187. The *traditio-redditio symboli* (the handing over and giving back of the Creed) is an important element of the baptismal catechumenate. The bipolarity of this gesture expresses the double dimension of the faith: the received gift (*traditio)* and the personal and enculturated response (*redditio)*. Cf. CT 28 for an adequate use in catechesis of this most expressive rite.

[223] Cf. LG 64.

[224] CCC 169. The relation between the *maternity of the Church* and her *educative function* is expressed very well by St Gregory the Great: *"Having been made fruitful by conceiving her children thanks to the ministry of preaching, causes them to grow in her womb by her teaching. Moralia* XIX, c. 12, 9; PL 76, 108).

The object of catechesis: communion with Jesus Christ

632   80. "The definitive aim of catechesis is to put people not only in touch, but also in communion and intimacy, with Jesus Christ".[225] All evangelizing activity is understood as promoting communion with Jesus Christ. Starting with the "initial"[226] conversion of a person to the Lord, moved by the Holy Spirit through the primary proclamation of the Gospel, catechesis seeks to solidify and mature this first adherence. It proposes to help those who have just converted "to know better this Jesus to whom he has entrusted himself: to know his 'mystery', the kingdom of God proclaimed by him, the requirements and comments contained in his Gospel message, and the paths that he has laid down for anyone who wishes to follow him".[227] Baptism, the sacrament by which "we are configured to Christ",[228] sustains this work of catechesis with the help of its grace.

633   81. Communion with Jesus Christ, by its own dynamic, leads the disciple to unite himself with everything with which Jesus Christ himself was profoundly united: with God his Father, who sent him into the world, and with the Holy Spirit, who impelled his mission; with the Church, his body, for which he gave himself up, with mankind and with his brothers whose lot he wished to share.

The object of catechesis is expressed in profession of faith in the one God: Father, Son and Holy Spirit

634   82. Catechesis is that particular form of the ministry of the word which matures initial conversion to make it into a living, explicit and fruitful confession of faith: "*Catechesis has its origin in the confession of faith and leads to confession of faith.*"[229]

The profession of faith inherent in Baptism[230] is eminently Trinitarian. The Church baptizes "*in the name of the Father and*

---

[225] CT 5; cf. CCC 426; AG 14a. In relation to this christological end of catechesis see Part I, chap. I and Part II, chap. I. *Jesus Christ mediator and fulness of Revelation* and that which is said in II part, chapter 1 *Christianity of the evagelical mission.*

[226] AG 13b.

[227] CT 20c.

[228] LG 7b.

[229] MPD 8; CCC 185-197.

[230] Cf. CCC 189.

of the Son and of the Holy Spirit" (Matt 28:19)[231] the triune God to whom the Christian entrusts his life. Initiatory catechesis – both before and after the reception of Baptism – prepares for this decisive undertaking. Continuing catechesis helps to mature this profession of faith, to proclaim it in the Eucharist and to renew the commitments which it entails. It is important that catechesis should unite well the confession of christological faith, *"Jesus is Lord",* with the trinitarian confession, *"I believe in the Father, the Son and the Holy Spirit",* in such a way that there are not two modes of expressing the Christian faith. He who is converted to Jesus Christ and recognizes him as Lord through the primary proclamation of the Gospel begins a process which, aided by catechesis, necessarily leads to explicit confession of the Trinity.

In the confession of faith in the one God, the Christian rejects all service of any human absolute; "power, pleasure, race, ancestors, state, wealth...",[232] and is thus liberated from the enslavement of any idol. It is the proclamation of his will to serve God and man without any ties. In proclaiming faith in the Trinity, which is a communion of Persons, the disciple of Jesus Christ shows at once that the love of God and neighbour is the principle which informs his being and his action.

83. The confession of faith is complete only in reference to **635** the Church. All the baptized individually proclaim the *Credo,* for no action can be more personal than this. However, they recite it in the Church and through the Church, because they do so as members of the Church. *'Credo'* and *'Credimus'* necessarily imply each other.[233] In fusing his confession of faith with that of the Church, the Christian is incorporated into her mission: to be the "universal sacrament of salvation" for the life of the world. He who makes the profession of faith takes on responsibilities that not infrequently provoke persecution. In Christian history the martyrs are proclaimers and witnesses par excellence.[234]

The tasks of catechesis accomplish its objective

84. The object of catechesis is realized by diverse, **636**

---

[231] Cf. CCC 180-190 and 197.
[232] Cf. CCC 2113.
[233] Cf. CCC 166-67; CCC 196.
[234] Cf. RM 45.

interrelated tasks.[235] To carry them out, catechesis is certainly inspired by the manner in which Jesus formed his disciples. He made known to them the different dimensions of the Kingdom of God: "to you it has been given to know the secrets of the Kingdom of heaven" (Matt 13:11).[236] He taught them to pray (*"When you pray, say Father... Luke 11:2).[237]* He impressed upon them evangelic attitudes (*"learn from me for I am gentle and lowly in heart"* Matt 11:29) He prepared them for mission (*"He sent them on ahead of him two by two..."* Luke 10:1).[238]

The duties of catechesis correspond to education of the different dimensions of faith, for catechesis is integral Christian formation, *"open to all the other factors of Christian life"*.[239] In virtue of its own internal dynamic, the faith demands to be known, celebrated, lived and translated into prayer. Catechesis must cultivate each of these dimensions. The faith, however, is lived out by the Christian community and proclaimed in mission: it is a shared and proclaimed faith. These dimensions must also be encouraged by catechesis. The Second Vatican Council expresses these duties as follows: "...catechetical instruction, which illumines and strengthens the faith develops a life in harmony with the Spirit of Christ, stimulates a conscious and fervent participation in the liturgical mystery and encourages men to take an active part in the apostolate".[240]

Fundamental tasks of catechesis: helping to know, to celebrate and to contemplate the mystery of Christ

637   85. The fundamental tasks of catechesis are:
– Promoting knowledge of the faith

Who has encountered Christ desires to know him as much as possible, as well as to know the plan of the Father which he revealed. Knowledge of the faith *(fides quae)* is required by

---

[235] The DCG (1971) 21-29 also distinguishes between the end *(finis)* and the means *(munera)* of catechesis. These are the specific objectives in which the end is concretized.
[236] Cf. *Mark* 4:10-12.
[237] Cf. *Matt* 6: 5-6.
[238] Cf. Matt 10:5-15.
[239] CT 21b.
[240] "GE 4; cf. RICA 19, CIC 788,2.

adherence to the faith *(fides qua).*[241] Even in the human order the love which one person has for another causes that person to wish to know the other all the more. Catechesis, must, therefore, lead to "the gradual grasping of the whole truth about the divine plan",[242] by introducing the disciples of Jesus to a knowledge of Tradition and of Scripture, which is *"the sublime science of Christ".*[243] By deepening knowledge of the faith, catechesis nourishes not only the life of faith but equips it to explain itself to the world. The meaning of the Creed, which is a compendium of Scripture and of the faith of the Church, is the realization of this task.

– Liturgical education

Christ is always present in his Church, especially in "liturgical celebrations".[244] Communion with Jesus Christ leads to the celebration of his salvific presence in the sacraments, especially in the Eucharist. The Church ardently desires that all the Christian faithful be brought to that full, conscious and active participation which is required by the very nature of the liturgy[245] and the dignity of the baptismal priesthood. For this reason, catechesis, along with promoting a knowledge of the meaning of the liturgy and the sacraments, must also educate the disciples of Jesus Christ "for prayer, for thanksgiving, for repentance, for praying with confidence, for community spirit, for understanding correctly the meaning of the creeds...",[246] as all of this is necessary for a true liturgical life.

– Moral formation: Conversion to Jesus Christ implies walking in his footsteps. Catechesis must, therefore, transmit to the disciples the attitudes of the Master himself. The disciples thus undertake a journey of interior transformation, in which, by participating in the paschal mystery of the Lord, "they pass from the old man to the new man who has been made perfect in Christ".[247] The Sermon on the Mount, in which Jesus takes up the

---

[241] Cf. DCG (1971) 36a.
[242] Cf. DCG (1971) 24.
[243] DV 25a.
[244] SC 7.
[245] Cf. SC 14.
[246] DCG (1971) 25b.
[247] AG 13.

Decalogue, and impresses upon it the spirit of the beatitudes,[248] is
an indispensable point of reference for the moral formation which
is most necessary today. Evangelisation which "involves the proclamation and presentation of morality",[249] displays all the force
of its appeal where it offers not only the proclaimed word but the
lived word too. This moral testimony, which is prepared for by
catechesis, must always demonstrate the social consequences of
the demands of the Gospel.[250]

– Teaching to pray: Communion with Jesus Christ leads the
disciples to assume the attitude of prayer and contemplation
which the Master himself had. To learn to pray with Jesus is to
pray with the same sentiments with which he turned to the Father:
adoration, praise, thanksgiving, filial confidence, supplication and
awe for his glory. All of these sentiments are reflected in the *Our
Father*, the prayer which Jesus taught his disciples and which is
the model of all Christian prayer. The *"handing on of the Our
Father"*[251] is a summary of the entire Gospel[252] and is therefore a
true act of catechesis. When catechesis is permeated by a climate
of prayer, the assimilation of the entire Christian life reaches its
summit. This climate is especially necessary when the
catechumen and those to be catechized are confronted with the
more demanding aspects of the Gospel and when they feel weak
or when they discover the mysterious action of God in their lives.

*Other fundamental tasks of catechesis: initiation and education in
community life and to mission*

638   86. Catechesis prepares the Christian to live in community
and to participate actively in the life and mission of the Church.
The Second Vatican Council indicates the necessity for pastors
"to form genuine Christian communities"[253] and for catechumens
"[to] learn to co-operate actively in building up the Church and its

---

[248] Cf. LG 62; CCC 1965-1986. The CCC 1697 specifies in particular the
characteristics which catechesis must assume in moral formation.
[249] VS 107.
[250] Cf. CT 29f.
[251] RCIA 25 and 188-191.
[252] Cf. CCC 2761.
[253] PO 6d.

work of evangelisation".[254]

– Education for Community Life:

a) Christian community life is not realized spontaneously. It is necessary to educate it carefully. In this apprenticeship, the teaching of Christ on community life, recounted in the Gospel of St Matthew, calls for attitudes which it is for catechesis to inculcate: the spirit of simplicity and humility (*"unless you turn and become like little children..."* Matt 18:3); solicitude for the least among the brethren (*"but whoever causes one of these little ones who believe in me to sin..."* Matt 18:6); particular care for those who are alienated (*"Go and search of the one that went astray..."* Matt 18:12); fraternal correction (*"Go and tell him his fault..."* Matt 18:15); common prayer (*"if two of you agree on earth to ask about anything..."* Matt 18:19); mutual forgiveness (*"but seventy times seven..."* Matt 18:22). Fraternal love embraces all these attitudes (*"love one another; even as I have loved you..."* John 13:34).

b) In developing this community sense, catechesis takes special note of the ecumenical dimension and encourages fraternal attitudes toward members of other Christian churches and ecclesial communities. Thus catechesis in pursuing this objective should give a clear exposition of all the Church's doctrine and avoid formulations or expressions that might give rise to error. It also implies "a suitable knowledge of other confessions",[255] with which there are shared elements of faith: "the written word of God, the life of grace, faith, hope and charity, and the other interior gifts of the Holy Spirit".[256] Catechesis will possess an ecumenical dimension in the measure in which it arouses and nourishes "a true desire for unity",[257] not easy irenicism, but perfect unity, when the Lord himself wills it and by those means by which he wishes that it should be brought about.

– Missionary initiation

a) Catechesis is also open to the missionary dimension.[258] This seeks to equip the disciples of Jesus to be present as

---

[254] AG 14d.
[255] DCG (1971) 27.
[256] UR 3b.
[257] CT 32; cf. CCC 821; CT 34.
[258] Cf. CT 24b and DCG (1971) 28.

Christians in society through their professional, cultural and social lives. It also prepares them to lend their cooperation to the different ecclesial services, according to their proper vocation. This task of evangelisation originates, for the lay faithful, in the sacraments of Christian initiation and in the secular character of their vocation.[259] It is also important that every means should be used to encourage vocations to the Priesthood, and to the different forms of consecration to God in religious and apostolic life and to awaken special missionary vocations. The evangelical attitudes which Jesus taught his disciples when he sent them on mission are precisely those which catechesis must nourish: to seek out the lost sheep, proclaim and heal at the same time, to be poor, without money or knapsack; to know how to accept rejection and persecution; to place one's trust in the Father and in the support of the Holy Spirit; to expect no other reward than the joy of working for the Kingdom.[260]

b) In educating for this missionary sense, catechesis is also necessary for interreligious dialogue, if it renders the faithful capable of meaningful communication with men and women of other religions.[261] Catechesis shows that the link between the Church and non-Christian religions is, in the first place, the common origin and end of the human race, as well as the "many seeds of the word which God has sown in these religions". Catechesis too helps to reconcile and, at the same time, to distinguish between "the proclamation of Christ" and "inter-religious dialogue". These two elements, while closely connected, must not be confused or identified.[262] Indeed, "dialogue does not dispense from evangelisation".[263]

Observations on the totality of these tasks

639   87. The tasks of catechesis, consequently, constitute a

---

[259] Cf. LG 31b and ChL 15; CCC 898-900.

[260] Cf. *Matt* 10:5-42 and *Luke* 10:1-20.

[261] Cf. EN 53 and RM 55-57.

[262] Cf. RM 55b; Congregation for the Evangelisation of Peoples and the Pontifical Council for inter-religious dialogue, *Dialogue and Proclamation* (19 may 1991), nn. 14-54; AAS 84 (1992), pp. 419-432. CCC 839-845; Part IV, chap. 4 of this Directory refers to those to whom catechesis is addressed and returns to the topic *Catechesis in the context of other religions*.

[263] RM 55a.

totality, rich and varied in aspect. On this point it is opportune to make some observations.

– "All of these tasks are necessary. As the vitality of the human body depends on the proper function of all of its organs, so also the maturation of the Christian life requires that it be cultivated in all its dimensions: knowledge of the faith, liturgical life, moral formation, prayer, belonging to community, missionary spirit. When catechesis omits one of these elements, the Christian faith does not attain full development.

– Each task realizes, in its own way, the object of catechesis. Moral formation, for example, is essentially christological and trinitarian. It is deeply ecclesial, while also open to social concerns. The same is true of liturgical formation. While essentially religious and ecclesial, it also strongly demands commitment to the evangelisation of the world.

– These tasks are interdependent and develop together. Each great catechetical theme – catechesis of God the Father, for example – has a cognitive dimension as well as moral implications. It is interiorized in prayer and appropriated in witness. One task echoes the other: knowledge of the faith prepares for mission; the sacramental life gives strength for moral transformation.

– To fulfil its tasks, catechesis avails of two principal means: transmission of the Gospel message and experience of the Christian life.[264] Liturgical formation, for example, must explain what the Christian liturgy is, and what the sacraments are. It must also however, offer an experience of the different kinds of celebration and it must make symbols, gestures, etc. known and loved. Moral formation not only transmits the content of Christian morality, but also cultivates active evangelical attitudes and Christian values.

– The different dimensions of faith are objects of formation, as much of being given as received. Knowledge of the faith, liturgical life, the following of Christ are all a gift of the Spirit which are received in prayer, and similarly a duty of spiritual and moral study and witness. Neither aspect may be neglected.[265]

– Every dimension of the faith, like the faith itself as a whole,

---

[264] Cf. CIC 773 and 778 § 2.
[265] Cf. DCG (1971) 22 and 23.

must be rooted in human experience and not remain a mere adjunct to the human person. Knowledge of the faith is significant. It gives light to the whole of existence and dialogues with culture. In the liturgy, all personal life becomes a spiritual oblation. The morality of the Gospel assumes and elevates human values. Prayer is open to all personal and social problems.[266]

As the 1971 Directory indicates, "it is very important that catechesis retain the richness of these various aspects in such a way that one aspect is not separated from the rest to the detriment of the others".[267]

The baptismal catechumenate: structure and progression

640   88. Faith, moved by divine grace and cultivated by the action of the Church, undergoes a process of maturation. Catechesis, which is at the service of this growth, is also a gradual activity. "Good catechesis is always done in steps".[268] In the baptismal catechumenate, formation is articulated in four stages:

– *the pre-catechumenate*,[269] characterized as the locus of first evangelisation leading to conversion and where the *kerygma* of the primary proclamation is explained;

– *the catechumenate*,[270] properly speaking, the context of integral catechesis beginning with "the handing on of the Gospels";[271]

– a time of *purification and illumination*[272] which affords a more intense preparation for the sacraments of initiation and in which the "the handing on of the Creed"[273] and "the handing on of the Lord's Prayer" take place;[274]

– a time of *mystagogy*,[275] characterized by the experience of the sacraments and entry into the community.

641   89. These stages, which reflect the wisdom of the great catech-

---

[266] Cf. DCG (1971) 26.

[267] DCG (1971) 31b.

[268] Cf. RCIA 19.

[269] RCIA 9-13.

[270] RCIA 14-20; 68-72; 98-105.

[271] RCIA 93; cf. MPD 8c.

[272] RCIA 21-26; 133-142; 152-159.

[273] RCIA 25 and 183-187.

[274] RCIA 25 and 188-192.

[275] RCIA 37-40; 35-239.

umenal tradition, also inspire the gradual nature of catechesis.[276] In the patristic period properly, catechumenal formation was realized through biblical catechesis, based on recounting the history of salvation; immediate preparation for Baptism by doctrinal catechesis, explaining the Creed and the *Our Father* which had just been handed on, together with their moral implications; and through the phase following the sacraments of initiation, a period of mystagogical catechesis which help the newly baptized to interiorize these sacraments and incorporate themselves into the community. This patristic concept continues to illuminate the present catechumenate and initiatory catechesis itself. This latter, in so far as it accompanies the process of conversion, is essentially gradual and, in so far as it is at the service of one who has decided to follow Christ, it is eminently Christocentric.

The baptismal catechumenate: inspiration for catechesis in the Church

90. Given that the *missio ad gentes* is the paradigm of all the Church's missionary activity, the baptismal catechumenate, which is joined to it, is the model of its catechizing activity.[277] It is therefore helpful to underline those elements of the catechumenate which must inspire contemporary catechesis and its significance. **642**

By way of premise, however, it must be said that there is a fundamental difference between catechumens those being catechized,[278] between the *pre-baptismal* catechesis and the *post-baptismal* catechesis, which is respectively imparted to them. The latter derives from the sacraments of initiation which were

---

[276] This gradual nature is also apparent in the names which the Church uses to designate those who are in the various stages of the baptismal catechumenate: *sympathizers* (RCIA 12), those who are disposed to the faith but do not yet fully believe; *catechumens* (RCIA 17-18), those who have firmly decided to follow Jesus; *elect* (RCIA 24), those called to receive Baptism; *neophytes* (RCIA 31-36) those just born into the light by the grace of Baptism; *the Christian faithful* (RCIA 39), those who are mature in the faith and active members of the Christian community.

[277] Cf. MPD 8; EN 44; ChL 61.

[278] In this DCG the expressions 'catechumens' and 'those being catechized' are used to make this distinction. For its part the CIC, canons 204-206, notes the different ways by which catechumens and the Christian faithful have union with the Church.

received as infants, "who have been already introduced into the Church and have been made sons of God by means of Baptism. The basis of their conversion is the Baptism which they have already received and whose power they must develop".[279]

643   91. In view of this substantial difference, some elements of the baptismal catechumenate are now considered, as the source of inspiration for post-baptismal catechesis.

– the baptismal catechumenate constantly reminds the whole Church of the fundamental importance of the function of initiation and the basic factors which constitute it: catechesis and the sacraments of Baptism, Confirmation and Eucharist. The pastoral care of Christian initiation is vital for every particular Church.

– The baptismal catechumenate is the responsibility of the entire Christian community. Indeed "this Christian initiation which takes place during the catechumenate should not be left entirely to the priests and catechists, but should be the care of the entire Christian community, especially the sponsors".[280] The institution of the catechumenate thus increases awareness of the spiritual maternity of the Church, which she exercises in every form of education in the faith.[281]

– The baptismal catechumenate is also completely permeated by the *mystery of Christ's Passover*. For this reason, "all initiation must reveal clearly its paschal nature.[282] The Easter Vigil, focal point of the Christian liturgy, and its spirituality of Baptism inspire all catechesis.

– The baptismal catechumenate is also an initial locus of inculturation. Following the example of the Incarnation of the Son of God, made man in a concrete historical moment, the Church receives catechumens integrally, together with their cultural ties. All catechetical activity participates in this function of

---

[279] RCIA 295. The same *Rite of Christian Initiation of Adults,* chap. 4, ponders the question of those baptized adults who need initiatory catechesis. CT 44 specifies the diverse circumstances in which this catechesis may be deemed necessary.

[280] AG 14d.

[281] Methodius of Olympus, for example, speaks of this *maternal action* of the Christian community when he says: With regard to those who are still imperfect (in the Christian life), it is for the more mature to form them and to bring them to birth as a mother. (*Symposium,* III, 8; GCS 27, 88). See also St Gregory the Great *Homilia in Evangelia,* I, III, 2; PL 76,1086 D).

[282] RCIA 8.

incorporating into the catholicity of the Church, authentic "seeds of the word", scattered through nations and individuals.[283]

– Finally, the concept of the baptismal catechumenate as *a process of formation and as a true school of the faith* offers post-baptismal catechesis dynamic and particular characteristics: comprehensiveness and integrity of formation; its gradual character expressed in definite stages; its connection with meaningful rites, symbols, biblical and liturgical signs; its constant references to the Christian community.

Post-baptismal catechesis, without slavishly imitating the structure of the baptismal catechumenate, and recognizing in those to be catechized the reality of their Baptism, does well, however, to draw inspiration from "this preparatory school for the Christian life",[284] and to allow itself to be enriched by those principal elements which characterize the catechumenate.

Part Two: The Gospel Message

The Gospel Message

"And this is eternal life, that they know thee the only true God, and Jesus Christ whom thou has sent" (Jn 17:3).

"Jesus came into Galilee, preaching the Gospel of God, and saying, 'The time is fulfilled, and the kingdom of God is at hand; repent and believe in the Gospel'" (Mk 1:14-15).

"Now I would remind you, brethren, in what terms I preached to you the Gospel, which you received, in which you stand, by which you are saved, if you hold it fast – unless you believed in vain. For I delivered to you as of first importance what I also received, that Christ died for our sins in accordance with the Scriptures, that he was buried, that he was raised on the third day to life in accordance with the Scriptures" (1 Cor 15:1-4).

The meaning and purpose of Part Two

92. The Christian faith, through which a person says "Yes" to   **644**

---

[283] Cf. CT 53.

[284] DCG (1971) 130. This article begins with the affirmation: "The catechumenate for adults, which at one and the same time includes catechesis, liturgical participation and community living, is an excellent example of an institute that springs from the cooperation of diverse pastoral functions".

Jesus Christ, may be analysed thus:

– as an adherence, which is given under the influence of grace, to God who reveals himself; in this case the faith consists in believing the word of God and committing oneself to it (*fides qua*);

– as the content of Revelation and of the Gospel message; in this sense, faith is expressed in its endeavour to understand better the mystery of the word (*fides quae*).

Both aspects, by their very nature, cannot be separated. Maturation and growth in the faith require their comprehensive and coherent development. For methodological purposes, however, they can be regarded separately.[285]

645   93. *Part Two*, considers the content of the Gospel message (*fides quae*).

– The first chapter sets out the norms and criteria which catechesis must follow so as to find, formulate and present its contents. Indeed every form of the ministry of the word is ordered to the presentation of the Gospel message according to its own character.

– The second chapter examines the content of the faith as it is presented in the *Catechism of the Catholic Church*, which is the doctrinal point of reference for all catechesis. It also presents some observations which may help the assimilation and interiorization of the Catechism and locate it within the catechetical activity of the Church. In addition, some criteria are set out to assist particular Churches in compiling catechisms based on the *Catechism of the Catholic Church*, which, while preserving the unity of the faith, must also take into account diversity of circumstances and cultures.

Chapter One: Norms and criteria for presenting the Gospel message in catechesis

"Hear, O Israel: The Lord our God is one Lord; and you shall love the Lord your God with all your heart, and with all your soul, and with all your might. And these words which I command you this day shall be upon your heart; and you shall teach them diligently to your children, and shall talk of them when you sit in

---

[285] Cf. DCG (1971) 36a.

your house, and when you walk by the way, and when you lie down, and when you rise. And you shall bind them as a sign upon your hand, and they shall be as frontlets between your eyes. And you shall write them on the doorposts of your house and on your gates" (Deut 6:4-9).

"And the Word became flesh and dwelt among us" (Jn 1:14).

The word of God: source of catechesis

94. The source from which catechesis draws its message is the word of God: **646**

"Catechesis will always draw its content from the living source of the word of God transmitted in Tradition and the Scriptures, for sacred Tradition and sacred Scripture make up a single sacred deposit of the word of God, which is entrusted to the Church".[286]

This "deposit of faith"[287] is like the treasure of a householder; it is entrusted to the Church, the family of God, and she continuously draws from it things new and old.[288] All God's children, animated by his Spirit, are nourished by this treasure of the Word. They know that the Word is Jesus Christ, the Word made man and that his voice continues to resound in the Church and in the world through the Holy Spirit. The Word of God, by wondrous divine "condescension"[289] is directed toward us and reaches us by means of human "deeds and words", "just as the Word of the eternal Father, when he took on himself the flesh of human weakness, became like men".[290] And so without ceasing to be the word of God, it is expressed in human words. Although close to us, it still remains veiled, in a "kenotic" state. Thus the Church, guided by the Holy Spirit, has to interpret the word continually. She contemplates the word with a profound spirit of faith, "listens to [it] devotedly, guards it with dedication and expounds it faithfully".[291]

---

[286] CT 27.
[287] Cf. DV 10 a e b; cf. *1 Tim* 6:20 and *2 Tim* 1:14.
[288] Cf. *Matt* 13:52.
[289] DV 13.
[290] *Ibid.*
[291] DV 10.

The source and the "sources" of the message of catechesis[292]

647   95. The *word of God,* contained in Sacred Tradition and in Sacred Scripture:

– is mediated upon and understood more deeply by means of the sense of faith of all the people of God, guided by the Magisterium which teaches with authority;

– is celebrated in the Sacred Liturgy, where it is constantly proclaimed, heard, interiorized and explained;

– shines forth in the life of the Church, in her two-thousand-year history, especially in Christian witness and particularly in that of the saints;

– is deepened by theological research which helps believers to advance in their vital understanding of the mysteries of faith;

– is made manifest in genuine religious and moral values which, as "seeds of the word", are sown in human society and diverse cultures.

648   96. These are all the sources, principle or subsidiary, of catechesis but must not be understood in a narrow sense.[293] Sacred Scripture "is the speech of God as it is put down in writing under the breath of the Holy Spirit",[294] Sacred Tradition "transmits in its entirety the word of God which has been entrusted to the apostles by Christ the Lord and the Holy Spirit".[295] The Magisterium has the duty of "giving an authentic interpretation of the word of God",[296] and in doing so fulfils, in the name of Christ, a fundamental ecclesial service. Tradition, Scripture and the Magisterium, all three of which are closely connected, are "each according to its own way",[297] the principle sources of catechesis. Each of the subsidiary sources of catechesis has its own proper language which has been shaped by a rich variety of "documents

---

[292] As can be seen both expressions, the source and the *sourcees,* are used. The term 'the source of catechesis' is used to underline the oneness of the word of God and recalls the concept of Revelation in *Dei Verbum.* CT 27 also speaks of 'the source' of catechesis. Nonetheless following general catechetical usage the expression 'the sources' is used to denote those concrete loci from which catechesis draws its message; cf. DCG (1971) 45.

[293] Cf. DCG (1971) 45b.

[294] DV 9.

[295] *Ibid.*

[296] DV 10b.

[297] DV 10c.

of the faith". Catechesis is a living tradition of such documents:[298] biblical excerpts, liturgical texts, patristic writings, formulations of the Magisterium, creeds, testimonies of the saints and theological reflections.

The living source of the word of God and the "sources" deriving from it, and through which it is expressed, provide catechesis with those criteria for the transmission of its message to all who have made their decision to follow Jesus Christ.

Criteria for the presentation of the message

97. The criteria for presenting the Gospel message in catechesis are closely inter-connected with each other as they spring from the same source.
649

– The message centred on the person of Jesus Christ *(christo-centricity),* by its inherent dynamic, introduces the trinitarian dimension of the same message.

– The proclamation of the Good News of the Kingdom of God, centred on the *gift of Salvation,* implies a message of *liberation.*

– The *ecclesial* character of the message reflects its *historic* nature because catechesis – as with all evangelisation – is realized within "the time of the Church".

– The Gospel message seeks *inculturation* because the Good News is destined for all peoples. This can only be accomplished when the Gospel message is presented in its *integrity and purity.*

– The Gospel message is a *comprehensive message,* with its own hierarchy of truth. It is this harmonious vision of the Gospel which converts it into a profoundly *meaningful* event for the human person.

Although these criteria are valid for the entire ministry of the word, here they are developed in relation to catechesis.

The christocentricity of the Gospel message

98. Jesus Christ not only transmits the word of God: he *is* the Word of God. Catechesis is therefore completely tied to him. Thus what must characterize the message transmitted by catechesis is, above all, its "christocentricity".[299] This may be
650

---

[298] Cf. MPD 9.
[299] Cf. CCC 426-429; CT 5-6; DCG (1971) 40.

understood in various senses.

    – It means, firstly, that "at the heart of catechesis we find, in essence, a person, the Person of Jesus of Nazareth, the only Son of the Father, full of grace and truth".[300] In reality, the fundamental task of catechesis is to present Christ and everything in relation to him. This explicitly promotes the following of Jesus and communion with him; every element of the message tends to this.

    – Secondly, christocentricity means that Christ is the "centre of salvation history",[301] presented by catechesis. He is indeed the final event toward which all salvation history converges. He, who came "in the fulness of time" is "the key, the centre and end of all human history".[302] The catechetical message helps the Christian to locate himself in history and to insert himself into it, by showing that Christ is the ultimate meaning of this history.

    – Christocentricity, moreover, means that the Gospel message does not come from man, but is the Word of God. The Church, and in her name, every catechist can say with truth: "my teaching is not from myself: it comes from the one who sent me" (John 7:16). Thus all that is transmitted by catechesis is "the teaching of Jesus Christ, the truth that he communicates, or more precisely, the Truth that he is".[303] Christocentricity obliges catechesis to transmit what Jesus teaches about God, man, happiness, the moral life, death etc. without in any way changing his thought.[304]

    The Gospels, which narrate the life of Jesus, are central to the catechetical message. They are themselves endowed with a "catechetical structure".[305] They express the teaching which was proposed to the first Christian communities, and which also transmits the life of Jesus, his message and his saving actions. In catechesis, "the four Gospels occupy a central place because Christ Jesus is their centre".[306]

---

[300] CT 5.
[301] DCG (1971) 41a; cf. DCG (1971) 39, 40, 44.
[302] *GS* 10.
[303] CT 6.
[304] Cf. *1 Cor* 15:1-4; EN 15e, f.
[305] CT 11b.
[306] CCC 139.

The trinitarian christocentricity of the Gospel message

651 99. The Word of God, incarnate in Jesus of Nazareth, Son of the Blessed Virgin Mary, is the Word of the Father who speaks to the world through his Spirit. Jesus constantly refers to the Father, of whom he knows he is the Only Son, and to the Holy Spirit, by whom he knows he is anointed. He is 'the Way' that leads to the innermost mystery of God.[307] The christocentricity of catechesis, in order of its internal dynamic, leads to confession of faith in God, Father, Son and Holy Spirit.

It is essentially a trinitarian christocentricity. Christians, at Baptism, are configured to Christ, "One of the Trinity",[308] and constituted "sons in the Son", in communion with the Father and the Holy Spirit. Their faith is, therefore, radically Trinitarian. "The mystery of the Most Holy Trinity is the central mystery of Christian faith and life".[309]

652 100. The trinitarian christocentricity of the Gospel message leads catechesis to attend amongst others, to the following points.

- The internal structure of catechesis: every mode of presentation must always be christocentric-trinitarian: "Through Christ to the Father in the Holy Spirit".[310] "If catechesis lacks these three elements or neglects their close relationship, the Christian message can certainly lose its proper character".[311]

- Following the pedagogy of Jesus in revelation of the Father, of himself as the Son, and of the Holy Spirit, catechesis shows the most intimate life of God, starting with his salvific works for the good of humanity.[312] The works of God reveal who he is and the mystery of his inner Being throws light on all of his works. It is analogous with human relationships: people reveal themselves by their actions and, the more deeply we know them, the better we understand what they do.[313]

- The presentation of the innermost being of God, revealed

---

[307] Cf. *John* 14:6.
[308] The term 'one of the Trinity' was used by the Fifth Ecumenical Council (Constantinople 533): cf. Constantinopolitanum II, Session VIII, can. 4, *Dz* 424. It is also used in CCC 468.
[309] CCC 234; cf. CCC 2157.
[310] DCG (1971) 41; cfr. *Eph* 2:18.
[311] Cf. DCG (1971) 41.
[312] Cf. CCC 258, 236 and 259.
[313] Cf. CCC 236.

by Jesus, the mystery of being one in essence and three in Person, has vital implications for the lives of human beings. To confess belief in one God means, that "man should not submit his personal freedom in an absolute manner to any earthly power".[314] It also implies that humanity, made in the image and likeness of God who is a "communion of persons", is called to be a fraternal society, comprised of sons and daughters of the same Father, and equal in personal dignity.[315] The human and social implications of the Christian concept of God are immense. The Church, in professing her faith in the Trinity and by proclaiming it to the world, understands herself as "a people gathered together in the unity of the Father, Son and Holy Spirit".[316]

A message proclaiming salvation

653   101. The message of Jesus about God is Good News for humanity. Jesus proclaimed the Kingdom of God;[317] a new and definitive intervention by God, with a transforming power equal and even superior to his creation of the world.[318] In this sense, "Christ proclaims salvation as the outstanding element and, as it were, the central point of his Good News. This is the great gift of God which is to be considered as comprising not merely liberation from all those things by which man is oppressed, but especially liberation from sin and from the domination of the evil one, a liberation which incorporates that gladness enjoyed by every man who knows God and is known by him, who sees God and who surrenders himself trustingly to him".[319] Catechesis transmits this message of the Kingdom, so central to the

---

[314] CCC 450.
[315] Cf. CCC 1878; CCC 1702. SRS uses the term model of unity when referring to this question. CCC 2845 calls the communion of the Blessed Trinity "the source and criterion of truth in every relationship".
[316] The term comes from St Cyprian *De orat. dom.,* 23; PL, 4:553; LG 4b.
[317] Cf. EN 11-14; RM 12-20; cf. CCC 541-556.
[318] In the liturgy of the Church it is expressed in the Easter Vigil: "Almighty and eternal God you created all things in wonderful beauty and order. Help us now to perceive how still more wonderful is the new creation by which in the fulness of time you redeemed your people through the sacrifice of our Passover, Jesus Christ, who lives and reigns forever and ever" (*Missale Romanum,* Easter Vigil, prayer after the first reading).
[319] EN 9.

preaching of Jesus. In doing so, the message "is gradually deepened, developed in its implicit consequences",[320] and thus manifests its great repercussions for man and the world.

102. In its drawing out the Gospel *kerygma* of Jesus, catechesis underlines the following basic aspects:

654

– Jesus, with the Kingdom, proclaims and reveals that God is not a distant inaccessible Being, "a remote power without a name"[321] but a Father, who is present among his creatures and whose power is his love. This testimony about God as Father, offered in a simple and direct manner, is fundamental to catechesis.

– Jesus shows, at the same time, that God, with the coming of his Kingdom offers the gift of integral salvation, frees from sin, brings one to communion with the Father, grants divine sonship, and in conquering death, promises eternal life.[322] This complete salvation is at once, immanent and eschatological, because "it has its beginning certainly in this life, but which achieves its consummation in eternity".[323]

– Jesus, in announcing the Kingdom, proclaims the justice of God: he proclaims God's judgement and our responsibility. The proclamation of this judgement, with its power to form consciences, is a central element in the Gospel, and Good News for the world: for those who suffer the denial of justice and for those who struggle to re-instate it; for those who have known love and existence in solidarity, because penance and forgiveness are possible, since in the Cross of Christ we all receive redemption from sin. The call to conversion and belief in the Gospel of the Kingdom – a Kingdom of justice, love and peace, and in whose light we shall be judged – is fundamental for catechesis.

– Jesus declares that the Kingdom of God is inaugurated in him, in his very person.[324] He reveals, in fact, that he himself, constituted as Lord, assumes the realization of the Kingdom until he consigns it, upon completion, to the Father when he comes

---

[320] CT 25.

[321] EN 26.

[322] This gift of Salvation confers on us, *justification* by means of the grace of faith and of the Church's Sacraments, This grace frees us from sin and introduces us to communion with God" (LC 52).

[323] EN 27.

[324] Cf. LG 3 and 5.

again in glory.[325] "Here on earth the Kingdom is mysteriously present; when the Lord comes it will enter into its perfection".[326]

– Jesus shows, equally, that the community of his disciples, the Church, "is, on earth, the seed and the beginning of that Kingdom"[327] and, like leaven in the dough, what she desires is that the Kingdom of God grow in the world like a great tree, giving shelter to all peoples and cultures. "The Church is effectively and concretely at the service of the Kingdom".[328]

– Finally, Jesus manifests that the history of humanity is not journeying towards nothingness, but, with its aspects of both grace and sin, is in him taken up by God and transformed. In its present pilgrimage towards the Father's house, it already offers a foretaste of the world to come, where, assumed and purified, it will reach perfection. "Accordingly, evangelisation will include a prophetic proclamation of another's life, that is of man's sublime and eternal vocation. This vocation is at once connected with and distinct from his present state".[329]

A message of liberation

655   103. The Good News of the Kingdom of God, which proclaims salvation, includes a "message of liberation".[330] In preaching this Kingdom, Jesus addressed the poor in a very special way: "Blessed are you poor, yours is the kingdom of God. Blessed are you that hunger now, for you shall be satisfied. Blessed are you that weep now, for you shall laugh" (Luke 6:20-21). The Beatitudes of Jesus, addressed to those who suffer, are an eschatological proclamation of the salvation which the Kingdom brings. They note that painful experience to which the Gospel is so particularly sensitive: poverty, hunger and the suffering of humanity. The community of the disciples of Jesus, the Church, shares today the same sensitivity as the Master himself showed them. With great sorrow she turns her attention to those "peoples who, as we all know, are striving with all their

---

[325] Cf. RM 16.
[326] GS 39.
[327] LG 5.
[328] RM 20.
[329] EN 28.
[330] Cf. EN 30-35.

power and energy to overcome all those circumstances which compel them to live on the border line of existence: hunger, chronic epidemics, illiteracy, poverty, injustice between nations... economic and cultural neo-colonialism".[331] All forms of poverty, "not only economic but also cultural and religious"[332] are a source of concern for the Church.

As an important dimension of her mission, "the Church is duty bound – as her bishops have insisted – to proclaim the liberation of these hundreds of millions of people, since very many of them are her children. She has the duty of helping this liberation, of bearing witness on its behalf and of assuring its full development".[333]

104. To prepare Christians for this task, catechesis is attentive, amongst other things, to the following aspects:

656

– it shall situate the message of liberation in the prospective of the "specifically religious objective of evangelisation",[334] since it would lose its raison d'être "if it were divorced from the religious basis by which it is sustained which is the kingdom of God in its full theological sense;[335] thus, the message of liberation "cannot be confined to any restricted sphere whether it be economic, political, social or doctrinal. It must embrace the whole man in all his aspects and components, extending to his relation to the absolute, even to the Absolute which is God";[336]

– catechesis, in the ambit of moral education, shall present Christian social morality as a demand and consequence of the "radical liberation worked by Christ";[337] in effect, the Good News which Christians profess with hearts full of hope is: Christ has liberated the world and continues to liberate it; this is the source of Christian praxis, which is the fulfilment of the great commandment of love;

– at the same time, in the task of initiating mission,

---

[331] EN 30.

[332] CA 57; cf. CCC 2444.

[333] EN 30.

[334] EN 32; cf. SRS 41 and RM 58.

[335] EN 32.

[336] EN 33. Cf. LC. This Instruction is an obligatory point of reference for catechesis.

[337] LC 71.

catechesis shall arouse in catechumens and those receiving catechesis "a preferential option for the poor",[338] which "far from being a sign of individualism or sectarianism, makes manifest the universality of the Church's nature and mission. This option is not exclusive"[339] but implies "a commitment to justice, according to each individual's role, vocation and circumstances".[340]

The ecclesial nature of the Gospel message

657   105. The ecclesial nature of catechesis confers on the transmitted Gospel message an inherent ecclesial character. Catechesis originates in the Church's confession of faith and leads to the profession of faith of the catechumen and those to be catechized. The first official word of the Church addressed to those about to be baptized, having called them by name, is: "What do you ask of God's Church?" The candidates' reply is *"Faith"*.[341] The catechumen who has discovered the Gospel and desires to know it better, realizes that it lives in the hearts of believers. Catechesis is nothing other than the process of transmitting the Gospel, as the Christian community has received it, understands it, celebrates it, lives it and communicates it in many ways.

Hence, when catechesis transmits the mystery of Christ, the faith of the whole people of God echoes in its message throughout the course of history: the faith received by the Apostles from Christ himself and under the action of the Holy Spirit; that of the martyrs who have borne witness to it and still bear witness to it by their blood; that of the saints who have lived it and live it profoundly; that of the Fathers and doctors of the Church who have taught it brilliantly; that of the missionaries who proclaim it incessantly; that of theologians who help to understand it better; that of pastors who conserve it with zeal and love and who interpret it authentically. In truth, there is present in catechesis the faith of all those who believe and allow themselves to be guided by the Holy Spirit.

658   106. This faith, transmitted by the ecclesial community, is

---

[338] SRS 42; CA 57; LC 68. Cf. CCC 2443-2449.

[339] LC 68.

[340] SRS 41; cf. LC 77. For its part the 1971 Synod devoted attention to a theme of fundamental importance to catechesis: Education in Justice (III, 2). Cf. Documents of the Synod of Bishops, II *De Iustitia in mundo III*, 835-937.

[341] RCIA 75; cf. CCC 1253.

one. Although the disciples of Jesus Christ form a community dispersed throughout the whole world, and even though catechesis transmits the faith in many different cultural idioms, the Gospel which is handed on is one. The confession of faith is the same. There is only one Baptism: "one Lord, one Faith, one Baptism one God and Father of us all" (Eph 4:5). Catechesis, in the Church, therefore, is that service which introduces catechumens and those to be catechized to the unity of the profession of faith.[342] By its very nature, it nourishes the bond of unity[343] and brings about an awareness of belonging to a great community which cannot be limited by space or time: "From Abel the just to the last of the chosen ones to the end of the earth, to the close of the age.[344]

The historical character of the mystery of salvation

107. The confession of faith of the disciples of Jesus Christ **659** springs from a pilgrim Church which has been sent on mission. It is not yet that of the glorious proclamation of the journey's end; rather, it is one which corresponds to the *"times of the Church"*.[345] The *"economy of Salvation"* has thus an historical character as it is realized in time: *"...in time past it began, made progress, and in Christ reached its highest point; in the present time it displays its force and awaits its consummation in the future.*[346] For this reason, the Church, in transmitting today the Christian message, begins with the living awareness which she carries of it, has a constant "memory" of the saving events of the past and makes them known. In the light of these, she interprets the present events of human history, where the Spirit of God is continually renewing the face of the earth, and she awaits with faith for the Lord's coming. In Patristic catechesis, the narration *(narratio)* of the

---

[342] Cf. CCC 172-175 where, inspired by St Irenaeus of Lyon there is an analysis of all the riches contained in the reality of one faith.

[343] CCC 815: "...the unity of the pilgrim Church is also assured by visible bonds of communion: profession of one faith received from the apostles; common celebration of divine worship, especially of the sacraments; apostolic succession through the sacrament of Holy Orders, maintaining the fraternal concord of God's family".

[344] EN 61, which takes up St Gregory the Great and the Didaché.

[345] CCC 1076.

[346] DCG (1971) 44.

wonderful deeds of God and the awaiting *(expectatio)* of Christ's return always accompanied the exposition of the mysteries of faith.[347]

660   108. The historical character of the Christian message requires that catechesis attend to the following points:

– presentation of salvation history by means of Biblical catechesis so as to make known the "deeds and the words" with which God has revealed himself to man: the great stages of the Old Testament by which he prepared the journey of the Gospel;[348] the life of Jesus, Son of God, born of the Virgin Mary who by his actions and teaching brought Revelation to completion;[349] the history of the Church which transmits Revelation: this history, read within the perspective of faith, is a fundamental part of the content of catechesis;

– in explaining the Creed and the content of Christian morality by means of doctrinal catechesis, the Gospel message should illuminate the 'today' of the history of salvation; indeed, "...in this way the ministry of the Word not only recalls the revelation of God's wonders which was made in time...but at the same time, in the light of this revelation, interprets human life in our age, the signs of the times, and the things of this world, for the plan of God works in these for the salvation of men";[350]

– it should situate the sacraments within the history of salvation by means of a mystagogy which "...re-lives the great events of salvation history in the 'today' of her liturgy";[351] reference to the historico-salvific 'today' is essential to such catechesis, and thus helps catechumens and those to be catechized "to open themselves to this 'spiritual' understanding of the

---

[347] The Fathers basing the content of catechesis on the narration of the events of salvation, wish to root Christianity in time by showing that it was a salvation history and not a mere religious philosophy. They also wished to emphasize that Christ was the centre of this history.

[348] CCC 54-64. At this point the catechism deals with the most important phases of revelation and in them the idea of Covenant is a key concept. These texts are a fundamental reference for biblical catechesis. Cf. CCC 1081 and 1093.

[349] Cf. DV 4.

[350] DCG (1971) 11.

[351] CCC 1095. Cf. CCC 1075; CCC 1116; cf. CCC 129-130 and 1093-1094.

economy of Salvation...";[352]

– the *"deeds and words"* of Revelation point to the *"mystery contained in them"*;[353] catechesis helps to make the passage from sign to mystery; it leads to the discovery of the mystery of the Son of God behind his humanity; behind the history of the Church, it uncovers the mystery of her being the "sacrament of salvation;" behind the "signs of the times", it encounters the traces of God's presence and plan: catechesis, thus, shall exhibit that knowledge which is typical of faith, which "is knowledge through signs".[354]

Inculturation of the Gospel message[355]

109. The Word of God became man, a concrete man, in space **661** and time and rooted in a specific culture: "Christ by his incarnation committed himself to the particular social and cultural circumstances of the men among whom he lived".[356] This is the original "inculturation" of the word of God and is the model of all evangelisation by the Church, "called to bring the power of the Gospel into the very heart of culture and cultures".[357]

'Inculturation'[358] of the faith, whereby in a wonderful exchange are comprised, "all the riches of the nations which have been given to Christ as an inheritance",[359] it is a profound and global process and a slow journey.[360] It is not simply an external adaptation designed to make the Christian message more attractive or superficially decorative. On the contrary, it means the penetration of the deepest strata of persons and peoples by the Gospel which touches them deeply, "going to the very centre and

---

[352] CCC 1095. CCC 1075 indicates the inductive nature of this "mystagogical catechesis" since it proceeds "from the visible to the invisible, from the sign to the thing signified, from the 'sacraments' to the 'mysteries'".
[353] DV 2.
[354] DCG (1971) 72; cf. CCC 39-43.
[355] Cf. Part IV, chp 5.
[356] AG 10; cf. AG 22a.
[357] CT 53; cf. EN 20.
[358] The term "inculturation" is taken from diverse documents of the Magisterium. See CT 53; RM 52-54. The concept of culture, either in a general or an ethnological or sociological sense is clarified in GS 53. Cf. also ChL 44a.
[359] AG 22a; cf. LG 13 and 17; GS 53-62; DCG (1971) 37.
[360] Cf. RM 52b which speaks of the "long time" required for inculturation.

roots"[361] of their cultures.

In this work of inculturation, however, the Christian community must discern, on the one hand, which riches to "take"[362] up as compatible with the faith; on the other, it must seek to "purify"[363] and "transform"[364] those criteria, modes of thought and lifestyles which are contrary to the Kingdom of God. Such discernment is governed by two basic principles: "compatibility with the Gospel and communion with the universal Church".[365] All of the people of God must be involved in this process which "...needs to take place gradually, in such a way that it really is an expression of the community's Christian experience".[366]

662 110. In this inculturation of the faith, there are different concrete tasks for catechesis. Amongst these mention must be made of:

– looking to the ecclesial community as the principal factor of inculturation: an expression and efficient instrument of this task is represented by the catechist who, with a profound religious sense, also possesses a living social conscience and is well rooted in his cultural environment;[367]

– drawing up local catechisms which respond to the demands of different cultures[368] and which present the Gospel in relation to the hopes, questions and problems which these cultures present;

– making the Catechumenate and catechetical institutes into "centres of inculturation", incorporating, with discernment, the language, symbols, and values of the cultures in which the catechumens and those to be catechized live;

– presenting the Christian message in such a way as to prepare those who are to proclaim the Gospel to be capable "of giving reasons for their hope" (1 Pet 3:15) in cultures often pagan or post-Christian: effective apologetics to assist the faith-culture dialogue is indispensable today.

---

[361] EN 20; cf. EN 63; RM 52.
[362] LG 13 uses the expression *to foster and to take (fovet et assumit)*.
[363] LG 13 expresses it in this way: *she purifies, strengthens and elevates them (sanare, elevare et consummare)*.
[364] EN 19 affirms: *to acquire and almost to overturn*.
[365] RM 54a.
[366] RM 54b.
[367] Cf. *Guide for catechists*, 12.
[368] Cf. CCC 24.

The integrity of the Gospel message

663 111. In its task of inculturating the faith, catechesis must transmit the Gospel message in its integrity and purity. Jesus proclaimed the Gospel integrally: "...because I have made known to you all that I have heard from my Father" (John 15:15) This same integrity is demanded by Christ of his disciples in his sending them on mission to preach the Gospel: "... and teaching them to observe all that I have commanded you" (Matt 28:19). A fundamental principle of catechesis, therefore, is that of safeguarding the integrity of the message and avoiding any partial or distorted presentation: "In order that the sacrificial offering of his or her faith should be perfect, the person who becomes a disciple of Christ has the right to receive 'the words of faith,' not in mutilated, falsified or diminished form but whole and entire, in all its rigour and vigour".[369]

664 112. Two closely connected dimensions underlie this criterion.

– The *integral* presentation of the Gospel message, without ignoring certain fundamental elements, or without operating a selectivity with regard to the deposit of faith.[370] Catechesis, on the contrary, "must take diligent care faithfully to present the entire treasure of the Christian message".[371] This is accomplished, gradually, by following the example of the divine pedagogy with which God revealed himself progressively and gradually. Integrity must also be accompanied by adaptation. Consequently catechesis starts out with a simple proposition of the integral structure of the Christian message, and proceeds to explain it in a manner adapted to the capacity of those being catechized. Without restricting itself to this initial exposition, it gradually and increasingly proposes the Christian message more amply and with greater explicitness, in accordance with the capacity of those being catechized and with the proper character of catechesis.[372] These two levels of the integral exposition of the Gospel message are called: *intensive integrity* and *extensive integrity.*

– The presentation of the authentic Gospel message, in all of its purity, without reducing demands for fear of rejection and

---

[369] CT 30.
[370] *Ibid.*
[371] DCG (1971) 38a.
[372] DCG (1971) 38b.

without imposing heavy burdens which it does not impose, since the yoke of Jesus is light.[373] The criterion of authenticity is closely connected with that of inculturation since the latter is concerned to "translate"[374] the essentials of the Gospel message into a definite cultural language. There is always tension in this necessary task: "Evangelisation will lose much of its power and efficacy if it does not take into consideration the people to whom it is addressed.". However "it may lose its very nature and savour if on the pretext of transposing its content into another language that content is rendered meaningless or is corrupted...[375]

665   113. In the complex relationship between inculturation and the integrity of the Christian message, the criterion to be applied is a Gospel attitude of "a missionary openness to the integral salvation of the world".[376] This must always unite acceptance of truly human and religious values with the missionary task of proclaiming the whole truth of the Gospel, without falling either into closed inflexibility or into facile accommodations which enfeeble the Gospel and secularize the Church. Gospel authenticity excludes both of these attitudes which are contrary to the true meaning of mission.

A comprehensive and hierarchical message

666   114. This message transmitted by catechetics has a "comprehensive hierarchical character",[377] which constitutes a coherent and vital synthesis of the faith. This is organized around the mystery of the Most Holy Trinity, in a christocentric perspective, because this is "the source of all the other mysteries of faith, the light that enlightens them".[378] Starting with this point, the harmony of the overall message requires a "hierarchy of truths",[379] in so far as the connection between each one of these and the foundation of the faith differs. Nevertheless, this

---

[373] Cf. *Matt* 11:30.

[374] EN 63 uses the expressions *transferre* and *traslatio;* cf. RM 53b.

[375] EN 63c; cf. CT 53c and CT 31.

[376] Synod 1985, II, D, 3; cf. EN 65.

[377] CT 31 which expounds the integrity and organization of the message; cf. DCG (1971) 39 and 43.

[378] CCC 234.

[379] UR 11.

hierarchy "does not mean that some truths pertain to Faith itself less than others, but rather that some truths are based on others as of a higher priority and are illumined by them".[380]

115. All aspects and dimensions of the Christian message **667** participate in this hierarchical system.

– The history of salvation, recounting the "marvels of God" (*mirabilia Dei*), what He has done, continues to do and will do in the future for us, is organized in reference to Jesus Christ, the "centre of salvation history".[381] The preparation for the Gospel in the Old Testament, the fulness of Revelation in Jesus Christ, and the time of the Church, provide the structure of all salvation history of which creation and eschatology are its beginning and its end.

– The Apostles' Creed demonstrates how the Church has always desired to present the Christian mystery in a vital synthesis. This Creed is a synthesis of and a key to reading all of the Church's doctrine, which is hierarchically ordered around it.[382]

– The sacraments, which, like regenerating forces, spring from the paschal mystery of Jesus Christ, are also a whole. They form "an organic whole in which each particular sacrament has its own vital place".[383] In this whole, the Holy Eucharist occupies a unique place to which all of the other sacraments are ordained. The Eucharist is to be presented as the "sacrament of sacraments".[384]

– The double commandment of love of God and neighbour is – in the moral message – a hierarchy of values which Jesus himself established: "On these two commandments depend all the Law and the Prophets" (Matt 22:40). The love of God and neighbour, which sum up the Decalogue, are lived in the spirit of

---

[380] DCG (1971) 43.

[381] DCG (1971) 41.

[382] St Cyril of Jerusalem affirms with regard to the Creed: "This synthesis of faith was not made to accord with human opinions but rather what was of the greatest importance was gathered from all the Scriptures, to present the one teaching of the faith in its entirety. And just as a mustard seed contains a great number of branches in a tiny grain, so too the summary of faith encompassed in a few words the whole knowledge of the true religion contained in the Old and New Testaments".

[383] CCC 1211.

[384] *Ibid.*

the Beatitudes and constitute the *magna carta* of the Christian life proclaimed by Jesus in the Sermon on the Mount.[385]

– The Our Father gathers up the essence of the Gospel. It synthesizes and hierarchically structures the immense riches of prayer contained in Sacred Scripture and in all of the Church's life. This prayer, given by Jesus to his disciples, makes clear the child-like trust and the deepest desires with which one can turn to God.[386]

A meaningful message for the human person

668   116. The Word of God, in becoming man, assumed human nature in everything, except sin. In this way Jesus Christ, who is "the image of the invisible God", (Col 1:15) is also the perfect man. From this it follows that "in reality it is only in the mystery of the Word made flesh that the mystery of man truly becomes clear".[387]

Catechesis, in presenting the Christian message, not only shows who God is and what his saving plan is, but, as Jesus himself did, it reveals man to man and makes him more aware of his sublime vocation.[388] Revelation, in fact, "... is not... isolated from life or artificially juxtaposed to it. It is concerned with the ultimate meaning of life and it illumines the whole of life with the light of the Gospel, to inspire it or to question it".[389]

The relationship between the Christian message and human experience is not a simple methodological question. It springs from the very end of catechesis, which seeks to put the human person in communion with Jesus Christ. In his earthly life he lived his humanity fully: "He worked with human hands, he thought with a human mind, he acted with a human will, and with a human heart he loved".[390] Therefore, "Christ enables us to live

---

[385] St Augustine presents the Sermon on the Mount as "the perfect charter of the Christian life and contains all the appropriate precepts necessary to guide it" (*De Sermone Domini in Monte* I, 1; PL 34, 1229-1231); cf. EN 8.

[386] The Our Father is, in truth, the summing up of the entire Gospel (Tertullian, *De oratione,* 1, 6). "Go through all the prayers in the Scriptures and I do not believe that it is possible to find anyone, anywhere, that is not included in the Lord's Prayer" (St Augustine, *Epistolas,* 130, 12; PL, 33, 502); cf. CCC 2761.

[387] GS 22a.

[388] Cf. *Ibid.*

[389] CT 22c; cf. EN 29.

[390] GS 22b.

in him all that he himself lived, and he lives it in us".[391] Catechesis operates through this identity of human experience between Jesus the Master and his disciple and teaches to think like him, to act like him, to love like him.[392] To live communion with Christ is to experience the new life of grace.[393]

117. For this reason, catechesis is eminently christological in presenting the Christian message and should therefore "be concerned with making men attentive to their more significant experiences, both personal and social; it also has the duty of placing under the light of the Gospel, the questions which arise from those experiences so that there may be stimulated within men a right desire to transform their ways of life".[394] In this sense:

– in first evangelisation, proper to the pre-catechumenate or to pre-catechesis, the proclamation of the Gospel shall always be done in close connection with human nature and its aspirations, and will show how the Gospel fully satisfies the human heart;[395]

– in biblical catechesis, it shall help to interpret present-day human life in the light of the experiences of the people of Israel, of Jesus Christ and the ecclesial community, in which the Spirit of the Risen Jesus continually lives and works;

– in explaining the Creed, catechesis shall show how the great themes of the faith (creation, original sin, Incarnation, Easter, Pentecost, eschatology) are always sources of life and light for the human being;

– moral catechesis, in presenting what makes life worthy of the Gospel[396] and in promoting the Beatitudes as the spirit that must permeate the Decalogue, shall root them in the human virtues present in the heart of man;[397]

– liturgical catechesis shall make constant reference to the great human experiences represented by the signs and symbols of liturgical actions originating in Jewish and Christian culture.[398]

669

---

[391] CCC 521; cf. CCC 519-521.
[392] Cf. CT 20b.
[393] Cf. *Rm* 6:4.
[394] DCG (1971) 74; cf. CT 29.
[395]Cf. AG 8a.
[396] Cf. *Phil* 1:27.
[397] Cf. CCC 1697.
[398] Cf. CCC 1145-1152 concerning the importance of signs and symbols in liturgical action.

Methodological principle for the presentation of the message[399]

670   118. The norms and criteria indicated in this chapter and
those concerning the "exposition of the content of catechesis,
must be applied in the various forms of catechesis, that is to say,
in biblical and liturgical catechesis, in doctrinal summaries, in the
interpretation of the conditions of human existence and so on.[400]

From these, however, it is not possible to deduce the order
that should be observed in the exposition of catechetical content.
Indeed, "it can happen that in the present situation of catechesis
reasons of method or pedagogy may suggest that the
communication of the riches of the content of catechesis should
be organized in one way rather than another".[401] It is possible to
begin with God so as to arrive at Christ, and vice versa. Equally,
it is possible to start with man and come to God, and conversely.
The selection of a particular order for presenting the message is
conditioned by circumstances, and by the faith level of those to be
catechized. It will always be necessary to elaborate with care that
pedagogical method which is most appropriate to the circumstances of an ecclesial community or of those to whom catechesis
is specifically addressed. Hence derives the need to investigate
correctly in order to find those means which best respond to
different situations.

It is a matter for Bishops to draw up more particular norms
for this and to apply them by means of Catechetical Directories
and catechisms which cater for different ages and cultural
conditions, as well as in other ways deemed more appropriate.[402]

Chapter Two: "This is our faith this is the faith of the Church"

"All Scripture is inspired by God and profitable for teaching,
for reproof, for correction, and for training in righteousness" (2
Thess 2:15).

"So then, brethren, stand firm and hold to the tradition which
you were taught by us, either by word of mouth or by letter" (2
Thess 2:15).

---

[399] Cf. part III, chapter 2.
[400] DCG (1971) 46.
[401] CT 31.
[402] Cf. CIC 775, §§ 1-3.

119. This chapter reflects on the content of catechesis as **671** presented by the Church in the syntheses of faith which are officially drawn up and presented in her catechisms. The Church has always used formulations of faith which, in short forms, contain the essentials of what she believes and lives: New Testament texts, creeds or professions of faith, liturgical formulas, Eucharistic prayers. At a later period, it was considered useful to provide more ample explanations of the faith in organic synthesis, through the catechisms compiled in numerous local Churches in recent centuries. In two historical moments, at the Council of Trent and in our own times, it was considered opportune to furnish a comprehensive presentation of the faith in a catechism of a universal nature, which would serve as a reference point for catechesis throughout the Church. It was with this intention that Pope John Paul II promulgated the *Catechism of the Catholic Church* on 11 October 1992.

The present chapter seeks to situate these official instruments of the Church, which is what catechisms are, in relation with catechetical activity and praxis.

In the first place, it will reflect on the *Catechism of the Catholic Church* and seek to clarify its role in the overall catechesis of the Church. It will, then, analyse the need for local catechisms to adapt the content of the faith to different circumstances and cultures. Some directions will be given to assist the preparation of such catechisms. The Church, contemplating the richness of the content of faith, which the Bishops propose to the people of God and which they express like a "symphony"[403] celebrates, lives and proclaims what she believes: "This is our faith, this is the faith of the Church".

The Catechism of the Catholic Church and the General Directory for Catechesis

120. The *Catechism of the Catholic Church* and the *General* **672** *Catechetical Directory* are two distinct but complementary instruments at the service of the Church's catechetical activity.

– The *Catechism of the Catholic Church* is "a statement of the Church's faith and of Catholic doctrine, attested to or illuminated

---

[403] Cf. FD 2d.

by Sacred Scripture, the Apostolic Tradition and the Church's Magisterium.[404]

– The *General Directory for Catechesis* provides "the basic principles of pastoral theology taken from the Magisterium of the Church, and in a special way from the Second Vatican Council by which pastoral action in the ministry of the word can be more fittingly directed and governed".[405]

Both instruments, each taken in accordance with its specific nature and authority, are mutually complementary. The *Catechism of the Catholic Church* is an act of the Magisterium of the Pope, by which, in our times, in virtue of Apostolic Authority, he synthesizes normatively the totality of the Catholic faith. He offers the *Catechism of the Catholic Church*, in the first place, to the Churches as a point of reference for the authentic presentation of the content of the faith. The *Catechetical Directory,* for its part, carries that authority normally vested by the Holy See in instruments of orientation by approving them and confirming them. It is an official aid for the transmission of the Gospel message and for the whole of catechetical activity. The complementary nature of both of these instruments justifies the fact, as already mentioned in the *Preface*, that this *General Catechetical Directory* does not devote a chapter to the presentation of the contents of the faith, as was the case in the 1971 *General Catechetical Directory for Catechesis* under the title: *"The more outstanding elements of the Christian message"*.[406] Such is explained by the fact that this Directory, as far as the content of the Christian message is concerned, simply refers to the Catechism of the Catholic Church", which is intended as a methodological norm for its concrete application. The following exposition of the *Catechism of the Catholic Church* seeks neither to summarize its contents nor to explain this instrument of the Magisterium. It simply seeks to facilitate a better understanding and use of the *Catechism of the Catholic Church* in catechetical practice.

The Catechism of the Catholic Church: Nature and purpose of the

---

[404] FD 4a.
[405] DCG (1971) *Introduction*.
[406] DCG (1971) Part III, chap. 2.

Catechism

121. The *Prologue* to the *Catechism of the Catholic Church* **673** states its purpose: "This catechism aims at presenting an organic synthesis of the essential and fundamental contents of Catholic doctrine, as regards both faith and morals, in the light of the Second Vatican Council and the whole of the Church's Tradition".[407] The Magisterium of the Church intends to render an ecclesial service for our times with the *Catechism of the Catholic Church*, recognizing that it is:

– "a valid and legitimate instrument for *ecclesial communion*":[408] it desires to promote the bond of unity in the faith by helping the disciples of Jesus Christ to make "the profession of one faith received from the Apostles";[409]

– "a sure norm for *teaching the faith*":[410] the *Catechism of the Catholic Church* offers a clear response to the legitimate right of all the baptized to know from the Church what she has received and what she believes; it is thus an obligatory point of reference for catechesis and for the other forms of the ministry of the word.

– "a sure and authentic reference text for teaching Catholic doctrine and particularly for preparing local catechisms":[411] the *Catechism of the Catholic Church,* in fact, "is not intended to replace the local catechism (duly approved)"[412] but "to encourage and assist in the writing of new local catechisms which take into account various situations and cultures, while carefully preserving the unity of faith and fidelity to Catholic doctrine".[413]

The nature or character proper to this document of the Magisterium consists in the fact that it is a comprehensive synthesis of the faith and thus it is of universal value. In this, it differs from other documents of the Magisterium, which do not set out to present such a synthesis. It differs also from local Catechisms, which, within the context of ecclesial communion, are destined for the service of a particular portion of the people of God.

---

[407] CCC 11.
[408] FD 4a; cf. FD 4b.
[409] CCC 815.
[410] FD 4a; cf. FD 4c.
[411] FD 1f; cf. FD 4c.
[412] FD 4d.
[413] *Ibid.*

Structure of the Catechism of the Catholic Church

674 122. The *Catechism of the Catholic Church* is structured around four fundamental dimensions of the Christian life: the profession of faith; the celebration of the liturgy; the morality of the Gospel; and prayer. These four dimensions spring from a single source, the *Christian mystery*. This is:

– the object of the faith *(Part One);*

– celebrated and communicated in liturgical actions *(Part Two);*

– present to enlighten and sustain the children of God in their actions *(Part Three);*

– the basis of our prayer, whose supreme expression is the *Our Father*, and the object of our supplication, praise and intercession *(Part Four);*[414]

This four part structure develops the essential aspects of the faith:

– belief in the Triune God and in his saving plan;

– sanctification by him in the sacramental life;

– loving him with all one's heart and one's neighbour as oneself;

– prayer while waiting for the coming of his Kingdom and our meeting with him face to face.

The *Catechism of the Catholic Church* thus refers to the faith as believed, celebrated, lived and prayed. It is a call to integral Christian education. The structure of the *Catechism of the Catholic Church* derives from the profound unity of the Christian life. It maintains an explicit interrelation between *"lex orandi"*, *"lex credendi"* and *"lex vivendi"*. "The Liturgy itself is prayer; the confession of faith finds its proper place in the celebration of worship. Grace, the fruit of the sacraments, is the irreplaceable condition for Christian living, just as participation in the Church's Liturgy requires faith. If faith is not expressed in works it is dead and cannot bear fruit into eternal life".[415]

Structured around the four pillars[416] which sustain the transmission of the faith *(the Creed, the Sacraments, the Decalogue,*

---

[414] FD 3d.

[415] FD 2e.

[416] Cf.CCC 13.

the Our Father), the *Catechism of the Catholic Church* is presented as a doctrinal point of reference for education in the four basic tasks of catechesis,[417] and for the drawing up of local catechisms. It does not, however, impose a predetermined configuration on the one or on the other. "The best structure for catechesis must be one which is suitable to particular concrete circumstances and cannot be established for the entire Church by a common catechism".[418] Perfect fidelity to Catholic doctrine is compatible with a rich diversity of presentation.

The inspiration of the Catechism of the Catholic Church:
Trinitarian Christocentricity and the nobility of the vocation of
the human person
    123. The axis of the *Catechism of the Catholic Church* is **675** Jesus Christ, "the Way, the Truth and the Life" (John 14:6). Centred on him, it is orientated in two directions: toward God and toward the human person.
    – The mystery of the Triune God and of his economy of salvation inspires and organizes the internal structure of the *Catechism of the Catholic Church* in general and in particular. The profession of faith, the liturgy, the morality of the Gospel and prayer in the *Catechism of the Catholic Church* all have a trinitarian inspiration, which runs through the entire work.[419]
    – The mystery of the human person is presented throughout the *Catechism of the Catholic Church* and specifically in some particularly significant chapters: "Man is capable of God", "The creation of Man", "The Son of God became Man", "The vocation of Man and life in the Spirit"... and others.[420] This doctrine, contemplated in the light of the humanity of Jesus, the perfect man, demonstrates the highest vocation and the ideal of perfection to which every human person is called.
    Indeed, the doctrine of the *Catechism of the Catholic Church*

---

[417] Cf. Part One, chap. 3.
[418] Cardinal Joseph Ratzinger, *Il Catechismo della Chiesa Cattolica e l'ottimismo dei redenti in* J. Ratzinger-C. Schönborn, *Brief introduction to the Catechism of the Catholic Church* (original title *Kleine Hinfürung zum Catechismus der Katolischen Kirche,* München 1993) Roma 1994, pp. 26-27.
[419] Cf. CCC 189-190; 1077-1109; 1693-1695; 2564; etc.
[420] Cf. CCC 27-49; 355-379; 456-478; 1699-1756; etc.

can be distilled into the following remark of the Council: "Jesus Christ, by revealing the mystery of the Father and of his love, fully reveals man to himself and brings to light his most high calling".[421]

The literary genre of The Catechism of the Catholic Church

676   124. It is important to understand the literary genre of the *Catechism of the Catholic Church* in order to foster the role which the Church's authority gives to it in the exercise and renewal of catechetical activity in our time. The principal characteristics of this follow:

– The *Catechism of the Catholic Church* is above all a catechism; that is to say, an official text of the Church's Magisterium, which authoritatively gathers in a precise form, and in an organic synthesis the events and fundamental salvific truths which express the faith common to the People of God and which constitute the indispensable basic reference for catechesis.

– In virtue of being a catechism, the *Catechism of the Catholic Church* collects all that is fundamental and common to the Christian life without "presenting as doctrines of the faith special interpretations which are only private opinions or the views of some theological school".[422]

– The *Catechism of the Catholic Church* is, moreover, a catechism of a universal nature and is offered to the entire Church. It presents an updated synthesis of the faith which incorporates the doctrine of the Second Vatican Council as well as the religious and moral concerns of our times. However, "by design this Catechism does not set out to provide the adaptation of doctrinal presentations and the catechetical methods required by the differences of culture, age, spiritual maturity and social and ecclesial condition amongst all those to whom it is addressed. Such indispensable adaptations are the responsibility of particular catechisms and, even more, of those who instruct the faithful".[423]

---

[421] GS 22a.
[422] Cf. DCG (1971) 119.
[423] CCC 24.

The Deposit of Faith and the Catechism of the Catholic Church

125. The Second Vatican Council set as one of its principal **677** tasks the "better conservation and presentation of the precious deposit of Christian doctrine so as to render it more accessible to Christ's faithful and to all men of good will". The content of that deposit is the word of God which is safeguarded in the Church. The Magisterium of the Church, having decided to draw up "a reference text" for the teaching of the faith, has chosen from this precious treasure "things new and old" which it considers suitable for accomplishing this task. The *Catechism of the Catholic Church* thus constitutes a fundamental service by encouraging the proclamation of the Gospel and the teaching of the faith, which both draw their message from Tradition and Sacred Scripture entrusted to the Church, so as to achieve this function with complete authenticity. The *Catechism of the Catholic Church* is not the only source of catechesis, since as an act of the Magisterium, "it is not superior to the word of God but at its service". However it is a particularly authentic act of interpretation of that word, such that the Gospel may be proclaimed and transmitted in all its truth and purity.

126. In the light of this relationship between the *Catechism of* **678** *the Catholic Church* and the *"deposit of faith"*, it may be useful to clarify two questions of vital importance for catechesis:
– the relationship between Sacred Scripture and the *Catechism of the Catholic Church* as points of reference for the content of catechesis;
– the relationship between the catechetical tradition of the Fathers of the Church, with its rich content and its profound understanding of the catechetical process, and the *Catechism of the Catholic Church*.

Sacred Scripture, the Catechism of the Catholic Church, and Catechesis

127. The Constitution *Dei Verbum* of the Second Vatican **679** Council emphasizes the fundamental importance of Sacred Scripture in the Church's life. Together with tradition, it is the "supreme rule of faith", since it transmits "the very word of God"

and makes "to resound... the voice of the Holy Spirit".[424] For this reason the Church desires that in the ministry of the word, Sacred Scripture should have a pre-eminent position. In concrete terms, catechesis should be "an authentic introduction to *lectio divina,* that is, to a reading of the Sacred Scriptures done in accordance to the Spirit who dwells in the Church".[425] "In this sense, to describe Tradition and Scripture as sources for catechesis means that catechesis must imbibe and permeate itself with biblical and evangelical thought, spirit and attitudes by constant contact with them. It also means that catechesis will be as rich and as effective only to the extent that these texts are read with the mind and heart of the Church".[426] In this ecclesial reading of the Scriptures, done in the light of Tradition, the *Catechism of the Catholic Church* plays a most important role.

680

128. Sacred Scripture and the *Catechism of the Catholic Church* are presented as two basic sources of inspiration for all catechetical activity in our time.

– Sacred Scripture as, "the word of God written under the inspiration of the Holy Spirit",[427] and the *Catechism of the Catholic Church,* as a significant contemporary expression of the living Tradition of the Church and a sure norm for teaching the faith, are called, each in its own way and according to its specific authority, to nourish catechesis in the Church of today.

– Catechesis transmits the content of the word of God according to the two modalities whereby the Church possesses it, interiorizes it and lives it: as a narration of the history of salvation and as an explanation of the Creed. Both Sacred Scripture and the *Catechism of the Catholic Church* must inform biblical as well as doctrinal catechesis so that they become true vehicles of the content of God's word.

– In the ordinary development of catechesis it is important that catechumens and those to be catechized can have trust in both Sacred Scripture and the local catechism. Catechesis, by definition, is nothing other than the living and meaningful transmission of

---

[424] DV 21.
[425] MPD 9c. Cf. Pontifical Biblical Commission, *The Interpretation of the Bible in the Church,* IV, c, 3 l.c.
[426] CT 27; cf. Synod 1985, II B, a, 1.
[427] DV 9.

these "documents of faith".[428]

The catechetical tradition of the Fathers and the Catechism of the Catholic Church

129. The whole Tradition of the Church together with Scripture **681** is contained in the *"deposit of faith"*. "The sayings of the holy Fathers are a witness to the life-giving presence of this Tradition, showing how its riches are poured out in the practice and life of the Church, in her belief and in her prayer".[429] With regard to this doctrinal and pastoral richness, some aspects merit special attention:

– the decisive importance which the Fathers attribute to the baptismal catechumenate in the structure of the particular churches;

– the gradual and progressive conception of Christian formation, arranged in stages:[430] The Fathers model the catechumenate on the divine pedagogy; in the catechumenal process the catechumen, like the people of Israel, goes through a journey to arrive at the promised land: Baptismal identification with Christ.[431]

– The organization of the content of catechesis in accordance with the stages of that process; in patristic catechesis a primary role is devoted to the *narration* of the history of salvation; as Lent advanced, the *Creed* and the *Our Father* were handed on to the catechumens together with their meaning and moral implications; after the celebration of the sacraments of initiation, mystagogical catechesis helped interiorize them and to savour the experience of

---

[428] Cf. MPD 9.

[429] DV 8c.

[430] When the Second Vatican Council called for the restoration of the adult catechumenate it underlined its necessary gradual nature: "The Adult Catechumenate arranged in various stages will be re-established" (SC 64).

[431] The witness of Origen is significant: "When you abandon the darkness of idolatry and when you wish to arrive at a knowledge of the Divine Law then you begin your exodus from Egypt. When you are counted among the multitude of the catechumens, when you have started to obey the commandments of the Church, then you have crossed the Red Sea. During the sojourn in the desert, everyday, when you apply yourself to listen to the Law of God and to contemplate the face of Moses who uncovers for you the glory of the Lord. But when you arrive at the baptismal font, having crossed the Jordan, then you will enter into the Promised Land" (*Homiliae in Iesu Nave,* IV, 1: SCh 71, 149).

configuration to Christ and of communion with him.

682   130. The *Catechism of the Catholic Church,* for its part, brings to catechesis "the great tradition of catechisms".[432] In the richness of this tradition the following aspects deserve attention:

– The cognitive or truth dimension of the faith: this is not only living attachment to God but also assent of intellect and will; the catechisms constantly remind the Church of the need for the faithful to have an organic knowledge of the faith, however simple in form;

– An education in the faith, which is well rooted in all its sources, embraces all the different dimensions of faith profession, celebration, life and prayer.

The wealth of the patristic tradition and the tradition of catechisms comes together in the actual catechesis of the Church, enriching her in her own concept of catechesis and of its contents. These traditions bring to catechesis the seven basic elements which characterize it: the three phases in the narration of the history of salvation (the Old Testament, the life of Jesus Christ and the history of the Church) and the four pillars of its exposition (the Creed, the Sacraments, the *Decalogue* and the *Our Father*). With these seven foundation stones, both of initiatory catechesis and of continuing Christian development, various schemes and styles may be devised, in accordance with the different cultural situations of those to whom catechesis is addressed.

Catechisms in the local Churches: Local Catechisms: their necessity[433]

683   131. The *Catechism of the Catholic Church* is given to all the faithful and to those who wish to know what the Catholic Church believes.[434] It is "meant to encourage and assist in the writing of new local catechisms, which take into account various situations and cultures, while carefully preserving the unity of faith and

---

[432] CCC 13.

[433] This section refers exclusively to official catechisms, that is those catechisms which are proper to the diocesan bishop or Episcopal Conference (CIC 775). Non official catechisms (CIC 827) and other catechetical aids (DCG (1971) 116) will be considered in Part V, chap. 4.

[434] FD 4c.

Catholic doctrine".[435]

Local catechisms, prepared or approved by diocesan Bishops or by Episcopal Conferences,[436] are invaluable instruments for catechesis which are "called to bring the power of the Gospel into the very heart of culture and cultures".[437] For this reason Pope John Paul II has offered a warm encouragement "to the Episcopal Conferences of the whole world to undertake, patiently but resolutely, the considerable work to be accomplished, in agreement with the Apostolic See, in order to prepare genuine catechisms which will be faithful to the essential content of Revelation and up to date in method, and which will be capable of educating the Christian generations of the future to a sturdy faith".[438]

By means of local catechisms, the Church actualizes the "divine pedagogy"[439] used by God himself in Revelation, adapting his language to our nature with thoughtful concern.[440] In local catechisms, the Church communicates the Gospel in a manner accessible to the human person so that it may be really perceived as the "Good News" of salvation. Local catechisms are palpable expressions of the wonderful "condescension"[441] of God and of his "ineffable"[442] love for the world.

The literary genre of the local catechism

132. Three principal traits characterize every catechism **684** adopted by a local Church: its official character, its organic and fundamental synthesis of the faith, and the fact that, along with Sacred Scripture, it is offered as a reference point for catechesis.

– The local catechism is an official text of the Church. In a certain sense, it makes visible the "handing on of the Creed" and the "handing on of the Our Father" to catechumens and those to

---

[435] FD 4d.
[436] Cf. CIC 775.
[437] CT 53a; cf. CCC 24.
[438] CT 50.
[439] DV 15.
[440] Cf. DV 13.
[441] DV 13.
[442] DV 13. *Ineffable kindness, providence and care, condescension* are terms which define the divine pedagogy in Revelation. They show God's desire *to adapt Himself* (synkatabasis) to human beings. This same spirit should guide the redaction of local catechisms.

be baptized. For this reason, it is an act of *tradition*. The official character of local catechisms establishes a qualitative difference from other instruments which may be useful for catechetical pedagogy *(didactic texts, non-official catechisms, catechetical guides etc.)*

– Moreover, every catechism is a synthetic and basic text, in which the events and fundamental truths of the Christian mystery are presented in an organic way and with regard to the "hierarchy of truths". The local catechism presents, in its organic structure, "an ensemble of the documents of Revelation and Christian Tradition",[443] made available in the rich diversity of "languages" in which the word of God is expressed.

– The local catechism, finally, is given as a reference point to inform catechesis. The Sacred Scriptures and the catechism are the two basic doctrinal texts for the process of catechesis and must always be to hand. While both of these texts are of the greatest importance, they are not the only texts available. Indeed, other more immediate aids are necessary.[444] It is, therefore, a valid question to ask if an official catechism should contain pedagogical elements or, on the contrary, should be limited to giving a doctrinal synthesis and a presentation of sources.

In any case, the catechism, being an instrument of catechetical activity, which is an act of communication, always reflects a certain pedagogical inspiration and must always make apparent, in its own way, the divine pedagogy.

More purely methodological questions are obviously more appropriate to other instruments.

Aspects of adaptation in a local catechism[445]

685 133. The *Catechism of the Catholic Church* indicates those aspects which must be taken into account when adapting or contextualizing the organic synthesis of the faith which every

---

[443] DCG (1971) 119.

[444] In catechesis apart from catechetical aids there are other decisive factors: the person of the catechist, his method of transmission, the rapport between catechist and those being catechized, respect for the receptive capacity of those being catechized, an atmosphere of love and faith in communication, active involvement of the Christian community, etc.

[445] Cf. part IV, chapter 1.

local catechism must offer. This synthesis of the faith must exhibit the adaptations which are required by "the differences of culture, age, spiritual maturity, and social and ecclesial conditions among all those to whom it is addressed".[446] The Second Vatican Council also emphatically affirms the need for adapting the Gospel Message: "Indeed, this kind of adaptation and preaching of the revealed word must ever be the law of all evangelisation".[447] Hence:

– The local catechism must present the synthesis of the faith with reference to the particular culture in which catechumens and those to be catechized are immersed. It will, however, incorporate all those "original expressions of life, of celebrations and of thought which are Christian",[448] proper to a particular cultural tradition and are the fruits of the work and inculturation of the local Church.

– The local catechism, "faithful to the message and to the human person",[449] presents the Christian message in a meaningful way and is close to the psychology and mentality of those for whom it is intended. Consequently, it will refer clearly to the fundamental experiences of their lives.[450]

– It shall pay attention in a special way to the concrete manner in which religion is lived in a given society. It is not, for example, the same thing to prepare a catechism for a society permeated by religious indifference as it is for a profoundly religious context.[451] The relationship between belief and science must be treated with great care in every catechism.

– Problems arising from social conditions, especially those arising from its more profound structural elements (economics, politics, family) are a factor in the contextualization of a catechism. Drawing inspiration from the social teaching of the Church, the Catechism will offer criteria, motivations and modes

---

[446] CCC 24.
[447] GS 44.
[448] CT 53a.
[449] Cf. CT 55c; MPD 7; DCG (1971) 34.
[450] Cf. CT 36-45.
[451] Local catechisms must give attention to the question and orientation of popular devotions (cf. EN 48; CT 54 and CCC 1674-1676). Equally they should be concerned with ecumenical dialogue (cf. CT 32-34; CCC 817-822) and with inter-religious dialogue (cf. EN 53; RM 55-57 and CCC 839-845).

of action to highlight the Christian presence in these critical situations.[452]

– Finally, the concrete ecclesial situation lived by a particular Church shall provide the context to which a catechism must make reference. Obviously one does not refer hereby to contingent situations, which are addressed by other magisterial documents, but to the more permanent situation which demands a more specific and appropriate evangelisation.[453]

The creativity of local Churches in the elaboration of catechesis

686   134. Local Churches, in fulfilling the task of adapting, contextualizing and inculturating the Gospel message by means of catechisms, for different ages, situations and cultures must exercise a mature creativity. From the *depositum fidei* entrusted to the Church, local Churches select, structure and express, under the guidance of the Holy Spirit, their inner Master, all those elements which transmit the Gospel in its complete authenticity in a given situation.

For this difficult task, the *Catechism of the Catholic Church* is a "point of reference" to guarantee the unity of the faith. This present *General Catechetical Directory*, for its part, offers the basic criteria which govern the presentation of the Christian message.

687   135. In elaborating local catechisms it will be useful to remember the following points:

– it is a question, above all, of elaborating genuine catechisms, adapted and inculturated: in this sense, a distinction must be drawn between a catechism which adapts the Christian message to different ages, situations and cultures, and one which is a mere summary of the *Catechism of the Catholic Church* and serves as an introduction to its study. These are two different types.[454]

---

[452] LC 72 distinguishes between "principles of reflection", "criteria of judgement" and "directives for action" which the Church offers in her social doctrine. A catechism should also distinguish these various levels.

[453] It refers fundamentally to "the different socio-religious situations" faced by evangelisation. These are examined in Part I, chap. I.

[454] On the distinction between local catechisms and syntheses of the *Catechism of the Catholic Church* see *"Orientamenti sulle sintesi del Catechismo della Chiesa Cattolica"*, of the Congregation for the Clergy and the Congregation for the Doctrine of the Faith. Among other things it notes: "syntheses of the *Catechism of the Catholic Church* can be erroneously understood to be

– Local catechisms may be diocesan, regional or national in character.[455]

– with regard to the structuring of contents, different Episcopates publish catechisms of various structures and configurations; as has been said, the *Catechism of the Catholic Church* is proposed as a point of doctrinal reference, but, does not impose on the entire Church a determined structure on other catechisms: there are catechisms with a trinitarian structure; others are planned according to the stages of salvation; others again are organized along a biblical or theological theme (Covenant, Kingdom of God, etc.); some are structured around an aspect of the faith, while others again follow the liturgical year;

– with regard to the manner of expressing the Gospel message, the creativity of a catechism will have a bearing on its formulation and content,[456] evidently a catechism must be faithful to the deposit of faith in its method of expressing the doctrinal substance of the Christian message: "The individual churches – which are involved not only with men but also with their aspirations, their wealth and their poverty, with their manner of praying and living and their outlook on the world – must make their own the substance of the evangelical message. Without any sacrifice of the essential truths they must transpose this message into an idiom which will be understood by the people they serve and those who proclaim it";[457]

---

substitutes for local catechisms even to the extent of discouraging these latter. However, they lack those adaptations to local situations particular to those who are catechized which is required of catechesis".

[455] Cf. CIC 775 §§ 1-2.

[456] The question of language both in local catechisms and in catechetical activity is of supreme importance. Cf. CT 59.

[457] EN 63. In the delicate task of assimilation and translation mentioned in this text it is most important to bear in mind the observation of the Congregation for the Doctrine of the Faith and of the Congregation for the Clergy *Orientamenti sulle sintesi del Catechismo della Chiesa Cattolica,* 3: "The preparation of local catechisms, which have the *Catechism of the Catholic Church* as an authoritative and secure reference text (FD 4), remains an important objective for the various Episcopates. However, the foreseeable difficulties which can arise in such an undertaking can only be overcome by an adequate assimilation of the *Catechism of the Catholic Church.* Such assimilation even when it is accomplished over a long period of time prepares the theological, catechetical and linguistic ground for a work that really inculturates the contents of the Catechism".

The principle to be followed in this delicate task is indicated by the Second Vatican Council: "to seek out more efficient ways – provided the meaning and understanding of them is safeguarded – of presenting their teaching to modern man: for the deposit of faith is one thing, the manner of expressing it is quite another".[458]

The Catechism of the Catholic Church and local catechisms: the symphony of faith

688

136. The *Catechism of the Catholic Church* and local catechisms, each, with its own specific authority, naturally, form a unity. They are a concrete expression of the "unity of the same apostolic faith",[459] and, at the same time, of the rich diversity of formulations of the same faith. To those who contemplate this harmony, the *Catechism of the Catholic Church* and local catechisms together express a "symphony" of faith, a symphony inherent above all in the *Catechism of the Catholic Church* which has been drawn up with the collaboration of the entire Episcopate of the Catholic Church, a symphony harmonized with this and manifested in local catechisms. This symphony, this "chorus of voices of the universal Church",[460] heard in the local catechisms and faithful to the *Catechism of the Catholic Church*, has a very important theological significance.

– It manifests the Catholicity of the Church: the cultural riches of the peoples is incorporated into the expression of the faith of the one Church.

– The *Catechism of the Catholic Church* and local catechisms make manifest to the ecclesial communion of which "the profession of the one faith"[461] is one of the visible links, "in which and formed out of which the one and unique visible Church of Christ exists".[462] The particular Churches, "parts of the one Church of Christ", form with the whole, the universal Church, "a peculiar relationship of mutual interiority"[463] The unity which

---

[458] GS 62b.
[459] FD 4b.
[460] RM 54b.
[461] CCC 815.
[462] LG 23a.
[463] Congregation for the Doctrine of the Faith, Letter *Communionis notio*, n. 19 *l. c.* 843.

thus exists between the *Catechism of the Catholic Church* and local catechisms makes visible this communion.

– The *Catechism of the Catholic Church* and local catechisms equally express, clearly, the reality of episcopal collegiality. The Bishops, each in his own diocese and together as a college, in communion with the Successor of Peter, have the greatest responsibility for catechesis in the Church.[464]

The *Catechism of the Catholic Church* and local catechisms, by their profound unity and rich diversity, are called to be a renewing leaven of catechesis in the Church. Contemplating them with her Catholic and universal gaze, the Church, that is, the entire community of the disciples of Christ, can say in truth: "This is our faith, this is the faith of the Church".

Part Three: The Pedagogy of the Faith

The pedagogy of the faith

"Yet it was I who taught Ephraim to walk, I took them up in my arms; but they did not know that I healed them. I lead them with cords of compassion, with the bands of love, and I became to them as one who eases the yoke on their jaws, and I bent down to them and fed them" (Hos 11:3-4).

"And when he was alone, those who were about him with the twelve asked him concerning the parables. And he said to them, 'to you has been given the secret of the kingdom of God'". "But privately to his own disciples he explained everything" (Mark 4:10-11, 34).

"You have one Master, the Christ" (Matt 23:10)

137. Jesus gave careful attention to the formation of the disciples whom he sent out on mission. He presented himself to them as the only teacher and, at the same time, a patient and faithful friend.[465] He exercised real teaching "by means of his whole life".[466] He stimulated them with opportune questions.[467] He explained to them in a more profound manner what he had

689

---

[464] Cf. CT 63b.
[465] Cf. *John* 15:15; *Mark* 9:33-37; 10:41-45.
[466] Cf. CT 9.
[467] Cf. *Mark* 8:14-21; 8:27.

proclaimed to the crowds.[468] He introduced them to prayer.[469] He sent them out on a missionary apprenticeship.[470] He promised to them the Spirit of his Father whom he sent to bring them to the complete truth,[471] and to sustain them in inevitable moments of difficulty.[472] Jesus Christ is "the Teacher who reveals God to Man and Man to himself, the Teacher who saves, sanctifies and guides. He is the Teacher who lives, who speaks, rouses, moves, redresses, judges, forgives and walks with us day by day on the path of history. He is also the Teacher who comes and will come in glory".[473] In Jesus Christ, Lord and Teacher, the Church finds transcendent grace, permanent inspiration and the convincing model for all communication of the faith.

The meaning and purpose of Part Three

690   138. In the school of Jesus the Teacher, the catechist closely joins his action as a responsible person with the mysterious action of the grace of God. Catechesis is thus an exercise in "the original pedagogy of the faith".[474]

The transmission of the Gospel through the Church remains before all else and forever the work of the Holy Spirit and has in Revelation a fundamental witness and norm.

This will be found in chapter one. But the Holy Spirit works through people who receive the mission to proclaim the Gospel and whose competence and human experience form part of the pedagogy of the faith.

Hence arises a series of questions which have been fully explored in the history of catechesis. These are concerned with catechetical activity, its sources, its methods, those to whom it is addressed and the process of inculturation.

The second chapter is not intended to be an exhaustive examination of all of these aspects but it will deal with those points which today appear to have particular importance for the

---

[468] Cf. *Mark* 4:34; *Luke* 12:41.
[469] Cf. *Luke* 11:1-2.
[470] Cf. *Luke* 10:1-20.
[471] Cf. *John* 16:13.
[472] Cf. *Matt* 10:20; *John* 15:26; *Acts* 4:31.
[473] CT 9.
[474] CT 58.

whole Church. It is the task of the various directories and other catechetical instruments of the particular Churches to respond to specific problems in an appropriate manner.

Chapter One: Pedagogy of God, source and model of the pedagogy of the faith[475]

Pedagogy of God

139. "God is treating you as sons; for what son is there whom **691** his father does not discipline?" (*Heb* 12:7) The salvation of the person, which is the ultimate purpose of Revelation, is shown as a fruit of an original and efficacious "pedagogy of God" throughout history. Similar to human usage and according to the cultural categories of time, God in Scripture is seen as a merciful Father, teacher and sage.[476] He assumes the character of the person, the individual and the community according to the conditions in which they are found. He liberates the person from the bonds of evil and attracts him to himself by bonds of love. He causes the person to grow progressively and patiently towards the maturity of a free son, faithful and obedient to his word. To this end, as a creative and insightful teacher, God transforms events in the life of his people into lessons of wisdom,[477] adapting himself to the diverse ages and life situations. Thus he entrusts words of instruction and catechesis which are transmitted from generation to generation.[478] He admonishes with reward and punishment, trials and sufferings, which become a formative influence.[479] Truly, to help a person to encounter God, which is the task of the catechist, means to emphasize above all the relationship that the person has with God so that he can make it his own and allow himself to be guided by God.

The pedagogy of Christ

140. When the fulness of time had come God sent his Son, **692**

---

[475] DV 15; DCG (1971) 33; CT 58; ChL 61; CCC 53, 122, 684, 708, 1145, 1609, 1950, 1964.

[476] Cf. *Deut* 8:5; *Hos* 11:3-4; *Prov* 3:11-12.

[477] Cf. *Deut* 4:36-40; 11:2-7.

[478] Cf. *Ex* 12:25-27; *Deut* 6:4-8; 6:20-25; 3:12-13; *Jos* 4:20.

[479] Cf. *Amos* 4:6; *Hos* 7:10; *Jer* 2:30; *Prov* 3:11-12; *Heb* 12:4-11; *Apoc* 3:19.

Jesus Christ, to humanity. He brought to the world the supreme gift of salvation by accomplishing his redemptive mission in a manner which continued "the pedagogy of God", with the perfection found in the newness of his Person. In his words, signs and works during his brief but intense life, the disciples had direct experience of the fundamental traits of the "pedagogy of Jesus", and recorded them in the Gospels: receiving others, especially the poor, the little ones and sinners, as persons loved and sought out by God; the undiluted proclamation of the Kingdom of God as the good news of the truth and of the consolation of the Father; a kind of delicate and strong love which liberates from evil and promotes life; a pressing invitation to a manner of living sustained by faith in God, by hope in the Kingdom and by charity to one's neighbour; the use of all the resources of interpersonal communication, such as word, silence, metaphor, image, example, and many diverse signs as was the case with the biblical prophets. Inviting his disciples to follow him unreservedly and without regret,[480] Christ passed on to them his pedagogy of faith as a full sharing in his actions and in his destiny.

The pedagogy of the Church

693   141. From her very beginnings the Church, which "in Christ, is in the nature of a Sacrament",[481] has lived her mission as a visible and actual continuation of the pedagogy of the Father and of the Son. She, "as our Mother is also the educator of our faith".[482]

These are the profound reasons for which the Christian community is in herself living catechesis. Thus she proclaims, celebrates, works, and remains always a vital, indispensable and primary *locus* of catechesis.

Throughout the centuries the Church has produced an incomparable treasure of pedagogy in the faith: above all the witness of saints and catechists; a variety of ways of life and original forms of religious communication such as the catechumenate, catechisms, itineraries of the Christian life; a

---

[480] Cf. *Mark* 8:34-38; *Matt* 8:18-22.
[481] LG 1.
[482] CCC 196; cf. GE 3c.

precious patrimony of catechetical teaching of faith culture, of catechetical institutions and services. All of these aspects form part of the history of catechesis and, by right, enter into the memory of the community and the praxis of the catechist.

Divine pedagogy, action of the Holy Spirit in every Christian

694

142. *"Blessed is the man whom thou dost chasten, O Lord, and whom thou dost teach out of thy law" (Ps* 94:12). In the school of the word of God, received in the Church, the disciple, thanks to the gift of the Holy Spirit sent by Christ, grows like his Teacher "in wisdom, stature, and in favour with God and men" (Luke 2:52). He is also assisted in developing in himself "the divine education" received by means of catechesis and by means of knowledge and experience.[483] In this way, by knowing more about the mystery of salvation, by learning to adore God the Father, and "by living in the truth according to charity", the disciple seeks "to grow in all things towards him, who is the Head, Christ" (Eph 4:15). The pedagogy of God can be said to be completed when the disciple shall "become the perfect Man, fully mature with the fulness of Christ himself" (Eph 4:13). For this reason there cannot be teachers of the faith other than those who are convinced and faithful disciples of Christ and his Church.

Divine pedagogy and catechesis

695

143. Catechesis, as communication of divine Revelation, is radically inspired by the pedagogy of God, as displayed in Christ and in the Church. Hence, it receives its constitutive characteristics and under the guidance of the Holy Spirit, it sets out a synthesis to encourage a true experience of faith, and thus a filial encounter with God. In this way, catechesis:

– is a pedagogy which serves and is included in the "dialogue of salvation" between God and the person, while giving due emphasis to the universal end of this salvation; with regard to God it underlines divine initiative, loving motivation, gratuity and respect for our liberty; with regard to man it highlights the dignity

---

[483] Cf. GE 4.

of the gift received and the demand to grow continually therein;[484]

– it accepts the principle of the progressiveness of Revelation, the transcendence and the mysterious nature of the word of God and also its adaptation to different persons and cultures;

– it recognizes the centrality of Jesus Christ, the Word of God made man, who determines catechesis as "a pedagogy of the incarnation", and through whom the Gospel is to be proposed for the life and in the life of people;

– it values the community experience of faith, which is proper to the people of God, the Church;

– it is rooted in inter-personal relations and makes its own the process of dialogue;

– it conducts a pedagogy of signs, where words and deeds, teaching and experience are interlinked;[485]

– draws its power of truth and its constant task of bearing witness to it, since the love of God is the ultimate reason for his self-revelation, from the inexhaustible divine love, which is the Holy Spirit.[486]

Thus catechesis takes the form of a process or a journey of following the Christ of the Gospel in the Spirit towards the Father. It is undertaken to reach the maturity of the faith "given as Christ allotted it" (Eph 4:7) and according to the possibilities and the needs of everyone.

The original pedagogy of faith[487]

696   144. Catechesis, which is therefore active pedagogy in the faith, in accomplishing its tasks, cannot allow itself to be inspired by ideological considerations or purely human interests.[488] It does not confuse the salvific action of God, which is pure grace, with the pedagogical action of man. Neither, however, does it oppose them and separate them. The wonderful dialogue that God undertakes with every person becomes its inspiration and norm.

---

[484] Cf. Paul VI, Ecyclical Letter, *Ecclesiam Suam* (6 August 1964), III: AAS 56 (1964), 637-659.

[485] Cf. DV 2.

[486] Cf. RM 15; CCC 24b-25; DCG (1971) 10.

[487] Cf. MPG 11; CT 58.

[488] Cf. CT 52.

"Catechesis becomes an untiring echo" of this. It continually seeks dialogue with people in accordance with the directions offered by the Magisterium of the Church.[489] The precise objects which inspire its methodological choices are:

– to promote a progressive and coherent synthesis between full adherence of man to God *(fides qua)* and the content of the Christian message *(fides quae)*;

– to develop all the dimensions of faith through which it conveys faith which is known, celebrated, lived and prayed;[490]

– to move the person to abandon himself "completely and freely to God":[491] intelligence, will, heart and memory;

– to help the person to discern the vocation to which the Lord calls him.

Catechesis therefore carries out a complete work of initiation, education and teaching.

Fidelity to God and to the person[492]

145. Jesus Christ is the living and perfect relationship of God with man and of man with God. From him the pedagogy of the faith receives "a law which is fundamental for the whole of the Church's life", and therefore for catechesis: "the law of fidelity to God and of fidelity to man in a single, loving attitude".[493]   **697**

Genuine catechesis therefore is that catechesis which helps to perceive the action of God throughout the formative journey. It encourages a climate of listening, of thanksgiving and of prayer.[494] It looks to the free response of persons and it promotes active participation among those to be catechized.

The "condescension" of God,[495] a school for the person

146. God, wishing to speak to men as friends,[496] manifests in a special way his pedagogy by adapting what he has to say by   **698**

---

[489] Cf. Paul VI, Lett. enc. *Ecclesiam Suam, l.c.* 609-659.
[490] Cf. MPD 7-11; CCC 3; 13; DCG (1971) 36.
[491] DV 5.
[492] Cf. MPD 7; CT 55; DCD (1971) 4.
[493] CT 55.
[494] Cf. DCG (1971) 10 and 22.
[495] DV 13; CCC 684.
[496] Cf. DV 2.

solicitous providence for our earthly condition.[497] This implies for
catechesis the never-ending task of finding a language capable of
communicating the word of God and the creed of the Church,
which is its development, in the various circumstances of those
who hear it.[498] At the same time, it maintains the certainty that, by
the grace of God, this can be done and that the Holy Spirit will
give us the joy of doing it. Therefore pedagogical instructions
adequate for catechesis are those which permit the communication of the whole word of God in the concrete existence of
people.[499]

Evangelize by educating and educate by evangelizing[500]

699   147. Being inspired by the pedagogy of faith, catechesis
presents its service as a designated educative journey in that, on
the one hand it assists the person to open himself to the religious
dimension of life, while on the other, it proposes the Gospel to
him. It does so in such a manner as to penetrate and transform the
processes of intelligence, conscience, liberty and action making
of existence a gift after the example of Jesus Christ. Thus the
catechist knows and avails of the contribution of the sciences of
education, understood always in a Christian sense.

---

[497] Cf. DV 13.
[498] Cf. EN 63; CT 59.
[499] Cf. CT 31.
[500] Cf. GE 1-4; CT 58.

Chapter Two: Elements of methodology

Diversity of methods in catechesis[1]

148. The Church, in transmitting the faith, does not have a **700** particular method nor any single method. Rather, she discerns contemporary methods in the light of the pedagogy of God and uses with liberty "everything that is true, everything that is noble, everything that is good and pure, everything that we love and honour and everything that can be thought virtuous or worthy of praise" (*Phil* 4:8). In short, she assumes those methods which are not contrary to the Gospel and places them at its service. This is amply confirmed in the Church's history. Many charisms of service of the word have given rise to various methodological directions. Hence, the "variety of methods is a sign of life and richness" as well as a demonstration of respect for those to whom catechesis is addressed. Such variety is required by "the age and the intellectual development of Christians, their degree of ecclesial and spiritual maturity and many other personal circumstances".[2] Catechetical methodology has the simple objective of education in the faith. It avails of the pedagogical sciences and of communication, as applied to catechesis, while also taking account of the numerous and notable acquisitions of contemporary catechesis.

The content-method relationship in catechesis[3]

149. The principle of "fidelity to God and fidelity to man" **701** leads to an avoidance of any opposition or artificial separation or presumed neutrality between method and content. It affirms, rather, their necessary correlation and interaction. The catechist recognizes that method is at the service of revelation and conversion[4] and that therefore it is necessary to make use of it. The catechist knows that the content of catechesis cannot be in-differently subjected to any method. It requires a process of trans-mission which is adequate to the nature of the message, to its sources and language, to the concrete circumstances of ecclesial

---

[1] CT 51.
[2] Cf. CT 51.
[3] Cf. CT 31, 52, 59.
[4] Cf. CT 52.

communities as well as to the particular circumstances of the faithful to whom catechesis is addressed.

Because of its intrinsic importance both in tradition and in present day catechesis, mention must be made of the method of approaching the Bible,[5] of "documentary pedagogy", especially of the Creed, since catechesis is a transmission of the faith;[6] of the method of liturgical and ecclesial signs; and of methods proper to the mass media. A good catechetical method is a guarantee of fidelity to content.

Inductive and deductive method[7]

702 150. The communication of the faith in catechesis is an event of grace, realized in the encounter of the word of God with the experience of the person. It is expressed in sensible signs and is ultimately open to mystery. It can happen in diverse ways, not always completely known to us. With regard to the history of catechesis, there is common reference today to inductive method and deductive method. Inductive method consists of presenting facts (biblical events, liturgical acts, events in the Church's life as well as events from daily life) so as to discern the meaning these might have in divine Revelation. It is a method which has many advantages, because it conforms to the economy of Revelation. It corresponds to a profound urge of the human spirit to come to a knowledge of unintelligible things by means of visible things. It also conforms to the characteristics of knowledge of the faith, which is knowledge by means of signs. The inductive method does not exclude deductive method. Indeed it requires the deductive method which explains and describes facts by proceeding from their causes. The deductive synthesis, however, has full value, only when the inductive process is completed.[8]

703 151. In reference to operative means, it has another sense: one is called "*kerygmatic*" *(descending),* which begins with the proclamation of the message, expressed in the principle documents of the faith *(Bible, liturgy, doctrine...)* and applies it to life;

---

[5] Cf. Pontifical Biblical Commission, *The Interpretation of the Bible in the Church, l.c..*
[6] MPD 9.
[7] DCG (1971), 72.
[8] Cf. DCG (1971), 72.

the other is called "existential" *(ascending),* which moves from human problems and conditions and enlightens them with the word of God. By themselves, these are legitimate approaches, if all factors at play have been duly observed; the mystery of grace and human data, the understanding of faith and the process of reason.

Human experience in catechesis [9]

152. Experience has different functions in catechesis. For this reason, it must be continuously and duly evaluated. **704**

a) It arouses in man, interests, questions, hopes, anxieties, reflections and judgements which all converge to form a certain desire to transform his existence. It is a task of catechesis to make people more aware of their most basic experiences, to help them to judge in the light of the Gospel the questions and needs that spring from them, as well as to educate them in a new way of life. Thus, the person becomes capable of behaving in a responsible and active way before the gift of God.

b) Experience promotes the intelligibility of the Christian message. This corresponds well to the actions of Jesus. He used human experiences and situations to point to the eschatological and transcendent, as well as to show the attitude to be adopted before such realities. From this point of view, experience is a necessary medium for exploring and assimilating the truths which constitute the objective content of Revelation.

c) The above functions indicate that experience, assumed by faith, becomes in a certain manner, a *locus* for the manifestation and realization of salvation, where God, consistently with the pedagogy of the Incarnation, reaches man with his grace and saves him. The catechist must teach the person to read his own lived experience in this regard, so as to, accept the invitation of the Holy Spirit to conversion, to commitment, to hope, and to discover more and more in his life God's plan for him.

153. Interpreting and illuminating experience with the data of faith is a constant task of catechetical pedagogy – even if with difficulty. It is a task that cannot be overlooked without falling into artificial juxtapositions or closed understandings of the truth. It is **705**

---

[9] Cf. DCG (1971), 74; CT 22.

made possible, however, by a correct application of the correlation and interaction between profound human experiences[10] and the revealed message. It is this which has amply borne witness to the proclamation of the prophets, the preaching of Christ, the teaching of the Apostles, which constitutes the basic normative criterion for every encounter of faith and human experience in the time of the Church.

Memorization in catechesis[11]

706   154. Catechetics forms part of that "memory" of the Church which vividly maintains the presence of the Lord among us.[12] Use of memory, therefore, forms a constitutive aspect of the pedagogy of the faith since the beginning of Christianity. To overcome the risk of a mechanical memorization, mnemonic learning should be harmoniously inserted into the different functions of learning, such as spontaneous reaction and reflection, moments of dialogue and of silence and the relationship between oral and written work.[13]

In particular, as objects of memorization, due consideration must be given to the principal formulae of the faith. These assure a more precise exposition of the faith and guarantee a valuable common doctrinal, cultural and linguistic patrimony. Secure possession of the language of the faith is an indispensable condition for living that same faith. Such formulae, however, should be proposed as syntheses after a process of explanation and should be faithful to the Christian message. To be numbered amongst them are some of the major formulae and texts of the Bible, of dogma, of the liturgy, as well as the commonly known prayers of Christian tradition: *(Apostles' Creed, Our Father, Hail Mary...)*.[14]

"The blossoms – if we may call them that – of faith and piety

---

[10] By this we mean those experiences linked with the "great questions" of life, reality and especially about the person: the existence of God, the destiny of the human person, the origin and end of history, the truth about good and evil, the meaning of suffering, of love and of the future...; cf. EN 53; CT 22 and 39.

[11] Cf. Part I, chap. III; DCG (1971) 73; CT 55.

[12] Cf. MPD 9.

[13] Cf. CT 55.

[14] Cf. CCC 22.

do not grow in the desert places of a memoryless catechesis. What is essential is that texts that are memorized must at the same time be taken in and gradually understood in depth, in order to become a source of Christian life on the personal level and on the community level".[15]

155. Again, more importantly, the learning of the formulae of the faith and their profession must be understood in the traditional seed-bed or context of the *traditio* and the *redditio,* for which the handing on of the faith in catechesis *(traditio)* corresponds to the response of the subject during the catechetical journey and subsequently in life *(redditio).*[16]

707

This process encourages a greater participation in received truth. That personal response is correct and mature which fully respects the datum of faith and shows an understanding of the language used to express it *(biblical, liturgical, doctrinal).*

The role of the catechist[17]

156. No methodology, no matter how well tested, can dispense with the person of the catechist in every phase of the catechetical process. The charism given to him by the Spirit, a solid spirituality and transparent witness of life, constitutes the soul of every method. Only his own human and Christian qualities guarantee a good use of texts and other work instruments.

708

The catechist is essentially a mediator. He facilitates communication between the people and the mystery of God, between subjects amongst themselves, as well as with the community. For this reason, his cultural vision, social condition and lifestyle must not be obstacles to the journey of faith. Rather, these help to create the most advantageous conditions for seeking out, welcoming and deepening the Christian message. He does not forget that belief is a fruit of grace and liberty. Thus, he ensures that his activities always draw support from faith in the Holy Spirit and from prayer. Finally, the personal relationship of the catechist with the subject is of crucial importance.

---

[15] CT 55.

[16] Cf. Part I, chap. 3. *The baptismal Catechumenate: structure and progression.*

[17] DCG (1971), 71; cf. Part V, Chaps. 1 and 2.

The activity and creativity of the catechized[18]

709   157. The active participation of all the catechized in their formative process is completely in harmony, not only with genuine human communication, but specifically with the economy of Revelation and salvation. Believers, indeed, in the ordinary state of Christian life, individually or in age groups, are called to respond to the gift of God through prayer, participation in the sacraments, the liturgy, ecclesial and social commitment, works of charity and promotion of human values, such as liberty, justice and peace and the protection of creation. In catechesis, therefore, subjects take on a commitment in activities of faith, hope and charity, to acquire the capacity and rectitude of judges, to strengthen their personal conversion, and to a Christian praxis in their lives. The same subjects, especially if adults, can contribute to catechesis, by pointing out the most effective ways of understanding and expressing the message such as: "learning while doing", by employing research 'and dialogue, by exchanging challenging points of view.

Community, person and catechesis[19]

710   158. Catechetical pedagogy will be effective to the extent that the Christian community becomes a point of concrete reference for the faith journey of individuals. This happens when the community is proposed as a source, *locus* and means of catechesis. Concretely, the community becomes a visible place of faith-witness. It provides for the formation of its members. It receives them as the family of God. It constitutes itself as the living and permanent environment for growth in the faith.[20]

Besides public and collective proclamation of the Gospel, person-to-person contact, after the example of Jesus and the Apostles, remains indispensable. In this way, personal conscience is more easily committed. The gift of the Holy Spirit comes to the subject from one living person to another. Thus, the power of persuasion becomes more effective.[21]

---

[18] DCG (1971) 75.
[19] Cf. Part V Chap. 1.
[20] Cf. AG 14; DCG (1971), 35; CT 24.
[21] EN 46.

The importance of the group[22]

159. Groups play an important function in the development processes of people. The same is true of catechesis, both for children where it fosters a rounded sociability, and for young people where groups are practically a vital necessity for personality formation. The same is true of adults where they promote a sense of dialogue and sharing as well as a sense of Christian co-responsibility. The catechist who participates in such groups and who evaluates and notes their dynamics recognizes and plays the primary specific role of participating in the name of the Church as an active witness to the Gospel, capable of sharing with others the fruits of his mature faith as well as stimulating intelligently the common search for faith. Apart from its didactic aspect, the Christian group is called to be an experience of community and a form of participation in ecclesial life. It finds its goal and fullest manifestation in the more extended Eucharistic community. Jesus says: "Where two or three are gathered in my name, there am I in their midst" (Matt 18:20).

711

Social communication[23]

160. "The first areopagus of the modern age is the world of communication, which is unifying humanity... The means of social communication have become so important as to be for many the chief means of information and education, of guidance and inspiration in their behaviour as individuals, families and within society at large".[24] For this reason, in addition to the numerous traditional means in use, the media has become essential for evangelisation and catechesis.[25] In fact, "the Church would feel herself guilty before God if she did not avail of those powerful instruments which human skill is constantly developing and perfecting... In them she finds in a new and more effective forum a platform or pulpit from which she can address the multitudes".[26]

712

---

[22] DCG (1971), 76.
[23] Cf. DCG (1971) 122-123; EN 45; CT 46; FC 76; ChL 44; RM 37; Pontifical Council for Social Communications, Instruction *Aetatis Novae* (22 Feb. 1992): AAS 84 (1992) pp. 447-468; EA 71; 122-124.
[24] RM 37.
[25] Cf. *Aetatis novae, l.c.,* 11.
[26] Cf. EN 45.

In this respect, the following can be considered: television, radio, press, discs, tape recordings, video and audio cassettes, Compact Discs, as well as the entire range of audio-visual aids.[27]All of these media offer a particular service and everybody will have his own specific use for them. It is therefore necessary to appreciate their importance and to respect their demands.[28] In every well planned catechesis, such aids cannot be absent. Reciprocal assistance between the Churches, so as to defray the rather high costs of acquiring and running such aids, is a true service to the Gospel.

713   161. Good use of the media requires of catechists a serious commitment to knowledge, competence, training and up to date use of them. But, above all, because of the strong influence of the mass media and culture, it must be remembered that "it is not enough to use the media simply to spread the Christian message and the Church's authentic teaching. It is also necessary to integrate that message into the "new culture" created by modern communications... with new languages, new techniques and a new psychology".[29] Only by this, with the grace of God, can the Gospel message have the capacity to penetrate the consciousness of all and obtain a personal acceptance as well as a complete personal commitment.[30]

714   162. Those who work in the mass media, as well as those who make use of them should be able to receive the grace of the Gospel. This should cause catechists to consider particular groups of people: media professionals to whom the Gospel can be pointed out as a great horizon of truth, of responsibility and of inspiration; families – who are so much exposed to the influence of the media – for their defence, but more so in view of a growing critical and educational capacity;[31] the younger generations, who are the users and creative subjects of mass media communications. All are reminded that "the use of these instruments by professionals in communication and their reception by the public demand both a work of education in a critical sense, animated by

---

[27] Cf. CT 46.
[28] Cf. DCG (1971), 122.
[29] RM 37.
[30] Cf. EN 45.
[31] Cf. FC 76.

a passion for the truth, and a work of defence of liberty, respect for the dignity of individuals, and the elevation of the authentic culture of peoples".[32]

Part Four: Those to be Catechized

Those to be catechized

"I will give you as a light to the nations, that my salvation may reach to the ends of the earth" (Is 49:6).

"And he came to Nazareth, where he had been brought up; and he went to the synagogue, as his custom was, on the sabbath day. And he stood up to read; and there was given to him the book of the prophet Isaiah. He opened the book and found the place where it was written, 'The spirit of the Lord is upon me, because he has anointed me to preach good news to the poor. He has sent me to proclaim release to the captives and recovering of sight to the blind, to set at liberty those who are oppressed, to proclaim the acceptable year of the Lord'. And he closed the book, and gave it back to the attendant, and sat down; and the eyes of all in the synagogue were fixed on him. And he began to say to them: 'Today this scripture has been fulfilled in your hearing'" (Lk 4:16-21).

"The Kingdom is for all"[33]

163. At the beginning of his ministry, Jesus proclaimed that he had been sent to announce a joyful message[34] to the poor, making it plain and confirming by his life that the Kingdom of God is for all men, beginning with those who are most disadvantaged. Indeed he made himself a *catechist* of the Kingdom of God for all categories of persons, great and small, rich and poor, healthy and sick, near and far, Jews and pagans, men and women, righteous and sinners, rulers and subjects, individuals and groups. He is available to all. He is interested in the needs of every person, body and soul. He heals and forgives, corrects and encourages, with words and deeds.

715

---

[32] ChL 44.
[33] Cf. RM 15; EN 49-50; CT 35s; RM 14; 23.
[34] Cf. *Luke* 4:18.

Jesus concluded his earthly life by sending his disciples to do the same, to preach the Gospel to every creature on earth,[35] to "all nations" (Matt 28:19; Luke 24:47) "to the end of the earth", (Acts 1:8) for all time, "to the close of the age" (Matt 28:20).

716   164. Throughout her two-thousand-year history, the Church, continually prompted by the Holy Spirit, has accomplished the task of paying her obligation of evangelizing "both to Greeks, and to Barbarians, both to the wise and the foolish" (Rom 1:14) with an immense variety of experience in proclamation or catechesis. In this way the characteristics of a pedagogy of the faith have been articulated in which the universal openness of catechesis and its visible incarnation in the world of those to whom it is addressed, are clearly linked.

The meaning and purpose of Part Four

717   165. Attention to the diverse life situations of people[36] moves catechesis to employ many different approaches to meet them and to adapt the Christian message and the pedagogy of the faith to different needs.[37] The catechesis of initial faith is for catechumens and neophytes. Attention to the development in faith of the baptized gives rise to catechesis designed to deepen faith or indeed to recover faith, for those who need to discover that essential orientation again. When considering the physical and psychological development of those to be catechized, catechesis is developed according to age. In socio-cultural contexts, again, catechesis is developed within these categories.

718   166. Because it impossible to deal with every type of catechesis, this Part will restrict itself to a consideration of those aspects of catechesis which are of importance in any situation:

– general aspects of catechetical adaptation *(chapter 1)*;

– catechesis based on age *(chapter 2)*;

– catechesis for those who live in special circumstances *(chapter 3)*;

– catechesis in various contexts *(chapters 4 and 5)*.

The question of inculturation will also be approached in general

---

[35] Cf. *Mark* 16:15.
[36] Cf. the General Introduction.
[37] Cf. DCG (1971), 77.

terms, especially with reference to the content of the faith to persons and to cultural contexts. It is for particular Churches, in their national and regional catechetical directories, to give more specific directions with regard to concrete conditions and local needs.

Chapter One: Adaptation to those to be catechized: General aspects

The need and right of every believer to receive a valid catechesis[38]

167. All the baptized, because they are called by God to maturity of faith, need and have therefore a right to adequate catechesis. It is thus a primary responsibility of the Church to respond to this in a fitting and satisfactory manner. Hence it must be recalled that those to be evangelized are "*concrete* and historical persons",[39] rooted in a given situation and always influenced by pedagogical, social, cultural, and religious conditioning. They may or may not be aware of this.[40] In the catechetical process, the recipient must be an active subject, conscious and co-responsible, and not merely a silent and passive recipient.[41]

719

A community need and a community right[42]

168. In giving attention to the individual, it should not be overlooked that the recipient of catechesis is the whole Christian community and every person in it. If indeed it is from the whole life of the Church that catechesis draws its legitimacy and energy, it is also true that "her inner growth and correspondence with God's plan depend essentially on catechesis".[43]

The adaptation of the Gospel both concerns and involves the community as a community.

720

Adaptation requires that the content of catechesis be a healthy and adequate food[44]

169. The "adaptation of the preaching of the revealed word

721

---

[38] EN 49-50; CT 14; 35s.
[39] RH 13; cf. EN 31.
[40] Cf. RH 13-14; CCC 24.
[41] Cf. DCG (1971), 75.
[42] Cf. DCG (1971), 21.
[43] CT 13.
[44] Cf. GS 44; EN 63; CT 31; CCC 24-25.

must always remain a law for all evangelisation".[45] There is an intrinsic theological motivation for this in the Incarnation. It corresponds to the elementary, pedagogical demands of healthy human communications and reflects the practice of the Church throughout the centuries. Such adaptation must be understood as a maternal action of the Church, who recognizes people as "the field of God" (1 Cor 3:9) not to be condemned but to be cultivated in hope. She sets out to meet each person, taking into serious account diversity of circumstances and cultures and maintains the unity of so many in the one saving Word. Thus the Gospel is transmitted as genuine, satisfying, healthy and adequate food. All particular initiatives must therefore be inspired by this criterion and the creativity and talent of the catechist must bow to it.

Adaptation takes account of diverse circumstances

722   170. Adaptation is realized in accordance with the diverse circumstances in which the word of God is transmitted.[46] These are determined by "differences of culture, age, spiritual maturity and social and ecclesial conditions amongst all of those to whom it is addressed".[47] Much careful attention shall be given to them. It shall be remembered that, in the plurality of situations, adaptation must always keep in mind the totality of the person and his essential unity, in accordance with the vision of the Church. For this reason catechesis does not stop with a consideration of the merely exterior elements of a given situation, but is always mindful of the interior world of the person, the truth of being human, "the first fundamental way of the Church".[48] In this manner a process of adaptation is determined which becomes the more suitable, the more the questions, aspirations and interior needs of the person are considered.

---

[45] GS 44. In this Part the terms *adaptation* and *inculturation* are used because they are employed in the Magisterium and for practical purposes. The first term mainly applies to attention given to persons while the second term is applied to cultural contexts.

[46] Cf. RM 33.

[47] CCC 24.

[48] RH 14.

Chapter Two: Catechesis according to age

General observations

171. Catechesis based on different age groups is an essential **723** task of the Christian community. On the one hand, faith contributes to the development of the person; on the other, every phase of life is open to the challenge of dechristianization and must above all be reinforced by ever new responses of Christian vocation.

Catechesis, therefore, is given by right on the basis of diverse and complementary age groups, on account of the needs and capacity of its recipients.[49]

For this reason it is necessary to pay attention to all the factors involved, whether anthropological-evolutionary or theological-pastoral, including also up to date scientific data and pedagogical methods prepared for different age groups. The various stages in the journey of faith must be prudently integrated, with care that successive phases of catechesis harmoniously complete catechesis received in childhood. Hence it is pedagogically useful to make reference to adult catechesis and, in that light, orientate catechesis for other times of life.

This chapter seeks to set out purely general elements, by way of example, and leaves further details to be worked out by the Catechetical Directories of particular Churches and of the Episcopal Conferences.

The catechesis of adults[50]

Adults to whom catechesis is directed[51]

172. The discourse of faith with adults must take serious **724** account of their experience, of their conditioning and of the challenges which they have encountered in life. Their questions of faith as well as their needs are many and varied.[52] Consequently, the following categories may be distinguished:

– adult Christians who consistently live their faith option and

---

[49] Cf. CT 45.
[50] Cf. Part I, chap. II, nn. 142-144; DCG (1971), 20; 92-97; CT 43-44; COINCAT, *The catechesis of adults in the Christian community,* 1990.
[51] Cf. DCG (1971), 20; CT 19; 44; COINCAT, 10-18.
[52] Cf. COINCAT 10-18.

sincerely desire to deepen it;

– adults who have been baptized but who have not been sufficiently catechized, or have not brought to fulfilment the journey begun at Christian initiation, or who have fallen away from the faith, to such a degree that they may be called 'quasi catechumens';[53]

– non-baptized adults, to whom the catechumenate truly and properly corresponds.[54]

Mention must also be made of those adults who come from Christian confessions which are not in full communion with the Catholic Church.

Elements and criteria proper to adult catechesis[55]

725   173. Adult catechesis concerns persons who have a right and a duty to bring to maturity the seed of faith sown in them by God.[56] It is addressed to individuals who are charged to fulfil social responsibilities of various types and to those who are also prey to all kinds of changes and crises, sometimes profound. The faith of adults, therefore, must be continually enlightened, developed and protected, so that it may acquire that Christian wisdom which gives sense, unity, and hope to the many experiences of personal, social, and spiritual life. Adult catechesis requires the accurate identification of the typical characteristics of Christian adults. It must translate them into objectives and content, and determine certain constants of presentation. It must establish the most effective methodological approaches and choose formats and models. The role and identity of the catechists who work with adults and their formation – the people who are responsible for the catechesis of adults in the community – are vitally important.[57]

726   174. Among the criteria which assure an authentic and effective adult catechesis, mention must be made of the following:[58]

– attention to those to whom it is addressed, to their condition

---

[53] CT 44.

[54] Cf. CT 19.

[55] Cf. DCG (1971), 92-94; COINCAT, 20-25; 26-30; 33-84.

[56] Cf. *1 Cor* 13:11; *Eph* 4:13.

[57] Cf. COINCAT, 33-84.

[58] Cf. COINCAT, 26-30.

as adult men and women, requires taking account of their problems and experiences, their spiritual and cultural resources, with full respect for their differences;

– attention to the lay condition of adults, on whom Baptism confers the task of "seeking the Kingdom of God by engaging in temporal affairs and directing them according to God's Will",[59] and whom it calls to holiness;[60]

– attention to the involvement of the community so that it may be a welcoming and supportive environment;

– attention to ensure systematic pastoral care of adults, with which liturgical formation and the service of charity have been integrated.

General and particular tasks of adult catechesis[61]

175. So as to respond to the more profound needs of our **727** time, adult catechesis must systematically propose the Christian faith in its entirety and in its authenticity, in accordance with the Church's understanding. It must give priority to the proclamation of salvation, drawing attention to the many difficulties, doubts, misunderstandings, prejudices and objections of today. It must introduce adults to a faith-filled reading of Sacred Scripture and the practice of prayer. A fundamental service to adult catechesis is given by the *Catechism of the Catholic Church* and by those adult catechisms based on it by the particular Churches. In particular, the tasks of adult catechesis are:

– *to promote formation and development of life in the Risen Christ* by adequate means: pedagogy of the sacraments, retreats, spiritual direction...

– *to educate toward a correct evaluation of the socio-cultural changes of our societies in the light of faith*: thus the Christian community is assisted in discerning true values in our civilization, as well as its dangers, and in adopting appropriate attitudes;

– *to clarify current religious and moral questions*, that is, those questions which are encountered by the men and women of our time: for example, public and private morality with regard to

---

[59] LG 31; cf. EN 70; ChL 23.
[60] Cf. ChL 57-59.
[61] Cf. DCG (1971), 97.

social questions and the education of future generations;

– *to clarify the relationship between temporal actions and ecclesial action*, by demonstrating mutual distinctions and implications and thus due interaction; to this end, the social doctrine of the Church is an integral part of adult catechesis;

– *to develop the rational foundations of the faith*: that the right understanding of the faith and of the truths to be believed are in conformity with the demands of reason and the Gospel is always relevant; it is therefore necessary to promote effectively the pastoral aim of Christian thought and culture: this helps to overcome certain forms of fundamentalism as well as subjective and arbitrary interpretations;

– to encourage adults to assume responsibility for the Church's mission and to be able to give Christian witness in society:

The adult is assisted to discover, evaluate and activate what he has received by nature and grace, both in the Christian community and by living in human society; in this way, he will be able to overcome the dangers of standardization and of anonymity which are particularly dominant in some societies of today and which lead to loss of identity and lack of appreciation for the resources and qualities of the individual.

Particular forms of adult catechesis[62]

728 176. Certain situations and circumstances require special forms of catechesis:

– catechesis for the Christian initiation or catechumenate of adults: this has its own express form in the RCIA;

– traditional forms of catechesis of the people of God, duly adapted to the liturgical year or in the extraordinary form of missions;

– the on-going catechesis of those who have a task of formation in the community: catechists and those involved in the lay apostolate;

– catechesis for use in particularly significant events in life, such as Marriage, the Baptism of children and the other sacraments of initiation, at critical times during youth, in sickness

---

[62] Cf. Part I, chap. 2; DCG (1971), 96.

etc.: in such circumstances, people are disposed more than ever to seek out the true meaning of life;

– is for special events and experiences, such as beginning work, military service, emigration etc.: these are changes which can give rise to interior enrichment or bewilderment and in which the need of God's saving word should be emphasized;

– catechesis for the Christian use of leisure time, especially during holidays and travel;

– catechesis for special events in the life of the Church and society.

These and many other forms of special catechesis, complement, but do not replace, the ongoing, systematic, catechetical courses which every ecclesial community must provide for all adults.

The catechesis of infants and young children.[63] The important context of infancy and childhood[64]

729

177. This age group, traditionally divided into early infancy or pre-school age and childhood, possesses, in the light of faith and reason, the grace of the beginnings of life, from which "valuable possibilities exist, both for the building up of the Church and for the making of a more humane society".[65] As a child of God, in virtue of the gift of Baptism, the child is proclaimed by Christ to be a privileged member of the Kingdom of God.[66] For various reasons today, rather more than in the past, the child demands full respect and help in its spiritual and human growth. This is also true in catechesis which must always be made available to Christian children. Those who have given life to children and have enriched them with the gift of Baptism have the duty continually to nourish it.

Characteristics of catechesis for infants and children[67]

730

178. The catechesis of children is necessarily linked with their life situation and conditions. It is the work of various but

---

[63] Cf. DCG (1971) 78-81; CT 36-37.
[64] DCG (1971) 78-79; ChL 47.
[65] Cf. ChL 47.
[66] *Mark* 10:14.
[67] Cf. DCG (1971) 78-79; CT 37.

complementary educational agents. Some factors of universal relevance may be mentioned:

– Infancy and childhood, each understood according to its own peculiarities, are a time of primary socialization as well as of human and Christian education in the family, the school and the Church. These must then be understood as a decisive moment for subsequent stages of faith.

– In accordance with accepted tradition, this is normally the time in which Christian initiation, inaugurated with Baptism, is completed. With the reception of the sacraments, the first organic formation of the child in the faith and his introduction into the life of the Church is possible.[68]

– The catechetical process in infancy is eminently educational. It seeks to develop those human resources which provide an anthropological basis for the life of faith, a sense of trust, of freedom, of self-giving, of invocation and of joyful participation. Central aspects of the formation of children are training in prayer and introduction to Sacred Scripture.[69]

– Finally attention must be devoted to the importance of two vital educational *loci*: the family and the school. In a certain sense nothing replaces family catechesis, especially for its positive and receptive environment, for the example of adults, and for its first explicit experience and practice of the faith.

731   179. Beginning school means, for the child, entering a society wider than the family, with the possibility of greater development of intellectual, affective and behavioural capacities. Often specific religious instruction will be given in school. All this requires that catechesis and catechists constantly co-operate with parents and school teachers as suitable opportunities arise.[70] Pastors should remember that, in helping parents and educators to fulfil their mission well, it is the Church who is being built up. Moreover this is an excellent occasion for adult catechesis.[71]

---

[68] Cf. CT 37.
[69] Cf. Sacred Congregation for Divine Worship, *Directory for Masses with children*; AAS 66 (1974) pp. 30-46.
[70] Cf. DCG (1971) 79.
[71] Cf. DCG (1971) 78, 79.

Infants and children without religious support in the family or
who do not attend school[72]

180. There are indeed many gravely disadvantaged children **732**
who lack adequate religious support in the family, either because
they have no true family, or because they do not attend school, or
because they are victims of dysfunctional social conditions or
other environmental factors. Many are not even baptized; others
do not bring to completion the journey of initiation. It is the
responsibility of the Christian community to address this situation
by providing generous, competent and realistic aid, by seeking
dialogue with the families, by proposing appropriate forms of
education and by providing catechesis which is proportionate to
the concrete possibilities and needs of these children.

Catechesis of young people.[73] *Pre-adolescence, adolescence and*
young adulthood.[74]

181. In general it is observed that the first victims of the **733**
spiritual and cultural crisis gripping the world[75] are the young. It
is also true that any commitment to the betterment of society finds
its hopes in them. This should stimulate the Church all the more
to proclaim the Gospel to the world of youth with courage and
creativity. In this respect experience suggests that it is useful in
catechesis to distinguish between pre-adolescence, adolescence
and young adulthood, attending to the results of scientific
research in various countries. In developed regions the question
of pre-adolescence is particularly significant: sufficient account is
not taken of the difficulties, of the needs and of the human and
spiritual resources of pre-adolescents, to the extent of defining
them a *negated age-group.* Very often at this time the pre-
adolescent, in receiving the sacrament of Confirmation, formally
concludes the process of Christian initiation but from that
moment virtually abandons completely the practice of the faith.
This is a matter of serious concern which requires specific
pastoral care, based on the formative resources of the journey of
initiation itself. With regard to the other two categories, it is

---

[72] Cf. DCG (1971) 80-81; CT 42.
[73] Cf. DCG (1971) 82-91; EN 72; CT 38-42.
[74] Cf. DCG (1971) 83.
[75] Cf. General Introduction, 23-24.

helpful to distinguish between adolescence and young adulthood even though it is difficult to define them strictly. They are understood together as the period of life which precedes the taking up of responsibilities proper to adults. Youth catechesis must be profoundly revised and revitalized.

The importance of youth for society and the Church[76]

734
182. The Church, while regarding young people as "hope", also sees them as "a great challenge for the future of the Church"[77] herself. The rapid and tumultuous socio-cultural change, increase in numbers, self-affirmation for a consistent period before taking up adult responsibilities, unemployment, in certain countries conditions of permanent under-development, the pressures of consumer society – all contribute to make of youth a world in waiting, not infrequently a world of disenchantment, of boredom, of angst and of marginalization. Alienation from the Church, or a least diffidence in her regard, lurks in many as a fundamental attitude. Often this reflects lack of spiritual and moral support in the family and weaknesses in the catechesis which they have received. On the other hand, many of them are driven by a strong impetus to find meaning, solidarity, social commitment and even religious experience.

735
183. Some consequences for catechesis arise from this. The service of the faith notes above all the contrasts in the condition of youth as found concretely in various regions and environments. The heart of catechesis is the explicit proposal of Christ to the young man in the Gospel;[78] it is a direct proposal to all young people in terms appropriate to young people, and with considered understanding of their problems. In the Gospel young people in fact speak directly to Christ, who reveals to them their "singular richness" and calls them to an enterprise of personal and community growth, of decisive value for the fate of society and of the Church.[79] Therefore young people cannot be considered only objects of catechesis, but also active subjects and protagonists of

---

[76] Cf. DCG (1971) 82; EN 72; MDP 3; CT 38-39; ChL 46; TMA 58.

[77] GE 2; ChL 46.

[78] Cf. *Matt* 19:16-22; cf. John Paul II, Apostolic Letter to Youth *Parati Semper* (31 March 1985): AAS 77 (1985), pp. 579-628.

[79] Cf. John Paul II, *"Parati semper"*, 3.

evangelisation and artisans of social renewal.[80]

Characteristics of catechesis for young people[81]

184. Given the extent of this task, the Catechetical **736** Directories of particular Churches and national and regional Episcopal Conferences must, taking into account different contexts, determine more specifically suitable measures for these areas. Some general directions, however, may be indicated.

– The diversity of the religious situation should be kept in mind: there are young people who are not even baptized, others have not completed Christian initiation, others are in grave crises of faith, others are moving towards making a decision with regard to faith, others have already made such a decision and call for assistance.

– It should also be remembered that the most successful catechesis is that which is given in the context of the wider pastoral care of young people, especially when it addresses the problems affecting their lives. Hence, catechesis should be integrated with certain procedures, such as analysis of situations, attention to human sciences and education, the co-operation of the laity and of young people themselves.

– Well organized group action, membership of valid youth associations[82] and personal accompaniment of young people, which should also include spiritual direction as an important element, are useful approaches for effective catechesis.

185. Among the diverse forms of youth catechesis, provision **737** should be made, in so far as circumstances permit, for the youth catechumenate during school years, catechesis for Christian initiation, catechesis on specific themes, as well as other kinds of occasional and informal meetings.

Generally youth catechesis should be proposed in new ways which are open to the sensibilities and problems of this age group. They should be of a theological, ethical, historical and social nature. In particular, due emphasis should be given to education in truth and liberty as understood by the Gospel, to the formation

---

[80] ChL 46; DCG (1971) 89
[81] DCG (1971) 84-89; CT 38-40.
[82] DCG (1971) 87.

of conscience and to education for love. Emphasis should also be placed on vocational discernment, Christian involvement in society and on missionary responsibility in the world.[83] It must be emphasized, however, that frequently contemporary evangelisation of young people must adopt a *missionary dimension* rather than a strictly *catechumenal* dimension. Indeed, the situation often demands that the apostolate amongst young people be an animation of a *missionary or humanitarian nature,* as a necessary first step to bringing to maturity those dispositions favourable to the strictly catechetical moment. Very often, in reality, it is useful to *intensify pre-catechumenal activity within the general educational process.* One of the difficulties to be addressed and resolved is the question of "language" (*mentality, sensibility, tastes, style, vocabulary*) between young people and the Church (*catechesis, catechists*). A necessary "adaptation of catechesis to young people" is urged, in order to translate into their terms "the message of Jesus with patience and wisdom and without betrayal".[84]

Catechesis for the aged.[85] Old age, gift of God to the Church

738   186. In many countries, the growing number of old people represents a new and specific pastoral challenge for the Church. Not infrequently the old are seen as passive objects and possibly even as an encumbrance. In the light of faith, however, they must be understood as a gift of God to the Church and to society, and must also be given adequate catechetical care. In catechesis, they have the same rights and duties as all Christians.

Attention must always be paid to the diversity of personal, family and social conditions. In particular, account must be taken of factors such as isolation and the risk of marginalization. The family has a primary function, since it is here that the proclamation of the faith can take place in an environment of acceptance and of love which best confirm the validity of the word. In any event, catechesis addressed to the aged will

---

[83] Other important themes include: the relationship between faith and reason; the existence and meaning of God; the problem of evil; the Church; the objective moral order in relation to personal subjectivity; the encounter between man and woman; the social doctrine of the Church.

[84] CT 40.

[85] Cf. DCG (1971) 95; ChL 48.

associate with the content of faith the caring presence of the catechist and of the community of believers. For this reason, it is most desirable that the aged participate fully in the catechetical journey of the community.

Catechesis of fulfilment and hope

739

187. Catechesis for the aged pays particular attention to certain aspects of their condition of faith. An aged person may have a rich and solid faith, in which case catechesis, in a certain sense, brings to fulfilment a journey of faith in an attitude of thanksgiving and hopeful expectation. Others live a faith weakened by poor Christian practice. In this case, catechesis becomes a moment of new light and religious experience. Sometimes people reach old age profoundly wounded in body and soul. In these circumstances, catechesis can help them to live their condition in an attitude of prayer, forgiveness and inner peace.

At any rate, the condition of the old calls for a catechesis of hope, which derives from the certainty of finally meeting God. It is always a personal benefit and an enrichment of the Christian community, when the old bear witness to a faith which grows even more resplendent as they gradually approach the great moment of meeting the Lord.

Wisdom and dialogue[86]

740

188. The Bible presents us with the figure of the old man as the symbol of a person rich in wisdom and fear of God, and as a repository of an intense experience of life, which, in a certain sense, makes him a natural "catechist" in the community. He is a witness to a tradition of faith, a teacher of life, and a worker of charity. Catechesis values this grace. It helps the aged to discover the riches within themselves and to assume the role of catechists among children – for whom they are often valued grandparents – and for young people and adults. Thus a fundamental dialogue between the generations can be promoted both within the family and within the community.

---

[86] Cf. ChL 48.

Chapter Three: Catechesis for special situations, mentalities and environments

Catechesis for the disabled and the handicapped[87]

741   189. Every Christian community considers those who suffer handicaps, physical or mental, as well as other forms of disability – especially children – as persons particularly beloved of the Lord. A growth in social and ecclesial consciousness, together with undeniable progress in specialized pedagogy, makes it possible for the family and other formative centres to provide adequate catechesis for these people, who, as baptized, have this right and, if non-baptized, because they are called to salvation. The love of the Father for the weakest of his children and the continuous presence of Jesus and His Spirit give assurance that every person, however limited, is capable of growth in holiness.

Education in the faith, which involves the family above all else, calls for personalized and adequate programmes. It should take into account the findings of pedagogical research. It is most effectively carried out in the context of the integral education of the person. On the other hand, the risk must be avoided of separating this specialized catechesis from the general pastoral care of the community. It is therefore necessary that the community be made aware of such catechesis and be involved in it. The particular demands of this catechesis require a special competence from catechists and render their service all the more deserving.

The catechesis of the marginalized

742   190. The catechesis of the marginalized must be considered within the same perspective. It addresses itself to immigrants, refugees, nomads, travelling people, the chronically ill, drug addicts, prisoners. The solemn word of Jesus, which acknowledged, as done to him any good work done to "the least of the brethren" (Matt 25:40;45) guarantees the grace needed to work well in difficult environments. Permanent signs of the strength of catechesis are its capacity to identify different situations, to meet the needs and questions of everyone, to stress the value of generous and patient

---

[87] Cf. DCG (1971) 91; CT 41.

personal contact, to proceed with trust and realism, sometimes turning to indirect and occasional forms of catechesis. The Christian community fraternally supports those catechists who dedicate themselves to this service.

Catechesis for different groups

191. Catechesis, today, is confronted by subjects who, because of professional training or more broadly cultural formation, require special programmes. These include catechesis for workers, for professionals, for artists, for scientists and for university students. This is warmly recommended within the common journey of the Christian community. Clearly, all these sectors demand a competent approach and language adapted to those being catechized, while always maintaining fidelity to the message which catechesis transmits.[88]

743

Environmental catechesis

192. The service of the faith today takes careful note of the environment and human habitats. It is in these that the person lives his concrete existence. It is here that he is influenced and that he influences. Here too he exercises his responsibilities. Very broadly, two major environments must be mentioned: rural and urban. Both call for different forms of catechesis. The catechesis of country people will necessarily reflect needs experienced in the country. Such needs are often linked with poverty, sometimes with fear and superstition, but also rich in simplicity, trust in life, a sense of solidarity, faith in God and fidelity to religious traditions. Urban catechesis must take account of a variety of social conditions, sometimes so extreme as to extend from exclusive areas of prosperity to pockets of poverty and marginalization. Stress can dominate the rhythm of life. Mobility is easy. There are many temptations to escapism and irresponsibility. Oppressive anonymity and loneliness are widespread.

744

For both of these environments the service of the faith requires adequate planning, trained catechists, useful aids and familiarity with the resources of the mass-media.

---

[88] Cf. CT 59.

Chapter Four: Catechesis in the socio-religious context

Catechesis in complex and pluralistic situations[89]

745   193. Many communities and individuals are called to live in a pluralistic and secularized world,[90] in which forms of unbelief and religious indifference may be encountered together with vibrant expressions of religious and cultural pluralism. In many individuals the search for certainty and for values appears strong. Spurious forms of religion, however, are also evident as well as dubious adherence to the faith. In the face of such diversity, some Christians are confused or lost. They become incapable of knowing how to confront situations or to judge the messages which they receive. They may abandon regular practice of the faith and end by living as though there were no God – often resorting to surrogate or pseudo-religions. Their faith is exposed to trials. When threatened it risks being extinguished altogether, unless it is constantly nourished and sustained.

746   194. In these circumstances, a catechesis of evangelisation becomes indispensable: a catechesis "which must be impregnated with the spirit of the Gospel and imparted in language adapted to the times and to the hearers".[91] Such catechesis seeks to educate Christians in a sense of their identity as baptized, as believers, as members of the Church, who are open to dialogue with the world. It reminds them of the fundamental elements of the faith. It stimulates a real process of conversion. For them, it deepens the truth and the value of the Christian message in the face of theoretical and practical objections. It helps them to discern the Gospel and to live it out in every-day life. It enables them to give the reasons for the hope that is theirs.[92] It encourages them to exercise their missionary vocation by witness, dialogue and proclamation.

Catechesis and popular devotion[93]

747   195. As a vital dimension in Catholic life, there exists in

---

[89] Cf. EN 51-56; MPD 15.
[90] Cf. General Introduction.
[91] Cf. EN 54.
[92] Cf. *1 Pet* 3:15.
[93] Cf. DCG (1971) 6; EN 48; CT 54.

Christian communities, particular expressions of the search for God and the religious life which are full of fervour and purity of intention, which can be called "popular piety". "For it does indicate a certain thirst for God such as only those who are simple and poor in spirit can experience. It can arouse in them a capacity for self-dedication and for the exercise of heroism when there is a question of professing the faith. It gives men a keen sensitivity by virtue of which they can appreciate the ineffable attributes of God: his fatherly compassion, his providence, his benevolence and loving presence. It can develop in the inmost depths of man habits of virtue rarely to be found otherwise in the same degree, such as patience, acceptance of the Cross in daily life, detachment, openness to other men and a spirit of ready service".[94] This is a rich yet vulnerable reality in which the faith at its base may be in need of purification and consolidation. A catechesis, therefore, is required which is of such religious richness as to be quick to appreciate its inherent nature and its desirable qualities and zealous to direct it so that the dangers arising out of its errors or fanaticism, superstition, syncretism, or religious ignorance may be avoided. "When it is wisely directed popular piety of this kind can make a constantly increasing contribution towards bringing the masses of our people into contact with God in Jesus Christ".[95]

196. Multiple forms of devotion to the Mother of God have **748** developed in different circumstances of time and place, in response to popular sensibilities and cultural differences. Certain forms of Marian devotion however, because of long usage, require a renewed catechesis to restore to them elements that have become lost or obscured. By such catechesis the perennial value of Marian devotion can be emphasised, doctrinal elements gleaned from theological reflection and the Church's Magisterium assimilated. Catechesis on the Blessed Virgin Mary should always express clearly the intrinsic Trinitarian, Christological and ecclesiological aspects of mariology. In revising or drawing up materials for use in Marian piety account should be taken of

---

[94] EN 48.
[95] EN 48.

biblical, liturgical, ecumenical and anthropological orientation.[96]

Catechesis in the context of ecumenism[97]

749   197. Every Christian community, by the mere fact of being what it is, is moved by the Spirit to recognize its ecumenical vocation in the circumstances in which it finds itself, by participating in ecumenical dialogue and initiatives to foster the unity of Christians. Catechesis, therefore, is always called to assume an "ecumenical dimension"[98] everywhere. This is done, firstly, by an exposition of all of Revelation, of which the Catholic Church conserves the deposit, while respecting the hierarchy of truths.[99] In the second place, catechesis brings to the fore that unity of faith which exists between Christians and explains the divisions existing between them and the steps being taken to overcome them.[100] Catechesis also arouses and nourishes a true desire for unity, particularly with the love of Sacred Scripture. Finally, it prepares children, young people and adults to live in contact with brothers and sisters of other confessions, by having them cultivate both their own Catholic identity and respect for the faith of others.

750   198. In the context of different Christian confessions, the Bishops may deem opportune or necessary specific ecumenical co-operation in the area of religious instruction. It is important, however, that Catholics are guaranteed, at the same time, a genuinely Catholic catechesis, by specific provisions and with all the more care.[101]

The teaching of religion in schools attended by Christians of diverse confessions can also have an ecumenical value when Christian doctrine is genuinely presented. This affords the

---

[96] Cf. Paul VI, Apostolic Exhortation *Marialis cultus* (2 February 1974), nn. 24, 25, 29, AAS 66 (1979), pp. 134-136, 141.

[97] Cf. DCG (1971) 27; MPG 15; EN 54; CT 32-34; Pontifical Council for the Promotion of Christian Unity, *Directory for the application of principles and norms concerning Ecumenism,* 61 AAS 85 (1993) pp. 1063-1064; TMA 34; (cf. *Ut Unum sint* (25 May 1995) 18 AAS 87 (1995), p. 932.

[98] CT 32.

[99] Cf. UR 11.

[100] Cf. *Directory for the application of principles and norms concerning Ecumenism,* 190; *l.c.,* p. 1107.

[101] Cf. CT 33.

opportunity for dialogue through which prejudice and ignorance can be overcome and a greater openness to better reciprocal understanding achieved.

Catechesis in relation to Judaism

199. Special attention needs to be given to catechesis in relation to the Jewish religion.[102] Indeed "when she delves into her own mystery, the Church, the People of God in the New Covenant, discovers her links with the Jewish People, the first to hear the word of God".[103]

751

"Religious instruction, catechesis, and preaching should not form only towards objectivity, justice and tolerance but also in understanding and dialogue. Both of our traditions are too closely related to be able to ignore each other. It is necessary to encourage a reciprocal consciousness at all levels".[104] In particular, an objective of catechesis should be to overcome every form of anti-semitism.[105]

Catechesis in the context of other religions[106]

200. For the most part, Christians today live in multi-religious contexts; many, indeed, in a minority position. In this context, especially with relation to Islam, catechesis takes on a particular importance and is called to assume a delicate responsibility which is expressed in several duties. Above all, it deepens and strengthens, by means of appropriate adaptation or inculturation, the identity of believers – particularly where they constitute a minority – who find themselves in an obligatory encounter between the Gospel of Jesus Christ and the message of other religions. For this exchange, solid, fervent, Christian communities and well prepared, native catechists are

752

---

[102] *Nostra Aetate,* Segretariat for Christian Unity, Commission for religious relations with Judaism, *Jews and Judaism in Catholic preaching and catechesis* 24 June 1985.

[103] CCC 839.

[104] *Jesus and Judaism in Catholic preaching and Catechesis,* VII.

[105] Cf. *Nostra Aetate,* 4.

[106] Cf. EN 53; MPD 15; ChL 35; RM 55-57; CCC 839-845; TMA 53; Sacred Congregation for the Evangelisation of Peoples – Pontifical Council for inter-religious dialogue, *Dialogue and Proclamation* (19 May 1991): AAS 84 (1992), pp. 414-446; 1263.

indispensable. In the second place, catechesis assists in creating awareness of the presence of other religions. It necessarily facilitates Christians in discerning the elements in those religions which are contrary to the Christian message, but also educates them to accept the seeds of the Gospel *(semina Verbi)* which are found in them and which can sometimes constitute an authentic *preparation for the Gospel.*

In the third instance, catechesis promotes a lively missionary sense among believers. This is shown by clear witness to the faith, by an attitude of respect and mutual understanding, by dialogue and cooperation in defence of the rights of the person and of the poor and, where possible, with explicit proclamation of the Gospel.

Catechesis in relation to "new religious movements"[107]

753   201. In a climate of cultural and religious relativism, and sometime because of the inappropriate conduct of Christians, a proliferation of "new religious movements" has occurred. These are sometimes called sects or cults but, because of the abundance of names and tendencies, are difficult to categorize in a comprehensive and precise framework. From available data, movements of Christian origin can be identified, while others derive from oriental religions, and others again appear to be con-nected with esoteric traditions. Their doctrines and their practices are of concern because they are alien to the content of the Christian faith. It is therefore necessary to promote among Christians exposed to such risks "a commitment to evangelisation and integral systematic catechesis which must be accompanied by a witness which translates these into life".[108] Thus it is necessary to overcome the danger of ignorance and prejudice, to assist the faithful in engaging correctly with the Scriptures, to awaken in them a lively experience of prayer, to defend them from error, to educate them in responsibility for the faith which they have received, confronting

---

[107] Report of the Secretariat for Christian Unity, the Secretariat for non-Christians and the Secretariat for non-believers and the Pontifical Council for Culture *The Phenomenon of Sects or new religious movements: pastoral challenge,* *L'Osservatore Romano,* 7 May 1986.
[108] *The Phenomenon of Sects or new religious movements: pastoral challenge,* cit., 5. 4.

dangerous situations of loneliness, poverty and suffering with the love of the Gospel. Because of the religious yearning which these movements can express, they should be considered "a market place to be evangelized", in which some of the most pressing questions can find answers. "The Church has an immense spiritual patrimony to offer mankind, a heritage in Christ, who called himself 'the way, and the truth, and the life' (John 14:6)".[109]

Chapter Five: Catechesis in the socio-cultural context[110]

Catechesis and contemporary culture[111]

754

202. "We can say of catechesis, as well as of evangelisation in general, that it is called to bring the power of the Gospel into the very heart of culture and cultures".[112] The principles governing the adaptation and inculturation of catechesis have already been discussed.[113] It suffices to reaffirm that the catechetical discourse has as its necessary and eminent guide "the rule of faith", illuminated by the Magisterium of the Church and further investigated by theology. It must always be remembered that the history of catechesis, particularly in the patristic period, from several perspectives, is the history of the inculturation of the faith, and as such it merits careful study and meditation. It is, at the same time, an open-ended history which will continue to require long periods of ongoing assimilation of the Gospel. In this chapter, some methodological directions will be expounded concerning this task, as demanding as it is necessary, ever easy and open to the risks of syncretism and other misunderstandings.

---

[109] RM 38.

[110] Cf. Part II, chap. 1; DCG (1971) 8; EN 20; CT 53; RM 52-54; John Paul II, Discourse to members of the International Council for catechesis, *L'Osservatore Romano,* of 27 September 1992; cf. Congregation for Divine Worship and the discipline of the Sacraments, *The Roman liturgy and Inculturation,* 1994; International Theological Commission, *Document on the faith and inculturation:* (25 Janury, 1985); AAS 87 (1995), pp. 288-319 *Commissio Theologica* on the Faith and Inculturation (3-8 October, 1988). Apostolic Exhortation *Ecclesia in Africa* (1995); cf. Discourses of John Paul II to the various Churches in his pastoral visits.

[111] Cf. EN 20; 63; CT 53; RM 52-54; CCC 172-175.

[112] CT 53.

[113] Cf. Part II, chap. 1.

It can indeed be said on this subject, which is particularly important today, that there exists a need for greater systematic and universal reflection on catechetical experience.

Duties of catechesis for inculturation of the faith[114]

755   203. These duties form an organic whole and are briefly expressed as follows:

– to know in depth the culture of persons and the extent of its penetration into their lives;

– to recognize a cultural dimension in the Gospel itself, while affirming, on the one hand, that this does not spring from some human cultural *humus,* and recognizing, on the other, that the Gospel cannot be isolated from the cultures in which it was initially inserted and in which it has found expression through the centuries;

– to proclaim the profound change, the conversion, which the Gospel, as a "transforming and regenerating"[115] force works in culture;

– to witness to the transcendence and the non-exhaustion of the Gospel with regard to culture, while at the same time discerning those seeds of the Gospel which may be present in culture;

– to promote a new expression of the Gospel in accordance with evangelized culture, looking to a language of the faith which is the common patrimony of the faithful and thus a fundamental element of communion;

– To maintain integrally the content of the faith and ensure that the doctrinal formulations of tradition are explained and illustrated, while taking into account the cultural and historical circumstances of those being instructed, and to avoid defacing or falsifying the contents.

Methodological processes

756   204. Catechesis, while avoiding all manipulation of culture, is not limited to a mere juxtaposition of the Gospel with culture in some "decorative manner". Rather it proposes the Gospel "in a vital way, profoundly, by going to the very roots of culture and

---

[114] CT 53.
[115] Cf. CT 53.

the cultures of mankind".[116] This defines a dynamic process consisting of various interactive elements: a listening in the culture of the people, to discern an echo (omen, invocation, sign) of the word of God; a discernment of what has an authentic Gospel value or is at least open to the Gospel; a purification of what bears the mark of sin (passions, structures of evil) or of human frailty; an impact on people through stimulating an attitude of radical conversion to God, of dialogue, and of patient interior maturation.

The need for and criteria of evaluation

205. In the evaluation phase, particularly in cases of initial attempts or experimentation, careful attention must always be given to ensuring that the catechetical process is not infiltrated by syncretistic elements. In instances where this happens, attempts at inculturation will prove dangerous and erroneous and must be corrected. In positive terms, a catechesis which inspires not only intellectual assimilation of the faith, but also touches the heart and transforms conduct is correct. Catechesis, thus, generates a dynamic life which is unified by the faith. It bridges the gap between belief and life, between the Christian message and the cultural context, and brings forth the fruits of true holiness.

757

Those with responsibility for the processes of inculturation

206. "Inculturation must involve the whole People of God, and not just a few experts, since the people reflect the authentic '*sensus fidei*' which must never be lost sight of. Inculturation needs to be guided and encouraged, but not forced, lest it give rise to negative reactions among Christians. It must be an expression of the community's life, one which must mature within the community itself and not be exclusively the result of erudite research".[117] The thrust to incarnate the Gospel which is the specific task of inculturation requires the co-operation in catechesis of all who live in the same cultural condition – clergy, pastoral workers (catechists) and laity.

758

---

[116] EN 20.
[117] RM 54.

Privileged forms and means

759   207. Among the forms most apt to inculturate the faith, it is helpful to bear in mind catechesis of the young and adult catechesis on account of the possibilities which they offer of better correlating faith and life. Neither can inculturation be neglected in the Christian initiation of children precisely because of the important cultural implications of this process: acquiring new motivations in life, education of conscience, learning a biblical and sacramental language, knowledge of the historical density of Christianity.

A privileged means of this is liturgical catechesis with its richness of signs in expressing the Gospel message and its accessibility to so great a part of the people of God. The Sunday homily, the content of the Lectionary and the structure of the liturgical year should be valued afresh, along with other occasions of particularly significant catechesis *(marriages, funerals, visits to the sick, feasts of patron saints etc.)*. The care of the family always remains central, since it is the primary agent of an incarnate transmission of the faith.

Catechesis also places special emphasis on multi-ethnic and multi-cultural situations in that it leads to a greater discovery and appreciation of the resources of diverse groups to receive and express the faith.

Language[118]

760   208. Inculturation of the faith, under certain aspects, is a linguistic task. This implies that catechesis respect and value the language proper to the message, especially biblical language, as well as the historical-traditional language of the Church *(creed, liturgy)* and doctrinal language *(dogmatic formulations)*. It is also necessary for catechesis to enter into dialogue with forms and terms proper to the culture of those to whom it is addressed. Finally, catechesis must stimulate new expressions of the Gospel in the culture in which it has been planted. In the process of inculturating the Gospel, catechesis should not be afraid to use traditional formulae and the technical language of the faith, but it must express its meaning and demonstrate its existential

---

[118] Cf. CT 59.

importance. Similarly, it is also the duty of catechesis "to speak a language suited to today's children and young people in general and to other categories of people – the language of students, intellectuals and scientists; the language of the illiterate or of people of simple culture; the language of the handicapped, and so on".[119]

The media of communication

209. Intrinsically connected with the question of language is that of the means of communication. One of the most effective and pervasive means is the *mass media.* "The very evangelisation of modern culture depends to a great extent on the influence of the media".[120]

761

While not repeating what has already been said of the *mass media* elsewhere,[121] some indications are proposed as useful in inculturation: a greater appreciation of the media for their specific communication quality, while realizing the importance of balancing the language of image and that of word; the safeguarding of the genuine religious meaning of selected forms of expression; the promotion of critical maturity among audiences, stimulating them to a deep, personal discernment of what has been received from the media; the production of catechetical aids congruent with this aim and the effective co-operation of all those engaged in pastoral initiatives.[122]

210. The catechism and, above all, the *Catechism of the Catholic Church* is central to the process of inculturation, and it must be used so as to evince a "vast range of services... which aim at inculturation, which, to be effective, must never cease to be true".[123]

762

The *Catechism of the Catholic Church* expressly calls for the preparation of appropriate local catechisms, incorporating those adaptations required by difference of culture, age, spirituality and in the social and ecclesial situations of those to whom catechesis is addressed.[124]

---

[119] CT 59.
[120] RM 37.
[121] Cf. Part III, chap. 2.
[122] Cf. DCG (1971), 123.
[123] John Paul II, to the members of COINCAT *l.c.*
[124] CCC 24; John Paul II, *Fidei Depositum* 4.

Anthropological environments and cultural tendencies

763   211. The Gospel seeks a catechesis which is open, generous and courageous in reaching people where they live, especially in encountering those *nuclei* in which the most elementary and fundamental cultural exchanges take place, such as the family, the school, the work environment and free time.

It is important for catechesis to discern and penetrate these environments, as it is there that the major cultural tendencies have greater impact in creating and popularizing such models of life as urban life, migratory or tourist influxes, the world of youth and other socially relevant phenomena. Indeed "there are so many sectors to enlighten with the light of the Gospel",[125] especially those cultural areas denominated 'modern *areopagi*' like communications; civil campaigns for peace, development and liberation of peoples; the protection of creation; the defence of human rights, especially of minorities, women and children; scientific research and international relations.

Intervention in concrete situations

764   212. The process of inculturation operated by catechesis is continually called to confront many, different concrete situations. Here some of the more frequent and relevant are mentioned. In the first place, it is necessary to distinguish inculturation in countries of recent Christian origin, where the primary proclamation of the Gospel must yet be consolidated, from inculturation in countries of long Christian tradition which have need of new evangelisation.

Account must also be taken of situations which are open to conflict and tension deriving from factors such as ethnic pluralism, religious pluralism, differences of development which sometimes are strident; urban and extra-urban life-styles, dominant thought-systems, which in some countries are strongly influenced by massive secularization and by strong religiosity in others. Finally, inculturation seeks to respect the significant cultural tendencies of a particular country, represented in the various social and professional strata, such as men and women of science and culture, the world of workers, the youth, the marginalized, foreigners and

---

[125] Cf. RM 37.

the disabled. In more general terms, "the formation of Christians will take the greatest account of local human culture, which contributes to formation itself, and will help to discern the value, whether implanted in tradition or proposed in modern affairs. Attention should be paid to diverse cultures which can exist in one and the same people or nation at the same time".[126]

Tasks of the local Churches[127]

213. Inculturation is a task for the particular churches and is referred to by all areas of the Christian life. Precisely because of the nature of inculturation which takes place in concrete and specific circumstances, "a legitimate attention to the particular Churches cannot but enrich the Church. It is indeed pressing and indispensable".[128] To this end, and most opportunely, Episcopal Conferences, almost everywhere, are proposing Catechetical Directories (and analogous instruments), catechisms and aids, work-shops and centres of formation. In the light of what has been expressed in the present Directory, an updating and revision of local directories becomes necessary. This should stimulate competition between centres of research, whilst availing of the experience of catechists and encouraging the participation of the people of God.

765

Guided initiatives

214. The importance of the matter, as well as, the indispensable phase of research and experimentation requires initiatives guided by legitimate Pastors. These include:

– promotion of widespread catechesis which serves to overcome ignorance and misinformation, the great obstacle of every attempt at inculturation: this permits that dialogue and direct involvement of persons who can best indicate effective ways of proclaiming the Gospel;

– carrying out pilot-schemes of inculturation of the faith within a programme established by the Church: the Catechumenate of adults according to the RCIA assumes a particularly

766

---

[126] ChL 63.
[127] Cf. Part V, chap. 4.
[128] EN 63.

influential role in this respect;

    – if, in the same ecclesial area there are several linguistic or ethnic groups, it is always useful to provide for the translation of guides and directories into the various languages, promoting, by means of catechetical centres, an homogenous catechetical service for each group;

    – setting up a dialogue of reciprocal learning and of communion between the Churches, and between these and the Holy See: this allows for the certification of experiences, criteria, programmes, tools and for a more valid and up to date inculturation.

Part Five: Catechesis in the Particular Church

Catechesis in the particular Church

    "And he went up into the hills, and called to him those whom he desired; and they came to him. And he appointed twelve, to be with him, and to be sent out to preach and have authority to cast out demons" (Mk 3:13-15).

    "Blessed are you, Simon Bar-Jonah! For flesh and blood has not revealed this to you, but my Father who is in heaven. And I tell you, you are Peter, and on this rock I will build my Church" (Mt 16:17-18).

    The Church of Jerusalem moved by the Holy Spirit gave birth to the Churches: "The Church of God which is at Corinth" (1 Cor 1:2); "The Churches of Asia" (1 Cor 16:19); "The Churches of Christ in Judaea" (Gal 1:22); "The seven Churches: Ephesus, Smyrna, Pergamum, Thyatira, Sardis, Philadelphia, Laodicea" (cf. Rev 2:1-3:22).

The meaning and purpose of Part Five

767   215. From what has been said in the preceding parts concerning the nature of catechesis, its content, pedagogy, and those to whom it is addressed, there arises the nature of catechetical pastoral work, which is done in the particular Church. Part Five of this Directory presents its more important elements.

768   216. The first chapter reflects upon the catechetical ministry and its agents. Catechesis is a shared but differentiated responsibility. Bishops, priests, deacons, religious and the lay faithful play their part, each according to their respective responsibilities and charisms.

The second chapter analyses catechists' formation, a decisive element in catechetical activity. If it is important that catechesis be provided with valid catechetical material, yet more important is the preparation of suitable catechists. The third chapter studies the *loci* where catechesis is realized.

The fourth chapter studies the more organizational aspects of catechesis: the structures of responsibility, the co-ordination of catechesis and some tasks specific to catechetical service. The directives and suggestions offered in this section cannot find immediate and contemporary application in all parts of the Church. For those nations or regions in which catechetical activity has not yet had the means of reaching a sufficient level of development, these orientations and suggestions offer but a series of goals to be achieved gradually.

Chapter One: The ministry of catechesis in the particular Churches and its agents

The particular Church[129]

217. The proclamation, transmission and lived experience of the Gospel are realized in the particular Church[130] or Diocese.[131] The particular Church is constituted by the community of Christ's disciples,[132] who live incarnated in a definite socio-cultural space. Every particular Church "makes present the universal Church together with all of its essential elements".[133] In reality the universal Church, made fruitful by the Holy Spirit on the first Pentecost, "brings forth the particular Churches as children and is

769

---

[129] In Part Five as in the rest of the document the term *particular Church* refers to dioceses and there equiparates (CIC Canon 368). The term local Church refers to a group of particular Churches delineated in terms of Region or Nation or group of Nations united by special links. Cf. Part I, chap. III and Part II, chap. I. "The ecclesial nature of the Gospel message".

[130] As mentioned in LG 26a the term *Churches* in the NT is used to denote lawful groups of the faithful; see the biblical texts with which this part opens.

[131] Cf. CD 11.

[132] The particular Church is described before all else as *Populi Dei portio* or "a portion of the people of God".

[133] Congregation for the Doctrine of the Faith, Lettera *Communionis Notio,* 7 (AAS 85 -1993), 842.

expressed in them".[134] The universal Church, as the Body of Christ, is thus made manifest as "a Body of Churches".[135]

770   218. The proclamation of the Gospel and the Eucharist are the two pillars on which is built and around which gathers the particular Church. Like the universal Church she also "exists for evangelisation".[136] Catechesis is a basic evangelizing activity of every particular Church. By means of it the Diocese gives to all its members, and to all who come with a desire to give themselves to Jesus Christ, a formative process which permits knowledge, celebration, living and proclamation within a particular cultural horizon. In this way the confession of faith – the goal of catechesis – can be proclaimed by the disciples of Christ "in their own tongues".[137] As at Pentecost, so also today, the Church of Christ, "present and operative"[138] in the particular Churches, "speaks all languages",[139] since like a growing tree she extends her roots into all cultures.

The ministry of catechesis in the particular Church

771   219. In all the ministries and services which the particular Church performs to carry out its mission of evangelisation, catechesis occupies a position of importance.[140] In this the following traits are underlined:

a) In the Diocese catechesis is a unique service[141] performed jointly by priests, deacons, religious and laity, in communion with the Bishop. The entire Christian community should feel responsible for this service. Even if priests, deacons, religious and laity

---

[134] *Communionis Notio,* 9b.

[135] LG 23b refers to St Hilary of Poitiers In *Ps 14:3* (PL 9, 206) and St Gregory the Great *Moralia:* IV, 7, 12 (PL 75, 643 C).

[136] EN 14.

[137] Cf. *Acts* 2:11.

[138] *Communionis Notio* 7.

[139] *Ibid.* 9b: *l.c.,* p. 843; cf. AG 4.

[140] The expression *ministry of catechesis* is used in CT 13.

[141] It is important to underline the nature of the one service which catechesis has in the particular Church. The subject of evangelizing activity is the particular Church. She proclaims and transmits the Gospel, which celebrates... The agents of catechesis "serve" this ministry and work "in the name of the Church." The theological, spiritual and pastoral implications of the ecclesial nature of catechesis are considerable.

exercise catechesis in common, they do so in different ways, each according to his particular condition in the Church *(sacred ministers, consecrated persons and the Christian faithful).*[142] Through them all and their differing functions, the catechetical ministry hands on the word in a complete way and witnesses to the reality of the Church. Were one of these forms absent catechesis would lose something its richness as well as part of its proper meaning;

b) On the other hand it is a fundamental ecclesial service, indispensable for the growth of the Church. It is not an action which can be realized in the community on a private basis or by purely personal initiative. The ministry of catechesis acts in the name of the Church by its participating in mission.

c) The catechetical ministry – among all ministries and ecclesial services – has a proper character which derives from the specific role of catechetical activity within the process of evangelisation. The task of the catechist, as an educator in the faith, differs from that of other pastoral agents *(liturgical, charitable and social)* even if he or she always acts in coordination with them.

d) In order that the catechetical ministry in the Diocese be fruitful, it needs to involve other agents, not specifically catechists, who support and sustain catechetical activity by performing indispensable tasks such as: the formation of catechists, the production of catechetical material, reflection, organization and planning. These agents, together with catechists, are at the service of a single diocesan catechetical ministry even if all do not play the same roles or act on the same basis.

The Christian community and responsibility for catechesis
220. Catechesis is a responsibility of the entire Christian community. Christian initiation, indeed, "should not be the work of catechists and priests alone, but of the whole community of the faithful".[143] Continuing education in the faith is a question which

772

---

[142] CT 16: "Shared but differentiated responsibility". Cf. also note 54, as well as note 50 for a clarification of the term "ministry of the Word".

[143] AG 14. In this sense CT 16 says: "Catechesis always has been, and always will be a work for which the whole Church must feel responsible and must wish to be responsible." Cf. also 1977 Synod; MPG 12; RCIA 12; CIC 774 § 1.

concerns the whole community; catechesis, therefore, is an educational activity which arises from the particular responsibility of every member of the community, in a rich context of relationships, so that catechumens and those being catechized are actively incorporated into the life of the community. The Christian community follows the development of catechetical processes, for children, young people and adults, as a duty that involves and binds it directly.[144] Again, at the end of the catechetical process, it is the Christian community that welcomes the catechized in a fraternal environment, "in which they will be able to live in the fullest way what they have learned".[145]

773   221. The Christian community not only gives much to those who are being catechized but also receives much from them. New converts, especially adolescents and adults, in adhering to Jesus Christ, bring to the community which receives them new religious and human wealth. Thus the community grows and develops. Catechesis not only brings to maturity the faith of those being catechized but also brings the community itself to maturity.

Yet, while the entire Christian community is responsible for Christian catechesis and all of it members bear witness to the faith, only some receive the ecclesial mandate to be catechists. Together with the primordial mission which parents have in relation to their children, the Church confers the delicate task of organically transmitting the faith within the community on particular, specifically called members of the people of God.[146]

The Bishop has primary responsibility for catechesis in the particular Church

774   222. The Second Vatican Council gave much importance to the proclamation and transmission of the Gospel in the episcopal ministry. "Among the principal duties of Bishops, that of

---

[144] Catechesis must be supported by the *witness* of the ecclesial community, DCG (1971) 35; cf. part IV, chapter 2.

[145] CT 24.

[146] "Besides this apostolate, which belongs to absolutely every Christian, the laity can be called in different ways to more immediate co-operation in the apostolate of the hierarchy, like those men and women who helped the apostle Paul in the Gospel, labouring much in the Lord" (LG 33). This conciliar doctrine is adopted by CIC 228 and 759.

preaching the Gospel excels".[147] In carrying out this task, Bishops are, above all, "heralds of the faith",[148] seeking new disciples for Jesus Christ, and "authentic teachers",[149] transmitting the faith to be professed and lived to those entrusted to their care. Missionary proclamation and catechesis are two closely united aspects of the prophetic ministry of Bishops. To perform this duty Bishops receive "the charism of truth".[150] The Bishops are "beyond all others the ones primarily responsible for catechesis and catechists par excellence".[151] In the Church's history the preponderant role of great and saintly Bishops is evident. Their writings and initiatives mark the richest period of the catechumenate. They regarded catechesis as one of the most fundamental tasks of their ministry.[152]

223. This concern for catechetical activity will lead the Bishop to assume "the overall direction of catechesis"[153] in the particular Church, which implies among other things:

– that he ensure *effective priority* for an active and fruitful catechesis in his Church "putting into operation the necessary personnel, means and equipment, and also financial resources";[154]

– that he exercise solicitude for catechesis by direct intervention in the transmission of the Gospel to the faithful, and that he be vigilant with regard to the authenticity of the faith as well as with regard to the quality of texts and instruments being used in catechesis;[155]

– "that he bring about and maintain... *a real passion for catechesis,* a passion embodied in a pertinent and effective organization",[156] out of a profound conviction of the importance of catechesis for the Christian life of the diocese;

– that he ensure "*that catechists are adequately prepared for their task,* being well instructed in the doctrine of the Church and

775

---

[147] LG 25; cf. CD 12a; EN 68c.
[148] LG 25.
[149] *Ibid.*
[150] DV 8.
[151] CT 63b.
[152] Cf. CT 12a.
[153] CT 63c.
[154] CT 63c; CIC 775 § 1.
[155] Cf. CT 63c; CIC 823 § 1.
[156] CT 63c.

possessing both a practical and theoretical knowledge of the laws of psychology and educational method";[157]

– that he establish an *articulated, coherent and global programme* in the Diocese in order to respond to the true needs of the faithful: it should be integrated into the diocesan pastoral plan and co-ordinated with the programmes of the Episcopal Conference.

Priests, pastors and educators of the Christian community

776   224. The function proper to the presbyterate in the catechetical task arises from the sacrament of Holy Orders which they have received. "Through that sacrament priests, by the anointing of the Holy Spirit, are signed with a special character and so are configured to Christ the priest, in such a way that they are able to act in the person of Christ the head".[158] In virtue of this ontological configuration to Christ, the ministry of the priest is a service which forms the Christian community and co-ordinates and strengthens other charisms and services. In catechesis the sacrament of Holy Orders constitutes priests as "educators of the faith".[159] They work, therefore, to see that the faithful are properly formed and reach true Christian maturity.[160] Conscious, on the other hand, that their "ministerial Priesthood"[161] is at the service of "the common Priesthood of the faithful",[162] priests foster the vocation and work of catechists and assist them in carrying out a function which springs from Baptism and is exercised in virtue of a mission entrusted to them by the Church. Thus priests put into effect the request which the Second Vatican Council made of them: "to recognize and promote the dignity of the laity and their specific role in the Church's mission".[163]

777   225. The catechetical tasks proper to the presbyterate and

---

[157] CD 14b; CIC 780.

[158] Cf. PO 8; 6; 12a; John Paul II, Post synodal exhortation *Pastores dabo vobis* (25 March 1992), 12 *l.c.* 675-677.

[159] PO 6b.

[160] Cf. CIC 773.

[161] LG 10.

[162] LG 10. Concerning the "two ways of participating in the single priesthood of Jesus Christ", cf. CCC 1546-1547.

[163] PO 9b.

particularly to parish priests are:[164]

– to foster a sense of *common responsibility* for catechesis in the Christian community, a task which involves all, and a recognition and appreciation for catechists and their mission;

– to care for the *basic orientation of catechesis* and its planning by giving emphasis to active participation of catechists and by insisting that catechesis be "well structured and oriented";[165]

– to promote and to discern *vocations* to the service of catechesis and, as catechist of catechists, attend to their formation by giving the greatest attention to this duty;

– to integrate catechetical activity into his programme of *community evangelisation*; and foster the link between catechesis sacraments and the liturgy;

– to secure the bonds between the catechesis of his community and the *diocesan pastoral programme* by helping catechists become active co-operators in a common diocesan programme.

Experience bears out that the quality of catechesis in a community depends very largely on the presence and activity of the priest.

Parents, primary educators of their children[166]

226. The witness of Christian life given by parents in the **778** family comes to children with tenderness and parental respect. Children thus perceive and joyously live the closeness of God and of Jesus made manifest by their parents in such a way that this first Christian experience frequently leaves decisive traces which last throughout life. This childhood religious awakening which

---

[164] Cf. CIC 776-777.

[165] CT 64. With respect to this basic orientation which priests must collaborate in giving to catechesis, the Second Vatican Council indicates two basic requirements: "their role is to teach not their own wisdom but the word of God", (PO 4) and "to expound the word of God not merely in a general and abstract way but by an application of the eternal truth of the Gospel to the concrete circumstances of life" (*Ibid.*).

[166] Cf. chap. 3 of this Part, *The family as an environment or means of growth in the faith,* where the characteristics of family catechesis are analysed; here, more consideration is given to parents as agents of catechesis. Cf. CIC 226 § 2; 774 § 2.

takes place in the family is irreplaceable.[167] It is consolidated when, on the occasion of certain family events and festivities, "care is taken to explain in the home the Christian or religious content of these events".[168] It is deepened all the more when parents comment on the more methodical catechesis which their children later receive in the Christian community and help them to appropriate it. Indeed, "family catechesis precedes...accompanies and enriches all forms of catechesis".[169]

779   227. Parents receive in the sacrament of Matrimony "the grace and the ministry of the Christian education of their children",[170] to whom they transmit and bear witness to human and religious values. This educational activity which is both human and religious is "a true ministry",[171] through which the Gospel is transmitted and radiated so that family life is transformed into a journey of faith and the school of Christian life. As the children grow, exchange of faith becomes mutual and "in a catechetical dialogue of this sort, each individual both receives and gives".[172] It is for this reason that the Christian community must give very special attention to parents. By means of personal contact, meetings, courses and also adult catechesis directed toward parents, the Christian community must help them assume their responsibility – which is particularly delicate today – of educating their children in the faith. This is especially pressing in those areas where civil legislation does not permit or makes difficult freedom of education in the faith.[173] In this case "the domestic Church"[174] is virtually the only environment in which children and young people can receive authentic catechesis.

The role of religious in catechesis

780   228. In a special way the Church calls those in consecrated life to catechetical activity and wishes that "religious communities

---

[167] CT 68.
[168] *Ibid.*
[169] *Ibid.*
[170] Cf. ChL 62; cf. FC 38.
[171] FC 38.
[172] CT 68; cf. EN 71b.
[173] Cf. CT 68.
[174] LG 11; FC 36b.

dedicate as much as possible of what ability and means that they have to the specific work of catechesis".[175] The particular contribution to catechesis of religious and of members of societies of apostolic life derives from their specific condition. The profession of the evangelical counsels, which characterizes the religious life, constitutes a gift to the whole Christian community. In diocesan catechetical activity their original and particular contribution can never be substituted for by priests or by laity. This original contribution is born of public witness to their consecration, which makes them a living sign of the reality of the Kingdom: "it is the profession of these counsels, within a permanent state of life recognized by the Church, that characterizes the life consecrated to God".[176] Although evangelical values must be lived by every Christian, those in consecrated life "incarnate the Church in her desire to abandon herself to the radicalism of the beatitudes".[177] The witness of religious united to the witness of the laity shows forth the one face of the Church which is a sign of the Kingdom of God.[178]

229. "Many religious institutes for men and women came into being for the purpose of giving Christian education to children and young people, especially the most abandoned".[179] That same charism of the founders is such that many religious collaborate today in diocesan adult catechesis. Throughout history many men and women religious "have been committed to the Church's catechetical activity".[180] The founding charisms[181] are not a marginal consideration when religious assume catechetical tasks. While maintaining intact the proper character of catechesis, the charisms of the various religious communities express this common task but with their own proper emphases, often of great religious, social and pedagogical depth. The history of catechesis demonstrates the vitality which these charisms have brought to the Church's educational activity.

781

---

[175] CT 65; cf. CIC 778.
[176] CCC 915; cf. LG 44.
[177] EN 69; cf. VC 33.
[178] Cf. VC 31 concerning *"the relationship between the diverse states of life of the Christian"*; cf. CCC 932.
[179] CT 65; cf. RM 69.
[180] CT 65.
[181] Cf. *1 Cor* 12:4; cf. LG 12b.

Lay catechists

782   230. The catechetical activity of the laity also has a proper character which is due to their condition in the Church: "their secular character is proper and peculiar to the laity".[182] The laity engage in catechesis on the basis of their insertion in the world, sharing all the demands of humanity and bringing to the transmission of the Gospel specific sensitivity and nuances: "this evangelisation, that is, the proclamation of Christ by word and the testimony of life, acquires a specific property and peculiar efficacy because it is accomplished in the ordinary circumstances of the world".[183] Indeed by sharing the same form of life as those whom they catechize, lay catechists have a special sensitivity for incarnating the Gospel in the concrete life of men and women. Catechumens and those receiving catechesis can find in them a Christian model for their future as believers.

783   231. The vocation of the laity to catechesis springs from the sacrament of Baptism. It is strengthened by the sacrament of Confirmation. Through the sacraments of Baptism and Confirmation they participate in the "priestly, prophetic and kingly ministry of Christ".[184] In addition to the common vocation of the apostolate, some lay people feel called interiorly by God to assume the service of catechist. The Church awakens and discerns this divine vocation and confers the mission to catechize. The Lord Jesus invites men and women, in a special way, to follow him, teacher and former of disciples. This personal call of Jesus Christ and its relationship to him are the true moving forces of catechetical activity. "From this loving knowledge of Christ springs the desire to proclaim him, to 'evangelize,' and to lead others to the 'Yes' of faith in Jesus Christ".[185] To feel called to be a catechist and to receive this mission from the Church acquires different levels of dedication in accordance with the particular characteristics of individuals. At times the catechist can collaborate in the service of catechesis over a limited period or

---

[182] LG 31. ChL 15 contains a detailed analysis of the *secular character* of the lay faithful.
[183] LG 35.
[184] AA 2b. cf. *Rituale Romanum, Ordo Baptisimi Parvulorum,* 62, Editio Typica, Typis Polyglottis Vaticanis 1969; RCIA 224.
[185] CCC 429.

purely on an occasional basis, but it is always a valuable service and a worthy collaboration. The importance of the ministry of catechesis, however, would suggest that there should be in a Diocese a certain number of religious and laity publicly recognized and permanently dedicated to catechesis who, in communion with the priests and the Bishop, give to this diocesan service that ecclesial form which is proper to it.[186]

Various types of catechists particularly necessary today
232. The figure of the catechist in the Church, has different modes, just as, the needs of catechesis are varied. **784**

– "The *catechists in missionary countries*",[187] to whom this title is applied in a special way: "Churches that are flourishing today would not have been built up without them".[188] There are those who have the "specific responsibility for catechesis";[189] and there are those who collaborate in various forms of apostolate.[190]

– In some Churches of ancient Christian tradition but where there is a shortage of clergy, there is need for catechists in some way analogous to those of missionary countries. This requires confronting urgent needs: the community animation of *small rural populations* deprived of the constant presence of a priest, the helpfulness of a missionary presence "in areas of *large cities*".[191]

– In countries of Christian tradition which require a "new evangelisation"[192] the *catechist for young people* and the *catechist for adults* become indispensable, in promoting the process of initiatory catechesis. The catechists must provide for continuing catechesis. In such tasks the role of the priest is equally fundamental.

---

[186] The *Code of Canon Law* establishes that ecclesiastical authority may officially entrust an office or an ecclesial service to the laity, prescinding from the fact that this service is or is not a formally instituted *non-ordained ministry*: "lay people, who are found to be suitable, are capable of being admitted by the sacred pastors to those ecclesiastical offices and functions which, in accordance with the provisions of law, they can discharge" (CIC 228 § 1); cf. EN 73; ChL 23.
[187] CT 66b; cf. GCM.
[188] CT 66b.
[189] GCM 4.
[190] *Ibid.*
[191] CT 45; cf. RM 37, ab, par. 2.
[192] RM 33.

– *The catechist for children and adolescents* continues to be indispensable. This catechist has the delicate mission of giving "the first notions of catechism and preparation for the sacrament of Penance, for First Communion and Confirmation".[193] This responsibility is all the more pressing today if children and adolescents "do not receive adequate religious formation within the family".[194]

– A catechist who must also be formed is the *catechist for pre-sacramental encounter*,[195] for adults on occasions such as the Baptism or the First Holy Communion of their children or the celebration of the sacrament of Matrimony. It is a specific and original task comprising the welcome of the faithful, of primary proclamation to them and of accompanying them on the journey of faith.

– Other catechists urgently needed in delicate human situations include catechists for the old[196] who need a presentation of the Gospel adapted to their condition; for handicapped or disabled people who require a special pedagogy,[197] in addition to their total integration into the community; for *migrants* and those *marginalized* by the evolution of modern society.[198]

– Other types of catechists may also be advisable. Every local Church, by analysing her own cultural and religious situation, will discover her own needs and will realistically foster those kinds of catechists which she needs. The organization and orientation of the formation of catechists is a fundamental responsibility.

Chapter Two: Formation for the service of catechesis

Pastoral care of catechists in a Particular Church

785   233. To ensure the working of the catechetical ministry in a local Church, it is fundamental to have adequate pastoral care of catechists. Several elements must be kept in mind in this respect.

---

[193] CT 66a.

[194] *Ibid.;* cf. CT 42.

[195] Cf. DCG (1971) 96.

[196] Cf. CT 45; cf. DCG (1971) 95.

[197] Cf. DCG (1971) 91; cf. CT 41.

[198] CT 45a.

Indeed efforts must be made:

 – to encourage in parishes and Christian communities *vocations* for catechesis. Today, because the needs of catechesis are so varied, it is necessary to promote different kinds of catechists. "There is therefore a need for specialised catechists".[199] In this respect selection criteria must be established;

 – to try to provide a certain number of *full time catechists* so that these can devote their time intensely and in a more stable way to catechesis,[200] in addition to fostering *part-time catechists* who are likely to be more numerous in the ordinary course of events;

 – to organize a *more balanced distribution of catechists*, among the various groups who require catechesis. Awareness of the needs of adult catechesis and catechesis for young people, for example, can help to establish a greater balance in relation to the number of catechists who work with children and adolescents.

 – to foster *animators of catechetical activity* with responsibility at diocesan level, in regions and in parishes.[201]

 – to organize adequately the *formation of catechists,* both in relation to basic training and continuing formation.

 – to attend to the *personal and spiritual needs of catechists as well as to the group of catechists as such.* This activity is principally and fundamentally the responsibility of the priests of the respective Christian communities.

 – to *co-ordinate catechists* with other pastoral workers in Christian communities, so that the entire work of evangelisation will be consistent and to ensure that catechists will not be isolated from or unrelated to the life of the community.

Importance of the formation of Catechists

234. All of these tasks are born of the conviction that the **786** quality of any form of pastoral activity is placed at risk if it does

---

[199] GMC, 5.
[200] In missionary territories (CT 66) the Second Vatican Council distinguishes two types of catechist: full time catechists and auxiliary catechists (cf. AG 17). This distinction is taken up in the *Guide for Catechists* 4, which refers to them as full-time catechists and part-time catechists.
[201] Cf. GMC, 5.

not rely on truly competent and trained personnel. The instruments provided for catechesis cannot be truly effective unless well used by trained catechists. Thus the adequate *formation of catechists* cannot be overlooked by concerns such as the updating of texts and the re-organization of catechesis.[202]

Consequently, diocesan pastoral programmes must give absolute priority to the *formation of lay catechists.* Together with this, a fundamentally decisive element must be the *catechetical formation of priests* both at the level of seminary formation as well as at the level of continuing formation. Bishops are called upon to ensure that they are scrupulously attentive to such formation.

Nature and purpose of the formation of catechists

787   235. Formation seeks to enable catechists to transmit the Gospel to those who desire to entrust themselves to Jesus Christ. The purpose of formation, therefore, is to make the catechist capable of communicating: "The summit and centre of catechetical formation lies in an aptitude and ability to communicate the Gospel message".[203]

The christocentric purpose of catechesis, which emphasizes the communion of the convert with Jesus Christ, permeates all aspects of the formation of catechists.[204] This aim is nothing other than to lead the catechist to know how to animate a catechetical journey of which, the necessary stages are: the proclamation of Jesus Christ; making known his life by setting it in the context of salvation history; explanation of the mystery of the Son of God, made man for us; and finally to help the catechumen, or those being catechized, to identify with Jesus Christ through the sacraments of initiation.[205] With continuing catechesis, the catechist merely tries to deepen these basic elements. This

---

[202] DCG (1971) 108a.

[203] Cf. DCG (1971) 111.

[204] Cf. CT 5c. This text defines the christocentric end of catechesis. This fact determines the Christocentric content of catechesis. It also determines the christocentricity of the response of those to whom catechesis is addressed (the 'Yes' to Jesus Christ) and the christocentricity of the spirituality of the catechist and of his formation.

[205] The four stages of the baptismal catechumenate are cultivated in a christocentric prospective.

christological perspective touches directly upon the identity of the catechist and his preparation. *"The unity and harmony of the catechist must be read in this christocentric light and built around a profound familiarity with Christ and the Father, in the Spirit".*[206]

236. By virtue of the fact that formation seeks to make the catechist capable of transmitting the Gospel in the name of the Church, all formation has an ecclesial nature. The formation of catechists is nothing other than an assistance for them in identifying with the living and actual awareness that the Church has of the Gospel, in order to make them capable of transmitting it in his name. **788**

In concrete terms, the catechist – in his formation – enters into communion with that aspiration of the Church which, like a spouse, "keeps pure and intact the faith of the Spouse"[207] and which, as "mother and teacher" desires to transmit the Gospel by adapting it to all cultures, ages, and situations. This truly ecclesial quality of the transmission of the Gospel permeates the entire formation of catechists and gives to that formation its true nature.

The inspiring criteria of the formation of catechists
237. An adequate conception of the formation of catechists must always take prior note of some of the criteria which inspire and configure with varying emphases relevant to the formation of catechists: **789**

– Firstly, it is a question of forming catechists for the need to evangelize in the present historical context, with its values, challenges and disappointments. To accomplish this task, it is necessary for catechists to have a deep faith,[208] a clear Christian and ecclesial identity;[209] as well as a great social sensitivity.[210] All formation programmes must accommodate these points.

– *In formation, account must also be taken of the concept of catechesis,* proposed by the Church today. It is a question of forming catechists so as to be able to transmit not only a teaching

---

[206] Guide for Catechists, 20.
[207] LG 64.
[208] DCG (1971) 114.
[209] Cf. *Guide for Catechists,* 7.
[210] Cf. *Guide for Catechists,* 13.

but also an integral Christian formation, by developing "tasks of initiation, of education, and of teaching".[211] Catechists must be able to be, at one and the same time, teachers, educators and witnesses of the faith.

   – The present *catechetical moment* being lived by the Church requires catechists who can "integrate", who are capable of overcoming "unilateral divergent tendencies"[212] and who are able to provide a full and complete catechesis. They must know how to link the dimension of truth and meaning of the faith, orthodoxy and orthopraxis, ecclesial and social meaning. Formation must contribute to the enrichment of these factors lest tensions arise between them.

   – The formation of lay catechists cannot ignore the *specific character of the laity in the Church,* and cannot be regarded as merely a synthesis of the mission received by priests and religious. Rather, "their apostolic training acquires a special character precisely from the secular nature of the lay state and from its particular type of spirituality".

   – Finally, the *pedagogy* used in this formation is of fundamental importance. As a general criterion, it is necessary to underline the need for a coherence between the general pedagogy of formation of catechists and the pedagogy proper to the catechetical process. It would be very difficult for the catechist in his activity to improvise a style and a sensibility to which he had not been introduced during his own formation.

The dimensions of formation: being, knowing, and savoir-faire

790   238. The formation of catechists is made up of different dimensions. The deepest dimension refers to the very being of the catechist, to his human and Christian dimension. Formation, above all else, must help him to mature as a person, a believer and as an apostle. This is what the catechist must know so as to be able to fulfil his responsibilities well. This dimension is permeated by the double commitment he has to the message and to man. It requires the catechist to have a sufficient knowledge of the message that he transmits and of those to whom he transmits

---

[211] DCG (1971) 31.
[212] CT 52; cf. CT 22.

the message and of the social context in which they live. This then is the dimension of *savoir-faire,* of knowing how to transmit the message, so that it is an act of communication. The formation of the catechist tends to make of him an "educator of man and of the life of man".[213]

The human, Christian and apostolic maturity of catechists.

239. On the basis of this initial human maturity,[214] the exercise of catechesis, by constant consideration and evaluation, allows the catechist to grow in a balanced and in a critical outlook, in integrity, in his ability to relate, to promote dialogue, to have a constructive spirit, and to engage in group work.[215] It will cause him to grow in respect and in love for catechumens and those being catechized: "What is this love? It is the love, not so much of a teacher as of a father, or rather of a mother. It is the Lord's wish that every preacher of the Gospel, every builder up of the Church should have this love".[216] Formation also assumes that the faith of the catechist is fostered and nourished by the exercise of catechesis, making him thus to grow as a believer. The formation, above all, nourishes the *spirituality* of the catechist,[217] so that his activity springs in truth from his own witness of life. Every theme covered by formation should feed, in the first place, the faith of the catechist. It is true that catechists catechize others by firstly catechizing themselves.

Formation also constantly nourishes the *apostolic conscious-ness of the catechist,* that is, his sense of being an evangelizer. For this reason he should be aware of and live out the concrete evangelisation efforts being made in his own diocese, as well as those of his own parish so as to be in harmony with the awareness that the particular Church has of its own mission. The best way to feed this apostolic awareness is by identifying with the figure of

791

---

[213] CT 22d.
[214] Cf. GCM, 21.
[215] The following human qualities are suggested by the *Guide for Catechists*: facility in human relationships and dialogue facilitating communication, a disposition to collaboration, a willingness to act as a guide, serenity of judgement, understanding and realism, a capacity to give consolation and hope (cf. 21).
[216] EN 79.
[217] Cf. ChL 60.

Jesus Christ, teacher and former of disciples by seeking to acquire the zeal which Jesus had for the Kingdom. Beginning with the exercise of catechesis, the apostolic vocation of the catechist – constantly fostered by continuing formation – will progressively mature.

The biblico-theological formation of the catechist

792   240. Besides being a witness, the catechist must also be a teacher who teaches the faith. A biblico-theological formation should afford the catechist an organic awareness of the Christian message, structured around the central mystery of the faith, Jesus Christ.

The context of this doctrinal formation should be drawn from the various areas that constitute every catechetical programme;

– the three great eras in the history of Salvation: the Old Testament, the life of Christ and the history of the Church.

– the great nuclei of the Christian message: the Creed, the Liturgy, the moral life and prayer.

In its own level of theological instruction, the doctrinal content of the formation of a catechist is that which the catechist must transmit. For its part, "Sacred Scripture should be the very soul of this formation".[218] The *Catechism of the Catholic Church* remains the fundamental doctrinal reference point together with the catechism proper to the particular Church.

793   241. This biblico-theological formation must contain certain qualities:

a) In the first place, it should be of a summary nature and correspond to the message to be transmitted. The various elements of the Christian faith should be presented in a well structured way and in harmony with each other by means of an organic vision that respects the "hierarchy of truths".

b) This synthesis of faith should be such as to help the catechist to mature in his own faith and enable him to offer an explanation for the present hope in this time of mission: "The situation today points to an ever-increasing urgency for doctrinal

---

[218] Cf. DCG (1971) 112. *Guide for Catechists*, 23, underlines the primary importance of Sacred Scripture in the formation of catechists: "May Sacred Scripture continue to be the principal subject of teaching and may it become the soul of all theological study. Where necessary may this be actualized".

formation of the lay faithful, not simply for a better understanding which is natural to faith's dynamism, but also in enabling them to give a reason for their hope in view of the world and its grave and complex problems".[219]

c) It must be a theological formation that is close to human experience and capable of correlating the various aspects of the Christian message with the concrete life of man "both to inspire it and to judge it in the light of the Gospel".[220] While remaining theological it must in some fashion adopt a catechetical style.

d) It must be such that the catechist "will be able not only to communicate the Gospel accurately, but also able to make those being taught capable of receiving it actively and of discerning what in their spiritual journey agrees with the faith".[221]

The human sciences and the formation of catechists

242. The catechist also acquires a knowledge of man and the reality in which he lives through the human sciences which have greatly developed in our own time. "In pastoral care sufficient use should be made, not only of theological principles, but also of secular findings, especially in the fields of psychology and sociology: in this way the faithful will be brought to a more mature living of the faith".[222]

794

It is necessary for the catechist to have some contact, with at least some of the fundamental elements of psychology: the psychological dynamics motivating man; personality structure; the deepest needs and aspirations of the human heart; progressive psychology and the phases of the human life-cycle; the psychology of religion and the experiences which open man to the mystery of the sacred.

The social sciences provide an awareness of the socio-cultural context in which man lives and by which he is strongly influenced. It is therefore necessary that in the formation of catechists that there take place "an analysis of the religious situation as well as of the sociological, cultural and economic conditions to the extent that these facts of collective life can

---

[219] ChL 60c.
[220] CT 22.
[221] DCG (1971) 112.
[222] GS 62b.

greatly influence the success of evangelisation".[223] In addition to these sciences, explicitly recommended by the Second Vatican Council, other human sciences should be used in one way or another in the formation of catechists, particularly the sciences of education and communication.

Various criteria which can inspire the use of human sciences in the formation of catechists

795   243. These are:

a) Respect for the autonomy of the sciences: "the Church... affirms the legitimate autonomy of culture and especially of the sciences".[224]

b) Evangelical discernment of the different tendencies or schools in psychology, sociology, and pedagogy: their values and their limitations.

c) The study of the human sciences – in the formation of catechists – is not an end in itself. Acquiring awareness of the existential, psychological, cultural and social situation of man is accomplished in the light of the faith in which man must be educated.[225]

d) In forming catechists, theology and the human sciences should mutually enrich each other. Consequently it is necessary to avoid a situation in which these materials are converted into the only norm for the pedagogy of the faith apart from the theological criteria deriving from the divine pedagogy. While these are fundamental and necessary disciplines, they are always at the service of evangelisation which is more than a human activity.[226]

---

[223] DCG (1971) 100.

[224] GS 59.

[225] "In the teaching of human sciences, given their very great number and diversity there are difficult problems in regard to choosing from among them and in regard to the method of teaching them. Since the question here is one of training catechists, not experts in psychology, the norm to be followed is this: determine and choose that which can directly help them to acquire facility in communication." DCG (1971) 112.

[226] A fundamental text for use of the human sciences in the formation of catechists continues to be that recommended by the Second Vatican Council in GS 62: "The faithful ought to work in close conjunction with their contemporaries and try to get to know that their ways of thinking and feeling, as they find them expressed in current culture. Let the faithful incorporate the

Pedagogical formation

244. Together with those dimensions which refer to being **796** and knowledge, the formation of catechists must also cultivate *technique.* The catechist is an educator who facilitates maturation of the faith which catechumens and those being catechized obtain with the help of the Holy Spirit.[227] The first reality of which account must be taken in this decisive area of formation is that concerning the original pedagogy of faith. The catechist is prepared or formed so as to facilitate a growth in the experience of faith, which he himself has not implanted for it is God who has sown it in the heart of man. The responsibility of the catechist is merely to cultivate this gift by nourishing it and by helping it to grow.[228] Formation seeks to mature an educational capacity in the catechist which implies: an ability to be attentive to people, an ability to interpret or respond to educational tasks or initiatives in organizing learning activities and the ability of leading a human group toward maturity. As with any other art the most important factor is that the catechist should acquire his own style of imparting catechesis by adapting the general principles of catechetical pedagogy to his own personality.[229]

245. More concretely: it must enable the catechist and **797** particularly the full-time catechist to know how to organize in the group of catechists, educational activity by carefully considering the circumstances, by elaborating a realistic catechetical plan and – having drawn it up – to know how to evaluate it critically.[230] It must be capable of animating a group by applying with discernment the techniques of group dynamics offered by psych-

---

findings of new sciences and teachings and the understanding of the most recent discoveries with Christian morality and thought so that their practice of religion and their moral behaviour may keep abreast of their acquaintance with science and of the relentless progress of technology: in this way they will succeed in evaluating and interpreting everything with an authentically Christian sense of values".

[227] The importance of pedagogy is underlined by CT 58: "Among the many prestigious sciences of man that are nowadays making immense advances, pedagogy is certainly one of the most important... the science of education and the art of teaching are continually being subjected to review, with a view to making them better adapted or more effective, with varying degrees of success".

[228] Cf. CT 58.

[229] Cf. DCG (1971) 113.

[230] *Ibid.*

ology. This educational capacity and this "know-how" along with the knowledge, attitudes and techniques which it involves "can be better acquired if they are taught simultaneously while the apostolic works are being performed (for example, during sessions when lessons of catechesis are being prepared and tested)".[231] The goal or ideal is that catechists should be the protagonists of their own learning by being creative in formation and not by just applying external rules. This formation must be closely related to praxis: one must start with praxis to be able to arrive at praxis.[232]

The formation of catechists within the Christian community

798 246. Among the ways of forming catechists, those of their own Christian community are all important. It is in this community that catechists test their own vocation and continually nourish their own apostolic awareness. The figure of the priest is fundamental in the task of assuring their progressive maturation as believers and witnesses.[233]

799 247. A Christian community can develop various types of formative activities for their own catechists:

a) One of these is the constant fostering of the ecclesial vocation of catechists by keeping alive in them an awareness of being sent by the Church;

b) It is also important to ensure catechists have a mature faith, through the usual means by which the Christian community educates in the faith its own pastoral workers and its more committed lay members.[234] When the faith of catechists is not yet mature it is advisable that they should participate in a catechumenal programme designed for young people and adults. This can be organized by the community itself, or one specifically created for them.

c) Immediate preparation for catechesis, done with a group of catechists, is an excellent means of formation especially when

---

[231] DCG (1971) 112.

[232] Cf. GCM, 28.

[233] "Priests and religious ought to assist the lay faithful in their formation. In this regard the Synod Fathers have invited priests and candidates for Orders "to be prepared carefully so they are ready to foster the vocation and mission of the lay faithful"". ChL 61.

[234] Cf. ChL 61.

accompanied with an evaluation of all that has been experienced in the sessions of catechesis.

d) Within the community other formative activities can also be realized: courses in awareness of catechesis, for example, at the beginning of the pastoral year; retreats and living in community at the important liturgical times of the year;[235] dissertations on more pressing and necessary themes; systematic doctrinal formation, for example, studying the *Catechism of the Catholic Church.* These are activities of continuing formation, which together with the personal work of the catechist, would appear very useful.[236]

Schools for catechists and centres for higher learning for experts in catechesis

248. Attendance at a *school for catechists*[237] is a particularly important moment in the formation of a catechist. In many places such schools are organized on two levels: one for catechists who are "ordinary";[238] the other for those who have "responsibility for catechesis". **800**

Schools for ordinary catechists

249. The purpose of such schools is to give an compre- **801**
hensive and systematic catechetical formation of a basic nature over a period of time during which the specifically catechetical dimensions of formation are promoted: the Christian message; knowledge of man and his socio-cultural situation; the pedagogy of the faith. Such a systematic formation has notable advantages amongst which the following can be numbered:

– its systematic nature which is not so absorbed in the immediate concerns of catechetical activity;
– its quality which is assured by trained specialists;

---

[235] "Also to be recommended are those parochial initiatives that promote the interior formation of catechists, such as prayer groups, the fraternal life, spiritual sharing and spiritual retreats. These initiatives do not isolate catechists but they help them to grow in their own spirituality and in communion with one another" (GCM, 22).

[236] Cf. DCG (1971) 110

[237] Cf. concerning schools for catechists in the missions: AG 17c; RM 73; CIC 785 and GCM, 30. For the Church in general see: DCG (1971) 109.

[238] The expression 'ordinary catechist' is used in DCG (1971) 112c.

– integration with catechists from other communities, which promotes ecclesial communion.

Institutes for those with responsibility for catechesis

802   250. So as to prepare those who have responsibility for catechesis, in parishes and vicariates as well as full time catechists[239] it is useful to provide catechetical institutes either at diocesan or inter-diocesan level. Clearly, standards in these institutes will be more demanding. In addition to the courses of basic catechetical formation they will promote those specializations regarded as necessary for the particular circumstances in which they are located. It may prove opportune, even for reasons of rationalizing resources, that the orientation of such institutes be directed towards those with responsibility for various pastoral activities. In this event they can be transformed into centres of formation for pastoral workers. Commencing with a general basic formation (doctrinal and anthropological) those areas in which specialization is required should be determined in relation to the particular demands made on the various pastoral and apostolic works of the diocese in which its pastoral workers are involved.

Higher institutes for experts in catechesis

803   251. A higher level of catechetical formation to which priests, religious and laity might have access is of vital importance for catechesis. In this regard it is hoped that "higher institutes for training in pastoral catechetics should be promoted or founded, so that catechists capable of directing catechesis at the diocesan level, or within the area of activities to which religious congregations are dedicated, may be prepared. These higher institutes can be national or even international. They ought to function as a university so far as curriculum, length of course and requisites for admission are concerned".[240] In addition to the formation of those who must assume responsibility for catechesis, these institutes will also form those who teach catechesis in seminaries, houses of formation and in the catechetical schools. These institutes should devote themselves to a congruent level of

---

[239] Cf. DCG (1971) 109b.
[240] DCG (1971) 109a.

research in catechesis.

252. At this level of formation there is much opportunity for **804** fruitful co-operation between the Churches: "Here also the material aid provided by the richer Churches to their poorer sisters can show the greatest effectiveness, for what better assistance can one Church give to another than to help it to grow as a Church with its own strength?"[241] Obviously such collaboration has due respect for the particular circumstances of poorer Churches and their responsibilities. At diocesan and inter-diocesan levels it is most useful when there is an awareness of the need to form people at a higher level, just as there is a similar need for such in other ecclesiastical activities as well as in the teaching of other disciplines.

Chapter Three: Loci and means of catechesis

The Christian community is a home for catechesis[242]

253. The Christian community is the historical realization of **805** the gift of "communion" (*koinonia*),[243] which is a fruit of the Holy Spirit. "Communion" expresses the profound nucleus between the universal Church and the particular Churches which make up the Christian community. It is realized and made visible in the rich variety of immediate Christian communities in which Christians are born into the faith, educated in it and live it: the family; parish; Catholic schools; Christian associations and movements; basic ecclesial communities. These are the loci of catechesis, the community places where initiatory catechesis and continuing education in the faith are realized.[244]

254. The Christian community is the origin, locus and goal of **806** catechesis. Proclamation of the Gospel always begins with the Christian community and invites man to conversion and the following of Christ. It is the same community that welcomes those who wish to know the Lord better and permeate themselves with a new life. The Christian community accompanies catech-

---

[241] CT 71a.

[242] See Part Five, chap. 1 where mention is made of the community responsibility for catechesis. This is regarded as a locus of catechizing.

[243] Cf. Congregation for the Doctrine of the Faith, *Communionis notio*, 1: *l.c.* 838.

[244] Cf. MPD 13.

umens and those being catechized, and with maternal solicitude makes them participate in her own experience of the faith and incorporates them into herself.[245]

Catechesis is always the same. However the *loci*[246] of catechesis distinguish it, each in its own way. Hence it is important to know the role of each of these.

807

The family as an environment or means of growth in faith

255. Parents are the primary educators in the faith. Together with them, especially in certain cultures, all members of the family play an active part in the education of the younger members. It is thus necessary to determine more concretely the sense in which the Christian family community is a *locus* of catechesis. The family is defined as a "domestic Church",[247] that is, in every Christian family the different aspects and functions of the life of the entire Church may be reflected: mission; catechesis; witness; prayer etc. Indeed in the same way as the Church, the family "is a place in which the Gospel is transmitted and from which it extends".[248] The family as a *locus* of catechesis has an unique privilege: transmitting the Gospel by rooting it in the context of profound human values.[249] On this human base, Christian initiation is more profound: the awakening of the sense of God; the first steps in prayer; education of the moral conscience; formation in the Christian sense of human love, understood as a reflection of the love of God the Father, the Creator. It is, indeed, a Christian education more witnessed to than taught, more occasional than systematic, more on-going and daily than structured into periods. In this family catechesis, the role of grandparents is of growing importance. Their wisdom and sense of the religious is often times decisive in creating a true Christian climate.

---

[245] Cf. CT 24.
[246] CT 67a. This is a classic expression in catechesis. The Apostolic Exhortation speaks of the places of catechesis (*de locis catecheses*).
[247] Cf LG 11; cf AA 11; FC 49.
[248] EN 71.
[249] Cf. GS 52; FC 37a.

The baptismal catechumenate of adults[250]

256. The baptismal catechumenate is a typical *locus* of **808**
catechesis, instituted by the Church to prepare adults, who desire
to become Christians and to receive the Sacraments of Christian
initiation.[251] In the catechumenate, it is realized "that specific
formation by means of which the adult, converted to the faith, is
brought to a confession of baptismal faith during the Easter
Vigil".[252] The catechesis given in the catechumenate is closely
linked with the Christian community.[253] From the moment of their
entry into the catechumenate, the Church surrounds catechumens
"with her affection, her care, as though they are already her
children and joined to her: indeed, they belong to the family of
Christ".[254] Thus the Christian community assists "candidates and
catechumens during their initiation process, from the pre-
catechumenate to the catechumenate, to the period of mystagogy".[255] This continual presence of the Christian community is
expressed in different ways and appropriately described in the
Rite of Christian Initiation of Adults.[256]

The parish as an environment for catechesis

257. The parish is, without doubt, the most important locus in **809**
which the Christian community is formed and expressed. This is
called to be a fraternal and welcoming family where Christians
become aware of being the people of God.[257] In the parish, all
human differences melt away and are absorbed into the universality
of the Church.[258] The parish is also the usual place in which the
faith is born and in which it grows. It constitutes, therefore, a very

---

[250] See Part I, chap. III. Here the question of the baptismal catechumenate as a
locus of catechesis is addressed in relation to the continuing presence of the
community in it.

[251] Cf. DCG (1971), 130 which describes the end of the baptismal catechumenate. Cf. RCIA 4 indicates the connection between the baptismal catechumenate
and the Christian community.

[252] 1977 Synod, MPG 8c.

[253] Cf. RCIA 4, 41.

[254] RCIA 18.

[255] RCIA 41.

[256] Cf. RCIA 41.

[257] Cf. CT 67c.

[258] Cf. AA 10.

adequate community space for the realization of the ministry of the word at once as teaching, education and life experience.

Today, the parish is undergoing profound transformation in many countries. Social changes are having repercussions on the parish especially in big cities "shaken by the phenomenon of urbanization".[259] Despite this, "the parish is still a major point of reference for the Christian people, even for the non-practising".[260] It must however, continue "to be the prime mover and pre-eminent place for catechesis",[261] while recognising that in certain occasions, it cannot be the centre of gravity for all of the ecclesial functions of catechesis and must integrate itself into other institutions.

810   258. In order that the parish may succeed in activating effectively the mission of evangelisation, some conditions must be fulfilled:

a) Adult catechesis[262] must be given priority. This involves "a post-baptismal catechesis, in the form of a catechumenate, ...presenting again some elements from the *Rite of Christian Initiation of Adults* with the purpose of allowing a person to grasp and live the immense, extraordinary richness and responsibility received at Baptism".[263]

b) With renewed courage, the proclamation of the Gospel to those alienated or who live in religious indifference[264] must be planned. In this task, pre-sacramental meetings *(preparation for Marriage, Baptism and First Holy Communion of children)* can be fundamental.[265]

c) As a solid reference point for parochial catechesis it is necessary to have a nucleus of mature Christians, initiated into the faith, for whom the pastor should have an adequate and differentiated pastoral care. This objective can be more easily achieved by the formation of small ecclesial communities.[266]

---

[259] CT 67b.

[260] *Ibid.*

[261] *Ibid.*

[262] The importance of adult catechesis is underlined in CT 43 and DCG (1971) 20.

[263] ChL 61.

[264] Cf. EN 52.

[265] Cf. DCG (1971) 96c.

[266] It is important to state as Pope John Paul II does in ChL 61 the usefulness of small ecclesial groups in the context of parishes. They should not however be a parallel movement which absorbs the best members of parishes: "internal to the

d) While the preceding points refer mainly to adults, at the same time catechesis for children, adolescents, and young people – which is always indispensable – will also benefit greatly.

Catholic schools

259. The Catholic school[267] is a most important *locus* for human and Christian formation. The declaration of the Second Vatican Council, *Gravissimum Educationis* "makes a decisive change in the history of Catholic schools: the move from school as institution to school as community".[268] Catholic schools "are no less zealous than other schools in the promotion of culture and in the human formation of young people. It is however, the special function of the Catholic school to:

– develop in the school community an atmosphere animated by a spirit of liberty and charity;

– enable young people, while developing their own personality, to grow at the same time in that new life which has been given them in baptism;

– orientate the whole of human culture to the message of salvation";[269]

The educational task of Catholic schools is bound to be developed along the basis of this concept proposed by the Second Vatican Council. It is accomplished in the school community, to which belong all of those who are directly involved in it: "teachers, management, administrative and auxiliary staff, parents – central in that they are the natural and irreplaceable educators of their own children – and pupils, who are participants and active subjects too of the educational process".[270]

260. When most students attending a Catholic school belong to families who associate themselves with the school because of

811

812

---

parish, especially if vast and territorially extensive, small Church communities, where present, can be a notable help in the formation of Christians by providing a consciousness and an experience of ecclesial communion and mission which are more extensive and incisive".

[267] Cf. Congregation for Catholic Education, *The Catholic School,* Rome 1977.

[268] Congregation for Catholic Education, *The Religious dimension of Education in the Catholic School. Outlines for Reflection,* Rome 1988, 31.

[269] GE 28.

[270] Congregation for Catholic Education, *The Religious dimension of Education in the Catholic School,* 32: l.c.

its Catholic character, the ministry of the word can be exercised in it in multiple forms: primary proclamation, scholastic religious instruction, catechesis, homily. Two of these forms, however, have a particular importance in the Catholic school: religious instruction in the school and catechesis whose respective characteristics have already been discussed.[271] When students and their families become associated with Catholic schools because of the quality of education offered in the school, or for other possible reasons, catechetical activity is necessarily limited and even religious education – when possible – accentuates its cultural character. The contribution of such schools is always "a service of great value to men",[272] as well as an internal element of evangelisation of the Church. Given the plurality of socio-cultural and religious contexts in which the work of Catholic schools is carried on in different nations, it is opportune that the Bishops and the Episcopal Conferences specify the kind of catechetical activity to be implemented in Catholic schools.

Associations, movements and groups of the faithful

813
261. The purpose of the various "associations, movements and groups of the faithful"[273] which develop in a particular Church is to help the disciples of Jesus Christ to fulfil their lay mission in the world and in the Church. In such associations Christians devote themselves to "the practice of piety, the direct apostolate, charity and relief work, or a Christian presence in temporal matters".[274] In all of these associations and movements it is always necessary to provide formation of some kind, in order to cultivate the fundamental aspects of the Christian life: "In fact they have the possibility, each with its own method, of offering a formation through a deeply shared experience in the apostolic life as well as having the opportunity to integrate, to make concrete

---

[271] *"The special character of the Catholic school, the underlying reason for it, the reason why Catholic parents should prefer it, is precisely the quality of the religious instruction integrated into the education of the pupils"* (CT 69); cf Part I, Chap. 2, nn. 73-76.

[272] AG 12c

[273] Cf. CT 70.

[274] CT 70 mentions those associations, movements and groups of faithful in which the catechetical aspects of their formation are attended to but which do not give rise, properly speaking, to environments of catechizing.

and specific the formation that their members receive from other persons and communities".[275] Catechesis is always a basic dimension in the formation of the laity. Usually, these organizations have "special times for catechesis".[276] Such catechesis is not an alternative for Christian formation. Rather it is one of its fundamental aspects.

262. When catechesis is given in the context of these **814** associations and movements, some important aspects of it must be regarded as fundamental:

a) The "proper nature"[277] of catechesis must be respected by developing the richness of its content through the threefold dimension of word, memory and witness (doctrine, celebration and commitment in life).[278] Catechesis, whatever the "way" in which it is given, is always a basic organic formation in the faith. It must, however, include "a serious study of Christian doctrine",[279] and it must constitute a serious religious formation "open to all the... factors of the Christian life".[280]

b) This is not an impediment to accomplishing the objectives proper to the various associations and movements – with their own charisms. With different emphases, catechesis must always remain faithful to its own nature. Education in the spirituality proper to a particular movement or association enriches the Church and is a natural continuation of the basic formation received by all Christians. Firstly, it is necessary to educate in what is common to all the members of the Church, before educating in what is particular and diverse.

c) It is necessary to affirm that movements and associations, as far as catechesis is concerned, are not alternatives to the parish since this is the educational community to which reference must be made by catechesis.[281]

---

[275] ChL 62.
[276] CT 67.
[277] CT 47b.
[278] CT 47b.
[279] CT 47. In this text Pope John Paul II speaks of diverse groups of young people: groups of Catholic action, prayer groups, groups for Christian reflection... he asks that in these there should also be a serious study of Christian doctrine. Catechesis should always be considered an essential part in the apostolic life of the laity.
[280] Cf. CT 21.
[281] Cf. CT 67b-c.

Basic ecclesial communities

815   263. Basic ecclesial communities have experienced a great
diffusion in recent decades.[282] These are groups of Christians
which "arise because men want to live the life of the Church with
greater fervour or because they desire and seek a more human
way of life which large ecclesial communities cannot easily
provide".[283]

Basic ecclesial communities are a sign of the "Church's
vitality".[284] The disciples of Christ gather together in them so as
to hear the word of God, to develop fraternal bonds, to celebrate
the Christian mysteries in their lives and to assume responsibility
for transforming society. In addition to these specifically
Christian concerns other important human values emerge:
friendship, personal recognition, a spirit of co-responsibility,
creativity, vocational response, concern for the problems of the
world and of the Church. From them, an enriched community
experience can result, "a true expression of communion and a
means for the construction of a more profound communion".[285]
To be authentic, "every community must live in union with the
particular and the universal Church, in heartfelt communion with
the Church's Pastors and the Magisterium, with a commitment to
missionary outreach and without yielding to isolationism or
ideological exploitation".[286]

816   264. In basic ecclesial communities an extremely enriching
catechesis can be developed:

– The fraternal climate, in which it lives, is an environment
suitable for integral catechetical activity, providing that the proper
nature and character of catechesis is respected;

– On the other hand, catechesis must strive to deepen
community life so as to ensure a basis for the Christian life of the
faithful, without which basic Christian communities lack stability;

– The small Community is always a suitable place to receive
those who have concluded a catechetical journey.

---

[282] EN 58 indicates how basic ecclesial communities flourish nearly everywhere
in the Church. RM 51 refers to them as a phenomenon in rapid growth.
[283] EN 58c.
[284] RM 51a; cf. EN 58f; LC 69.
[285] RM 51c.
[286] *Ibid.,* RM 51; cf. EN 58; LC 69.

Chapter Four: The organization of catechetical pastoral care in the particular Churches

Organization and exercise of responsibilities: The diocesan service of catechesis

265. The organization of catechetical pastoral care has as its **817** reference point the Bishop and the Diocese. The diocesan catechetical office *(Officium Catechisticum)* is "the means which the Bishop as head of the community and teacher of doctrine utilizes to direct and moderate all the catechetical activities of the diocese".[287]

266. The principal competencies of the diocesan office are **818** the following:

a) to analyse the state of the diocese[288] with regard to education in the faith: such analysis must identify, amongst other things, the real needs of the diocese as far as catechetical praxis is concerned;

b) to develop a plan of action[289] which sets out clear objectives, proposes definite suggestions and shows concrete results;

c) to promote the formation of catechist: in this respect suitable centres shall be set up;[290]

d) to elaborate, or at least to indicate to parishes and to catechists, the necessary instruments for catechesis: catechisms, directories, programmes for different ages, guides for catechists, material for those being catechized, audio-visual aids etc.;[291]

e) to foster diocesan institutions of a specifically catechetical character *(catechumenate, parochial catechesis, groups responsible for catechesis)*: these are the "basic cells"[292] of catechetical activity;

---

[287] DCG (1971) 126. The diocesan office *(officium catechisticum)* was instituted in every diocese by the decree *Provido Sane* (1935): cf. AAS 27 (1935), p. 151; see also CIC 775 § 1.

[288] Cf. DCG (1971) 100; the general lines are suggested in the *Introduction* and also in this chapter under the heading: *Analysis of the situation and of needs.*

[289] Cf. DCG (1971) 103. See also in this chapter: *"Programmes of catechetical actions and orientation".*

[290] Cf. DCG (1971) 108-109. See also Part V, chapter II.

[291] Cf. DCG (1971) 116-124.

[292] DCG (1971) 126.

f) to improve personnel and material resources at diocesan level as well as at the level of the parish and the vicariates forane;[293]

g) to collaborate with the Liturgical Office given the relevance of Liturgy for catechesis, especially for catechumenal and initiatory catechesis.

819   267. To accomplish these responsibilities, the diocesan catechetical office should "have a staff of persons who have special competence. The extent and the diversity of the problems which must be handled demand that the responsibilities be divided among a number of truly skilled people".[294] Ordinarily, this diocesan service should be performed by priests, religious and laity. Catechesis is so basic to the life of every particular Church, that "no diocese can be without its own catechetical office".[295]

Services of inter-diocesan co-operation

820   268. This co-operation is extremely fruitful in our time. Shared catechetical endeavour is advisable not only for reasons of geographic proximity but also for reasons of cultural homogeneity. Indeed "it is useful for a number of Dioceses to combine their actions, bringing together for common benefit their experiences and undertakings, their offices and equipment; for the Dioceses that are better provided to give help to the others; and for a common action programme to be prepared for the region as a whole".[296]

The service of the Episcopal Conference

821   269. "The Episcopal Conference may establish a catechetical office, whose principal purpose is to assist individual dioceses in catechetical matters".[297] This possibility, which has been established by the *Code of Canon Law,* is in fact a reality in many

---

[293] Cf. CT 63. Pope John Paul II recommends that catechesis be given *"pertinent and effective organization, putting in to operation the necessary personnel, means and equipment, and also financial resources"*.

[294] DCG (1971) 126.

[295] *Ibidem.*

[296] DCG (1971) 127.

[297] CIC 775 § 3.

of the Episcopal Conferences. The catechetical office or national catechetical centre of the Episcopal Conference has a double function:[298]

– to be at the service of the catechetical needs of all Dioceses of a given territory: it oversees publications of national relevance, national congresses, relations with the mass media and, in general, those tasks and responsibilities which are beyond the means of Dioceses or regions;

– to be at the service of the Dioceses and regions by distributing information and catechetical projects, in order to co-ordinate activities and to lend assistance to Dioceses less well provided with catechetical materials.

If an Episcopate so determines, it is also within the competence of the catechetical office or the national catechetical centre to co-ordinate its activities with other catechetical institutions or to co-operate with catechetical activities at international level. All this, however, is always done as a means of assistance to the Bishops of an Episcopal Conference.

The service of the Holy See

270. "The command of Christ to preach the Gospel to every creature applies primarily and immediately to them (the Bishops) – with Peter, and subject to Peter".[299] The ministry of the Successor of Peter – in this collegial mandate of Jesus regarding the proclamation and transmission of the Gospel – assumes a basic responsibility. This ministry must be considered "not only as a global service reaching every Church *from the outside,* but *from inside* as something already belonging to the essence of every particular Church".[300]

822

The ministry of Peter in catechesis is exercised in an eminent way through its teachings. The Pope, in what regards catechesis, acts in an immediate and particular way through the Congregation

---

[298] Cf. DCG (1971) 129.

[299] AG 38a; cf. CIC 756 §§ 1-2.

[300] John Paul II, *Allocution* to the Bishops of the United States of America, during the meeting in the seminary of Our Lady of Los Angeles 16 September 1987: *Insegnamenti di Giovanni Paolo II,* X, 3 (1987), 556. The expression is taken from the Congregation for the Doctrine of the Faith, *Communionis Notio,* Rome 1992, 13, *l.c.* 846.

for Clergy, which assists "the Roman Pontiff in the exercise of his supreme pastoral office".[301]

823   271. The Congregation for the Clergy thus:

– "has the function of promoting the religious education of the Christian faithful of all ages and conditions;

– issues timely norms so that catechetical lessons be conducted according to a proper programme;

– maintains a watchful attention to the suitable delivery of catechetical instruction;

– grants, with the assent of the Congregation of the Doctrine of the Faith, the prescribed approbation of the Holy See for catechisms and other writings pertaining to catechetical instruction;[302]

– is available to catechetical offices and international initiatives on religious education, coordinates their activities and, where necessary, it lends assistance".[303]

The co-ordination of catechesis: The importance of an effective co-ordination of catechesis

824   272. The *co-ordination of catechesis* is an important internal responsibility of the local Church. It can be considered:

– from within catechesis itself, through its diverse forms, intended for different ages and social contexts;

– in reference to the link between catechesis and other forms of education in the faith and other evangelizing activities.

The co-ordination of catechesis is not merely a strategic factor, aimed at more effective evangelisation, but has a profound theological meaning. Evangelizing activity must be well co-ordinated because it touches on the *unity of faith,* which sustains all the Church's actions.

825   273. The purpose of this section is to consider:

– the internal co-ordination of catechesis, so that the particular Church can offer a coherent and unified catechetical service;

---

[301] Apostolic Constitution *Pastor Bonus,* art. 1. This constitution, of 28 June 1988, deals with the reform of the Roman Curia which had been requested by the Council: cf. CD 9. The first reform was promulgated by the Apostolic Constitution *Regimmini Ecclesiae* of Paul VI, 18 August 1967: AAS 59 (1967) pp. 885-928.

[302] See nn. 282 and 284 of this chapter.

[303] PB, 94.

– the link between missionary activity and catechumenal activity – which are mutually dependent – in the context of the mission *ad gentes*[304] or of "new evangelisation";[305]

– the need for well co-ordinated pastoral care in the area of education, taking account of the multiplicity of educators who address themselves to the same recipients, especially children and adolescents.

The Second Vatican Council recommended the co-ordination of all pastoral activity, so that the unity of the particular Church may shine forth all the more.[306]

Coherent diocesan catechetical programmes

274. The diocesan catechetical programme is the global catechetical project of a particular Church, which integrates, in a structured and coherent way, the diverse catechetical programmes addressed by the Diocese to different age groups.[307] In this sense, every particular Church, especially in relation to Christian initiation, should offer at least two services: **826**

a) a single, coherent, process of Christian initiation for *children, adolescents and young people*, intimately connected with the sacraments of initiation already received or about to be received and linked with educational pastoral care;

b) a catechetical programme for *adults,* addressed to those Christians who need to deepen their faith in order to complete the Christian initiation begun at Baptism.

In many countries, there is also a growing need for programmes of catechesis for the *old*, for those Christians who, in the last stage of their earthly lives, desire, perhaps for the first time, to lay a solid foundation for their faith.

275. These different programmes of catechesis, each with it **827**

---

[304] RM 33.

[305] *Ibid.*

[306] CD 17a: "... the various forms of the apostolate should be encouraged. Close collaboration and the co-ordination of all the apostolic works under the direction of the Bishop should be promoted in the diocese as a whole or in parts of it. Thus all the undertakings and organizations, whether their object be catechetical, missionary, charitable, social, family, educational, or any other pastoral end, will act together in harmony, and the unity of the diocese will be more closely demonstrated".

[307] Cf. Part IV, chap. 2: *"Catechesis according to age".*

own socio-cultural variations, should not be organized separately as though they were "separate compartments without any communication between them".[308] It is necessary that the catechesis offered by a particular Church be well co-ordinated. Among the diverse forms of catechesis "their perfect complementarity must be fostered".[309] As has been already mentioned, the *organizing principle*, which gives coherence to the various catechetical programmes offered by a particular Church, is attention to adult catechesis. This is the axis around which revolves the catechesis of childhood and adolescence as well as that of old age.[310]

The fact that a Diocese offers within a single diocesan programme different programmes of catechesis does not imply that those to whom it is addressed need follow them one after the other. A young person who has arrived at adulthood with a well rounded faith does not need a catechumenal type of catechesis for adults, but other more solid nourishment, to assist him in permanently maturing in the faith. The same is true of those who arrive at old age with well rooted faith. Along with the provision of initiatory programmes, which are absolutely indispensable, the local Church must also provide diversified programmes of permanent catechesis for Christians adults.

Catechetical activity in the context of new evangelisation

828   276. If catechesis is defined as a moment in the total process of evangelisation, the problem inevitably arises of co-ordinating catechetical activity with the missionary activity which necessarily precedes it, as well as with the pastoral activity which follows it. There are in fact "elements which prepare for catechesis as well as those deriving from it".[311] In this respect, the link between missionary proclamation which seeks to stir up the faith, and initiatory catechesis, which seeks to deepen its roots, is decisive for evangelisation. This link is, in a certain sense, more evident in the mission *ad gentes*.[312] Adults converted by the

---

[308] CT 45c.

[309] *Ibid.*

[310] Cf. DCG (1971) 20, where it is shown how the other forms of catechesis are ordered *(ordinantur)* to adult catechesis.

[311] CT 18d.

[312] RM 33.

primary proclamation enter the catechumenate where they are catechized. In situations requiring *"new evangelisation"*,[313] co-ordination becomes more complex because ordinary catechesis is, at times, offered to young people and adults who need a period of prior proclamation and awakening in their adherence to Christ.

Similar difficulties arise with regard to the catechesis of children and the formation of their parents.[314] At other times forms of ongoing catechesis are applied to adults who, in fact, require a true initiatory catechesis.

277. The current situation of evangelisation requires that both **829** activities, missionary proclamation and initiatory catechesis, be conceived in a co-ordinated manner and be given, in the particular Church, through a single programme of evangelisation which is both missionary and catechumenal. Today, catechesis must be seen above all as the consequence of an effective missionary proclamation. The directives of the decree *Ad Gentes* – which sets the catechumenate in the context of the Church's missionary activity – remain a particularly valid reference point for catechesis.[315]

Catechesis in educational pastoral work

278. Pastoral care offered by a particular Church in the area **830** of education should establish a necessary co-ordination between the different *loci* in which education in the faith takes place. It is extremely important that all catechetical means "should converge on the same confession of faith, on the same membership of the Church, and on commitments in society lived in the same Gospel spirit".[316] Educational co-ordination primarily concerns children, adolescents, and young adults. It is more than useful for the particular Church to integrate various educational sectors and environments in a single project at the service of the Christian education of youth. All of these *loci* complement each other, but no one of them, taken separately, can ensure a complete Christian education. Since it is always the same and unique person of the

---

[313] *Ibidem.*
[314] Cf. CT 19 and 42.
[315] Cf. AG 11-15. The concept of evangelisation as a process structured in stages was analysed in Part I, chap. I. *The process of evangelisation.*
[316] CT 67b.

child or young person who undergoes these different educational actions, it is important that the different influences always have the same fundamental inspiration. Any contradiction between these actions is harmful, in so far as each one of them has its own specificity and importance. Thus it is most important for the particular Church to provide a programme of Christian initiation which takes into account and integrates the various educational tasks as well as the demands of new evangelisation.

Some responsibilities proper to the catechetical ministry:
Analysis of the situation and its needs

831   279. The particular Church, in organizing its catechetical activity, must have as its point of departure an *analysis of the situation*. "The object of this investigation is multiple: included are examination of pastoral action and analysis of the religious situation as well as of the sociological, cultural, and economic conditions, to the extent that these facts of collective life can greatly influence the success of evangelisation".[317] This is nothing other than becoming aware of reality from the point of view of catechesis and its needs.

More concretely:

– there must be a clear awareness, in "*examining pastoral action*", of the state of catechesis: how, in fact, it is situated in the process of evangelisation; a distinct balance between the various catechetical sectors (children, adolescents, young people, adults); the co-ordination of catechesis with Christian education in the family, in schools and elsewhere; its internal quality; the contents imparted and the methodology used; the characteristics of catechists and their formation;

– an "*analysis of the religious situation*" of the Diocese includes three closely related levels: the *sense of the sacred*, that is those human experiences, which, because of their depth, tend to open to mystery; the *religious sense*, the concrete ways in which a particular people conceives of and communicates with God; and the *situation of the faith,* in the light of the various types of believer; in connection with these levels, it also investigates the *moral situation* as lived, inquiring into its emerging values and

---

[317] DCG (1971) 100.

evident ambiguities or counter values.

– *"socio-cultural analysis"*, about which much has already been said in relation to the human sciences in the formation of catechists,[318] is also necessary because catechumens and those being catechized must be prepared to constitute a Christian presence in society.

280. The analysis of the situation, from these various per- **832** spectives, "should also convince those who work in the ministry of the word that, so far as pastoral action is concerned, human situations are ambivalent. Therefore, workers in the service of the Gospel should learn to note the many possibilities that are opening up for their action in new and diverse circumstances... For always possible is a process of change which can make clear the way to the Faith".[319]

This analysis is a primary working instrument, of an informational nature, offered by the catechetical service to pastors and catechists.

Programme of catechetical actions and orientation
281. Following close study of the situation, it becomes **833** necessary to proceed to the formulation of a *programme of action.* This will determine the objectives, the means of pastoral catechesis and the norms governing it with reference to local needs and be in complete harmony with the objectives and norms of the universal Church. The programme or plan of action should be effective since its purpose is to orientate diocesan or inter-diocesan catechesis. Because of its nature, it is usually drawn up for a specific period, at the end of which it is revised, taking into account new emphases, objectives and means. Experience confirms the usefulness of such a programme of action for catechesis. By defining certain common objectives it encourages various interests to work together with a common purpose. Thus realism should be the first characteristic of a programme of action, then simplicity, conciseness and clarity.

282. Together with the programme of action – focused above **834** all on workable options – many Episcopates prepare, at national

---

[318] Cf. Part Five, chap. 5.
[319] DCG (1971) 102; cf. Introductory explanation, 16.

level, catechetical materials of a orientational or reflective nature which provide criteria for an adequate and appropriate catechesis. These instruments are called by various names: *Catechetical Directory, Catechetical Guidelines, Basic Document, Reference Text*, etc. These are mainly addressed to those responsible for catechesis and to catechists. They clarify the concept of catechesis: its nature, object, tasks, contents, method and those to whom it is addressed. These directories or general guidelines prepared by Episcopal Conferences or published with their authority are obliged to follow the same process of elaboration and approval as catechisms. That is, such documents, before their publication, must be submitted to the Apostolic See for its approbation.[320] These catechetical guidelines are a source of great inspiration for catechesis in the local Churches and their elaboration is useful and recommended, because, amongst other things, they are an important point of reference for the formation of catechists. This kind of aid is closely and directly related to episcopal responsibility.

Elaboration of instruments and didactic aids for catechetical activity

835   283. Along with those instruments dedicated to the orientation and general planning of catechetical activity (*analysis of the situation, plan of action, Catechetical Directory*), there are other instruments of more immediate use in catechetical activity. In the first place, mention must be made of *textbooks*,[321] which are placed directly in the hands of catechumens and those being catechized. Also helpful are the various catechetical *Guides* for both catechists and, in the case of the catechesis of children, for

---

[320] Cf. DCG (1971) 117 and 134; PB 94.

[321] With regard to this ensemble of catechetical books *Catechesi Tradendae* notes: "one of the major features of the renewal of catechetics today is the rewriting and multiplication of catechetical books taking place in many parts of the Church. Numerous very successful works have been produced and are a real treasure in this service of catechetical instruction" (CT 49). DCG (1971) 120 defines textbooks in the following way: "textbooks are aids offered to the Christian community that is engaged in catechesis. No text can take the place of a live communication of the Christian message; nevertheless, the texts do have great value in that they make it possible to present a fuller exposition of the witnesses of Christian tradition and of principles that foster catechetical activity".

parents.[322] *Audio-visual* aids too are important in catechesis and appropriate discernment should be exercised in their use.[323] The basic criterion for these work aids should be that of twofold fidelity to God and to man, a fundamental principle for the whole Church. This implies an ability to marry perfect doctrinal fidelity with a profound adaptation to man's needs, taking into consideration the psychology of age and the socio-cultural context in which he lives.

In short, catechetical aids must:

– be "linked with the real life of the generation to which they are addressed, showing close acquaintance with its anxieties and questionings, struggles and hopes";[324]

– try "to speak meaningfully to this generation";[325]

– "really aim to give to those who use them a better knowledge of the mysteries of Christ, aimed at true conversion and a life more in conformity with God's will".[326]

Preparation of local catechisms: a direct responsibility of the episcopal ministry

284. Among the aids available to catechesis, catechisms excel all others.[327] Their importance derives from the fact that the message transmitted by them is recognized as authentic by the Pastors of the Church. If the Bishop presides over the general catechetical activity of a particular Church, it is also true that the publication of catechisms is a direct responsibility of the episcopal ministry. National, regional, or diocesan catechisms,

836

---

[322] With regard to catechetical manuals DCG (1971) 121 indicates what they should contain: "an explanation of the message of Salvation (constant reference must be made to the sources and a clear distinction must be kept between those things which pertain to the faith and to the doctrine that must be held, and those things which are mere opinions of theologians); psychological and pedagogical advice; suggestions about methods".

[323] Cf. Part Three, chap. 2, *Social communication;* cf. DCG (1971) 122.

[324] CT 49b.

[325] *Ibid.*

[326] *Ibid.*

[327] The question of local catechisms has been dealt with in Part two, chap. II. Here we intend to present only some criteria for their elaboration. By the term "local catechisms" the present document refers to those catechisms which are proposed by particular Churches or by Episcopal Conferences.

drawn up in co-operation with catechetical workers, are ultimately the responsibility of the Bishops, who are catechists *par excellence* in the particular Churches.

In drawing up catechisms, the following two criteria must be carefully adhered to.

a) perfect harmony with the *Catechism of the Catholic Church*: "a sure and authentic reference... particularly for preparing local catechisms";[328]

b) due consideration for the norms and criteria for the presentation of the Gospel message contained in the *General Directory for Catechesis*, which is also a "standard of reference"[329] for catechesis.

837   285. The *"prior approbation of the Apostolic See"*[330] which is required for catechisms emanating from Episcopal Conferences – signifies that these are documents whereby the universal Church, in the differing socio-cultural contexts to which she is sent, proclaims and transmits the Gospel and "generates the particular Churches by manifesting herself in them".[331] The approbation of a catechism is a recognition of the fact that it is a text of the universal Church for a specific culture and situation.

Conclusion

838   286. In formulating the present guidelines and directives every possible effort has been made to ensure that they are based on the teachings of the Second Vatican Council and on the subsequent interventions of the Church's Magisterium. Particular attention has, moreover, been given to the experience of ecclesial life among different peoples in the interim. In the light of fidelity to the spirit of God the requisite discernment has been exercised, always, however, with a view to the renewal of the Church and the service of evangelisation.

839   287. This new Directory is offered to all the Pastors of the Church, to their fellow workers and to catechists in the hope that it may serve as an encouragement in the service which the Church

---

[328] FD 3c.

[329] CT 50.

[330] DCG (1971) 119, 134; CIC 775 § 2; PB 94.

[331] Congregation for the Doctrine of the Faith, *Communionis Notio,* 9; *l.c.* 843.

and the Holy Spirit entrusts to them, namely, fostering the growth of faith in those who believe. The guidelines, contained herein, are intended not only to clarify the nature of catechesis and the norms and criteria which govern this evangelizing ministry of the Church but to nurture, with the power of the word and the interior action of the Holy Spirit, the hope of those who labour in this privileged area of ecclesial activity.

288. The effectiveness of catechesis is and always will be a   **840** gift of God, through the operation of the Spirit of the Father and the Son. St Paul, in his letter to the Corinthians, confirms this total dependence on the intervention of God when he writes: *"I planted, Apollos watered, but God gave the growth. So neither he who plants nor he who waters is anything, but only God who gives the growth"* (*1 Cor* 3:6-7).

Neither catechesis nor evangelisation is possible without the action of God working through his Spirit.[332] In catechetical praxis neither the most advanced pedagogical techniques nor the most talented catechist can ever replace the silent and unseen action of the Holy Spirit.[333] "It is he who is in truth the protagonist of all the Church's mission";[334] it is he who is the principal catechist; it is he who is "the interior teacher" of those who grow in the Lord.[335] He is, in fact, "the principle inspiring all catechetical work and all who do this work".[336]

289. May patience and trust abide in the spirituality of the   **841** catechist, since it is God himself who sows, gives growth, and brings to fruition the seed of his word, planted in good soil and tended with love. St Mark, the Evangelist, is alone in recounting the parable by which Jesus makes us to understand the stages, one after the other, whereby the scattered seed gradually and constantly develops: *"The Kingdom of God is as if a man should scatter seed upon the ground, and should sleep and rise night and day, and, the seed should sprout and grow, he knows not know. The earth produces of itself, first the blade, then the ear, then the full grain in the ear. But when the grain is ripe, at once he puts in*

---

[332] Cf. EN 75a.
[333] Cf. EN 75d.
[334] RM 21.
[335] Cf. CT 72.
[336] CT 72.

the sickle, because the harvest has come" (Mark 4:26-29).

842   290. The Church, which has the responsibility of catechizing those who believe, invokes the Spirit of the Father and of the Son, begging him to give fruitfulness and interior strength to the toil which is everywhere undertaken for the growth of the faith and the fellowship of Our Saviour Jesus Christ.

843   291. Today as ever, all labourers of catechesis, trusting in her intercession, turn to the Blessed Virgin Mary, who saw her Son grow "in wisdom, age and grace" (Luke 2:52). They find in her the spiritual model for carrying out and strengthening the renewal of contemporary catechesis, in faith, hope and love. Through the intercession of the "Virgin of Pentecost",[337] there is born in the Church a new power, generating sons and daughters in the faith and educating them toward the fulness of Christ.

His Holiness Pope John Paul II, on 11 August 1997, approved this present General Directory for Catechesis and authorized its publication.

Darío Castrillón Hoyos
Archbishop Emeritus of Bucaramanga
Pro-Prefect
Crescenzio Sepe
Titular Archbishop of Grado
Secretary

---

[337] CT 73.

THE CATHOLIC SCHOOL ON THE THRESHOLD OF THE THIRD
MILLENNIUM

Congregation for Catholic Education (for Seminaries and Educational Institutions) 28 December 1997

Introduction

1. On the threshold of the third millennium education faces **844** new challenges which are the result of a new socio-political and cultural context. First and foremost, we have a crisis of values which, in highly developed societies in particular, assumes the form, often exalted by the media, of subjectivism, moral relativism and nihilism. The extreme pluralism pervading contemporary society leads to behaviour patterns which are at times so opposed to one another as to undermine any idea of community identity. Rapid structural changes, profound technical innovations and the globalization of the economy affect human life more and more throughout the world. Rather than prospects of development for all, we witness the widening of the gap between rich and poor, as well as massive migration from underdeveloped to highly-developed countries. The phenomena of multiculturalism and an increasingly multi-ethnic and multi-religious society is at the same time an enrichment and a source of further problems. To this we must add, in countries of long-standing evangelisation, a growing marginalization of the Christian faith as a reference point and a source of light for an effective and convincing interpretation of existence.

2. In the specifically educational field, the scope of **845**

educational functions has broadened, becoming more complex, more specialized. The sciences of education, which concentrated in the past on the study of the child and teacher-training, have been widened to include the various stages of life, and the different spheres and situations beyond the school. New requirements have given force to the demand for new contents, new capabilities and new educational models besides those followed traditionally. Thus education and schooling become particularly difficult today.

846   3. Such an outlook calls for courageous renewal on the part of the Catholic school. The precious heritage of the experience gained over the centuries reveals its vitality precisely in the capacity for prudent innovation. And so, now as in the past, the Catholic school must be able to speak for itself effectively and convincingly. It is not merely a question of adaptation, but of missionary thrust, the fundamental duty to evangelize, to go towards men and women wherever they are, so that they may receive the gift of salvation.

847   4. Accordingly, the Congregation for Catholic Education, during this time of immediate preparation for the great jubilee of the year 2000, and as it celebrates the thirtieth anniversary of the creation of the Schools Office[1] and the twentieth anniversary of *The Catholic School*, published on 19th March 1977, proposes to "focus attention on the nature and distinctive characteristics of a school which would present itself as *Catholic*".[2] It therefore addresses this circular letter to all those who are engaged in Catholic schooling, in order to convey to them a word of encouragement and hope. In particular, by means of the present letter, the Congregation shares their joy for the positive fruits yielded by the Catholic school and their anxiety about the difficulties which it encounters. Furthermore, the teachings of the

---

[1] The Sacred Congregation for Catholic Education was the new name given to the Sacred Congregation for Seminaries and Universities by the Apostolic Constitution *Regimini ecclesiae universae*, which was published on 15 August 1967 and in force as from 1 March 1968 (AAS, LIX [1967] pp. 885-928). The Congregation now comprised a third section, the Schools Office, intended "to develop further" the fundamental principles of education, especially in schools (Cf. Second Vatican Council, *Declaration on Christian Education GE*, Preface).

[2] S. Congregation for Catholic Education, *The Catholic School*, 2.

Second Vatican Council, innumerable interventions of the Holy Father, ordinary and extraordinary Assemblies of the Synod of Bishops, Episcopal Conferences and the pastoral solicitude of diocesan Ordinaries, as well as international Catholic organisations involved in education and schooling, all support our conviction that it is opportune to devote careful attention to certain fundamental characteristics of the Catholic school, which are of great importance if its educational activity is to be effectual in the Church and in society. Such are: *the Catholic school as a place of integral education of the human person through a clear educational project of which Christ is the foundation;*[3] its ecclesial and cultural identity; its mission of education as a work of love; its service to society; the traits which should characterize the educating community.

Joys and difficulties
  5. We retrace with satisfaction the positive course of the **848** Catholic school over the past decades. First and foremost, we must recognize the contribution it makes to the evangelizing mission of the Church throughout the world, including those areas in which no other form of pastoral work is possible. Moreover, in spite of numerous obstacles, the Catholic school has continued to share responsibility for the social and cultural development of the different communities and peoples to which it belongs, participating in their joys and hopes, their sufferings and difficulties, their efforts to achieve genuine human and communitarian progress. In this respect, mention must be made of the invaluable services of the Catholic school to the spiritual and material development of less fortunate peoples. It is our duty to express appreciation for the Catholic school's contribution to innovation in the fields of pedagogy and didactics, and the strenuous commitment of so many men and women, especially of all those religious and laity who see their teaching as a mission and true apostolate.[4] Finally, we cannot forget the part played by Catholic schools in organic pastoral work and in pastoral care for the family in particular, emphasizing in this respect their discreet insertion in the educational dynamics between

---

[3] Cf. S. Congregation for Catholic Education, *The Catholic School*, 34.
[4] Cf. Second Vatican Council, *Declaration on Christian Education GE*, 8.

parents and their children and, very especially the unpretentious yet caring and sensitive help offered in those cases, more and more numerous above all in wealthy nations, of families which are "fragile" or have broken up.

849   6. The school is undoubtedly a sensitive meeting-point for the problems which besiege this restless end of the millennium. The Catholic school is thus confronted with children and young people who experience the difficulties of the present time. Pupils who shun effort, are incapable of self-sacrifice and perseverance and who lack authentic models to guide them, often even in their own families. In an increasing number of instances they are not only indifferent and non-practising, but also totally lacking in religious or moral formation. To this we must add – on the part of numerous pupils and families – a profound apathy where ethical and religious formation is concerned, to the extent that what is in fact required of the Catholic school is a certificate of studies or, at the most, quality instruction and training for employment. The atmosphere we have described produces a certain degree of pedagogical tiredness, which intensifies the ever increasing difficulty of conciliating the role of the teacher with that of the educator in today's context.

850   7. Among existing difficulties, there are also situations in the political, social and cultural sphere which make it harder or even impossible to attend a Catholic school. The drama of large-scale poverty and hunger in many parts of the world, internal conflicts and civil wars, urban deterioration, the spread of crime in large cities, impede the implementation of projects for formation and education. In other parts of the world, governments themselves put obstacles in the way, when they do not actually prevent the Catholic school from operating, in spite of the progress which has been made as far as attitude, democratic practice and sensitivity to human rights are concerned. Finance is a source of further difficulties, which are felt more acutely in those states in which no government aid is provided for non state schools. This places an almost unbearable financial burden on families choosing not to send their children to state schools and constitutes a serious threat to the survival of the schools themselves. Moreover, such financial strain not only affects the recruiting and stability of teachers, but can also result in the exclusion from Catholic schools of those who cannot afford to pay, leading to a selection according to means which deprives the Catholic school of one of its distinguishing features, which is to be a school for all.

Looking ahead

8. This overview of the joys and difficulties of the Catholic school, although not pretending to exhaust its entire breadth and depth, does prompt us to reflect on the contribution it can make to the formation of the younger generation on the threshold of the third millennium, recognising, as John Paul II has written, that "the future of the world and of the Church belongs to the *younger generation*, to those who, born in this century, will reach maturity in the next, the first century of the new millennium".[5] Thus the Catholic school should be able to offer young people the means to acquire the knowledge they need in order to find a place in a society which is strongly characterized by technical and scientific skill. But at the same time, it should be able, above all, to impart a solid Christian formation. And for the Catholic school to be a means of education in the modern world, we are convinced that certain fundamental characteristics need to be strengthened.

851

The human person and his or her education

9. The Catholic school sets out to be a school for the human person and of human persons. "The person of each individual human being, in his or her material and spiritual needs, is at the heart of Christ's teaching: this is why the promotion of the human person is the goal of the Catholic school".[6] This affirmation, stressing man's vital relationship with Christ, reminds us that it is in His person that the fulness of the truth concerning man is to be found. For this reason the Catholic school, in committing itself to the development of the whole man, does so in obedience to the solicitude of the Church, in the awareness that all human values find their fulfilment and unity in Christ.[7] This awareness expresses the centrality of the human person in the educational project of the Catholic school, strengthens its educational endeavour and renders

852

---

[5] John Paul II, Apostolic Letter *Tertio Millennio Adveniente*, 58.
[6] Cf. John Paul II, *Address to the I National Meeting of the Catholic School in Italy*, in "L'Osservatore Romano", 24 November 1991, p. 4.
[7] Cf. S. Congregation for Catholic Education, *The Catholic School*, 35.

it fit to form strong personalities.

853 10. The social and cultural context of our time is in danger of obscuring "the educational value of the Catholic school, in which its fundamental reason for existing and the basis of its genuine apostolate is to be found".[8] Indeed, although it is true to say that in recent years there has been an increased interest and a greater sensitivity on the part of public opinion, international organizations and governments with regard to schooling and education, there has also been a noticeable tendency to reduce education to its purely technical and practical aspects. Pedagogy and the sciences of education themselves have appeared to devote greater attention to the study of phenomenology and didactics than to the essence of education as such, centred on deeply meaningful values and vision. The fragmentation of education, the generic character of the values frequently invoked and which obtain ample and easy consensus at the price of a dangerous obscuring of their content, tend to make the school step back into a supposed neutrality, which enervates its educating potential and reflects negatively on the formation of the pupils. There is a tendency to forget that education always presupposes and involves a definite concept of man and life. To claim neutrality for schools signifies in practice, more times than not, banning all reference to religion from the cultural and educational field, whereas a correct pedagogical approach ought to be open to the more decisive sphere of ultimate objectives, attending not only to "how", but also to "why", overcoming any misunderstanding as regards the claim to neutrality in education, restoring to the educational process the unity which saves it from dispersion amid the meandering of knowledge and acquired facts, and focuses on the human person in his or her integral, transcendent, historical identity. With its educational project inspired by the Gospel, the Catholic school is called to take up this challenge and respond to it in the conviction that "it is only in the mystery of the Word made flesh that the mystery of man truly becomes clear".[9]

---

[8] S. Congregation for Catholic Education, *The Catholic School*, 3.
[9] Second Vatican Council, Pastoral Constitution on the Church in the Modern World *GS*, 22.

The Catholic school at the heart of the Church

11. The complexity of the modern world makes it all the more **854** necessary to increase awareness of the ecclesial identity of the Catholic school. It is from its Catholic identity that the school derives its original characteristics and its "structure" as a genuine instrument of the Church, a place of real and specific pastoral ministry. The Catholic school participates in the evangelizing mission of the Church and is the privileged environment in which Christian education is carried out. In this way "Catholic schools are at once places of evangelisation, of complete formation, of inculturation, of apprenticeship in a lively dialogue between young people of different religions and social backgrounds".[10] The ecclesial nature of the Catholic school, therefore, is written in the very heart of its identity as a teaching institution. It is a true and proper ecclesial entity by reason of its educational activity, "in which faith, culture and life are brought into harmony".[11] Thus it must be strongly emphasized that this ecclesial dimension is not a mere adjunct, but is a proper and specific attribute, a distinctive characteristic which penetrates and informs every moment of its educational activity, a fundamental part of its very identity and the focus of its mission.[12] The fostering of this dimension should be the aim of all those who make up the educating community.

12. By reason of its identity, therefore, the Catholic school is **855** a place of ecclesial experience, which is moulded in the Christian community. However, it should not be forgotten that the school fulfils its vocation to be a genuine experience of Church only if it takes its stand within the organic pastoral work of the Christian community. In a very special way the Catholic school affords the opportunity to meet young people in an environment which favours their Christian formation. Unfortunately, there are instances in which the Catholic school is not perceived as an integral part of organic pastoral work, at times it is considered alien, or very nearly so, to the community. It is urgent, therefore, to sensitize parochial and diocesan communities to the necessity of

---

[10] John Paul II, Apostolic Exhortation *Ecclesia in Africa*, 102.

[11] Congregation for Catholic Education, *Religious Dimension of Education in a Catholic school*, 34.

[12] Cf. Congregation for Catholic Education, *Religious Dimension of Education in a Catholic school*, 33.

their devoting special care to education and schools.

856   13. In the life of the Church, the Catholic school is recognised above all as an expression of those Religious Institutes which, according to their proper charism or specific apostolate, have dedicated themselves generously to education. The present time is not without its difficulties, not only on account of the alarming decrease in numbers, but also of a serious misunderstanding which induces some Religious to abandon the teaching apostolate. In other words, on the one hand the commitment to schooling is separated from pastoral activity, while on the other it is not easy to reconcile concrete activities with the specific demands of religious life. The fertile intuitions of saintly founders and foundresses demonstrate, more radically than any other argumentation, the groundless and precarious nature of such attitudes. We should also remember that the presence of consecrated religious within the educating community is indispensable, since "consecrated persons are able to be especially effective in educational activities";[13] they are an example of the unreserved and gratuitous "gift" of self to the service of others in the spirit of their religious consecration. The presence of men and women religious, side by side with priests and lay teachers, affords pupils "a vivid image of the Church and makes recognition of its riches easier".[14]

Cultural identity of the Catholic school

857   14. From the nature of the Catholic school also stems one of the most significant elements of its educational project: the synthesis between culture and faith. Indeed, knowledge set in the context of faith becomes wisdom and life vision. The endeavour to interweave reason and faith, which has become the heart of individual subjects, makes for unity, articulation and coordination, bringing forth within what is learnt in school a Christian vision of the world, of life, of culture and of history. In the Catholic school's educational project there is no separation between time for learning and time for formation, between acquiring notions and growing in wisdom. The various school

---

[13] John Paul II, Apostolic Exhortation *Vita Consecrata*, 96.
[14] John Paul II, Apostolic Exhortation *Christifideles Laici,* 62.

subjects do not present only knowledge to be attained, but also values to be acquired and truths to be discovered.[15] All of which demands an atmosphere characterized by the search for truth, in which competent, convinced and coherent educators, teachers of learning and of life, may be a reflection, albeit imperfect but still vivid, of the one Teacher. In this perspective, in the Christian educational project all subjects collaborate, each with its own specific content, to the formation of mature personalities.

*"Care for learning means loving" (*Wis 6:17*)*

15. In its ecclesial dimension another characteristic of the Catholic school has its root: it is a school for all, with special attention to those who are weakest. In the past, the establishment of the majority of Catholic educational institutions has responded to the needs of the socially and economically disadvantaged. It is no novelty to affirm that Catholic schools have their origin in a deep concern for the education of children and young people left to their own devices and deprived of any form of schooling. In many parts of the world even today material poverty prevents many youths and children from having access to formal education and adequate human and Christian formation. In other areas new forms of poverty challenge the Catholic school. As in the past, it can come up against situations of incomprehension, mistrust and lack of material resources. The girls from poor families that were taught by the Ursuline nuns in the 15th Century, the boys that Saint Joseph of Calasanz saw running and shouting through the streets of Rome, those that De la Salle came across in the villages of France, or those that were offered shelter by Don Bosco, can be found again among those who have lost all sense of meaning in life and lack any type of inspiring ideal, those to whom no values are proposed and who do not know the beauty of faith, who come from families which are broken and incapable of love, often living in situations of material and spiritual poverty, slaves to the new idols of a society, which, not infrequently, promises them only a future of unemployment and marginalization. To these new poor the Catholic school turns in a spirit of love. Spurred on by the aim of offering to all, and especially to the poor and

858

---

[15] Cf. S. Congregation for Catholic Education, *The Catholic School*, 39.

marginalized, the opportunity of an education, of training for a job, of human and Christian formation, it can and must find in the context of the old and new forms of poverty that original synthesis of ardour and fervent dedication which is a manifestation of Christ's love for the poor, the humble, the masses seeking for truth.

The Catholic school at the service of society

859   16. The school cannot be considered separately from other educational institutions and administered as an entity apart, but must be related to the world of politics, economy, culture and society as a whole. For her part the Catholic school must be firmly resolved to take the new cultural situation in her stride and, by her refusal to accept unquestioningly educational projects which are merely partial, be an example and stimulus for other educational institutions, in the forefront of ecclesial community's concern for education. In this way the Catholic school's public role is clearly perceived. It has not come into being as a private initiative, but as an expression of the reality of the Church, having by its very nature a public character. It fulfils a service of public usefulness and, although clearly and decidedly configured in the perspective of the Catholic faith, is not reserved to Catholics only, but is open to all those who appreciate and share its qualified educational project. This dimension of openness becomes particularly evident in countries in which Christians are not in the majority or developing countries, where Catholic schools have always promoted civil progress and human development without discrimination of any kind.[16] Catholic schools, moreover, like state schools, fulfil a public role, for their presence guarantees cultural and educational pluralism and, above all, the freedom and right of families to see that their children receive the sort of education they wish for them.[17]

860   17. The Catholic school, therefore, undertakes a cordial and constructive dialogue with states and civil authorities. Such dialogue and collaboration must be based on mutual respect, on the reciprocal recognition of each other's role and on a common service to mankind. To achieve this end, the Catholic school

---

[16] Cf. Second Vatican Council, *Declaration on Christian Education GE*, 9.

[17] Cf. Holy See, *Charter of Rights of the Family*, art. 5.

willingly occupies its place within the school system of the different countries and in the legislation of the individual states, when the latter respect the fundamental rights of the human person, starting with respect for life and religious freedom. A correct relationship between state and school, not only a Catholic school, is based not so much on institutional relations as on the right of each person to receive a suitable education of their free choice. This right is acknowledged according to the principle of subsidiarity.[18] For "The public authority, therefore, whose duty it is to protect and defend the liberty of the citizens, is bound according to the principle of distributive justice to ensure that public subsidies are so allocated that parents are truly free to select schools for their children in accordance with their conscience".[19] In the framework not only of the formal proclamation, but also in the effective exercise of this fundamental human right, in some countries there exists the crucial problem of the juridical and financial recognition of non-state schools. We share John Paul II's earnest hope, expressed yet again recently, that in all democratic countries "concrete steps finally be taken to implement true equality for non-state schools and that it be at the same time respectful of their educational project".[20]

Climate of the educating community

18. Before concluding, we should like to dwell briefly on the climate and role of the educating community, which is constituted by the interaction and collaboration of its various components: students, parents, teachers, directors and non-teaching staff.[21] Attention is rightly given to the importance of the relations existing between all those who make up the educating community. During childhood and adolescence a student needs to experience personal relations with outstanding educators, and what is taught has greater influence on the student's formation when placed in a

861

---

[18] Cf. John Paul II, Apostolic Exhortation *Familiaris consortio,* 40; Cf. Congregation for the Doctrine of the Faith, Instruction *Libertatis conscientia,* 94.
[19] Second Vatican Council, *Declaration on Christian Education GE,* 6.
[20] John Paul II, *Letter to the Superior General of the Piarists,* in *L'Osservatore Romano,* 28 June 1997, p. 5.
[21] Cf. S. Congregation for Catholic Education, *Lay Catholics in Schools: Witnesses to Faith,* 22.

context of personal involvement, genuine reciprocity, coherence of attitudes, life-styles and day to day behaviour. While respecting individual roles, the community dimension should be fostered, since it is one of the most enriching developments for the contemporary school.[22] It is also helpful to bear in mind, in harmony with the Second Vatican Council,[23] that this community dimension in the Catholic school is not a merely sociological category; it has a theological foundation as well. The educating community, taken as a whole, is thus called to further the objective of a school as a place of complete formation through interpersonal relations.

862   19. In the Catholic school, "prime responsibility for creating this unique Christian school climate rests with the teachers, as individuals and as a community".[24] Teaching has an extraordinary moral depth and is one of man's most excellent and creative activities, for the teacher does not write on inanimate material, but on the very spirits of human beings. The personal relations between the teacher and the students, therefore, assume an enormous importance and are not limited simply to giving and taking. Moreover, we must remember that teachers and educators fulfil a specific Christian vocation and share an equally specific participation in the mission of the Church, to the extent that "it depends chiefly on them whether the Catholic school achieves its purpose".[25]

863   20. Parents have a particularly important part to play in the educating community, since it is to them that primary and natural responsibility for their children's education belongs. Unfortunately in our day there is a widespread tendency to delegate this unique role. Therefore it is necessary to foster initiatives which encourage commitment, but which provide at the same time the right sort of concrete support which the family needs and which involve it in the Catholic school's educational project.[26] The constant aim of the school therefore, should be contact and dialogue with the pupils' families, which should also

---

[22] Cf. *Ibid.*

[23] Cf. Second Vatican Council, *Declaration on Christian Education GE*, 8.

[24] Congregation for Catholic Education, *Religious Dimension of Education in a Catholic school*, 26.

[25] Cf. Second Vatican Council, *Declaration on Christian Education GE*, 8.

[26] Cf. John Paul II, Apostolic Exhortation *Familiaris consortio*, 40.

be encouraged through the promotion of parents' associations, in order to clarify with their indispensable collaboration that personalised approach which is needed for an educational project to be efficacious.

Conclusion

21. The Holy Father has pointed out in a meaningful **864** expression how "man is the primary and fundamental way for the Church, the way traced out by Christ himself".[27] This way cannot, then, be foreign to those who evangelize. Travelling along it, they will experience the challenge of education in all its urgency. Thus it follows that the work of the school is irreplaceable and the investment of human and material resources in the school becomes a prophetic choice. On the threshold of the third millennium we perceive the full strength of the mandate which the Church handed down to the Catholic school in that "Pentecost" which was the Second Vatican Council: "Since the Catholic school can be of such service in developing the mission of the

People of God and in promoting dialogue between the Church and the community at large to the advantage of both, it is still of vital importance even in our times".[28]

Pio Card. Laghi
Prefect
José Saraiva Martins
Tit. Archbishop of Tuburnica, Secretary
Rome, 28 December 1997, Solemnity of the Holy Family.

---

[27] Cf. John Paul II, Encyclical Letter *Redemptor hominis,* 14.
[28] Second Vatican Council, *Declaration on Christian Education GE,* 8.

FURTHER READING

General

The Holy Bible (Revised Standard Version or The Jerusalem Bible)

Catechism of the Catholic Church (Revised Edition, 1999), London: Geoffrey Chapman (available on-line at www.vatican.va)

Flannery A, *Vatican Council II Conciliar and Post-conciliar Documents* (1988), Boston, Paul Edition (All documents are available on-line at www.vatican.va)

Compendium of the Catechism of the Catholic Church, 2006, Catholic Truth Society, London (available on-line at www.vatican.va)

Apostolic Constitution of the Supreme Pontiff John Paul II on Catholic Universities (1990), *Ex corde ecclesiae* (available at www.vatican.va)

More relevant Church Documents

Sacred Congregation for Catholic Education (1983) *Educational Guidance in Human Love,* Catholic Truth Society

International Council for Catechesis (1990) *Adult Catechesis in the Christian Community,* St Paul Publications.

The Pontifical Council for the Family (1995) *The Truth and Meaning of Human Sexuality - Guidelines for Education within the Family,* London: Catholic Truth Society.

Sacred Congregation for Catholic Education (2002) *Consecrated Persons and their Mission in Schools: Reflections and Guidelines,* London: Catholic Truth Society.

The Pontifical Council for the Family (2004*) Enchiridion of the Family: A Compendium of Church Teaching on the Family and Life Issues,* Pauline Books and Media.

Pontifical Council for Justice and Peace, (2005) *Compendium of the Social Doctrine of the Church,* Continuum.

Some Recommended Books for General Reading

Conroy J (Ed.) (1999), *Catholic Education: Inside Out–Outside In,* Dublin: Lindisfarne

Ratzinger J (1997), *Gospel, Catechesis, Catechism – Sidelights on the Catechism of the Catholic Church,* San Francisco: Ignatius Press.

Redford J (Ed.) (2002), *Hear O Islands – Theology and Catechesis in the New Millennium*, Dublin: Veritas.

Journals
The Sower, Maryvale Institute, Old Oscott Hill, Birmingham B44 9AG,
    UK
Catholic Education: A Journal of Inquiry and Practice, University of
    Notre Dame, 150 I.E.I. Building Notre Dame, IN 46556-5682 USA

Useful Websites
www.vatican.va
www.ewtn.com
www.tere.org
www.ceo.melb.catholic.edu.au
www.zenit.org

APPENDIX 1

Code of Canon Law: schools

Can. 796 §1 Among the means of advancing education, Christ's faithful are to consider schools as of great importance, since they are the principal means of helping parents to fulfil their role in education.

§2 There must be the closest cooperation between parents and the teachers to whom they entrust their children to be educated. In fulfilling their task, teachers are to collaborate closely with the parents and willingly listen to them; associations and meetings of parents are to be set up and held in high esteem.

Can. 797 Parents must have a real freedom in their choice of schools. For this reason Christ's faithful must be watchful that the civil society acknowledges this freedom of parents and, in accordance with the requirements of distributive justice, even provides them with assistance.

Can. 798 Parents are to send their children to those schools which will provide for their Catholic education. If they cannot do this, they are bound to ensure the proper Catholic education of their children outside the school.

Can. 799 Christ's faithful are to strive to secure that in the civil society the laws which regulate the formation of the young, also provide a religious and moral education in the schools that is in accord with the conscience of the parents.

Can. 800 §1 The Church has the right to establish and to direct schools for any field of study or of any kind and grade.

§2 Christ's faithful are to promote Catholic schools, doing everything possible to help in establishing and maintaining them.

Can. 801 Religious institutes which have education as their mission are to keep faithfully to this mission and earnestly strive to devote themselves to Catholic education, providing this also through their own schools which, with the consent of the diocesan Bishop, they have established.

Can. 802 §1 If there are no schools in which an education is provided that is imbued with a Christian spirit, the diocesan

Bishop has the responsibility of ensuring that such schools are established.

§2 Where it is suitable, the diocesan Bishop is to provide for the establishment of professional and technical schools, and of other schools catering for special needs.

Can. 803 §1 A Catholic school is understood to be one which is under the control of the competent ecclesiastical authority or of a public ecclesiastical juridical person, or one which in a written document is acknowledged as Catholic by the ecclesiastical authority.

§2 Formation and education in a Catholic school must be based on the principles of Catholic doctrine, and the teachers must be outstanding in true doctrine and uprightness of life.

§3 No school, even if it is in fact Catholic, may bear the title 'Catholic school' except by the consent of the competent ecclesiastical authority.

Can. 804 §1 The formation and education in the Catholic religion provided in any school, and through various means of social communication is subject to the authority of the Church. It is for the Episcopal Conference to issue general norms concerning this field of activity and for the diocesan Bishop to regulate and watch over it.

§2 The local Ordinary is to be careful that those who are appointed as teachers of religion in schools, even non-Catholic ones, are outstanding in true doctrine, in the witness of their Christian life, and in their teaching ability.

Can. 805 In his own diocese, the local Ordinary has the right to appoint or to approve teachers of religion and, if religious or moral considerations require it, the right to remove them or to demand that they be removed.

Can. 806 §1 The diocesan Bishop has the right to watch over and inspect the Catholic schools situated in his territory, even those established or directed by members of religious institutes. He has also the right to issue directives concerning the general regulation of Catholic schools these directives apply also to schools conducted by members of a religious institute, although they retain their autonomy in the internal management of their schools.

§2 Those who are in charge of Catholic schools are to ensure, under the supervision of the local Ordinary, that the formation given in them is, in its academic standards, at least as outstanding as that in other schools in the area.

Catholic universities and other institutes of higher studies

Can. 807 The Church has the right to establish and to govern universities, which serve to promote the deeper culture and fuller development of the human person, and to complement the Church's own teaching office.

Can. 808 No university, even if it is in fact Catholic, may bear the title 'Catholic university' except by the consent of the competent ecclesiastical authority.

Can. 809 If it is possible and appropriate, Episcopal Conferences are to take care to have within their territories suitably located universities or at least faculties, in which the various disciplines, while retaining their own scientific autonomy, may be researched and taught in the light of Catholic doctrine.

Can. 810 §1 In Catholic universities it is the duty of the competent statutory authority to ensure that there be appointed teachers who are not only qualified in scientific and pedagogical expertise, but are also outstanding in their integrity of doctrine and uprightness of life. If these requirements are found to be lacking, it is also that authority's duty to see to it that these teachers are removed from office, in accordance with the procedure determined in the statutes.

§2 The Episcopal Conference and the diocesan Bishops concerned have the duty and the right of seeing to it that, in these universities, the principles of Catholic doctrine are faithfully observed.

Can. 811 §1 The competent ecclesiastical authority is to ensure that in Catholic universities there is established a faculty or an institute or at least a chair of theology, in which lectures are given to lay students also.

§2 In every Catholic university there are to be lectures which principally treat of those theological questions connected with the studies of each faculty.

Can. 812 Those who teach theological subjects in any institute of higher studies must have a mandate from the competent ecclesiastical authority.

Can. 813 The diocesan Bishop is to be zealous in his pastoral care of students, even by the creation of a special parish, or at least by appointing priests with a stable assignment to this care. In all universities, even in those which are not Catholic, the diocesan Bishop is to provide Catholic university centres, to be of assistance to the young people, especially in spiritual matters.

Can. 814 The provisions which are laid down for universities apply equally to other institutes of higher studies.

APPENDIX 2

This section contains some texts from Scripture and the Catechism of the Catholic Church. These serve as a reminder that the study of Catholic Education is not simply a matter of *learning information* but should be a time of formation in faith: no formation is complete without prayer.

On the Need for Faith in God

On that day, when evening had come, he said to them, "Let us go across to the other side." And leaving the crowd, they took him with them in the boat, just as he was. And other boats were with him. And a great storm of wind arose, and the waves beat into the boat, so that the boat was already filling.
But he was in the stern, asleep on the cushion; and they woke him and said to him, "Teacher, do you not care if we perish?"
And he awoke and rebuked the wind, and said to the sea, "Peace! Be still!" And the wind ceased, and there was a great calm.
He said to them, "Why are you afraid? Have you no faith?"
And they were filled with awe, and said to one another, "Who then is this, that even wind and sea obey him?" (Mark 4:35-41).

A Reflection on the Art of Catechesis

And when a great crowd came together and people from town after town came to him, he said in a parable:
"A sower went out to sow his seed; and as he sowed, some fell along the path, and was trodden under foot, and the birds of the air devoured it. And some fell on the rock; and as it grew up, it withered away, because it had no moisture.
And some fell among thorns; and the thorns grew with it and choked it. And some fell into good soil and grew, and yielded a hundredfold." As he said this, he called out, "He who has ears to hear, let him hear."
And when his disciples asked him what this parable meant, he said, "To you it has been given to know the secrets of the kingdom of God; but for others they are in parables, so that seeing they may not see, and hearing they may not understand.

Now the parable is this: The seed is the word of God.
The ones along the path are those who have heard; then the devil comes

*and takes away the word from their hearts, that they may not believe
and be saved.*
*And the ones on the rock are those who, when they hear the word,
receive it with joy; but these have no root, they believe for a while and
in time of temptation fall away.*
*And as for what fell among the thorns, they are those who hear, but as
they go on their way they are choked by the cares and riches and
pleasures of life, and their fruit does not mature.*
*And as for that in the good soil, they are those who, hearing the word,
hold it fast in an honest and good heart, and bring forth fruit with
patience (Luke 8: 4-15).*

On the mandate given by Jesus to the Church

*Now the eleven disciples went to Galilee, to the mountain to which Jesus
had directed them. And when they saw him they worshiped him; but
some doubted. And Jesus came and said to them, "All authority in
heaven and on earth has been given to me.*
*Go therefore and make disciples of all nations, baptizing them in the
name of the Father and of the Son and of the Holy Spirit, teaching them
to observe all that I have commanded you; and lo, I am with you always,
to the close of the age" (Mark 4:35-41).*

On Forgiveness and the Mercy of God

*Early in the morning he came again to the temple; all the people came
to him, and he sat down and taught them. The scribes and the Pharisees
brought a woman who had been caught in adultery, and placing her in
the midst*
*they said to him, "Teacher, this woman has been caught in the act of
adultery.*
*Now in the law Moses commanded us to stone such. What do you say
about her?"*
*This they said to test him, that they might have some charge to bring
against him. Jesus bent down and wrote with his finger on the ground.
And as they continued to ask him, he stood up and said to them, "Let
him who is without sin among you be the first to throw a stone at her."
And once more he bent down and wrote with his finger on the ground.
But when they heard it, they went away, one by one, beginning with the
eldest, and Jesus was left alone with the woman standing before him.
Jesus looked up and said to her, "Woman, where are they? Has no one
condemned you?"*
*She said, "No one, Lord." And Jesus said, "Neither do I condemn you;
go, and do not sin again" (John 8:2-11).*

A vision of the early Church
And they devoted themselves to the apostles' teaching and fellowship, to the breaking of bread and the prayers (Acts 2:42).

Texts on Catechesis from the Catechism of the Catholic Church

1697 Catechesis has to reveal in all clarity the joy and the demands of the way of Christ. Catechesis for the "newness of life" in him should be:

- a catechesis of the Holy Spirit, the interior Master of life according to Christ, a gentle guest and friend who inspires, guides, corrects, and strengthens this life;

- a catechesis of grace, for it is by grace that we are saved and again it is by grace that our works can bear fruit for eternal life;

- a catechesis of the beatitudes, for the way of Christ is summed up in the beatitudes, the only path that leads to the eternal beatitude for which the human heart longs;

- a catechesis of sin and forgiveness, for unless man acknowledges that he is a sinner he cannot know the truth about himself, which is a condition for acting justly; and without the offer of forgiveness he would not be able to bear this truth;

- a catechesis of the human virtues which causes one to grasp the beauty and attraction of right dispositions towards goodness;

- a catechesis of the Christian virtues of faith, hope, and charity, generously inspired by the example of the saints; -a catechesis of the twofold commandment of charity set forth in the Decalogue;

- an ecclesial catechesis, for it is through the manifold exchanges of "spiritual goods" in the "communion of saints" that Christian life can grow, develop, and be communicated.

1698 The first and last point of reference of this catechesis will always be Jesus Christ himself, who is "the way, and the truth, and the life. It is by looking to him in faith that Christ's faithful can hope that he himself fulfils his promises in them, and that, by loving him with the same love with which he has loved them, they may perform works in keeping with their dignity:

I ask you to consider that our Lord Jesus Christ is your true head, and that you are one of his members. He belongs to you as the head belongs to its members; all that is his is yours: his spirit, his heart, his body and soul, and all his faculties. You must make use of all these as of your own, to serve, praise, love, and glorify God. You belong to him, as members belong to their head, and so he longs for you to use all that is in you, as if it were his own, for the service and glory of the Father.

For to me, to live is Christ (Phil. 1:21).

APPENDIX 3

The Credo of the People of God
POPE PAUL VI, 3 June 1968

This relatively short document of Paul VI provides a comprehensive overview of the essential tenets of Catholic doctrine

With this solemn liturgy we end the celebration of the nineteenth centenary of the martyrdom of the holy apostles Peter and Paul, and thus close the Year of Faith. We dedicated it to the commemoration of the holy apostles in order that we might give witness to our steadfast will to be faithful to the deposit of the faith[1] which they transmitted to us, and that we might strengthen our desire to live by it in the historical circumstances in which the Church finds herself in her pilgrimage in the midst of the world.

We feel it our duty to give public thanks to all who responded to our invitation by bestowing on the Year of Faith a splendid completeness through the deepening of their personal adhesion to the word of God, through the renewal in various communities of the profession of faith, and through the testimony of a Christian life. To our brothers in the episcopate especially, and to all the faithful of the holy Catholic Church, we express our appreciation and we grant our blessing.

Likewise, we deem that we must fulfil the mandate entrusted by Christ to Peter, whose successor we are, the last in merit; namely, to confirm our brothers in the faith.[2] With the awareness, certainly, of our human weakness, yet with all the strength impressed on our spirit by such a command, we shall accordingly make a profession of faith, pronounce a creed which, without being strictly speaking a dogmatic definition, repeats in substance, with some developments called for by the spiritual condition of our time, the creed of Nicaea, the creed of the immortal tradition of the holy Church of God.

---

[1] Cf. 1 Tim. 6:20.
[2] Cf. Luke 22:32.

In making this profession, we are aware of the disquiet which agitates certain modern quarters with regard to the faith. They do not escape the influence of a world being profoundly changed, in which so many certainties are being disputed or discussed. We see even Catholics allowing themselves to be seized by a kind of passion for change and novelty. The Church, most assuredly, has always the duty to carry on the effort to study more deeply and to present, in a manner ever better adapted to successive generations, the unfathomable mysteries of God, rich for all in fruits of salvation. But at the same time the greatest care must be taken, while fulfilling the indispensable duty of research, to do no injury to the teachings of Christian doctrine. For that would be to give rise, as is unfortunately seen in these days, to disturbance and perplexity in many faithful souls.

It is important in this respect to recall that, beyond scientifically verified phenomena, the intellect which God has given us reaches that which is, and not merely the subjective expression of the structures and development of consciousness; and, on the other hand, that the task of interpretation – of hermeneutics – is to try to understand and extricate, while respecting the word expressed, the sense conveyed by a text, and not to recreate, in some fashion, this sense in accordance with arbitrary hypotheses.

Put above all, we place our unshakable confidence in the Holy Spirit, the soul of the Church, and in theological faith upon which rests the life of the Mystical Body. We know that souls await the word of the Vicar of Christ, and we respond to that expectation with the instructions which we regularly give. But today we are given an opportunity to make a more solemn utterance.

On this day which is chosen to close the Year of Faith, on this feast of the blessed apostles Peter and Paul, we have wished to offer to the living God the homage of a profession of faith. And as once at Caesarea Philippi the apostle Peter spoke on behalf of the twelve to make a true confession, beyond human opinions, of Christ as Son of the living God, so today his humble successor, pastor of the Universal Church, raises his voice to give, on behalf of all the People of God, a firm witness to the divine Truth entrusted to the Church to be announced to all nations.

We have wished our profession of faith to be to a high degree complete and explicit, in order that it may respond in a fitting way to the need of light felt by so many faithful souls, and by all those in the world, to whatever spiritual family they belong, who are in search of the Truth.

To the glory of God most holy and of our Lord Jesus Christ, trusting in the aid of the Blessed Virgin Mary and of the holy apostles Peter and Paul, for the profit and edification of the Church, in the name of all the pastors and all the faithful, we now pronounce this profession of faith, in full spiritual communion with you all, beloved brothers and sons.

We believe in one only God, Father, Son and Holy Spirit, creator of things visible such as this world in which our transient life passes, of things invisible such as the pure spirits which are also called angels,[3] and creator in each man of his spiritual and immortal soul.

We believe that this only God is absolutely one in His infinitely holy essence as also in all His perfections, in His omnipotence, His infinite knowledge, His providence, His will and His love. He is He who is, as He revealed to Moses,[4] and He is love, as the apostle John teaches us:[5] so that these two names, being and love, express ineffably the same divine reality of Him who has wished to make Himself known to us, and who, "dwelling in light inaccessible"[6] is in Himself above every name, above every thing and above every created intellect. God alone can give us right and full knowledge of this reality by revealing Himself as Father, Son and Holy Spirit, in whose eternal life we are by grace called to share, here below in the obscurity of faith and after death in eternal light. The mutual bonds which eternally constitute the Three Persons, who are each one and the same divine being, are the blessed inmost life of God thrice holy, infinitely beyond all that we can conceive in human measure.[7] We give thanks, however, to the divine goodness that very many believers can testify with us before men to the unity of God, even though they know not the mystery of the most holy Trinity.

---

[3] Cf Dz.-Sch. 3002.
[4] Cf Ep.3:14.
[5] Cf 1 John 4:8.
[6] Cf 1 Tim. 6:16.
[7] Cf Dz.-Sch. 804.

We believe then in the Father who eternally begets the Son, in the Son, the Word of God, who is eternally begotten; in the Holy Spirit, the uncreated Person who proceeds from the Father and the Son as their eternal love. Thus in the Three Divine Persons, *coaeternae sibi et coaequales,*[8] the life and beatitude of God perfectly one super-abound and are consummated in the supreme excellence and glory proper to uncreated being, and always "there should be venerated unity in the Trinity and Trinity in the unity."[9]

We believe in our Lord Jesus Christ, who is the Son of God. He is the Eternal Word, born of the Father before time began, and one in substance with the Father, *homoousios to Patri,*[10] and through Him all things were made. He was incarnate of the Virgin Mary by the power of the Holy Spirit, and was made man: equal therefore to the Father according to His divinity, and inferior to the Father according to His humanity;[11] and Himself one, not by some impossible confusion of His natures, but by the unity of His person.[12]

He dwelt among us, full of grace and truth. He proclaimed and established the Kingdom of God and made us know in Himself the Father. He gave us His new commandment to love one another as He loved us. He taught us the way of the beatitudes of the Gospel: poverty in spirit, meekness, suffering borne with patience, thirst after justice, mercy, purity of heart, will for peace, persecution suffered for justice sake. Under Pontius Pilate He suffered – the Lamb of God bearing on Himself the sins of the world, and He died for us on the cross, saving us by His redeeming blood. He was buried, and, of His own power, rose on the third day, raising us by His resurrection to that sharing in the divine life which is the life of grace. He ascended to heaven, and He will come again, this time in glory, to judge the living and the dead: each according to his merits – those who have responded to the love and piety of God going to eternal life, those who have refused them to the end going to the fire that is not extinguished.

---

[8] Cf Dz.-Sch. 75.

[9] Cf. *Ibid.*

[10] Cf Dz.-Sch. 150.

[11] Cf Dz.-Sch.76.

[12] Cf *Ibid.*

And His Kingdom will have no end.

We believe in the Holy Spirit, who is Lord, and Giver of life, who is adored and glorified together with the Father and the Son. He spoke to us by the prophets; He was sent by Christ after His resurrection and His ascension to the Father; He illuminates, vivifies, protects and guides the Church; He purifies the Church's members if they do not shun His grace. His action, which penetrates to the inmost of the soul, enables man to respond to the call of Jesus: Be perfect as your Heavenly Father is perfect (Matt 5:48).

We believe that Mary is the Mother, who remained ever a Virgin, of the Incarnate Word, our God and Savoir Jesus Christ,[13] and that by reason of this singular election, she was, in consideration of the merits of her Son, redeemed in a more eminent manner,[14] preserved from all stain of original sin[15] and filled with the gift of grace more than all other creatures.[16]

Joined by a close and indissoluble bond to the Mysteries of the Incarnation and Redemption,[17] the Blessed Virgin, the Immaculate, was at the end of her earthly life raised body and soul to heavenly glory[18] and likened to her risen Son in anticipation of the future lot of all the just; and we believe that the Blessed Mother of God, the New Eve, Mother of the Church,[19] continues in heaven her maternal role with regard to Christ's members, cooperating with the birth and growth of divine life in the souls of the redeemed.[20]

We believe that in Adam all have sinned, which means that the original offence committed by him caused human nature, common to all men, to fall to a state in which it bears the consequences of that offence, and which is not the state in which it was at first in our first parents – established as they were in

---

[13] Cf Dz.-Sch. 251-252.
[14] Cf *LG*, 53.
[15] Cf Dz.-Sch. 2803.
[16] Cf *LG*, 53.
[17] Cf *LG*, 53, 58, 61.
[18] Cf Dz.-Sch. 3903.
[19] Cf *LG*, 53, 58, 61, 63; Cf Paul VI, Alloc. for the Closing of the Third Session of the Second Vatican Council: *AAS* LVI [1964] 1016; Cf. Exhort. Apost. *Signum Magnum*, Introd.
[20] Cf *LG*, 62; cf Paul VI, Exhort. Apost. *Signum Magnum*, p 1, n. 1.

holiness and justice, and in which man knew neither evil nor death. It is human nature so fallen stripped of the grace that clothed it, injured in its own natural powers and subjected to the dominion of death, that is transmitted to all men, and it is in this sense that every man is born in sin. We therefore hold, with the Council of Trent, that original sin, is transmitted with human nature, "not by imitation, but by propagation" and that it is thus "proper to everyone."[21]

We believe that Our Lord Jesus Christ, by the sacrifice of the cross redeemed us from original sin and all the personal sins committed by each one of us, so that, in accordance with the word of the apostle, "where sin abounded grace did more abound."[22]

We believe in one Baptism instituted by our Lord Jesus Christ for the remission of sins. Baptism should be administered even to little children who have not yet been able to be guilty of any personal sin, in order that, though born deprived of supernatural grace, they may be reborn "of water and the Holy Spirit" to the divine life in Christ Jesus.[23]

We believe in one, holy, catholic, and apostolic Church built by Jesus Christ on that rock which is Peter. She is the Mystical Body of Christ; at the same time a visible society instituted with hierarchical organs, and a spiritual community; the Church on earth, the pilgrim People of God here below, and the Church filled with heavenly blessings; the germ and the first fruits of the Kingdom of God, through which the work and the sufferings of Redemption are continued throughout human history, and which looks for its perfect accomplishment beyond time in glory.[24] In the course of time, the Lord Jesus forms His Church by means of the sacraments emanating from His plenitude.[25] By these she makes her members participants in the Mystery of the Death and Resurrection of Christ, in the grace of the Holy Spirit who gives her life and movement.[26] She is therefore holy, though she has sinners in her bosom, because she herself has no other life but that

---

[21] Cf Dz.-Sch. 1513.

[22] Cf Rom. 5:20.

[23] Cf Dz.-Sch. 1514.

[24] Cf. *LG*, 8, 5.

[25] Cf *LG*, 7, 11.

[26] Cf *Sacrosanctum Concilium*, 5, 6; cf *LG*, 7, 12, 50.

of grace: it is by living by her life that her members are sanctified; it is by removing themselves from her life that they fall into sins and disorders that prevent the radiation of her sanctity. This is why she suffers and does penance for these offences, of which she has the power to heal her children through the blood of Christ and the gift of the Holy Spirit.

Heiress of the divine promises and daughter of Abraham according to the Spirit, through that Israel whose scriptures she lovingly guards, and whose patriarchs and prophets she venerates; founded upon the apostles and handing on from century to century their ever-living word and their powers as pastors in the successor of Peter and the bishops in communion with him; perpetually assisted by the Holy Spirit, she has the charge of guarding, teaching, explaining and spreading the Truth which God revealed in a then veiled manner by the prophets, and fully by the Lord Jesus. We believe all that is contained in the word of God written or handed down, and that the Church proposes for belief as divinely revealed, whether by a solemn judgment or by the ordinary and universal magisterium.[27] We believe in the infallibility enjoyed by the successor of Peter when he teaches *ex cathedra* as pastor and teacher of all the faithful,[28] and which is assured also to the episcopal body when it exercises with him the supreme magisterium.[29]

We believe that the Church founded by Jesus Christ and for which He prayed is indefectibly one in faith, worship and the bond of hierarchical communion. In the bosom of this Church, the rich variety of liturgical rites and the legitimate diversity of theological and spiritual heritages and special disciplines, far from injuring her unity, make it more manifest.[30]

Recognizing also the existence, outside the organism of the Church of Christ of numerous elements of truth and sanctification which belong to her as her own and tend to Catholic unity,[31] and believing in the action of the Holy Spirit who stirs up in the heart

---

[27] Cf Dz.-Sch. 3011.
[28] Cf Dz.-Sch. 3074.
[29] Cf *LG*, 25.
[30] Cf. *LG*, 23; cf *Orientalium Ecclesiarum* 2, 3, 5, 6.
[31] Cf *LG*, 8.

of the disciples of Christ love of this unity,[32] we entertain the hope that the Christians who are not yet in the full communion of the one only Church will one day be reunited in one flock with one only shepherd.

We believe that the Church is necessary for salvation, because Christ, who is the sole mediator and way of salvation, renders Himself present for us in His body which is the Church.[33] But the divine design of salvation embraces all men, and those who without fault on their part do not know the Gospel of Christ and His Church, but seek God sincerely, and under the influence of grace endeavour to do His will as recognized through the promptings of their conscience, they, in a number known only to God, can obtain salvation.[34]

We believe that the Mass, celebrated by the priest representing the person of Christ by virtue of the power received through the Sacrament of Orders, and offered by him in the name of Christ and the members of His Mystical Body, is the sacrifice of Calvary rendered sacramentally present on our altars. We believe that as the bread and wine consecrated by the Lord at the Last Supper were changed into His body and His blood which were to be offered for us on the cross, likewise the bread and wine consecrated by the priest are changed into the body and blood of Christ enthroned gloriously in heaven, and we believe that the mysterious presence of the Lord, under what continues to appear to our senses as before, is a true, real and substantial presence.[35]

Christ cannot be thus present in this sacrament except by the change into His body of the reality itself of the bread and the change into His blood of the reality itself of the wine, leaving unchanged only the properties of the bread and wine which our senses perceive. This mysterious change is very appropriately called by the Church transubstantiation. Every theological explanation which seeks some understanding of this mystery must, in order to be in accord with Catholic faith, maintain that in the reality itself, independently of our mind, the bread and wine

---

[32] Cf *LG*, 15.
[33] Cf *LG*, 14.
[34] Cf *LG*, 16.
[35] Cf Dz.-Sch. 1651.

have ceased to exist after the Consecration, so that it is the adorable body and blood of the Lord Jesus that from then on are really before us under the sacramental species of bread and wine,[36] as the Lord willed it, in order to give Himself to us as food and to associate us with the unity of His Mystical Body.[37]

The unique and indivisible existence of the Lord glorious in heaven is not multiplied, but is rendered present by the sacrament in the many places on earth where Mass is celebrated. And this existence remains present, after the sacrifice, in the Blessed Sacrament which is, in the tabernacle, the living heart of each of our churches. And it is our very sweet duty to honour and adore in the blessed Host which our eyes see, the Incarnate Word whom they cannot see, and who, without leaving heaven, is made present before us.

We confess that the Kingdom of God begun here below in the Church of Christ is not of this world whose form is passing, and that its proper growth cannot be confounded with the progress of civilization, of science or of human technology, but that it consists in an ever more profound knowledge of the unfathomable riches of Christ, an ever stronger hope in eternal blessings, an ever more ardent response to the love of God, and an ever more generous bestowal of grace and holiness among men. But it is this same love which induces the Church to concern herself constantly about the true temporal welfare of men. Without ceasing to recall to her children that they have not here a lasting dwelling, she also urges them to contribute, each according to his vocation and his means, to the welfare of their earthly city, to promote justice, peace and brotherhood among men, to give their aid freely to their brothers, especially to the poorest and most unfortunate. The deep solicitude of the Church, the Spouse of Christ, for the needs of men, for their joys and hopes, their griefs and efforts, is therefore nothing other than her great desire to be present to them, in order to illuminate them with the light of Christ and to gather them all in Him, their only Saviour. This solicitude can never mean that the Church conform herself to the things of this world, or that she lessen the ardour of

---

[36] Cf Dz.-Sch. 1642,1651-1654; Paul VI, Enc. *Mysterium Fidei*.
[37] Cf S.Th.,111,73,3.

her expectation of her Lord and of the eternal Kingdom.

We believe in the life eternal. We believe that the souls of all those who die in the grace of Christ – whether they must still be purified in purgatory, or whether from the moment they leave their bodies Jesus takes them to paradise as He did for the Good Thief – are the People of God in the eternity beyond death, which will be finally conquered on the day of the Resurrection when these souls will be reunited with their bodies.

We believe that the multitude of those gathered around Jesus and Mary in paradise forms the Church of Heaven, where in eternal beatitude they see God as He is,[38] and where they also, in different degrees, are associated with the holy angels in the divine rule exercised by Christ in glory, interceding for us and helping our weakness by their brotherly care.[39]

We believe in the communion of all the faithful of Christ, those who are pilgrims on earth, the dead who are attaining their purification, and the blessed in heaven, all together forming one Church; and we believe that in this communion the merciful love of God and His saints is ever listening to our prayers, as Jesus told us: Ask and you will receive.[40]

Thus it is with faith and in hope that we look forward to the resurrection of the dead, and the life of the world to come.

Blessed be God Thrice Holy. Amen.

Pope Paul VI

---

[38] Cf 1 John 3:2; Dz.-Sch. 1000.
[39] Cf LG, 49.
[40] Cf Luke 10:9-10; John 16:24

APPENDIX 4

PRAYERS

"A certain memorization of some essential prayers, far from opposing the dignity of young Christians, or obstructing personal dialogue with the Lord, constitutes a real need. What is memorized must at the same time be absorbed and gradually understood in depth, in order to become a source of Christian life."[1]

The Lord's Prayer

Our Father, who art in heaven, hallowed be thy name. Thy kingdom come; thy will be done on earth as it is in heaven.

Give us this day our daily bread; and forgive us our trespasses as we forgive those who trespass against us; and lead us not into temptation, but deliver us from evil. Amen.

Pater noster, qui es in cælis: sanctificétur nomen tuum; advéniat regnum tuum; fiat volúntas tua, sicut in cælo, et in terra.

Panem nostrum cotidiánum da nobis hódie; et dimítte nobis débita nostra sicut et nos dimíttimus debitóribus nostris; et ne nos indúcas in tentatiónem; sed líbera nos a malo. Amen.

Hail Mary

Hail, Mary, full of grace, the Lord is with thee; blessed art thou among women, and blessed is the fruit of thy womb Jesus.

Holy Mary, Mother of God, pray for us sinners, now and at the hour of our death. Amen.

Ave, María, grátia plena, Dóminus tecum; benedícta tu in muliéribus, et benedíctus fructus ventris tui, Iesus.

Sancta María, Mater Dei, ora pro nobis peccatóribus, nunc et in hora mortis nostræ. Amen

---

[1] CT, 55

Glory be

Glory be to the Father, and to the Son, and to the Holy Spirit.

As it was in the beginning, is now, and ever shall be, world without end. Amen.

Glória Patri, et Fílio, et Spirítui Sancto.

Sicut erat in princípio et nunc et semper et in saécula sæculórum. Amen.

The Apostles' Creed

I believe in God, the Father almighty,
creator of heaven and earth.
I believe in Jesus Christ, his only Son, our Lord.
He was conceived by the power of the Holy Spirit
and born of the Virgin Mary.
He suffered under Pontius Pilate,
was crucified, died, and was buried.
He descended to the dead.
On the third day he rose again.
He ascended into heaven,
and is seated the right hand of the Father.
He will come again to judge the living and the dead.
I believe in the Holy Spirit,
the holy Catholic Church,
the communion of saints,
the forgiveness of sins,
the resurrection of the body,
and the life everlasting. Amen.

Angelus

V. The angel of the Lord declared unto Mary;
R. And she conceived by the Holy Spirit.
Hail Mary . . .
V. Behold the handmaid of the Lord.
R. Be it done unto me according to your word.
Hail Mary . . .
V. And the Word was made flesh.
R. And dwelt among us.
Hail Mary . . .
V. Pray for us, O holy Mother of God.
R. That we may be made worthy of the promises of Christ.

Let us pray.

Pour forth, we beseech you, O Lord, your grace into our hearts, that we to whom the incarnation of Christ, your Son, was made known by the message of an angel, may by his passion and cross be brought to the glory of his resurrection, through the same Christ our Lord.

R. Amen.

Regina Cæli (For Easter Time)

V. Queen of heaven, rejoice! Alleluia.

R. For he whom you did merit to bear. Alleluia.

V. Has risen, as he said. Alleluia.

R. Pray for us to God. Alleluia.

V. Rejoice and be glad, O Virgin Mary. Alleluia.

R. For the Lord is truly risen. Alleluia.

Let us pray.

O God, who gave joy to the world through the resurrection of your Son our Lord Jesus Christ, grant, we beseech you, that through the intercession of the Virgin Mary, his Mother, we may obtain the joys of everlasting life, through the same Christ our Lord.

R. Amen.

Mysteries of the Rosary

Joyful Mysteries: Mondays and Saturdays

1. The Annunciation
2. The Visitation
3. The Nativity
4. The Presentation in the Temple
5. The Finding of the child Jesus in the Temple

Mysteries of Light: Thursdays

1. The Baptism of our Lord
2. The Wedding feast at Cana
3. The Proclamation of the Kingdom of God and the call to conversion
4. The Transfiguration
5. The Institution of the Eucharist

Sorrowful Mysteries: Tuesdays and Fridays
1. The Agony in the Garden
2. The Scourging at the Pillar
3. The Crowning with Thorns
4. The Carrying of the Cross
5. The Crucifixion and Death of our Lord

Glorious Mysteries: Wednesdays and Sundays
1. The Resurrection
2. The Ascension
3. The Descent of the Holy Spirit on the Apostles
4. The Assumption
5. The Coronation of the Blessed Virgin

Hail Holy Queen
Hail, holy Queen, mother of mercy,
our life, our sweetness, and our hope.
To you do we cry,
poor banished children of Eve.
To you do we send up our sighs
mourning and weeping in this valley of tears.
Turn then, most gracious advocate,
your eyes of mercy toward us,
and after this exile
show us the blessed fruit of your womb, Jesus.
O clement, O loving, O sweet Virgin Mary.

V.   Pray for us, O Holy Mother of God.
R.   That we may be made worthy of the promises of Christ.

Memorare
Remember, O most gracious Virgin Mary, that never was it
known that anyone who fled to your protection, implored your
help or sought your intercession, was left unaided. Inspired by
this confidence, I fly unto you, O Virgin of virgins, my Mother.
To you I come, before you I stand, sinful and sorrowful. O
Mother of the Word incarnate, despise not my petitions, but, in
your mercy, hear and answer me. Amen.

To one's Guardian Angel

Angel of God, my guardian dear, to whom his love commits me here, ever this day (or night) be at my side, to light and guard, to rule and guide. Amen.

Prayers of St. Thomas Aquinas

Before Mass

Almighty and ever-living God,
I approach the sacrament of your only-begotten son, our Lord Jesus Christ,
I come sick to the doctor of life,
unclean to the fountain of mercy,
blind to the radiance of eternal light,
and poor and needy to the Lord of heaven and earth.
Lord, in your great generosity,
heal my sickness, wash away my defilement,
enlighten my blindness, enrich my poverty,
and clothe my nakedness.
May I receive the bread of angels,
the King of kings and Lord of lords,
with humble reverence,
with the purity and faith,
the repentance and love,
and the determined purpose
that will help to bring me to salvation.
May I receive the sacrament of the Lord's body and blood,
and its reality and power.
Kind God,
may I receive the body of your only begotten Son, our Lord Jesus Christ,
born from the womb of the Virgin Mary,
and so be received into his mystical body
and numbered among his members.
Loving Father,
as on my earthly pilgrimage
I now receive your beloved Son
under the veil of a sacrament,
may I one day see him face to face in glory,
who lives and reigns with you for ever. Amen.

After Mass
Lord, Father all-powerful and ever-living God,
I thank you, for even though I am a sinner,
your unprofitable servant,
not because of my worth
but in the kindness of your mercy,
you have fed me with the precious body and blood of your Son
our Lord Jesus Christ.
I pray that this Holy Communion
may not bring me condemnation and punishment
but forgiveness and salvation.
May it be a helmet of faith
and a shield of good will.
May it purify me from evil ways
and put an end to my evil passions.
May it bring me charity and patience,
humility and obedience,
and growth in the power to do good.
May it be my strong defence
against all my enemies, visible and invisible,
and the perfect calming of all my evil impulses,
bodily and spiritual.
May it unite me more closely to you, the one true God,
and lead me safely through death
to everlasting happiness with you.
And I pray that you will lead me, a sinner,
to the banquet where you, with your Son and Holy Spirit
are true and perfect light,
total fulfillment, everlasting joy,
gladness without end,
and perfect happiness to your saints.
Grant this through Christ our Lord. Amen.

APPENDIX 5

Provido Sane Consilio – On the Better Care for Catechetical Teaching: Questionnaire regarding the teaching of Christian doctrine

A. For Children

(a) In the Parishes:

1. What is the number of children in the individual parishes, and how many of these attend catechetical instruction?
2. What diligence do the pastors display in the fulfillment of their task of giving the children religious instruction, and what pastors neglect this duty?
3. Have parochial schools been instituted in these same parishes? With what result, and what method do they follow in teaching Christian doctrine?
4. Do the priests and other clerics living within the territory of the parish assist the pastor in teaching Christian doctrine? In what way is this assistance given? Have any been negligent or recalcitrant?
5. Do the religious of both sexes assist the pastor in teaching catechism to the children? Have any shown themselves negligent or recalcitrant?
6. Has the Confraternity of Christian Doctrine been established in the separate parishes, and in what way does it cooperate with the pastor in teaching Christian doctrine to the children?
7. Do other societies of the laity, especially of Catholic Action, assist the pastor in this same duty?
8. Has a Catechetical Bureau (*Officium catechisticum*) or some similar institute been established in the diocese, or is it possible to establish such?
9. Is a Catechetical Day celebrated? In what manner?
10. Are catechetical gatherings (*coetus catechistici*) held? With what fruits? Are other conventions for religion schools held?
11. Are any means employed to stimulate both parents and children, so that the latter will attend the parish catechism class?

What means are employed?

12. Is there anything that interferes with the more abundant fruits of the teaching of Christian doctrine? What abuses have crept in, and what means are being employed, or may be employed, to remove them?

(b) In Catholic Schools and Colleges:

13. How many Catholic schools for boys and girls, especially of recent institution, are under the direction of the secular or regular clergy or of religious sisters?

14. How many pupils are there, day and boarders, in the individual Catholic schools and colleges?

15. How often during the week, and by what method and with what results, is religious instruction given in these schools?

16. How could this instruction be more efficaciously and usefully promoted?

(c) In Public Schools:

17. Is Christian doctrine being taught in the public schools? In what schools, and with what success?

18. Is the religious instruction subject to the authority and inspection of the Church? In what way and in what public schools?

19. In what public schools, and for what reason, is Christian doctrine not taught? How is the religious instruction of the pupils of these schools being provided for?

20. Are any means employed, or can there be, to secure that Christian doctrine may be taught in these schools?

B. For Adults

21. Besides the usual homily, is any catechetical instruction being given by the pastor to adults? When is this instruction given?

22. With what diligence, by what method, and at what time do the pastors fulfill this duty?

23. Do the faithful attend religious instruction in the individual parishes, and with what results?

24. In view of the circumstances of the time and place, what means are considered most suitable for promoting the more fruitful religious instruction of adults?

ADVANCE PRAISE FOR

AN ANTHOLOGY OF CATHOLIC TEACHING ON EDUCATION

"This collection of key Catholic texts on education and catechesis will be invaluable for informing and forming a new generation of Catholic educators."

> Dr Petroc Willey,
> Editor, *The Sower Review for Catechetics*, and
> Deputy Director, Maryvale Institute

"This collection will provide an excellent resource to teachers and all who care about Catholic education. By bringing together in a single volume the documents of the Church on this important theme over the last 100 years, the compilers show how the Church has constantly responded to the challenge of the age with a renewed attention to the vital task of formation.

It is to be hoped that this Anthology will prove to be a valued and oft-consulted reference point on the bookshelf of the family home, the classroom and the university library."

> +Mario Conti
> Archbishop of Glasgow

"Today as always, our central concern as Catholics must be the presentation of the person of Jesus Christ, with his call to repent and believe. We espouse crucifixion Christianity which leads to the resurrection and believe that everyone stands under the four last things of death and judgement, heaven and hell. Catholicism calls to faith and reason as well as love and hope. This is now profoundly countercultural. This is the ongoing challenge for education in the Catholic tradition.

This collection of official Catholic teaching on education is a rich body of work spanning almost a century."

> + Cardinal George Pell
> Archbishop of Sydney